THE TRUTH ABOUT CRIME

THE TRUTH ABOUT CRIME

Sovereignty, Knowledge, Social Order

◆

Jean Comaroff and John L. Comaroff

The University of Chicago Press ◆ Chicago and London

The University of Chicago Press, Chicago 60637
The University of Chicago Press, Ltd., London
© 2016 by The University of Chicago
All rights reserved. Published 2016.
Printed in the United States of America

25 24 23 22 21 20 19 18 17 16   1 2 3 4 5

ISBN-13: 978-0-226-42488-0 (cloth)
ISBN-13: 978-0-226-42491-0 (paper)
ISBN-13: 978-0-226-42507-8 (e-book)
DOI: 10.7208/chicago/9780226425078.001.0001

Library of Congress Cataloging-in-Publication Data

Names: Comaroff, Jean, author. | Comaroff, John L., 1945– author.
Title: The truth about crime : sovereignty, knowledge, social order / Jean Comaroff
    and John L. Comaroff.
Description: Chicago ; London : The University of Chicago Press, 2016. | Includes
    bibliographical references and index.
Identifiers: LCCN 2016034773 | ISBN 9780226424880 (cloth : alk. paper) | ISBN
    9780226424910 (pbk. : alk. paper) | ISBN 9780226425078 (e-book)
Subjects: LCSH: Crime. | Police administration.
Classification: LCC HV6035 .C657 2016 | DDC 364.01—dc23
    LC record available at https://lccn.loc.gov/2016034773

♾ This paper meets the requirements of ANSI/NISO Z39.48-
1992 (Permanence of Paper).

CONTENTS

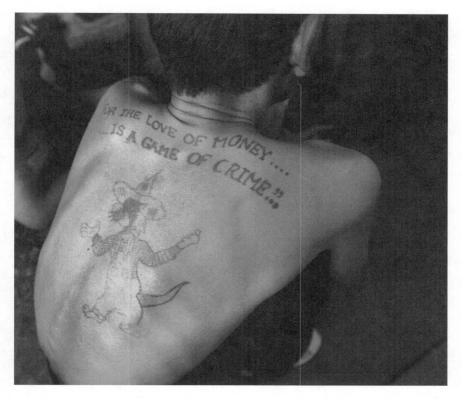

IMAGE 1. "For the love of money . . . is a game of crime . . ." (Esa Alexander, photographer)

PREFACE

Once upon a time, Michel Foucault famously wrote, public executions dramatized the deadly vengeance of the law. And, with it, the sublime power of the sovereign. All this changed, he said, in the late eighteenth century, when punishment-as-spectacle began to disappear—and the body to lose its salience as a visceral target of penality—in favor of a less immediately physical regime of discipline: a sober, modern "economy of suspended rights" (Foucault 1995, 11), administered in the name of civil authority and the crafting of the moral subject. The starkness of this archaeology has been disputed, of course. For one thing, torture never really went away (Hron 2008); it merely became less open to scrutiny, more secretive. For another, as the twentieth century drew to a close, punitive spectacle returned in a new guise: the ever more flagrant "expressive violence" of law enforcement almost everywhere (Simon 2001, 129; Meranze 2003). Think here of the beating of Rodney King in Los Angeles. Or the killing of unarmed black men in Ferguson, Missouri, in Baltimore, Maryland, and in Staten Island, New York. Or the deployment of brute force against "disorderly" youth in London, Paris, or Iguala, Mexico. Or the Marikana massacre in South Africa. All of these were more or less theatrically staged instances of punishment, even capital punishment, without due process. Part of a growing culture of cruelty, a culture driven by the reach of the digital media, they underscore the increasing centrality of "visible" enforcement to statecraft across much of the world nowadays; also the fact that policing, in the name of order, frequently makes felons *before*-the-fact, punishing them *prior* to their breaches being legally established. Or even committed. It is as if we are witnessing the ghost of Carl Schmitt—who was convinced that the intrinsic weakness of liberal democracy lies in its incapacity to wield the sovereign, primal force of the law—channeled into quasi-militarized cops who take control over the life and death of the (allegedly) unruly on behalf of respectable citizens.

Not that this is surprising. Citizenship these days, it seems, is framed less in terms of a social contract founded on liberty and the good life than with reference to the imperatives of safety, security, and righteous self-enrichment, which are seen to be imperiled from all sides: by the uncouth, the undocumented, and the undeserving, by the irresponsible and the unemployed, by criminals, itinerant migrants, terrorists, bent business(wo)men, states(wo)men, police(wo)men, and soldiers. "You paid your taxes, so where are the police?" asked a poster put up by the opposition Conservative Party before the British parliamentary elections of 2001; the question was superimposed over an image of a frail woman walking fearfully across a desolate housing estate, haunted by shadowy figures. The critique of government here, its failure to secure meaningful citizenship, could not have been starker. Similarly, if much more darkly, a cartoon from South Africa—the central focus of this study—where concern with state corruption and police malfeasance has become endemic, shows a terrified gas station attendant filling the tank of a car crammed with heavily armed hoods. Behind, waiting to be served, is a police vehicle. "Don't worry," one of the balaclava'd gangsters tells the attendant as he looks back apprehensively at the cops, "we'll protect you" (image 2).[1] The attendant had good reason to fear for his life. Five gas station workers had recently been killed—by a cop.

What this cartoon speaks to, what that election poster signifies, is a deep ambivalence, a paradox at the core of contemporary citizenship, a paradox of desire and distrust born of the phenomenology of fear. On the one hand, populations across the planet, even in relatively peaceful places, express a longing for the security of persons and property against the immanent danger of violation, real or imagined. And yet, on the other, they evince a deep suspicion of the state, of its interests and its capacities, of its will to protect against, rather than to commit or condone, corruption and predatory crime. This appears to be the corollary of two things, both of which we shall explore in extenso in the pages to come. The first is the outsourcing by governments of many of their functions, including some of those attendant on the means of violence, thus decentering and decentralizing their sovereignty and the jurisdiction/s of the law. The second is the growing difficulty, in many domains of everyday life, of discerning the lines that once were held to set apart the key domains of liberal-modern social order: of distinguishing, that is, the legal from the il-

IMAGE 2. Cartoon by Zapiro (Jonathan Shapiro) appearing in the *Mail & Guardian*

legal, the rightful from the reprobate, the clean from the corrupt, legitimate from illegitimate force, even crime-and-policing, which exist, in the here and now, in ever greater, hyphenated complicity. This blurring of lines is a feature of an age of capital made more opaque, less fathomable, even unknowable, by its increasingly complex, increasingly abstract, increasingly entangled technologies of production, communication, financialization, digitization, governance, and much else besides.

In the upshot, the line between order and unruliness, civility and chaos, has come to look very thin indeed. And it is perpetually rendered more so, tautologically, by the *perception*, factually grounded or not, of rising lawlessness, from street mugging, pilfering, vandalism, and vagrancy; through home invasion, identity theft, and "contact" felonies; to organized crime and corruption, international cyberattack, and multibillion-dollar scams perpetrated by "too-big-to-fail" financial houses. This, we shall argue, is why it is that, even where criminality appears, in measurable terms, *not* to threaten major social and material disruption or to endanger life and limb, mass anxiety about it is so rife; why, too, the phenomenology of fear is—in most places, for most people—so strikingly, so demonstrably, *dis*proportionate to risk. And why that phenomenology is more acutely attuned to the incidental and the graphic, to the singular act of violation, than to the much more insidious, much more dangerous structural violence—the "slow violence" (Nixon 2011)—of economic dispossession, ecological despoliation, and biophysical degradation.

As we show in part 1, the preoccupation these days with lawlessness finds focus ever more in dramas of crime and punishment, be they factual or fictional or mythic admixtures of the two. Ours, after all, is an epoch—if not the first, then certainly the latest—in which law-making, law-breaking, and law-enforcement are especially critical registers in which societies construct, contest, and confront truths about themselves. Hence the frank fascination with encounters, alike on the page and on the screen, between the forces of authority and variously ingenious outlaws. And with those epic courtroom trials, which become reflections, in the mode of a Dickens or a Hugo, on the condition of our times. Hence, too, the global obsession with mass-mediated crime stories, be they police procedurals, magico-scientist narratives of CSI-style forensics, or epic accounts of supercops. In these, unlike in everyday life, the mystery is always solved, the criminals always caught, and order always restored—thereby reenacting, over and over, the phantasm of sovereign authority successfully sustained. Real or mimetic, the play of crime and punishment evokes horror and fascination, staging a resolution to the paradox of desire and distrust, of im/possibility, that remains out of reach, for the most part, in the lifeworld of late modernity. Hence also, we see the assertive rise of an ironic counternarrative, new noir, whose dystopic zeitgeist engages much more skeptically, open-endedly, even surreally, with the anxieties, apprehensions, and indeterminacies of the day—thus to explore some of our deepest existential dilemmas about economy and society, about politics, personhood, and ethics. And about the frequent failure of conviction(s), in both senses of the term. In this genre, which resonates cogently with the mood of the moment, criminals are *not* always caught, cops are *not* necessarily clean, and the distinction between fealty and felony, law and its underside, is anything but decisive. In it, criminal antiheroes, the likes of Tony Soprano (*The Sopranos*), Walter White (*Breaking Bad*), and Omar Little (*The Wire*), appear as the dark, everyman sages of public fantasy, rogue capitalists in a neoliberal age. In it, too, the counterpoint of desire and distrust that surrounds policing and sovereign authority is well to the fore: far from being about the repair of normativity or the taming of transgression and breach, this new noir dwells upon the open secrets, the ambiguities, the contradictions of our lifeworld.

The Truth about Crime, then, poses a clutch of big questions, questions far bigger than we can answer here, but questions that beg nonetheless to be broached: If crime haunts our moral imaginary, if punishment-as-spectacle is once more a common technology of rule, why? What precisely does it—crime, that is—*mean* in this, our epoch-under-construction? What is new or different about it, about the way we understand it, about the workings of criminal justice, particularly of policing, in the history of the present? And how does crime fit into the long history of modernity, into its historical sociology of class, race, gender, generation, into its fetishism of the law and its conventional means of violence? What has happened, more broadly, to the nature of the police-function with its outsourcing, to a greater or lesser extent, to the private sector under the impact of the market and *its* managerial ideology, *its* sovereignty, and *its* claim to world-making? And, what, more fundamentally, might all these things have to do with shifting relations among, the shifting triangulation of, capital, the state, and governance in recent decades?

We address these questions comparatively, with South Africa as our primary focus. This is not just because we know it better than we know other places. It is also because, like other post-totalitarian societies, South Africa is struggling to build a democracy founded on the rule of law out of the wreckage wrought by long, violently oppressive years of rule *by* law. Like those other places, too, much of the crime committed here is global both in its nature and in its reach, as are the modes of enforcement that seek to combat it. In these societies, crime-and-policing provide especially fertile raw matter, elemental images both negative and positive, by means of which the very im/possibility of late modernist nationhood—of a moral public built on the commonweal, if not on horizontal fraternity (cf. Anderson 1991)—is being confronted and contested. But, we stress, it is not only in these societies that this is true. Anyone interested in what, at this historical conjuncture, makes civility, political society, personhood, community, the state, or a nation would do well to follow the well-trodden track to the "scene of the crime" (Benjamin 1999b).

Why? Because, as we shall argue in extenso, criminality has, in *this* Age of Global Capitalism, become *the* constitutive fact of contemporary life, *the* vernacular in terms of which politics is conducted, moral panics are voiced, and populations are ruled; because, moreover, it is being mobilized ever more centrally, not just to patrol normative margins, but to yield ethnosociological truths about a universe that appears to be growing increasingly inscrutable. This is why we draw attention throughout to the similarities and differences between our antipodean case and those of the global north, especially the United States and the United Kingdom. It is also why we return repeatedly to a claim made by Emile Durkheim, whose sociology was itself an embodiment of the ideology of liberal modernity: that criminality is a critical prism by means of which societies know themselves, take the measure of themselves, and contemplate ways of perfecting themselves—and, he might have added, argue among themselves along various, and variously empowered, lines of difference. Without law-breaking, he said, societies would resolve into chaos, since they would lack all signs of their own *sovereign* existence, their existence as an authoritative order. Given that sovereignty—authoritative order, that is—is in question in so many places right now, it is no wonder that the criminal obsessions of the moment are so widespread and so acute (Comaroff and Comaroff 2004a; cf. Caldeira 2000), at once surprisingly alike and yet locally inflected. No wonder, too, that so much sociology has run out of explanations for the late modern condition. Or that it is being displaced by criminology, broadly defined, as the privileged means by which the social world aspires to know itself; this at the cost of confronting critically, and theorizing anew, the structural conditions—economic and ecological, political and biophysical—that are remaking that world.

What we intend here, in recommissioning that critical prism, is, in short, a *criminal anthropology* of late modernity. Michel Foucault (1995, 18), recall, once used the same term, which he took to refer to the set of discursive terms and techniques deployed by penal systems to create their object and do their work. Ours is a rather different sort of criminal anthropology. It seeks to plumb the meaning of criminality and the sorts of social truths to which it gives rise; to interrogate the larger, more or less visible conditions that spawn phenomenologies of fear, the metaphysics of disorder in which they are embedded, and the forms of law-enforcement that they mandate; and to situate the practical epistemology of crime-and-policing in the changing lineaments of the history of the present. It is a criminal anthropology, in other words, that seeks, first, to make sense of the ways in which living societies—or, more accurately, their citizens and constituent publics—understand the social ecology of their lives and, second, to give account of the forces that persuade them to portray the world, and act upon it, as they do.

The Truth about Crime, in sum, is an excursion into the contemporary Order of Things—or, rather, into the metaphysic of disorder that has come to infuse the late modern world. It is, finally, a meditation on sovereignty and citizenship, on civility, class, and race, on the law and its transgression, on the political economy of representation.

◆

Precisely because criminality has become such a saturating fact of life in so many places, it is difficult to draw a priori lines of limitation around it or its analysis. Ours is *not*, we stress, a conventional history or sociology of crime-and-policing in late modern South Africa—or anywhere else. That task has been admirably undertaken by a cluster of scholars more qualified than are we; their highly informed work bears vibrant testimony, from a variety of theoretical and methodological perspectives, to the importance of the topic (e.g., on South Africa, see Marsh 1999; Steinberg 2001, 2008; Shaw 2002; Dixon and van der Spuy 2004; Altbeker 2005, 2010; Orford 2011; Grobler 2013; Hornberger 2013; Super 2013; Klatzow 2014; also the publications of the Institute for Security Studies). Rather, we have sought out a number of unorthodox angles from which to take on the questions we have posed about the meaning of crime-and-policing in the late modern world; about the part they play in the contemporary politics, economics, and culture of world-making, truth-making, knowledge-making, state-making, nation-making; about the ways in which they serve as allegory for addressing the mysteries, the insistent enigmas and specters, of our age; about the endless quest to recapture what, in retrospect, are believed to have been the sovereign certainties of modernity, certainties that seem to be slipping away, widely mourned, irrecoverable.

The Truth about Crime is not arranged into a sequence of chapters, but into two parts. The first is composed of three interlocking pieces, 1.1–1.3, which, together, explore the big picture, as it were: the impact on crime-and-policing of historical changes—a tectonic shift, we call it—in the triangulation of late modern capitalism, the state form, and so-called "neoliberal" governance. By "tectonic shift" we mean, quite specifically, a gradual, cumulative transformation, and rearticulation, of the foundational elements of our social, economic, political, juridical, ethical, and cultural universe, a shift that is part rupture and part intensification. We begin, in 1.1, by scrutinizing anew the part played by criminality—by law-making, law-breaking, and law-enforcement—in the rise of modernity, in its conception of society and in the sacralization of its regime of property, personhood, privilege, and power—and also in its equation of private ownership with bourgeois public order, such that a violation of the one was seen as a violation of the other. It is against this archaeology that we describe the tectonic shift and, in 1.2, direct our attention to a clutch of its critical effects: to the popular angst—about spreading lawlessness, about the deregulated excesses of laissez-faire, about the threat of social disorder—that it has spawned; to the ways in which it has rendered ever more murky, ever less decidable or enforceable, the line between the legal and the illegal, the ethical and the venal, leaving in its wake a "criminal specter," a sense of the immanence of lawlessness everywhere; to its creation of "new criminal types" (Siegel 1998), largely out of a decommissioned, disposable—and disproportionately racialized—population of former workers; to its techniques of managing that population; and to the recasting of the police-function, focusing state enforcement primarily on order, broadly defined, and privatizing much of the remainder. These processes become sharply visible by comparing criminal justice in the United States and South Africa, both of which see themselves as exceptional. Unexceptionally so. That comparison also illuminates the big picture in another register: the political economy and cultural ecology of representation. In 1.3, we turn to mass-mediated crime fiction—in literature, film, and television, in social media and public culture—which, we argue, has become a site in which are addressed some of the most weighty social and existential issues of late modern times. As we have already intimated, the image takes on a particular gravitas here, as conventional genres—those in which the felon is found, the mystery solved, order restored—are challenged by a new noir that, playing on the prevailing mood of our times, reflects on the impossibility of neat resolutions or easy answers when old sureties unravel, when abstraction, alienation, ambivalence, undecidability, and il/legality appear to become endemic to "life itself," when new truths demand to be probed.

If part 1 deals with the big picture, part 2 opens up unorthodox angles of narrower focal length, exploring, in five "uneasy pieces" (2.1–2.5), different yet interlocking dimensions of crime-and-policing. These pieces are based in part on ethnography, both thick and thin, in the North West Province, in the Western Cape Province, in the digital domain, print media, radio and television, theater and film, and in all the other places and spaces into which crime-and-policing have taken us, as they take all South Africans, over the past fifteen or so years. The first of these pieces, 2.1, picks up on the popular fascination with mythic forms of enforcement, personified in such figures as diviner-detectives, inspired supercops, and forensic crime busters with putatively preternatural powers. But *why* this fascination? What accounts for it? Might it have to do with the widespread coexistence of, on the one hand, a cynical distrust in the capacities of the state to protect its citizens and en- sure their survival with, on the other, the Durkheimian faith that criminal justice might yet beget social order? In order to address these questions, we explore the rise of alternative policing in South Africa, where it is more com- mon than commonly supposed, and where it is widely appealed to "to solve the mystery" that conventional crime detection cannot, does not, and usually will not deal with any more. Across the world, it turns out, unorthodox cops of various kinds have become stand-ins, surrogates of sorts, for a sense of loss, of absence: in prospect if not always in fact, as we shall see, they resolve the dialectic of desire and distrust—and address the metaphysic of disorder—that has grown up in the void left behind by the erosion, almost everywhere, of the liberal-democratic social contract.

That dialectic opens up another unorthodox angle, which we pursue in 2.2. It plays upon the growing murkiness of the line between the legal and the ille- gal, criminality and entrepreneurial self-making: imposture. In an age domi- nated by *The Culture of the Copy* (Schwartz 1996), by a sense that reality itself consists of "copies all the way down," technologies of the self, of self-making- by-faking, appear rampant. Why? Why does the late modern world, and par- ticularly a place like South Africa, seem so hospitable to impostors and fakes? What does it tell us about the legal person and the policing of personhood? Could the indeterminacy of identity be iconic of an epoch in which the self is the ultimate form of capital, an epoch in which the il/licit and the entrepre- neurial exist in mutually validating counterpoint? In which the murkiness of the il/legal is where *homo oeconomicus* is most at home? In which the cul- tural foundations of political economy—with its emphasis on rupture, rule- breaking, innovation, edginess—actually lie? How might the ambiguities sur- rounding personhood be related to the efforts of states to fix, discipline, and track their citizens by biometric means? And why do many of those citizens evince a strong impulse to elude that fixity, even though they may desire the benefits it confers?

The ambivalent relationship between citizens and the state takes us, in turn, to two further angles on crime-and-policing. In 2.3,[2] we explore the alchemy of crime statistics: how, across the world, they have become a charged cur- rency of public debate and a critical measure of both effective governance and transparent democracy; why, at times, they have been treated like state secrets in South Africa, seen by some as political capital, by others as a means to the redemptive reestablishment of order, and by yet others as mere mythostats; how, in the dialectic of dis/trust, they figure as objects of suspicion, at once disparaged for their endemic fallibility and their openness to manipulation, and yet believed to have the capacity, if honestly brokered, to yield the "real" truth about the national condition. Like alternative policing (2.1) and the policing of personhood (2.2), the politics of numbers illuminates the ways in which various publics inhabit the metaphysics of disorder: how they deploy crime-and-policing as a vernacular sociology through which to make sense of the world, tame its uncertainties, and reduce its ambiguities; how they take account of their own actions and those of others in that world; what they expect from the state and the social contract—and how they fear being failed by both.

This last clause leads us directly to 2.4. It deals with "informal justice," a phenomenon with a deep history in South Africa, one that, in the present, seems to be reaching epidemic proportions. It far outstrips policing under the official aegis of government—which says something profound about the twenty-first-century state; specifically, about the forfeiture of its monopoly over the means of sovereign violence, one of its defining features in the high age of modernity. The term itself, "informal justice," refers to a wide range of nonstate (mostly extralegal) enforcement, much of it highly physical, a good deal of it deadly. It stretches from private security offered by commercial companies, through "community action," nongovernmental organization (NGO) anticrime patrols, and "people's courts," to "vigilantism" and "alternative" protection undertaken by variously founded (often outlaw) organizations. At surface, this explosive spread appears attributable to the (relative) disengagement of the state from its conventional policing operations. On one level, this is true, but the story is more complicated. Quite commonly, publics that *complain* about being unpoliced, and call for the return of sovereign state violence against criminals, also *prevent* the cops from dealing with those very criminals, preferring to "take matters into their own hands." Or more accurately, they prefer to enact, even constitute, moral community by "taking responsibility"—seizing sovereignty, that is—for their own law/lore. Herein lies an obvious question: Why demand strong intervention on the part of the authorities and yet, counterintuitively, *refuse* policing? What does this tell us about the limits of criminal justice in an epoch when so many functions of state are being repurposed and/or privatized, ever more subject to bureaucratic displacement, corporate capture, and the disciplining effect of the market? And how does it inform the big picture, the thing with which we began, namely, the shifting triangulation of the state form, capital, and governance?

The pervasive preoccupation with crime-and-policing in South Africa and elsewhere may be rooted in the sociology, economics, and politics of our times. But it is also always, as we show in 2.5, a vector of human creativity, everyday aesthetics, and, wittingly or otherwise, parodic self-knowledge. Vide the uniquely South African domestic security device called *Eina* (Afrikaans, "Ouch!"). It consists of an unlikely confection of vicious iron spikes and luxuriant faux ivy. These are woven together and placed, in/visibly, atop the walled surrounds of residential properties—enclosure with lethal teeth, so to speak. Their purpose, patently, is to prevent intruders—standardized nightmares of the propertied, of whom most South Africans have a horror story—from doing their deadly work, from destroying social order, one person, one property, one home-and-garden at a time. *Eina*, in other words, is a dialectical image, after Walter Benjamin, a fragment in "a montage of history," one that, unbidden, critically interrupts the conventional appearance of things (Pensky 1993, 223). Juxtaposing civility with violation, beauty with cruelty, it is iconic of the fine line that separates law from lawlessness, serving as a cogent pointer to the psychic, social, and material costs of privatized protection as the state disinvests from ordinary policing. It also resonates with the public view of a world-turned-upside-down: a world in which criminals are thought to roam the streets freely while upright citizens—forced into never-ending, scopic vigilance (Feldman 1991)—are imprisoned behind walls. And left to ponder not merely how to keep violent criminals at bay but how to recuperate a legible, orderly society founded on ethical citizenship (cf. Muehlebach 2012), on the common good, and on sovereign authority committed to the protection of person and property. *Eina*, in sum, captures very sharply—if we may be forgiven the play on words—the murkiness of the late modern world, the difficulty, in it, of keeping apart il/legalities, un/certainties, un/knowns, insides from outsides, property from theft, freedom from capture. As such, it seemed to us an especially fitting image with which to conclude our effort to think South Africa, and the Order of Things in the history of the present, through crime-and-policing—at once at their most abstract, their most *heimlich*, their most immediate.

PART ONE

CRIME, CAPITAL, AND THE METAPHYSICS OF DISORDER: AN OVERVIEW, IN THREE MOVEMENTS

CHAPTER 1.1

CRIME, POLICING, AND
THE MAKING OF MODERNITY
The State, Sovereignty, and the Il/legal

Four fragments from different fronts in the so-called "War on Crime," variously imagined, variously deployed, distinctively diagnostic of their time and place:

The First: British Prime Minister David Cameron cut short his summer vacation Monday night and flew back to the U.K. in order to chair a crisis meeting with government ministers as the streets of London continued to see rioting and looting, and as the prospect of further violence spreading to other cities and towns intensified. In a Tuesday statement, the prime minister said that his government "will do everything necessary to restore order to the British streets" and characterized those behind the riots as "pure criminality." The prime minister said that 450 people had already been arrested and that more would follow.—Kim Hjelmgaard, *MarketWatch*, August 2011[1]

The Second: [In the wake of the shooting of the unarmed black youth Michael Brown by a police officer, the] people of Ferguson, Missouri, have caused serious complications for the US National Security State. By virtue of standing their ground in their own small city, the demonstrators have forced the police to show their true, thoroughly militarized colors. Ferguson's rebellious Black youth have succeeded in pinning down the armed forces of racist repression in full view, so that the whole world can bear witness to the truth of what another generation proclaimed nearly half a century ago: that, in the Black community, the police are an army of occupation. . . . The term "mass Black incarceration" had not yet been coined [then], but it was only a matter of time before a permanent, militarized police offensive against rebellion-prone ghettos would cause unprecedented numbers of Black prisoners to flow into the greatest gulag in the history of the world. Since America tells itself and the world that it does not make war on its own citizens, . . . the war against Black people had to be called something else—a War on Drugs, or simply a War on Crime.—Glen Ford, *Black Agenda Report*, August 2014[2]

The Third: **This website is called Turn It Around, South Africa, www.turn itaround.co.za.** On this website you can receive regular reports of crimes happening in a radius of your home or business and you can also report any suspicious activity or crime incidents online to inform others. . . . **If your neighbour was hijacked or robbed—would you even know about it?** High walls and security has [*sic*] made neighbors strangers to one another. With Turn it Around, you will be informed and aware of the crimes happening around you. . . . **We CAN use crime to bring us together and become one another's safety zones. . . . You are not alone**—everyone feels the way you do about crime.—Anonymous, Turn It Around, South Africa, October 2011[3]

The Fourth: CAPITA, plc [is] the UK's leading [private sector] provider of integrated professional support service solutions, with 64,000 staff across the UK, Europe, South Africa and India.

What we do: Police and justice

[We deliver] services to help protect the public, manage the rehabilitation and care of offenders, and support our police and justice services.

We've been working in the CRIMINAL JUSTICE sector since the early 1990s. . . . Our end-to-end services support the police and justice systems in delivering best of breed services to the public, helping both victims and offenders to get their lives back on track while enabling police officers and offender personnel to do their job efficiently and effectively.

We deliver a range of solutions directly to the frontline of the criminal justice system, from victim support and forensic services, through to custodial services and offender management and rehabilitation.

[We supply] products and services to 43 police forces in England, Ireland and Wales; and to Police Scotland.

We were the first providers of outsourced police custody services in the UK.

We process and look after 644,000 detainees for the UK police and Home Office annually.—Capita, plc, capita.co.uk, August 2014[4]

Crime is a major preoccupation across the world today. It always has been, more or less, since the dawn of modernity. Nor is this surprising, especially in Euro-America and its former colonies. The modernist nation-state, after all, was founded from the first on a scaffolding of legalities. To the degree that it conceived of itself, in classic liberal terms, as a body of free citizens living, normatively, according to the rule of law, its endemic nightmare was crime-run-amok, crime "out of control." Emile Durkheim long ago noted the epistemic corollary that follows from this: crime is a critical prism through which a society might come to know itself, might measure itself against its own ideal self-image, might contemplate ways and means of perfecting itself. As he once put it (1938, xxvii; cf. Greenhouse 2003, 276), "a society . . . free of crime would fall into chaos." Being "bereft of the signs of its own existence as an authoritative order," it would lack the means to reflect on, and to govern, itself. Hence the concern, obsession even, with breaches of the law.

Still, the sense that lawlessness *is* presently on the rise, dangerously so, seems to be evident almost everywhere. As David Garland (2001, 163) has noted, "high crime rates are regarded as a normal social fact," a "fact" that elicits "fascination as well as fear, anger, resentment." Already in May 2001, the director of the Europol went public with the statement that crime, both domestic and transnational, had come to pose a critical threat to the security of European countries; authorities in many southern nations had been saying the same thing of their parts of the world for some years. Governments, he went on, ought to rethink the prevailing paradigm of international geopolitics: "the resources that had previously been spent on military defense would be better invested" in dealing with that threat.[5] And, he might have added, domestic terror. Many agreed. In sedate Sweden, for example, citizens have come to see their country as "a place of dark crimes and vicious psychopaths, of fractured families and a fraying society," in which few have faith in either the police or the criminal justice system;[6] their dark imaginings being fed by a highly fertile, often-febrile crime fiction industry now known as Nordic noir (see below). Similarly in Britain, the "rule of lawlessness"[7] has been a major issue for two decades, to the extent that, at the millennium, the country was said to be on the verge of a "nervous breakdown";[8] since then, felony rates have dropped sharply, but two-thirds of the population believe the contrary.[9] Even in law-abiding Singapore, the state recently festooned its streets with public signage that read "Low Crime Doesn't Mean No Crime." By contrast, South Africa has much higher incidences of violent transgression. MURDER AND RAPE CAPITAL OF THE WORLD[10] is a boldfaced claim often made for it by its citizens (Masuku 2001, 16; de Haas 2000, 300). The uppercase attests to an odd mix of assertiveness and ignominy, the frisson that comes with living in a place taken to be, at once, terrifying and titillating (Malan 2002), a perilous paradise in which, as Goldberg et al. (2001, xii) have put it in another context, "romantic longing and the embrace of terror . . . stand as components of the sublime." In fact, South Africa, as we shall see, is not nearly as exceptional as its population thinks (de Haas 2000, 319; du Preez 2013 187). True, whites there have suffered more frequent attacks on persons and property since the late 1980s than they did during the apartheid years, when, to all intents and purposes, they lived in garrisoned residential enclaves; as the racial state gave way, crime spilled over the heavily policed boundaries of black neighborhoods, where—partly as a result of an economics of scarcity, partly out of a culture of criminal iconoclasm, partly a response to the violence and illegitimacy of the law—it had long been endemic. Nonetheless, beyond the most immiserated of those black neighborhoods, risk to life and limb still lies *less* in lawlessness than it does in other, more mundane things. And that risk has been decreasing. Over the past decade or so, rates of most felonies, especially serious "contact crimes,"[11] have dropped substantially, although murder and aggravated (i.e., armed) robbery numbers rose in 2013/14. Moreover, "Crime Capital of the World" is a crown that has also been claimed, in the Caribbean, for Kingston; in Latin America, for Barrancabermeja (Colombia) and Ciudad Juárez (Mexico); in the United States, for Washington, DC, and Gary, Indiana—even, oddly, for Adelaide in Australia.[12]

What is striking, though, is that, in *all* these places—in Sweden, Britain, Singapore, South Africa—the relationship between fear and danger is starkly disproportionate. Thus, in Cape Town, the homicide *ratio* in 2003 between its wealthier white suburbs and one of its poor black "townships"[13] was somewhere in the region of 1:358; in 2013 it was 0:262 (see 2.3); two-thirds of all murder victims are black males between the ages of twenty and thirty-nine (Bundy 2014, 125). Yet it is in the former, in the wealthier white suburbs, that angst about violence was, and still is, more marked. Thus, too, in Sweden, the United Kingdom, and Singapore—not to mention the United States, where, despite the claims of the New York Police Department to the contrary (see below), "violent crime is at its lowest level in a generation."[14] Those who discuss the threat of lawlessness and social disorder in such urgent terms rarely suffer it directly. This is not to deny that criminality *is* a gravely serious matter in many places. But so are chronic un(der)employment, poverty, disease, ecological and technological disaster, regional wars, and xenophobic outbreaks, which wreak demonstrably more devastation. Yet they seldom elicit the same measure of civic outrage, acrimonious political debate, severe penal sanction, or urgent policy-mongering.

Nor only is it that criminality is commonly perceived to be on the rise, thus to justify the mood of "popular punitiveness" that has gripped much of the late modern world (Bottoms 1995; Simon 2001; Haggerty 2001, 197).[15] The phenomenon itself, as a productive category of signifying practice (cf. Caldeira 2000, 19 et passim), appears to be metamorphosing. States are said to be "governing through crime" (Simon 2007; Super 2013)—indeed, to have become "penal states" in the Global North (Wacquant 2009b, 162 et passim) and "criminal states" in the Global South, especially in Africa (Bayart, Ellis, and Hibou 1999). They are also said to be managing large populations with reference to it (Kohler-Hausmann 2014, 611 et passim); to be deploying it to achieve the effects of civil—specifically, race and class and ethnoreligious—war (Packer 2011); to be legitimizing authoritative, forensic knowledge by means of it (Keenan and Weizman 2012); and to be justifying the digitization of entire nations under its biometric sign (Jain, Flynn, and Ross 2008; Breckenridge 2014a). Reciprocally, as the language of criminality becomes the vernacular in which politics is increasingly conducted, governments past and present are indicted by their citizens for corruption, war atrocities, human rights abuses, the violation of persons, the seizure of property, disagreeable and discriminatory legislation; even for history itself, which, these days, is redeemed fully for its victims only by subjecting its perpetrators to a judicial settling of accounts (in all senses of the term; Comaroff and Comaroff 2006b). What is more, those citizens tend increasingly to construe social reality in toto—in a dialectical dance with mass representations authored by the culture industry—through the allegory of law-making and law-breaking (cf. de Kock 2015).

As this implies, criminality, broadly conceived, serves not merely as an index of undoing, of things falling apart, of doubts about the legitimacy of the law itself. It is also the object of political demand, an alibi for assertive efforts to remake the authority of that law in pursuit of the liberal-democratic idyll of "the good life." Patently, this—the counterpoint between a fear of lawlessness and a felt need for law-enforcement, between a sense of immanent chaos and a desire for the recuperation of order—is not peculiar to the here and now either. As a secular resurrection narrative, it has been an enduring feature of modern state-making (C. Smith 2009). But criminality seems to be an especially urgent motif in public discourse at present. Listen to a cri de coeur from the New York Police Department. Dated 26 August 2014, it was published by the *New York Times* in a full-page open letter: "[The city] is lurching backwards to the bad old days of high crime, danger-infested public spaces, and families that walk our streets worried for their safety. . . . The degradation of our streets is on the rise."[16] This is in spite of the fact that in Camden, in the adjoining state of New Jersey, "notoriously one of the nation's poorest, most crime-ridden cities, . . . shootings [were] down 43 percent in two years, and violent crime down 22 percent";[17] also the fact that, as recent scholarly research shows (Roeder, Eisen, and Bowling 2015), crime has declined in New York City as well—although, to be fair, while the FBI released figures in late 2015 showing a fall in violent offenses, there *have* been recent reports of sharp spikes in a number of US cities.[18]

The problem, then, will be plain enough. While global felony rates may or may not have risen—some, like John Gray (1998), say they have, others disagree[19]—the preoccupation with lawlessness appears to have grown exponentially. It expresses itself in rising carceral rates, calls for tougher law-enforcement, moral panics about impending disorder, draconian strategies of social management—and an explosive economy of representation that reflects upon, and makes capital from, it. As this suggests, crime has become *the* metaphysical optic by means of which people across the planet understand and act upon their worlds.

But why? Why should this be so if the risk posed by lawlessness appears disproportionate to its incidence? If the imminent danger it poses to most people—other, ironically, than to the poor and the marginalized, those who are commonly seen as the prime perpetrators of crime, not its primary victims—is comparatively limited, perhaps receding? If, as a threat to social order, it pales into insignificance against other potential sources of public peril? After all, crime waves, real and imagined, are hardly unprecedented; they often spike in periods of social transition, as Steinberg (2001) has shown for South Africa, rupturing the flow of "ordinary times." But could it be that, with the end of "the long twentieth century" (Arrighi 1994), with the dawn of "the new way of the world" (Dardot and Laval 2014),[20] we are seeing a tectonic shift in the relationship between capital, governance, and the state, a cumulative reconfiguration of the long run, as we explained in the preface, involving the rearticulation of foundational elements of our social, economic, political, juridical, ethical, and cultural universe, a shift that is part intensification and part rupture? Could it be that this reconfiguration—made manifest in changes in the nation-state form, in its rapid privatization, and in the assault on it by an aggressively rising corporate sector—is recasting the line between the political and the il/legal? And blurring the distinction between the criminal economy and legitimate business? Could it be that this, by turn, is having an effect on the practices of sovereignty, on public perceptions of social dis/order, and on the ways in which populations are being defined, differentiated, managed, even commodified, all the more so as inequality appears to be reaching critical proportions? In which, finally, crime is being mobilized to frame new philosophical concerns, to yield new truths, and to explore new species of normative knowledge about a changing world?

In order to address these questions, to plumb the meaning of crime in the early twenty-first century—be it in South Africa, the United States, or elsewhere—let us first step briefly back into the past, into the archaeology of the relationship between criminality and modernity. And its theoretical scaffolding. A contrapuntal reading of the present against that past, of its play of continuities and discontinuities, turns out to be more than a little illuminating.

Criminality and the Making of Modernity

Classical understandings of criminality, as our opening citation of Durkheim underscores, have, ab initio, been integral to liberal-humanist ideas of law, sovereignty, and social order. For Hobbes (1994, 190–91), transgression might have been fired by human passions. But it did not qualify as crime until it breached a *jural* norm: while every crime was a sin, not every sin, nor every breach of morality, was a crime. *Lex naturae*, natural law, and the rules of moral behavior that derived from it, might be understood as universal and eternal, but not so the positive law of any sovereign political community. To be sure, "customary" legal systems, in Africa and elsewhere, have long tended to draw a sharp distinction between moral and legal infraction (Gluckman 1955). The text often held to have marked the advent of Western criminology, Beccaria's eighteenth-century *Dei delitti e delle pene* (*Crimes and Punishments*), aimed to separate crime as "harm to society" from sin as "offense to God" (Schneider and Schneider 2008, 352).[21] Without legality there could be no such thing as criminality, sensu stricto. And vice versa. Crime, in this original understanding, is inherently a *social* artifact, like a contract or a convention. As Derrida (2009, 42, original emphasis) once explained, Hobbes saw sovereignty, law, and the institution of the state itself as "prostheses." They were "historical and always provisional," he insisted, "deconstructible, essentially fragile or finite or mortal, even if sovereignty"—as the *fons et origo* of the law—"is *posited as immortal.*"

It was precisely because of the mortal, man-made quality of positive law that crime was taken, by John Locke (1988, 280–81) and other liberals, to be the archetypal violation of the social contract: it threatened to plunge society into a State of Warre[22]; this, long before states declared "wars on crime"—a hyperbolic amplification, says Robert Sullivan (2001, 31), that has its originary precursor in Locke's *Two Treatises of Government* (1988).[23] Here, prefigured, is one of the founding axioms of Durkheimian functionalism: that illegal acts are those that offend the *conscience collective*, rupture the given order of things, conjure up a nightmare of chaos, and, consequently, call for punishment—which, tautologically, becomes the negative against which the norm of civility, of society-as-moral-universe, sustains itself.

There is a deep historical irony in this.

State-Making, Law-Breaking, and the Dialectics of Dis/order

During the epoch when nation-states were becoming the dominant political form in the West, Charles Tilly (1985, 170) famously argued, state-making was, for all intents and purposes, a product of organized crime, of its raw coercive power in pursuit of self-legitimation. "Banditry, piracy, gangland rivalry, policing, and war-making," he observed, belonged on the same continuum. States, to extrapolate further, only sedimented into *sovereign* political institutions, only established their hegemony, when those who ruled in their name acquired the authority to make law and monopolize the means of violence, to protect private property and public assets, and to establish bureaucratic modes of managing official knowledge; in short, to transform extortion, expropriation, ransom, and clientage into de jure administrative practices such as taxation, military conscription and policing, social and legal services—and, most of all, the rights and responsibilities of citizenship as condensed in the liberal chimera of the social contract.

The received conceptions of criminality in play for much of the nineteenth and twentieth centuries in Euro-America, if less so in their colonies, are a corollary of this history or, at least, of the liberal nation-state form that emerged from it. Whether or not the nation-state had its origins in organized crime, it fashioned governmental regimes in which, to invoke the ghost of Max Weber, the making and preserving of law were founded on the exclusive exercise of authorized force and administrative oversight, on securing private and public property, on naturalizing distinctions of race, class, culture, and gender, and on delegitimating—even, at times, outlawing—political rivalry. In the process, law and crime, the interests they preserved and the truths they presumed, took on the sanctity of absolutes.

Hence the tendency of functionalist sociologies and anthropologies to replicate, as social science, the ideology of the liberal-modernist polity, treating law as the bedrock of civic order and the commonweal—and its violation as pathology, dysfunction, dystopia. Hence, specifically, the Weberian attribution to the state, as a *necessary* condition of its existence, of a monopoly over the means of legitimate coercion, a monopoly vested in police for purposes of law and in the military for purposes of war; the line between them, as Evans-Pritchard (1940, 278–79) reminds us, calling to mind Carl Schmitt, being synonymous with that between the polity and its exteriors, citizen and stranger, inclusion and annihilation—which is why the stakes in taking the one for the other have become so high.

Historically speaking, there have always been exceptions, exemptions, and exclusions from the Weberian norm: among them, imperial charter companies that ran their own constabularies and, later, their postcolonial progeny, translocal corporations licensed to extend sovereign dominion over enclaved sites of extraction (Ferguson 2006, 37; Kelly 1999). But, this aside, the idea that the state *ever* enjoyed exclusive control over legitimate force is questionable; legitimacy itself is always a claim, never a given, always open to contestation, rarely unequivocal. It is a claim, moreover, that law-enforcement agencies *themselves* have long had to expend a great deal of effort to make real, sometimes by the careful management of images, sometimes in spectacular pageants of the brute power to seize and subpoena and sequester. Of course, those agencies have also tended to portray themselves, simultaneously, as a pacific public service in the cause of social order: as early as the 1820s, when the original "Peelers" and "Bobbies" (named for Sir Robert Peel, founder of the modern police force in the United Kingdom) were introduced in England and Ireland, respectively, it was this aspect of their work that was emphasized, precisely because their role as a coercive institution, "a plague of blue locusts," provoked sustained civic protest (Storch and Engels 1975; Reiner 2012). This continues into the present: many twenty-first-century police departments, now saddled with an "impossible mandate" (Manning 1977; see below), devote substantial resources to "education" (Young 1991) and invest heavily in mass-mediated rituals of (self-)representation[24]—even to the extent of fabricating dramaturgies of violent disorder, thus to assert their right to enforce order by violent means (Comaroff and Comaroff 2004a). In short, whatever the de/merits of the Weberian model as a historical sociology of modern policing, it continues to mirror liberal ideology in depicting the state as an essentially benign institution: a sovereign entrusted with a monopoly over violence, legitimately exercised by its criminal justice system, in the name of protecting its citizenry from the threat of criminal disorder.

By contrast, critical theorists of various stripes—who have repeatedly stressed the degree to which modern legal regimes, and institutions of enforcement, have been an object of contestation—have tended to treat both law-making and law-breaking as a force altogether more political, oppressive, enigmatic, Janus faced. From their vantage, the rise of the bourgeois state during the Industrial Revolution was not motivated, as liberal theory would have it, by the tensile balance between private interest and the common good, between individual liberty and legal restraint. It was directed, rather, at developing a judicial apparatus designed to protect and reproduce the wealth of its dominant class fractions and, also, to put capital accumulation, and the dispossession it involved, "beyond incrimination."[25] For Mandel (1984, 135), its history was "[a history] of property and the negation of property, in other words, crime"; Proudhon (1994)—the socialist-inflected anarchist to whom is owed the cliché "property is theft"—would have concurred. Not without reason. Private property *was* presumed, in the bourgeois weltanschauung of "possessive individualism" (Macpherson 1962), to be the most inviolable, the most sacralized, of the rights of citizenship. It *was* held out as the material grounding of liberty, of social order and civil society, of the infrastructure of the modern nation and its moral economy (E. Thompson 1991, 185–351); in sum, of the practical philosophy, the collective mindscape, of a new liberalism and its rising Leviathan.

Which is why, as that practical philosophy established itself across Euro-America, it came to define law-breaking, above all, as "the negation of property," as the violation of its possession and the persons who laid legitimate claim to it. Those persons, as *right*eous citizens, were, above all else, "self-possessed"; it was in self-possession, after all, that their civility lay—which meant that any assault upon them was an assault on their most elemental of properties, their embodied selves. Apposite here is one of Locke's most cited phrases, from chapter 5 (no. 44) in the second of his *Two Treatises of Government*, that, "by being master of himself," *Man*, capitalized and italicized, is "*proprietor* of his own person." No wonder, then, that theft and assault were sanctioned as heavily as they were, or that even relatively minor infractions against persons and/or property called forth *capital* punishment until 1832: it repaid the capital of the victim with the *caput* of the perpetrator, his or her head.[26] As Peter Linebaugh (1991) has argued, new forms of capitalist exploitation produced new sorts of law-as-governance, and, with them, new sorts of crime. And new sorts of crime effected transformations in the nature of capitalism and the subjects who lived under its sway.

Concomitantly, from the same critical vantage, law-breaking could be, and often was, seen as a *positive* act of redistribution, survival, resistance, revolt, emancipation; this being the distaff side of the Janus face of criminal justice. Modern politics, goes the argument, was a product of the class struggle occasioned by the prevailing order of property relations that the legal system existed to protect; its transgression, therefore, was merely a contingent by-product of those politics, that struggle. Foucault (1995, 289), for example, points out that, in the wake of the French workers' movements of 1830–50, anti-penal polemicists saw crime as "an outburst of protest in the name of human individuality" and, thus, as a "political instrument." Its instrumentality, however, often had equivocal effects. While the bandit, noble or not, might have railed against a hardening regime of private privilege and the "blue locusts" that protected it, he was destined to be regarded, normatively, as no more than a common miscreant, a member of the "dangerous classes" (Schneider and Schneider 2008, 352; cf. Hobsbawm 1959) who called forth the violent response of bourgeois policing, warranted as a defense of social order at large.

Perhaps Marx (1993, 52–53) had this in mind when he wrote, apparently tongue-in-cheek (D. Greenberg 1993, 41), of the "usefulness" of crime. His droll account of its productivity—of the fact that it "produced" the police, the justice system, and a host of professions, forms of knowledge, and enterprises—anticipated not merely Foucault but a world in which the "prison-industrial complex" would come to fuel expansive economies in depleted, postindustrial landscapes (Lichtenstein 2011, 13; see below). The criminal "interrupts the . . . security of bourgeois life," Marx mused, "protect[ing] it from stagnation and bring[ing] forth that restless tension, that nobility of spirit without which the stimulus of competition would itself become blunted."[27] For Walter Benjamin (1978, 281), writing in the early twentieth century, that interruption made luminously visible, if only passingly, the manner in which government monopolized coercion under the sovereign sign of the law; the secret admiration for the "great criminal" on the part of the public, Benjamin argued, stemmed from the way in which he bore witness to, and cast himself against, state violence and legal repression (cf. Derrida 2002, 267). Adorno and Horkheimer

(1979, 225–26) also saw a libertine strain in lawlessness: to the extent that it ran counter to "bold progress," it partook of the same quality as sublime works of art. For them, though, the outlaw was devoid of resistance. In a reflection on the semiotics of crime that presaged Foucault and amplified Durkheim, they portrayed the modern felon as martyr, invisibly wasting away within the great prison houses of a state intent less on punishing the body, as had monarchies of old, than on attacking the soul. In this view, it is not so much the separation of the criminal from polite society, or even his reform, that motivated modern incarceration. Most important was his exemplary role: the man-in-jail was, first and foremost, a "virtual image" of alienated labor in its perfected form, an image of dispossession not yet fully realized beyond the penitentiary. For Adorno and Horkheimer (1979, 226), the highly controlled interior of the prison was nothing less than "an image of the bourgeois world of labor taken to its logical conclusion," an imagined world, never fully realized in fact, in which the laborer was rendered docile, disciplined, and delivered, more or less propertyless, to the factory and the farm—labor said to be "free," but carefully policed lest it lust after, lift, or seek to "liberate" the assets of the wealthy (cf. E. Thompson 1963). That labor, once it entered the productive process—which it was increasingly forced to do with the enclosure of the commons and the eclipse of noncapitalist modes of production—itself became the property of those who had purchased it by means of the wage; its withdrawal, as in "unauthorized" strike action or foot-dragging or absenteeism or vagrancy, was, hence, also a felony. An ironic twist, one might add, on the theme of "property as theft."

Policing, understood from this critical perspective, stands as a cogent counter to Weberian idealism, indeed to the romance of much functionalist criminology and its heavily masked "imperialist reason" (Agozino 2003, passim). Recall Walter Benjamin's *Critique of Violence* (1978, 286–87): police violence may "[exist] for *legal ends*," but in practice, it marks the point at which the capacities of the state run out, thus to intervene "where no clear legal situation exists." What is more, it "intervenes" in such a way as to erase the distinction between *preserving* the law and *making* it; to wit, "the 'law' of the police . . . marks the point at which the state . . . [cannot] guarantee through the legal system the empirical ends that it desires." As a result, enforcement, especially in democracies, is "formless," promiscuous, and "spectral," a pervasive, "brutal encumbrance" upon the citizen. Derrida (2002, 276) takes this yet further: the police, he says, actually "*are* the state . . . if not the lawmaker[s] of modern times" (emphasis added; cf. Jauregui 2013b, 127).

Much the same point has been made by a long line of criminologists in the Marxist tradition.[28] For them, the origins of modern policing, substantively speaking,[29] date to Hobsbawm's (1962) *Age of Revolution, 1789–1848*— specifically, to the "triumph" of a bourgeoisie whose hegemony, as we said a moment ago, was grounded in the legal sanctity of private property. As Ernest Mandel (1984) has put it, enforcement was dedicated less to the oppressive control of unruly populations than to the protection of the assets, effects, and interests of individuals, human and legal (i.e., corporations qua "legal persons"). But the Marxist perspective, in stressing both the *production* of class relations and the *protection* of class interests, has also paid attention to the ways in which criminal justice systems have been deployed to yield tractable human subjects as workers to the market—and to ensure their continued docility by policing dissent. Those subjects, we might add, were frequently marked by race and gender; biophysically typed, that is, as less than fully self-possessed and, therefore, as discountable, cheap labor, labor potentially unruly and uncivil(ized) and hence in constant need of discipline. Thus were interpolated race and gender into the core of capitalist modernity and its forms of criminalization.

Discipline, of course, is not merely about dissent or even about punishment. As Foucault famously argues in *Discipline and Punish* (1995), the archaeology of the modern subject, and of modernist subjection, lies in the productive establishment of a new kind of sovereignty, a sovereignty-under-the-skin, as it were: a move away from premodern punitive technologies, which emphasized spectacles of publically inflicted pain, toward the administrative microphysics of everyday surveillance, knowledge production, and self-regulation. Policing, from this alternative perspective, exceeds the work of the police per se. It is understood to diffuse itself, by various ways and means, deeply into the social and institutional order of things, becoming so normalized as to disseminate its effects, inter- and intrasubjectively, throughout a population. Taken to a reductio ad absurdum, as Caleb Smith (2013, 163) intimates, this would render imprisonment, indeed all enforcement, obsolete, which, obviously, policing has not done; there is a good deal more to social life than is captured by these disciplinary determinations. But the general point—that policing exceeds police work everywhere, that the (self-)disciplining of populations lies in a converging, capillary order of everyday institutional practices—is a point well, and widely, taken.

What these critical perspectives share, for all the differences among them, is a dialectical conception of the relationship between legality and criminality, between crime-and-policing, hyphenated and mutually constituting. The rising modernist polity might have sought to naturalize the rule of law, to render its absolutes hegemonic, to define transgression as its dysfunctional underside, to portray its penality as a necessary condition of social order. But no hegemony is ever complete. Beyond it there is always a remainder. Among that remainder were those who, although criminalized, *rejected* the Authority of the Law: the racketeer, the rebel, the trickster, the gangster, the indigent. As ambivalent signifiers, they had the capacity to reveal the justice system for what it was, for what its hegemony failed to hide. So, too, did another part of that remainder, this one on the side of justice, if not necessarily of the law: the private investigator, for example, often a rogue former cop, who, in both fact and fiction, showed up the shortcomings of ordinary enforcement, typically by working along the darker edges of il/legality.

We shall return to these figures, both past and present, in interrogating crime-as-culture. For now, however, a prior point: the archaeology of modern crime-and-policing points to the fact that, with the rise of the bourgeois state, law-making and law-breaking—whether they are read from a liberal or a critical perspective, whether they are seen in functionalist, normative terms or as a dialectic of authority and its transgression—hinged primarily on the protection of property and the (self-possessed) persons who owned it from variously criminalized others. A historically specific culture of legality, in other words, was intrinsic to and inseparable from the birth and maturation of industrial capitalism, of its sense of order. By extension, crime-and-punishment also concerned itself, at once figuratively and concretely, with disciplining labor, especially disciplining those who sought to undermine property and productive relations. But this archaeology, clearly, is Euro- and metropocentric. At the edges of empire things were rather different.

From Metropole to Colony, and Back

In Europe's colonies, labor and property relations were not as hedged around by the liberal contract as they were "at home." In spite of all the talk of a civilizing mission, of "humane" imperialism, their "natives," at least ab initio, were held to lack the civilized self-possession, the ambition for moral and material improvement, necessary for inclusion in "the body of corporate nations" (Comaroff and Comaroff 1991, 86–125)[30]—or in its common law. In the colonial fantasy, it was market relations, above all wage employment, that would civilize them and draw them into capitalist modernity. Until then, a "then" never fully realized, they remained racialized subjects, a reserve army of workers awaiting deployment. Here, the connection between modernity and criminality hinged less directly on matters of private property, especially once indigenes had been dispossessed of their land.[31] Among the colonized—whose "customary law" was not held by their imperial rulers to recognize private ownership per se (cf. Chanock 1991)—enforcement was primarily invested, for the state, in labor relations;[32] labor relations, here, broadly defined to include the insurrectionary violence, vandalism, and petty theft, especially directed against Europeans, that arose out of the refusal to work under prevailing conditions and could, therefore, be read as "political" (cf. Stoler 1985). Only later, when "native" middle classes arose, did property become a focus of criminal justice, and even then, as a secondary matter, often paid relatively less attention by the authorities. As this suggests, colonies abroad were, in many ways, the camera obscura image of the liberal nation-states of Europe. In them, the systematic exploitation of labor was more fully realized than it was at the metropole, the in world according to Adorno and Horkheimer (1979, 226): vide the spectral appearance, in the folklore of the Americas and Africa, of the zombie, the quintessential alienated worker, a body sans sentient self whose toil yielded value without cost. For those employed in the mines, plantations, and industries of Africa, South Asia, and the New World, the workplace *was* a prison; the labor, liberty, and civil rights of entire, racially marked populations were annexed under legally sanctioned arrangements of indenture and enslavement.

Across the diverse facets of the imperial mirror, then, was reflected a plainly visible picture of the connections between capitalism, race, legality, and criminality. Slavery provided the most explicit, most extreme instance, of course. The slave, wrote Frederick Douglass in 1846,[33] could "own nothing . . . but what must belong to another. To eat the fruit of his toil, to clothe his person with the work of his own hands, is considered stealing" (A. Davis 1999, 339); so, too, was his "laziness." Foreshadowings, here, of Adorno and Horkheimer's virtual man-in-jail, of the haunting image of docile, alienated labor in its perfected form, the dark inverse of the self-possessed bourgeois citizen of Euromodernity. When Douglass himself escaped from bondage, "both state and federal law constructed him as a criminal—a thief who absconded with his own body" (A. Davis 1999, 341). The Thirteenth Amendment of the US Constitution, which abolished slavery in 1865, had also declared involuntary servitude unconstitutional, *"except as a punishment for crime"* (A. Davis 1999, 341, original emphasis). It thereby established the judicial basis for an American institution of the *longue durée*: the forced labor of the incarcerated, flexibly adjusted over the decades to changing political and economic conditions, from convict leasing and chain gangs through penitentiary workshops to state- and privately contracted prison labor (see below). The passage of the so-called Black Codes by southern states[34] soon after the Civil War was aimed specifically at controlling the freedom and productive capacity of former slaves, declaring a range of quite-ordinary behavior, from vagrancy and drunkenness to "insulting gestures," as infractions for which only people of color could be convicted. This, in turn, yielded a prison population so large that public officials were soon authorized to "lease the labor of convicts to the highest bidder." For W. E. B. Du Bois (1901, 740–41), what emerged was the "Spawn of Slavery": the "state became a dealer in crime," he wrote, and "profited from it so as to derive a net annual income from her prisoners."

A similar story might be told of British governance in India and the Cape Colony, where the state took firm hold of enforcement, not merely to secure assets, but also to control the flow of labor. British India operated one of the largest prison systems in the world at the time, enabling the extensive use of incarcerated workers, especially those of low caste (Arnold 1994, 173). And at the Cape, the emancipation of slaves in 1834 triggered a penal policy that, as in the United States during the same period, sought to regulate the freedom of black populations in toto, yielding mounting numbers of offenders to be deployed in public works and private-sector agriculture. Elsewhere in South Africa, the story was somewhat more complicated. During the early, explosive years of the Industrial Revolution in the interior—initiated, in the Boer Republics, by the discovery of diamonds near Kimberley in 1867 and gold in the Transvaal in the 1880s—this frontier region saw an influx of adventurers and settlers. Many of them, like their counterparts in the New World, were the victims of processes of industrialization, rural dispossession, labor discipline, and criminalization in Europe. Some had been fugitives from the law; others had been convicts sold as indentured laborers to companies exploring and exploiting new territories, a pattern repeated across much of the colonial map (Ekirch 1987).

Iconic, here, were the Irish, the racialized, impoverished subjects of Britain's oldest "possession" (Ignatiev 1995), a good number of them driven into England's grim factories at midcentury. Charles van Onselen (2014, 2) points out that a significant proportion of these migrants chose to avoid the "enslavement of industry" by joining a motley mix of fortune hunters, vagabonds, and "hard men" at the edges of empire, where they preyed on expanding enterprises and exposed the fragility of local regimes of rule. As in the United States, a few of those fortune hunters—Irish, Jews, Italians—proved highly successful at climbing the "'crooked ladder' of social mobility" by transforming illicit operations into respectable wealth and prestige (Gladwell 2014, 37).[35] In places where the state lacked the capacity or the inclination to protect property or to prevent its expropriation, crime and capitalism fed voraciously off each other, inflected by the prism of race (van Onselen 2014, 163), giving these men plenty of scope for peddling, among other things, violence. Significantly, in those early days in Kimberley, mining consortia often relied more on Irish guns than on the police to defend their holdings. However, as they consolidated their control over the diamond fields in the 1880s, these cartels became the de facto proxies of the state. And, as they did, they developed the notorious closed-compound system, under which African workers were housed in fenced and guarded barracks, securing both their labor and the gemstones it produced; illicit dealings have always been held to plague the diamond industry, justifying the close surveillance of the bodies and movements of its employees. Here we see, in highly elaborated form, the urge to perfect the alienation of labor by means of a carceral workplace. As if to reinforce this, De Beers, the largest of the mining companies, sought and was granted the right by the authorities to build a privately administered jail on their premises—which ensured the additional availability of "convict" labor (Worger 2004).[36]

The urban compound system, and the flow of migrant workers that it managed, would endure, with modifications, for over a century in the South African extractive industries. As in the United States, Britain, and Britain's other colonies, moreover, most forms of contract wage labor were buttressed by master-and-servant acts: laws that made it a felony, punishable by imprisonment (often with hard labor), for employees either to leave their job without the express permission of their employer or to enter into "combinations" to press for better conditions (Hay and Craven 2004; Chanock 2004).[37] These arrangements laid the material and legal substrate of a modernist, highly industrialized national economy; rural black South Africa, tightly contained in "scheduled areas" (aka reservations), was its socially engineered underside, the wellspring that sustained its workforce—in major part through the agrarian toil of women, whose im/mobility was also regulated by official decree.

The broad lines of this quasi-carceral order were buttressed by means of a raft of statutes, among them the infamous pass laws, whose regulation of the lives, first of urban black male South Africans and then of all blacks, led to approximately 250,000 being imprisoned annually.[38] The passbook, which had to be carried at all times under threat of arrest, contained a photograph and the fingerprints of its bearer, as well as personal and official information, including, most significantly, employment details, official permission to be in a specified area to hold or to seek a job, and an employer's signature, accompanied by a report on work performance and general conduct. If an employer—who could *only* be white ("European," in bureau-speak)—refused to endorse the book, its bearer's right to remain in that specified area was terminated. Blacks could also be "endorsed out" by any government functionary for any reason whatsoever, without explanation or legal recourse. This meant "returning" to the economically immiserated countryside, which was reconstituted from the 1960s onward as a patchwork of "ethnic homelands," and which became its own quasi-carceral zone from which exit, for its "discarded people" (Desmond 1971), required formal permission—written into the same pass. The "dompas" ("stupid/dumb pass"), as it was known to black South Africans, was the object of innumerable protests; it was one of the primary causes of the notorious Sharpeville massacre of 1960. That it was so reviled derived in large part from the fact that, as an instrument of governance, it made any African who was not a docile, productive worker into a *protocriminal*, and every white employer into an agent of apartheid enforcement—in other words, an agent of the legal infrastructure of racial capitalism. That infrastructure remained intact until the late 1980s, when changes in the global economy and the deregulation that accompanied the end of apartheid began to dismantle established institutions of labor control (Moodie and Ndatshe 1994, 11ff.; Breckenridge 2014b), if not their penal implications.

In the United States, the counterpoint of race, labor, and the carceral was similarly oppressive, similarly convoluted, similarly colonial, and similarly implicated in the making of the national economy. It goes without saying that criminal justice here, or anywhere else, was not solely addressed to the policing of (especially racialized) labor and its refusal (indigence, vagrancy, and the like). It was integral to the management of social order writ large. Recall yet again Adorno and Horkheimer's "exemplary" figure of the man-in-jail as the negative "image of the bourgeois world." Another exemplary felon, of course, was the communist, who, insofar as she or he allegedly repudiated existing relations of both property and labor and intended the overthrow of the "free world," subsumed all American nightmares rolled into one, all the more so if she or he was black or working class; witness, in this respect, the often-illegal lengths to which the FBI, under J. Edgar Hoover, went to "catch" reds, real or imagined or fabricated. Other felonies and misdemeanors, including those of organized crime (Gladwell 2014, 40), were prosecuted *very* infrequently; they were treated as the predictable infractions of everyday life, arising out ordinary human emotions—need, greed, envy, hate, love, desire—as long as they did not involve civil rights, difference, labor discipline, or anything political.

The civil rights struggle of the 1960s and 1970s would strive to reverse this long history of de jure racism, inequality, and criminalization, a history that continued well beyond emancipation, under Jim Crow, to discipline and discount black labor. It would prove to be a Pyrrhic victory, however: as African Americans, along with women, began to win the right to equality in the workplace, capital was exporting ever more jobs offshore, thus transforming the reserve army of labor in the United States to a largely decommissioned, expendable one. But we are running ahead of ourselves. Our schematic archaeology—in which we have juxtaposed metropolitan Europe, colonial South Africa, and the United States—is intended to make four points about the articulation of crime-and-policing, the state, and capital under conditions of high modernity and its conception of social order: first, that, ordinary lawlessness arising out of "natural" passions and interests aside, it has taken, as its exemplary objects of enforcement, property and labor, albeit in varying proportions over time and place; second, that it has constructed, as its archetypical felons, the indigent, the savage, the stranger, the poor—often characterized, together, as "underclasses," often racialized—whose *structural* situation has made them most likely to violate existing property and/or labor relations; third, that crime has, from the first, been defined as a transgression against society under the trusteeship of the state, which, in terms of the social contract, has the sovereign right and ultimate responsibility to implement the rule of law; and fourth, that, to the degree that the political theology of the modernist nation-state has invested governance with a monopoly over the legitimate means of violence, its policing functions have been assumed to extend to *all* breaches of order within the borders of the political community, be they ordinary felonies, threats to public peace, the public purse, and public security, the violation of persons, places, property, and routes of passage, and so on.

These four features of the modernist conception of crime-and-policing—all of which are undergoing more or less radical transformation—long survived the insistence of critical theorists that state-making and law-making had their origins in organized crime, which entrenched itself in the process of exerting hegemony over the means of violence, the administration of populations, and the management of public finance; that, reciprocally, law-breaking may be seen as insurrectionary practice against the order of relations put in place by "bourgeois society"; that police, far from merely preserving or enforcing the law, make it all the time, especially in the zone of indistinction that lies at the edge of legality, the point at which the state "runs out," the point at which, as Derrida (see above) put it, they actually "are the state." It is because these four features, *as idealizations*, persist in the present—they have an active discursive afterlife, largely as a hankering for the return of an epoch of order, of a commonweal, that never really was—that we write about them in the past-continuous tense.

The Truth about Crime, in the Present Imperfect

If the truth about crime lies in its capacity to yield truths about the times in which we live, the heightened preoccupation with it in the present points to a number of hard "late" modern realities, realities that speak of an epoch-under-construction rather different from what came before, realities captured, in contrasting ways, by our opening fragments.

The first fragment concerned the "rioting and looting" in London in 2011. A political by-product of conservative austerity measures, this uprising was dismissed as "pure criminality" by then Prime Minister David Cameron, who promised to "restore order" to the British streets forthwith; those arrested, mainly youth, were characterized as wild, irresponsible, amoral, reprobate. This incident echoes others elsewhere in the world, among them the "water wars" of 2000 in Cochabamba, Bolivia, in which public demonstrations against privatization and price hikes were met with military action, mass arrests, and a state of emergency; there, too, protesters were portrayed as miscreants with a penchant for trespass, pillage, and plunder. Similarly, in August 2012, the Marikana massacre in South Africa, in which thirty-four striking platinum miners, all of them among the most poorly paid cadres in the industry, were shot to death by police. In an e-mail to the police commissioner, the national vice president, Cyril Ramaphosa, described the action of the workers, who sought moderate pay increases, as "dastardly criminal" and called for "concomitant [police] action." Ramaphosa is a former head of the National Union of Mineworkers, now a board member of Lonmin, the mining company involved, and one of the country's wealthiest businessmen.[39] Evidence submitted to the Commission of Inquiry into the massacre indicated that the "decision to go tactical" (i.e., to shoot to kill) had "to have been political," in short, to have come from the executive branch, although this has not been definitely established.[40] For their part, the police defended their actions by claiming that the strikers, crazed by *muti* (occult medicines), had threatened them with deadly violence, a claim that was credibly disputed at the Marikana Commission.[41] Note that, in each of these "incidents"—alike in England, Bolivia, and South Africa—mass action was treated by the state as, at once, a violation of private property, specifically corporate property, and a breach of public order; these two things being commensurated, equated, and given precedence over the lives, livelihoods, and common concerns of citizens, over their quest for justice and political recognition.

The second fragment, about the shooting of an unarmed black youth, Michael Brown, in Ferguson, Missouri, spoke angrily of the militarization of law-enforcement, of the mass incarceration of people of color, and of an unacknowledged civil war in the United States. This unrest was described as "revolution, plain and simple," by some of its participants.[42] By contrast, the governor of Missouri put it all down to "a violent criminal element intent upon terrorizing the community." Promising to "take action . . . to protect our citizens" against the "vandals and looters,"[43] he called in the National Guard to augment a police department already equipped much like an army, with mine-resistant trucks, combat-grade armor, and automatic rifles.[44] Talk of vandalism and looting, whether or not they actually occur, are archetypically implicated in the criminalization of political protest: they evoke the standardized nightmare of societies based on the sanctity of property. The events in Ferguson also have analogues elsewhere, if less precipitous ones. For example, Didier Fassin (2013) describes urban enforcement in the housing projects of Paris, where, despite a recent decline in violent felonies (xii), racialized populations are policed by cadres who see themselves caught up in a "war without mercy against criminality" (40), cadres who are "ineffective at dealing with everyday crime" (5–6) but who justify their "existence by demonstrating that youth of the *banlieue* are dangerous threats to the nation" (Owen 2014, 596). For Fassin, the "punitive state" (2013, xvii; see below, 1.2) conjures up the ghost of colonialism, being centrally about the assertion of order against the fantasy of impending anarchy (2013, passim; cf. Agozino 2003, 3).

The third of our fragments illuminates a quite-different face of contemporary social order: the absent-presence of the state for ordinary citizens. Taken from the website Turn It Around, South Africa, it is a summons to those who feel vulnerable and unprotected, who have been reduced by crime to a society of strangers, to come together to ensure each other's safety and to fight off disorder. Above all, it is an effort to create a knowledge commons—and to conjure up community as a kind of "cult of affliction" (after V. Turner 1957, 298)[45]—in the void left by a regime of governance that can no longer be relied upon to deliver trustworthy public information or ensure the security of its subjects. Nor is that void an illusion: a report in 2013 by PAIA CSN, a network of civil society organizations, documented the fact that 54 percent of requests for information from public bodies were simply ignored; and, of those that were not ignored, 65 percent were refused.[46] In the circumstances, many have come to believe that the knowledge of which they are being deprived is "being used in the service of the elite and the political class they represent" by a state "more obsessed with protecting [itself] than protecting its citizens."[47] Similar initiatives to that of Turn It Around have occurred in many other places. Typically, they too are born out of serial encounters with unresponsive, disengaged governmental institutions—in particular, with the criminal justice system— which conduce to the appearance, well founded or not, of an unwillingness on the part of the state to attend to a broad range of ordinary breaches and felonies (cf., on South Africa, Steinberg 2008). No wonder, then, that this leaves in its wake a sense of the fragility of public safety and social order, all the more so as people are encouraged to "take responsibility" for their own material, physical, and moral well-being; echoes here of Foucauldian theory, which treats "responsibilization" as an integral element of "neoliberal governmentality" (see below, p. 28). This, as we shall see in 2.4, is sometimes taken as a justification for meting out popular justice and, in the United States, for neighborhood watches, civic associations, and "stand your ground" laws.[48] But, as in the narrative fragment above, such efforts also evince a desire to produce trusting moral publics through the circulation of social knowledge that states—or, more precisely, that those who rule under their sign—frequently fail to provide or guard jealously as *their* secrets under the guise of security (Masco 2010; see 2.3), thus depriving their subjects of the wherewithal to construct zones of civility.

The fourth fragment speaks directly to the privatization of the state, specifically, to the outsourcing, *pace* Weberian orthodoxy, of its monopoly over legitimate violence. Capita, plc is a British company that retails "private indirect government," broadly conceived, if not exactly in the sense described for Africa in the 1990s by Achille Mbembe (2001, 66ff.). The "first [corporate] provider of police services in the UK," it "suppl[ies] end-to-end products" to law-enforcement departments within and beyond Britain, including "immigration and border" control, forensic expertise, and "secure justice applications."[49] But it is not the largest security firm on the planet. G4S is. So deep do its tendrils extend into British society that, in 2013, a *New Statesman* headline declared: "In the Future Our Police, Lawyers and Jails Will Be Run by G4S."[50] The privatization of the public sphere in general, and of the means of violence in particular, is partly a product of corporate capture, partly a corollary of an ideological imperative to "shrink" the state in favor of the market, the two things being intimately related. In the United States, argue Laurence Tribe and Joshua Matz (2014, 120), "government [has been] stripped of nearly all power over money in politics"—this as "social and economic policies [are] made by corporations and bankers"[51]—while police and businesses are now largely "[free] to act without the checks and balances of judicial oversight" (284). What is more, "three times as many persons are employed in private policing as in official law enforcement agencies" (Singer 2003, 69); in South Africa, whose security sector may be "the largest in the world" (Bundy 2014, 120), the ratio is roughly 4:1 (see 2.1), there being some 411,000 registered security guards in a population of ca. 54 million.[52] The outsourcing of government in North America, from the municipal to the federal levels, has increased steadily since the 1980s, despite its distinctly mixed effects (cf. Indiana University, School of Public and Environmental Affairs 2014); in July 2010, Maywood, a California town, became the first in the nation to be *fully* outsourced.[53] Of course, as we noted earlier, the privatization of policing, like the privatization of warfare (Singer 2003), has deep historical precedents. In its latest form, it has four variants: the hiring, by governments, of security companies to "assist" with enforcement; the establishment of their own police by institutions, associations, and corporations; the sale of "protection" by free-standing firms directly to residential consumers; and the meting out of "informal justice" by civic groups or by organized crime, both of which may or may not enjoy local legitimacy. Thus, for example, while we lived in Chicago (1979–2012), our environs were "protected" by city cops (and, on occasion, the FBI), the University of Chicago constabulary, surveillance units run by the Black Muslim community, several private companies, and so-called "street gangs." All of them sought to bring a sovereign sense of order to their slice of the neighborhood and, with it, a simulacrum of the law—this in the face of an obsessive fear of violent crime, and a metaphysic of disorder, that felt little different from South Africa. Thus is sovereignty in its late modern guise both pluralized and lateralized.

Taken together, these narrative fragments begin to illuminate the tectonic shift of which we spoke at the outset: the shift, that is, in the relationship among state, governance, and capital that began in the late twentieth century; the shift, we suggest, that is changing both the meaning of criminality and the nature of crime-and-policing.

The first two fragments give evidence of a redrawing of the line between crime and politics—and, by extension, between the legal and its transgression. In point of fact, that line has always been porous, partial, partisan; to wit, sovereign power resides precisely in the capacity to authorize and enforce it. This has been true since the dawn of modernity, both in Europe, as Foucault (1995, 289) noted of France ca. 1830–50 (see above), and in the Global South, as Claudio Lomnitz (2014, 85) reminds us of Mexico ca. 1810–21.[54] It has been said that, in the late modern world, the effort to redraw, to make, and to suspend the law—thus to delegitimize dissent and difference, inequity and inequality—has become *the* defining act of statecraft (Simon 2007; Scheingold 1991). Doing so in ever more expansive ways, arguably, has become a means of shoring up the edifice of governance under changing conditions everywhere (e.g., R. Wilson 2013, 450)[55]—hence Cochabamba in 2000, London in 2011, Marikana in 2012, Ferguson in 2014, and on and on. In the process, protest and poverty are treated as an unfortunate product of ir/rational choice, individual turpitude, delinquent behavior, affective excess, moral culpability; nor only, in the case of poverty, at moments of major public confrontation, also in the drear bathos of everyday existence. "People across America," says Sarah Stillman (2014, 52), although she could have been talking about many other places as well, "are routinely jailed for fees and fines that they are too poor to pay," fees and fines that often accrue usurious legal penalties for late payment, plus exorbitant "service" costs charged by the private companies to which the state outsources their collection. John Oliver took the point further on US television in his acerbically satirical *Last Week Tonight* (HBO, 22 March 2015),[56] pointing out how people caught up in this vortex of debt, petty transgression, and enforcement frequently lose their jobs, their homes, their families, their futures. Held responsible for their own immiseration—this being the negative face of "responsibilization"—they are also incarcerated for many other petty offenses associated with life on the lumpen undersides of civil society. Thus are social and structural determinations erased from the language of lawmaking and law-breaking. Thus, concomitantly, does criminology displace sociology as the social science that deals with—or, more precisely, after Foucault (1995), *disciplines* our knowledge practices concerning—dis/order at its most general.

To the degree that these two fragments speak to the way in which protest, poverty, difference, and dissent are criminalized, they emphasize the heavy-handed presence of the state in law-enforcement. Even more, they highlight the rising militarization of the police, itself a global phenomenon (A. Wright 2002, 66), which evoked considerable concern in the United States after Ferguson even among conservatives,[57] who, it seems, feared that the "war" on criminal violence had moved *visibly* from the metaphorical to the literal—a fact of which black Americans were well aware, having long seen the cops as an invading force (Goffman 2014, xii);[58] even worse, as an "occupying army" that treated them as "the enemy," according to a veteran of the Boston Police Department.[59] By striking contrast, the third and fourth narrative fragments stress the opposite: the absence of the state, its withdrawal from its subject-citizens, and the devolution of its signal policing functions into the private sector. This—the hyperpresence of the state in *and* its palpable absence from everyday law-enforcement—may appear paradoxical. It is not. Quite the contrary: it is a critical node in the ongoing transformation of crime-and-policing. But before we explain ourselves on that count, let us explore a bit further the implications of these last two fragments.

There is, of course, a close connection between the privatization of government, typified by Capita, plc, and the popular view, echoed at Turn It Around, South Africa, that the state, these days, is neither a guarantor of the security of persons and property nor an authoritative source of social truth—this, nostalgically, by contrast to its imagined past. Both, patently, are corollaries of Dardot and Laval's (2014) "new way of the world" (see above), of what has come to be described, loosely, as the global neoliberal order; loosely, because both "global" and "neoliberal" are, at best, slippery signifiers, at worst, polymorphous, incessantly contested terms. For present purposes, we are less concerned to characterize that order than to focus on one of its signature manifestations: the morphing of the state form and, in particular, its entailment in the changing nature of crime-and-policing.

Sovereignty, Citizenship, and the Criminal Specter

We have already alluded, both directly and indirectly, to several elements involved in the metamorphosis of the state form, all of them well recognized: the incursion into the state of corporate capital; the ideological ascendance of "the market" as the productive epicenter of material and social value; the rise of new species of property, propriety, and possession; transformations in, and the disempowerment of, labor; the widespread impetus to reduce government to an ensemble of institutions designed above all to secure, license, and promote the frictionless workings of a "free," more or less deregulated economy; and, again, the displacement of as many as feasible of its received functions into the private sector or into "public-private" collaborations—to the huge financial advantage of the likes of Capita, plc, G4S, et al. and the chagrin of

Turn It Around, South Africa. From these elements follow three corollaries, each of them also widely documented, all of them closely interrelated.

The first corollary, a function of the anti-etatism of our age, is the dispersal of state sovereignty, increasingly if unevenly across the world; specifically, its appropriation by business firms, nongovernmental organizations, religious movements, ethnopolities, organized crime, civic associations of various sorts, security conglomerates, and the like, all of which seek to control semienclaved terrains, their micro- and moral economies, and the lives (and sometimes the deaths) of those who fall under their sway. Typically, too, they erect facsimiles of criminal justice systems and administrative bureaucracies, and adopt the rhetorics and rituals of citizenship in order to make real their authority; some enact constitutions as well. These lateral sovereignties may be more or less complete, more or less enduring, more or less tolerated by ruling regimes, if they have a choice in the matter. Some of them assert themselves within the space of the nation, others transect its borders, but all of them complicate its jurisdictional geographies. We shall return to them, indeed to the matter of sovereignty tout court, repeatedly as we proceed.

The second corollary of the morphing state form is a transformation in the ecology of citizenship; we have already encountered it, with Turn It Around, South Africa, in talk of responsibilization. It places onus on persons "to give their lives a specific entrepreneurial form" (Lemke 2001, 202–3; cf. Foucault 2008) based on "self-care" and the assumption of responsibility for risk, for rational action, and for pursuing personal fulfillment as a series of cost-benefit calculations; also for their own safety, in a manner oddly reminiscent of ancient Rome, in which "protection of property and personal security were the responsibility of citizens themselves" (Nippel 1995, 113; cf. A. Wright 2002, 54). Accompanying this transformation—itself the realization of the utilitarian strain in capitalist modernity—is the displacement of "society" at the core of collective existence with such concrete abstractions as the "public," the "community," and, most of all, the "network," a global, digitally mediated phantasm constituted of self-possessed subjects (Castells 1996); subjects whose interests, even *within* the family, in which the unborn and nonhuman also have rights, are immanently ranged against one another. Thus does *homo oeconomicus*, a free-floating exosocial being, infuse the essence of humanity, made manifest in the equation of freedom with choice—choice among commodities, identities, moralities, sexualities, philosophies, religiosities, sensibilities—and, concomitantly, with the right and duty to optimize one's preferences. Thus, parenthetically, does the felon, as rational choice theorists argued a while back (e.g.,

G. Becker 1968; Posner 1981), come to be seen as a perfectly ordinary "rational-economic individual who invests, expects a certain profit, and risks . . . a loss" (G. Becker 1968, 198–99) from breaking the law (cf. Pierson 2014, 21). While a great deal has been made of late, especially in Europe, of the yielding of the social citizen to the ethical citizen under neoliberalism (cf. Muehlebach 2012), the latter has come to coexist, if awkwardly—sometimes out of conviction, sometimes to avoid it, often in un/easy complicity—with *homo oeconomicus* in the shifting ecology of citizenship.

There is a lot more to be said about that ecology, but for present purposes, we focus on just one further dimension: the erosion of the social contract, precarity, and the specter of inequality.

The turn of the state away from the business of welfare toward the welfare of business, its reluctance to redistribute, to raise minimum wages, or to regulate labor markets, and its stress on facilitating corporate profit—all of these things exported to the Global South as "structural adjustment"—have rendered large numbers of people disposable, bereft of any prospect of steady employment, or, if they are employed, with incomes insufficient to support dignified lives. In South Africa, for example, where inequality has become a leitmotif of public discourse and levels of debt are the highest in the world,[60] the official jobless count in late 2014, according to Statistics South Africa, was 25.43 percent,[61] although, by common consensus, the actual level is much higher—and racially disproportionate, radically so. The country's reserve army of labor, created under colonial capitalism (see above), has been, for the most part, decommissioned. Statistics South Africa also released a report a few months later that put at a staggering 53.8 the percentage of citizens living below the poverty line, currently calculated at approximately $2.25 per day; this despite the creation of a cash transfer system of social grants directed at softening, if not solving, the problem of a declining formal workforce.

Even where unemployment rates are low—in the United States, on 3 July 2014, the rate dropped to 6.1 percent, amid considerable fanfare—figures often mislead. They typically exclude incarcerated and otherwise-institutionalized populations, the technically disabled, and those who have ceased looking for jobs, usually as a result of chronic failure to find them—all of the above disproportionately racialized. They are also distorted by including, as employed, part-timers who would prefer to be full-time. What is more, with the effective depression of wages in low-paid sectors of many national economies, and with the casualization of work by businesses that seek to squeeze every last bit of profit from their operations, many are compelled to find multiple sources of income to survive. One actuarial analysis assessed the "real" US unemploy-ment rate at 19.9 percent in early 2012, although it also excluded the incar-cerated, institutionalized, and disabled, which would have raised this figure substantially; indeed, to global southern levels[62]—which is where it seems to be heading, given that 48.5 percent of all black children live in poverty, as does 22.1 percent of the population of Chicago (Mariner 2015, 14). Many ordinary middle-class families also hover hazardously at the edge of ruin, just one se-rious illness, accident, divorce, fire, flood, or loss of job away from destitu-tion (cf. Warren 2014, 32, 69). No wonder, in this light, that rising inequality, bloodlessly measured by Gini coefficients, is congealing into a proto-moral panic of planetary proportions, one that has even reached into the interiors of the International Monetary Fund;[63] hence the unusually agitated reaction, scholarly and lay, affirmative and critical, to Thomas Piketty's *Capital in the Twenty-First Century* (2014), which seeks to explain the wealth gap widening inexorably across much of the world.[64] Significantly, it opens with the Mari-kana massacre, using it as a paradigmatic instance of the distributional prob-lem at the core of contemporary capitalism—a problem, Piketty might have added, that is always explosively immanent in the "unholy trinity" of the state, capital, and criminal justice.[65]

Those on the wrong side of that gap, or threatened with falling into it, con-stitute what Guy Standing (2011), among others (e.g., Wacquant 2009a, 113; During 2015), has called the precariat, a growing mass of un- or underinsured, insecure, unwaged, at-risk citizens who, to the face of authority, appear as a "new dangerous class," aka "a new criminal type" (Siegel 1998). Although not a *klass-für-sich*, it is the population for which the liberal social contract is effec-tively under suspension, for which the Leviathan seems merely nasty, brutish, and shortsighted—being more concerned with surveillance, secrecy, securiti-zation, and servicing capital than with serving civil society—*pace* neoconser-vatives, who continue to see it as still too intrusive, too "big," too protective of the indigent and the alien. In absconding from the social contract, actually ex-isting states (or, rather, those who govern in their name, those who invoke "the state" to authorize its partisan provenance) appear ever more committed to forcing an ineffable distinction between respectable citizen-populations and lumpen-populations; again, those decommissioned, disposable workers. The latter are named and narrated as the enemy within, the enemy against whose very condition of being—poverty, disease, illiteracy, nonorthodox families, drug use, homelessness, vagrancy—"war" is to be waged under the sign of the law. Observe, yet again, the strategic confusion between law and war, citizen and stranger. It legitimizes the out*law*ing of entire populations—of that typically racialized precariat whose *law*lessness is taken to pose an immanent threat of disorder—by promulgating and enforcing *laws* that prohibit many of their ordinary survival practices; Eric Garner was killed by police in New York City in July 2014 while being arrested for allegedly selling loose cigarettes from an unstamped pack, a petty crime against a regressive tax regulation that disproportionately disadvantages the poor.[66] Therein lies the "criminalization of poverty" (see, e.g., Gustafson 2009), of race (A. Davis 2007; Hudson 2006; Goffman 2014; cf. Mauer 2006), and of immigration (e.g., Provine and Doty 2011). Therein, too, lie the interdiction, the exclusion, and negation, not to mention the gross inequities in access to justice and legal defense,[67] that they warrant. All this points to a politics of mutual mistrust, to the fraying bond between state and citizen that, ideologically, held the modernist nation together; indeed, to the sense, encountered earlier, of an un/civil war between the empowered and the disempowered. For many citizens, who believe that the state should protect them, that it has the means to do so—so vividly exemplified in the first two narrative fragments—this conduces to a sense of violation of their citizenship, a point to which we shall return.

The third corollary of the morphing state form with which we are concerned here is an especially critical one. It is the ever-growing murkiness, in the shadows of the rising global economy, of the line between the licit and the illicit, the entrepreneurial and the extralegal—and, with it, a pervasive sense that crime lurks everywhere, either immanent or in fact, either in plain sight or just beyond it. These two things, the murkiness of the line and the pervasive sense of lurking criminality, congeal into what may be characterized as the "criminal specter" of late modernity, of its metaphysics of disorder. In large part, this specter has its source in the uneven liberalization, deregulation, and deterritorialization of that economy, and its space-time compression, which have enhanced greatly the capacity of corporate and finance capital to keep moving in pursuit of legally lax, preferentially (or un-)taxed, relatively undocumented shelters.[68] This, plus the sheer complexity of commercial and administrative legal geographies and their jurisdictions of enforcement, has eventuated in a world ever more hospitable to what is conventionally perceived as corruption and fraud, a good proportion of which hides itself in jural black holes. Both have become endemic not just to business but also to government, even criminal justice, at all levels. As we noted earlier, crime and politics have never been hermetically separated from one another. However, as Aspinall and van Klinken (2010, 23) put it, speaking of Indonesia in particular, these forms of illegality are "not [any longer] an aberration"; rather, "they *are* the state." The same can be said of many other places.

This, in turn, is owed directly to the outsourcing of its functions, which has transformed the state, in many respects, into something akin to a holding company, a metacorporation under the sign of "Nationality, Inc." (Comaroff and Comaroff 2009, 122): a licensing authority, that is, in the game of franchising out social, security, financial, carceral, administrative, military, and other services to profit-seeking firms. To the degree that, in this capacity, it is a conduit for the redistribution of public funds into private hands, its legislators and bureaucrats, its politicians and its policeman become the agents of rentier government; their proceeds—as finders' and consultants' fees, as campaign contributions, as "informal" favors and influence, as shareholders of firms that "do business" with the state, even just in the delivery of votes—become indistinguishable from those of anyone else who harvests personal gain from office. This is precisely what is generally defined as "corruption." Which, typically, contemporary ruling regimes claim perpetually to be "combating," another metaphor from the argot of warfare, just as they seem perpetually to be afflicted by it. This is often seen to be a classically African "problem," its states having long been called "criminal," its rulers long characterized, generically, as kleptocratic or worse (Bayart, Ellis, and Hibou 1999). In South Africa, whose President Jacob Zuma has been dubbed a "thief" in Parliament (and "commander-in-thief" in the press; Poplak 2014, 58), allegations of gross corruption have been part and parcel of the transition from apartheid to democracy (see, e.g., du Preez 2013, 57, 70–71, 87–88; cf. Mbeki 2009). But many non-African ruling regimes, including the likes of Germany, the United States, the United Kingdom, and Russia—not to mention the European Union—have also had megascandals in recent decades; this even when, as in the United States and the United Kingdom, many of the things taken to be corrupt elsewhere are laundered in and by the law. Nor is it only African leaders who have been accused of serious illegalities. The head of the International Monetary Fund, Christine Lagarde, was placed under formal investigation by the French Court of Justice in August 2014 for her involvement in a "murky business affair" while she was the country's finance minister.[69] And her predecessor, Dominique Strauss-Kahn, notoriously, has faced criminal investigation more than once, most recently in France for aiding and abetting prostitution, aka "aggravated pimping."

But the "corruption" laced seamlessly into the fabric of the state—as we have implied, it is more accurately described as "rentier governance," being a *systemic* feature of contemporary political economy—is also both a corollary and a manifestation of something else, another face of the criminal specter. The morphing of the state form, and of the political economy of which it is part, has conduced to a world in which material, legal, and moral deregulation has obfuscated, perhaps more than before, received distinctions between conventional business practice and organized crime, brokerage and bribery, franchising and racketeering, proprietary rent-taking and piracy, legitimate and illegitimate force-for-sale, venture speculation and Ponzi-style skullduggery. Striking, in this last respect, is the rise, in South Africa, of the "tenderpreneur," an official "who abuses their political power and influence to secure government . . . contracts,"[70] and, in the United States, of new shell games that are viewed in the finance industry as "distasteful cousins in the high-rolling world of securities," thereby muddying the difference between criminal and merely unsavory practices.[71] Note, here, the capacity of those guilty of market malfeasance to escape arrest, a phenomenon especially marked in the wake of the economic quakes of 2007–8.[72] Not always, of course: hence the recent indictments for unprecedented kinds of felony—many of them quite ingenious, some of them so momentous as to put at risk the workings of the global financial order—handed down against respected businesses and banks that had long evaded sanction for shady dealings.[73] But they are remarkably few, all things considered; vide the Enron scandal of 2001, which illustrated not just the blurring of the line between licit dealings and fraud, nor just the capture of the state by the corporate sector, but the nefarious ways and means opened up for creative criminality by the new global laissez-faire.[74] Relatively rare, too, is the prosecution of high-end players in the world of organized crime, those who, as in the corporate sector, are "too big to fail." The point was forcibly made by the case of James "Whitey" Bulger in Boston in 2014, in which the collaboration of police and politicians, crime and government, made plain both the immunity of the powerful from prosecution and the difficulty of distinguishing enforcement from the commissioning of felonies (Cullen 2013; Keefe 2015, 96–99; see below, 1.3).

Indeed, perhaps the most striking feature of the criminal specter is the inseparability, a lot of the time, of policing from crime, crime from policing, a point poignantly captured in the cartoon by Zapiro cited in the preface (see image 2). This has both epic and mundane dimensions. Thus, for example, in the United States, according to Human Rights Watch, the FBI, in the course of setting up sting operations aimed at catching terrorists, has actually created them out of law-abiding citizens; in one case, said the judge, "[the government] came up with the crime, provided the means, and removed all relevant obstacles [to committing it]."[75] This is not new, of course—as we mentioned before and will return to again, J. Edgar Hoover's FBI regularly violated the law[76]—but the practice seems to have expanded exponentially and occurs at all levels of policing (see, e.g., Crank 1998, 249–50; Jackall 2005, 36; see below). In 2013 the FBI "disclosed that it had authorized [its] informants to break the law on 5,939 occasions" (Keefe 2015, 98), a number that does not include authorizations to its own officers. In Britain, in 2014, several senior policemen, including the police chiefs of Manchester, West Yorkshire, and Avon and Somerset were under criminal investigation for a variety of alleged felonies.[77] Even more dramatically, a recent head of Interpol—the World's Most Senior Cop, who happened also to be the South African police commissioner, Jackie Selebi—was imprisoned in 2010 for fifteen years for his illicit dealings with a notorious drug kingpin. Selebi, who had been active in the antiapartheid movement, died in 2015, after a medical parole; despite his criminal past, he was eulogized by the ruling African National Congress, which paid for his funeral.[78] At the time of writing, efforts are being made, in the upper echelons of the party, to argue that Selebi never broke the law to begin with, that, despite the decision of the court, he was the victim of an intelligence sting operation.[79] Farfetched, perhaps, but not unexpected in a world in which *law-breaking and law-enforcement are so entangled as often to be impossible to set apart*, a world in which, to recall Charles Tilly's (1985) archaeology of modern government, state-making was largely indistinguishable from organized crime. This, in turn, makes two generic points about the criminal specter: first, that at the edges of legality the distinction between the licit and the illicit is often undecidable, its determination depending not on the law but on political and economic externalities; and second—this being the other side of the redrawing of the line between crime and politics—that in many places these days accusations of criminal malfeasance, especially corruption, have become a conventional instrument, the hatchet of choice, in struggles among the rich and the powerful, much like accusations of witchcraft have long been in many parts of Africa (cf. Kondos 1987; Blundo 2007).

More mundanely, however, in both South Africa and the United States,[80] felony rates among cops—counted, uncounted, recounted, discounted—appear to be strikingly high. In South Africa, fully 10 percent of the police force, 14,600 officers, faced criminal charges in 2000 (Newham and Bruce 2000), a figure likely to be equaled in 2014 (see 2.1).[81] Some of these charges have been for brute violence against innocent citizens (cf. Altbeker 2005, 130–

34), and this is not to mention dramatic incidents like the Marikana massacre or the flagrant killing in public of political protesters, of which there have been several cases (see below). In May 2015 the heads of Crime Intelligence and the Independent Police Investigative Directorate (the body mandated to deal with malpractice in the South African Police Service, or SAPS), as well as two provincial police commissioners, were under investigation; the last national commissioner was recently removed after being accused of a serious breach of practice. A research report by the South African Institute of Race Relations (2015), *Broken Blue Line 2*, argues that there has long been "a pattern . . . of police planning and perpetrating violent crime" (2), that many of those who have been convicted remain on active duty (5), that the SAPS has been infiltrated by criminal syndicates (8), and, most intriguing perhaps, that gangs of "cloned" (fake) officers, enabled and equipped by one or more "real" ones, have used official cover to commit serious, serial offenses (4; see also 2.2),[82] a phenomenon that underscores, again, the illegibility, for the public, of the line between law-breaking and law-enforcement. Significantly, *Broken Blue Line 2* was preceded, just over a year earlier, by a damning study entitled *Crossing the Line: When Cops Become Criminals* (Grobler 2013). Clearly, the symbolism of the sundered line, less thin blue (Steinberg 2008) than ruptured red—which again calls to mind the Schmittian cleavage between friend and enemy—evokes Newham and Faull's (2011) question about the SAPS: protector or predator? No wonder that fully a third of the population admits to being afraid of the cops, or that 70 percent believe many of them to be felons.[83] Notwithstanding the fact that the majority of officers are perfectly honest, are more or less competent, and go about their daily business in good faith, it is often unclear who are *really* cops, who are crooked ones, and who are clones—all the more so since the real ones are poorly paid and, hence, thought to be perpetually open to the blandishments of the criminal economy. As a street thug puts it in K. Sello Duiker's (2000, 73) celebrated *Thirteen Cents*, "Ba Batla borotho [literally, "they want bread"]. They want to eat well. Streets are hard, hey. We give those arseholes a tough time." So rife is law-breaking within the realms of law-enforcement that, in one province, a local Anti-corruption Investigation Unit has been charged with stamping it out; this as, in February 2015, the provincial police commissioner promised zero tolerance of crime *within* the police force.[84]

We shall return to the SAPS below. But there are distinct parallels with the United States. According to the *Washington Post*, American cops have shown a growing proclivity to perpetrate "indefensible violence against civilians, including innocents";[85] this usually is excused by invoking not just the dire threat of disorder but also the mortal risks they ordinarily face—which is ironic, since, statistically, in the United States, their work has been shown to be less dangerous than that of farmers, truck drivers, construction workers, and garbage collectors.[86] Typically, they have gone unindicted and unpunished for their violence, which has "create[d] a culture of impunity," a point underscored by the killing of Michael Brown in Ferguson, Eric Garner in New York, and the thousands of others recorded by the Stolen Lives Project and the October 22 Coalition.[87] Said a former policeman from Saint Louis, not thirteen miles from Ferguson, the "problem is that cops aren't held accountable for their actions, and they know it. These officers violate rights with impunity."[88] Echoes of Walter Benjamin, almost a hundred years on: the cops are still making the law as they break it, but even more so, and in more militarized a manner. Here too, law-making, law-breaking, and law-enforcement are increasingly difficult to distinguish. These days, moreover, police almost everywhere call up the specter of security—of inscrutable terrors of sundry types, both home-grown and alien—to justify their deadly violence, their protection from prosecution, and their deployment of the dark edges of the law (cf., on Brazil, Caldeira 2000, 158ff.). Theirs, as we have said, is a universe erected on the pervasive, persuasive antinomies of good-and-evil, civility-and-chaos, dis/order, a universe in which they see themselves as taking on an unruly mass of anticitizens whose very physical presence appears to them to signal an inherent threat to civil order (cf. Butler 1993b).

Coda: From Im/possibility to the Pathological Public Sphere

These elemental shifts in the state form, in its relationship to capital, governance, and crime-and-policing, make plain why it is that lawlessness is presumed almost everywhere to be on the rise, almost everywhere a potential threat to order; this, patently, being an overdetermined corollary of the criminal specter, the succubus in the dark shadows of the rising global economy, that is eroding received sovereignties and truths. The very undecidability of the lines between the licit and the illicit, between law-making, law-breaking, and law-enforcement, presents itself, phenomenologically, as imminent, immanent disorder—whether or not, statistically, fear and risk *are* dis/proportionate, whether or not criminal violence *is* actually on the rise, whether or not it actually *does* present a clear and present danger to everyday life. Which, of course, it does in some places, albeit in varying, sometimes-counterintuitive measure. In short, the phenomenology of fear resides as much in the illegibilities of a world in which it is difficult ever to know where risks to person and property lie, who is the upright citizen and who the enemy within—or, for that matter, who is the righteous political dissident and who the common vandal, the looter, the violent opportunist (see 2.2). This, in turn, underscores the transcendent significance of crime as a lingua franca, an ethnosociological vernacular in which to debate, dissect, and diagnose the condition of "the" social order itself: to reflect on the quality of life and confront critical questions of governance and politics, of race and class and gender, of identity and civility, and much else besides. It is a hieroglyph, in other words, that demands decoding. Recall, once more, Durkheim's stress on the semiotic side of criminality, on its invocation as a critical medium, an instrument of divination almost, by means of which societies produce and posit knowledge about themselves. Thus, the lament by Turn It Around, South Africa, and in virtual public spheres like it, that the social contract has been abrogated by the state: that, as a result, the self-imagining of community, of cohesion born of collective consciousness and a unity of purpose, has been voided. And that civil society, absent reliable means of truth, has lost its moorings.

Absent that truth—given the emergent ecology of citizenship, with its stress on responsibilization and self-care—the question of who or what it is that might serve as the sovereign guarantor of safety, security, and moral order presents itself ever more urgently. The organs of state? Not really, as we have seen, for all but relatively few. The private sector? The mechanisms of "informal" or "people's" justice? Self-securitizing religious and ethnic communities? Corporate police forces? Organized crime? For large segments of national populations, this question is left perennially open, perennially to be negotiated, perennially the object of anxious uncertainty, intermittently the subject of calls to action. At the same time, the fantasy remains that if it *did* have the will, the state *could* recapture both its monopoly over the means of legitimate coercion and its patrimonial role in the protection of its citizens; after all, as our first two fragments show, when that will *is* present, states *do* show the capacity to police, to do so with considerable, often-theatrical authority, not to mention violence. What is more, they tend to talk constantly about winning the "war" on crime, about increased enforcement, about their resolve to secure their sovereign scapes; about "clean[ing] up the streets" and "reassert[ing] the authority of the state," as the Office of the Presidency in South Africa recently put it.[89] Herein lies the ostensible paradox of which we spoke earlier, the paradox of presence-and-absence. It is a source of deep ambivalence toward law-enforcement among publics in many places: on the one hand, a desire for effective policing and a faith in its possibility; yet, on the other, widespread disillusion about its efficacy in containing lawlessness, about the corruption, criminality, and excessive force of the cops themselves, about a lack of commitment on their part to the commonweal. And about the fact that even when they act in good faith, as Redi Tlhabi, a widely read black South African writer and columnist has put it, they are often badly outmanned and outgunned by felons "who do not give a damn about being caught," felons "in overdrive," felons who "have the upper hand" in a "surreal, . . . toxic mix of circumstances which gives [them] the upper hand."[90]

Popular desire, in short, runs constantly up against fear and distrust—which, dialectically, yields a pathological public sphere (cf. Seltzer 1997) born of the belief, simultaneously, in *both* the possibility *and* the impossibility of policing-as-panacea in defense of civility, property, liberty, and the good life. Or, put another way, in the representation of the police as *both* a positive necessity for the accomplishment of order *and* a popular nightmare, the negation of that very order (cf. Caldeira 2000, 158–59). It is in precisely this, in the pathological public sphere, that a metaphysic of disorder has taken root across so much of the geosphere of the late modern epoch. It is in this, too, that there has arisen what Robert Reiner (2010, 3, 4; also Reiner and Newburn 2007) refers to as "police fetishism," that is, the axiom that officers of the law are a "prerequisite of social order" despite their "debatable" contribution to its accomplishment or to the control of crime;[91] this in stark contrast to perceptions common half a century or so ago, when Michael Banton (1964, 1) could say, quite plausibly, that those officers "are relatively unimportant in the enforcement of law," or when Jane Jacobs (1961) could assert, with confidence, that "social order is *not* brought about by policemen" (see Scott 1998, 135–36).

The present-absence of policing, the dialectic of im/possibility to which it has given rise, and the gnawing ambivalence spawned by it, as will be clear by now, all flow from the parsing of the police function that has come with the seismic shift of the state form in its relation to capital and governance. While, normatively, government is still expected by its citizens to take responsibility for all aspects of protection and enforcement—thus to reproduce the ideological scaffolding on which the law was founded during the high age of modernity—the abdication of so much to the market and the self-care of citizens has opened up a rift between the past and the present. Much of the oversight of the persons and property of ordinary citizens, as we have seen, has migrated into the private sector, into the hands of everything from conglomerates like Capita, plc and smaller security firms to the NGOs, communal associations, and other sovereignty-seeking bodies mentioned earlier. At the same time, labor, in many places, is now disciplined directly by corporations—except where "indiscipline" comes to be defined as a threat to public order—largely through casualization, underemployment, wage controls,[92] threats of dismissal, the outlawing of unions, and, as in the colonial period (see above, p. 19), the operations of company security units largely autonomous of legal oversight; as early as 1983, Neil Kinnock, then soon to be head of the Labour Party in Britain, spoke presciently of the disciplinary function, of "the gibbet of unemployment," of its capacity to induce quiescence.[93] The outsourcing of the police function in these and other ways makes it plain why the present-absence of state enforcement is not a paradox at all: it is an endemic feature of the post-Weberian age of private indirect governance, of its division of social labor.[94] But this, in turn, raises an obvious question: if law-enforcement has been parsed—effectively leaving the everyday security of private property and persons to the commercial sector and to community self-protection (see 2.4), and the disciplining of labor to corporations—how are we to typify crime-and-policing as a state project in the history of the present? Once more taking as our prime examples the United States and South Africa, let us turn to this question, to what it tells us of the truth about crime.

CHAPTER 1.2

THE ORDER OF THINGS TO COME

Crime-and-Policing in the Present Continuous

We ended our archaeology of the relationship between criminality and modernity with the hard-won gains of the civil rights movement in the United States during the 1960s and 1970s. Much has changed since then. For one thing, rates of imprisonment have quadrupled since the 1980s (Garland 2001; Wacquant 2002); this in tandem with rising inequality, rising precarity, as post-Fordist America found either mechanical or foreign substitutes for domestic labor, thus to decommission the less skilled, disproportionately black and devalued fractions of its workforce (see, e.g., Western 2006). The United States is now home to some 25 percent of *all* the world's prisoners.[1] Depending on whose figures one treats as authoritative—indeed, to the degree that crime statistics are authoritative at all (see 2.3)—approximately 743 per 100,000 people languished in a correctional institution in mid-2011, over half of them for drug offenses. Rwanda (595) and Russia (568) come next, followed by other notoriously authoritarian states (in the 400+ range); South Africa has 316 per 100,000 people, but most nations commonly classified as democracies fall below 150. Already by the 1980s there was an alarming overrepresentation of the poor, the un(der)employed, and people of color in US penitentiaries (Lichtenstein 2011, 8; cf. Muhammad 2010; Western 2006). By 2007 African Americans were being imprisoned 5.6 times more than whites; and Hispanics, 1.8 times more. The proportion of women inmates, mostly African American and Hispanic, has also grown substantially since the late 1970s (Mauer and King 2007). The "new Jim Crow" (M. Alexander 2010), which reprises the post–Civil War era in a late liberal key, has deployed some very old mechanisms of criminalizing the indigent. But it also rests on newly intensified techniques of "hyperpolicing" (Tibbs 2010)—and on militarized enforcement, of which we spoke earlier—that has targeted narcotics, debt default, sex offenses, homelessness, illegal immigration, unsanctioned public gatherings, trespass, and many petty violations (e.g., Beckett and Herbert 2010). And has secured sentences of unprecedented length for them (Golden 2005, 45; Garland 2001, 168–69). These techniques have conduced to "the uniquely punitive social order of the United States" (Simon 2014, 62–63; but cf. Matthews 2005), where, adds Nicholas Kristof, "black men in their 20's without a high school diploma are more likely to be incarcerated today than employed."[2] Or worse. Which brings us up sharply into the present.

First, in the USA . . .

It is unnecessary here to trace any further the route by which—or the roots from which—the United States arrived at its here and now; there is a comprehensive, critical literature on the topic, some of which we have already alluded to. Suffice it to say that, in order to justify hyperpolicing, the precariat of the United States has come to be portrayed as an unruly, indolent, inherently violent, and expendable population; no longer productive workers, they are "matter-out-of-place"—Mary Douglas's (1966, 36) classic definition of what is archetypically perceived as dirt, disorder, and pollution—in the postindustrial city of the twenty-first century. The alleged crimogenic propensities of this population are regularly invoked in the cause of "sanitizing" urban landscapes that, outside their dark inner archipelagos (ghettos, *banlieues, favelas*, projects, townships), are home to postproletarian elites. The almost-iconic status accorded to the "broken-windows" approach,[3] its zero tolerance for even the most minor misdemeanors, its emphasis on "quality-of-life" policing, and its targeting of "high-crime hotspots" make evident the spatial, indeed socio-aesthetic, turn in law-enforcement—one that resonates with a gentrifying, class-segregated, order-obsessed politics of neighborhood civility-and-security (Beckett and Herbert 2010, 16; Wacquant 2009b, 16; C. Smith 2013, 164).

Policing, on the part of the state, in short, has come to be dedicated primarily to the preservation of social order, focusing, above all else, on the containment of those who, putatively at least, pose an imminent threat to peace, property, public assets, and polite society (cf., e.g., A. Wright 2002, 49–71); recall, in this respect, Fassin's (2013) account of Paris, where enforcement is directed less to crime fighting per se than to "controlling urban disorder" (above, 1.1). Public order has always been integral to the police function, of course, along with crime prevention and crime fighting. In the present, however, it appears to loom larger, proportionately, than it has done in the past, save for exceptional periods of unrest. What has emerged, suggests David Garland (2001), is a *"culture* of control" (169, emphasis added), sustained by "[p]roblem-oriented policing, community policing, order-maintenance policing, quality-of-life policing." Aspects of enforcement that do not fall within this purview, as we have noted, tend to be outsourced to the private sector. There are exceptions, patently. Notable among them are the forms of specialist policing aimed, with varying degrees of efficacy, at dealing with the complex financial practices that have arisen out of new forms of immaterial property, many of which hover in the spectral murk between the law and "creative" accounting (see, e.g., 2.1).

But the broad lines within which the police function has been parsed seem very clear. To the degree that officers of the law are drawn into operations typically dealt with by the private sector, they attend largely to their administrative side—recording felonies, for example, for insurance purposes—rather than to the prosecution of perpetrators or the recovery of property. Almost everywhere, only a small proportion of crimes reported to the cops are actively investigated; a much smaller proportion end in arrests. In the United States in 2006–10, to take one critical instance, "out of every 100 rapes, 32 [were] reported to the police, 7 [led] to an arrest, 3 [were] referred to prosecutors, 2 [ended in] a felony conviction."[4] In the United Kingdom, by way of a telling comparison, albeit for a slightly earlier period (1992), "47 per cent [of all "actual" crimes] were 'reported,' 27 per cent [were] 'recorded,' 5 per cent [were] 'cleared-up' and only 2 per cent result[ed] in conviction" (Mayhew, Mirrlees-Black, and Aye Maung 1994; cf. A. Wright 2002, 90). It is these figures—which will surprise South Africans, who believe the South African Police Service (SAPS) to be the least effective on the planet (above, 1.1; below, pp. 104, 151, 190)—that persuade many criminologists to discount crime fighting on the part of the police as pure "myth" (A. Wright 2002, 90). This is notwithstanding the fact that cops themselves, both real and fictional, overwhelmingly see it as their defining practice.[5]

These transformations in enforcement have been read in a variety of ways. Lichtenstein (2011, 9), for one, treats the spike in incarceration in the United States from the mid- 1970s—necessitating state contracts for building, staffing, and provisioning prisons—as a highly "successful public-works program" in the face of declining manufacture, excess immigration, periodic economic instability, and the rapid growth of a vulnerable, deskilled underclass; this by contrast to a previous era of penal welfarism (Garland 2001), in which the penitentiary was viewed as a site of rehabilitation. A more complex, no less conspiratorial narrative relates it directly to the retrenchment of the state, a process in which correctional services were quickly caught up (cf. Shapiro 2011). As the incidence of penal servitude began to rise dramatically at fin de siècle, goes this argument, private firms campaigned for its outsourcing, capitalizing—literally—on the fact that mass imprisonment was placing a heavy political and fiscal burden on public resources (cf. Gilmore 2007). Claiming that privatization "is always preferable to public ownership because of the purported efficiency of private markets," even where the evidence proves otherwise (Mason 2012, 12), those firms insisted that they could make confinement pay. Riding an ideological wave, their percentage of the penal population exploded after 1999 (Justice Policy Institute 2011, 1–2); by late 2014 they were said to be seeking to buy prisons in forty-eight states in exchange for exclusive management contracts and guaranteed occupancy. More to the present point, they are said to have lobbied aggressively, successfully, and profitably—two of the largest companies had combined revenues of $2.9 billion in 2010[6]—for legislation that would fill cells (Mason 2012, 13; Justice Policy Institute 2011, 15–30);[7] legislation that favors treating an ever-wider range of minor misdemeanors as problems of public dis/order. Corporations, moreover, have invested billions in the businesses that flourish inside correctional institutions, selling financial, telecommunication, and other services to inmates at highly inflated rates, free of the regulations that protect ordinary consumers.[8] The industry has also shown itself to be alive to new opportunities, including those that flow from its own internal contradictions and pressures to reform. For example, since 2008 a few states (New York, Michigan, California) have begun to shrink their carceral populations (Drucker 2013, 1103).[9] Talk now abounds of a new era of "America on probation,"[10] which has sparked an expanding, highly controversial, for-profit halfway house, parole, and reentry sector (Drucker 2013, 1109–10). This is in spite of a large literature to show that, in addition to increasing America's carceral and probation populations, these firms run low-quality penal institutions, prey on the poor, contribute to recidivism rates, and profit excessively themselves while actually costing the taxpayer money (see, e.g., Mason 2012). Crime, patently, has been made here to pay very well. It has become, in a grim parody of Marx (above, 1.1), a highly profitable mode of production in which persons are the commodities in question, secreting the relations of race and class embodied in them as it produces new truths about a society in which race-and-class are more or less unspeakable.

The emphasis of state policing on public order has also been narrated with reference to the vexed issue of carceral labor. It has been claimed that a new internal "offshore" enclave, even a gulag of "slave labor camps," has emerged within US penitentiaries, thus to deliver the nation's disposable, lumpen population into the maw of the corporate sector (Western 2006; E. Alexander 2008; Hallett and Sheldon 2006; Brewer and Heitzeg 2008; but cf. n.105 below). Steven Fraser and Joshua Freeman describe a prison "archipelago" that serves as a "niche market" for homegrown sweatshop work, an industry that employs "more people than any Fortune 500 corporation and operat[es] in 37 states."[11] Penal servitude is an endemic American institution, they argue, having played a similar role in subsidizing industrial power when the means of capital accumulation were in crisis during the late nineteenth century. Persuasive as this may seem, it cannot, in itself, account for the scale of incarceration here. A "prison-industrial complex" (Lichtenstein 2011, 13), indeed a highly profitable one, does exist. But only a small proportion of inmates actually work for private firms; the largest employer is Federal Prison Industries, a state-owned company, which supplies contract labor to government departments, like Defense and Homeland Security, often at a net loss (Wacquant 2009b, 85). As James Kilgore argues, convicts suffer more from purposeless warehousing than economic exploitation; the techniques necessary to enforce control over them in overcrowded facilities are incompatible with the rationalities of large-scale production.[12] Labor abuse *is* at the core of mass incarceration, he suggests. But it is the exclusion of the underclasses from mainstream employment through processes of deindustrialization—their *dis*employment, if we may coin a phrase—and ill-supported education that drives the process; he might have added to this the retraction of welfare, obligatory workfare, and the systemic erosion of wages. Drawing on his own years inside, Kilgore concludes that the "school to prison pipeline" is far more a reality than is the penitentiary as factory floor. The prison-industrial complex, he insists, is "more about politics than profits." In fact, it is about both, translated into the argot of public order.

For Loïc Wacquant (2009b, 162 et passim), all this signals a *structural* shift from the "social state" to the "penal state." It is part of a "hegemonic neoliberalism" that has made prisons the ur-mechanism for dealing with race, poverty, and precarity. Adds Wacquant, the broken-windows approach to enforcement—its zero-tolerance policing, which was branded by William Bratton in New York under Mayor Rudolph Giuliani (see Bratton 1998; Auletta 2015) and has become the paradigm du jour for much of the planet—targets the "subproletariat that mars the scenery and menaces or annoys the consumers of urban space." Note, again, the aesthetics of order, and the ordering aesthetic, entailed in policing the unruly and the unpropertied on behalf of polite, propertied American society; it involves a repertoire of technologies—think CCTV, GIS, and the like—that objectify and make visible, in a spatial syntax, those inner-city surplus populations in order, paradoxically, to put them "out of sight."

This account of the rise of the penal state, and of the global diffusion of a new "penal common sense," resonates broadly with what has been dubbed, internationally, the "managerial model" of criminal justice; Wacquant (2009a, 113) himself speaks of the "punitive *management* of poverty" (emphasis added)—poverty, we would add, arising out of changes in the nature and value of labor, in the nature and value of property, and in the law that protects it. That managerial model of criminal justice, as Issa Kohler-Hausmann (2014, 611 et passim) puts it, echoing the earlier Foucault, is intended less to "[punish] individual acts of lawbreaking" than to discipline targeted populations.[13] The stress on "management," moreover, gestures toward something else as well: the move from an older-style, bureaucratic-institutional culture of policing to a corporate-business one, stressing, in its self-representation, "service" instead of force (see Mawby 2002, 28–29 for the United Kingdom). Written in the rhetoric of cost-benefit efficiency, outsourcing, and risk reduction, it relies in its modus operandi on a data-driven, statistical model known as CompStat.

A friendly amendment here. The turn to a managerial model seems not so much an either/or, or a less/more, than a both/and in respect of penality/discipline: the "targeted population" in question, as Wacquant (2009a, 113) appears to appreciate, is *both* "targeted" *and* constituted as a "population"—even as a polis—in the course of its criminalization, effected in an infinite number of individual arrests that congeal into mass incarceration. Take, for example, a striking statistic, cited by Kohler-Hausmann (2014, 611 et passim) herself: in 2013, despite a receding crime rate, the New York Police Department (NYPD) made 394,539 individual arrests, tens of thousands more than in 1995, when there were three times as many murders and many more felonies overall[14]—although, "as [those] misdemeanor arrests climbed dramatically, . . . rates of criminal convictions [if not their raw incidence] fell sharply."[15] Also, while arrest may not end in conviction, it *is* itself a form of punishment: in the United States, it may involve battery, hard time in holding cells, even an extrajudicial death sentence. And mass arrest, as we have intimated, is both an enactment of and a justification for the focus of state policing on public order rather than on crime fighting per se; the latter, to the degree that it is pursued, is a means to the former. In the process, the line between civil and uncivil society is constantly redrawn along the axes of race and class. In the process, ethno-sociological truths about normativity and pathology are fabricated and naturalized (cf. C. Wilson 2000, 5), people are relentlessly categorized, and "criminal classes" are identified;[16] in the process, too, as Foucauldians would add, the "body politique" is transformed into that new behemoth, the "body demographic" (Vanderbilt 1997, 141), a reified abstraction founded on putative biophysical and psychogenetic characteristics. Thus are the geographical lineaments of nation-states—even, says Meg Stalcup (2013), of the world at large—recast, defining axes of sovereign jurisdiction anew, mapping vulnerable borders, pinpointing so-called hot spots, cordoning off zones of entropy and anarchy from those of social, commercial, and domestic order. And creating such new political theaters as "the street."

The criminal anthropology of this managerial model of enforcement not only concretizes "targeted populations." It also interpolates, into the body demographic and its aestheticized geography, "communities" as *both* objects and subjects of oversight. This explains the spread, under the rubric of community policing, of such things as Neighborhood Watch, Business Watch, CCTV, and, on a larger scale, Crime Stoppers International, which implores digitized publics to act upon their "collective responsibility"—"responsibilization," once again—by reporting "neighbors, relatives, or friends . . . [who may be] involved in crime."[17] The "community" is also the carefully bounded terrain, in up-class precincts, of friendly beat cops, would-be latter-day versions of peelers and bobbies, and, in less salubrious ones, of officers who command the wary familiarity of "close-distance" (Ahmed 2000). The people upon whom police continue to inflict more or less graphic violence, against whom they draw the line, are construed, by contrast, as anticitizens who live in "hoods," a double entendre of self-evident semiotic overload. These people also conjure with "community," with potential spaces of collective action, moral solidarity, even uncaptured subjectivities. But they often experience such spaces as a battleground for sovereignty, contending with local politicians, organized crime, street gangs, religious associations, civic self-help groups, and the like—a battleground, more often than not, that the state neither pacifies nor protects but from whose overspill it protects others.

The focus of criminal justice on public order, effected largely through mass penality, laissez-faire racism (Bobo and Smith 1998), and the management of the body demographic—which, again, Foucauldians might wish to subsume under the concepts of governmentality and biopower, but which, being embedded deeply in the contradictions of contemporary political economy, exceeds both—has been greatly abetted by developments in biometrics, that is, the "physiognomy of identity" (Lebovic 2015, 841ff., after Benjamin 1999a, 434). By means of its technologies, citizens and anticitizens alike are digitized in order better to know them, to document them, to assert truths about them, to incriminate them, to control them. In the mass-mediated *imaginaire*, science has come to be the panacea for the policing of everything. But despite its mythologizing in popular discourse, its methods, for all their utility, do not remove the doubts, difficulties, deficits, and indeterminacies that beset enforcement everywhere; vide the epic debates about the reading of the Rodney King video (Gooding-Williams 1993) and other visual evidence of police actions—likely to recur, in future, over the images captured by body cams, despite the widespread faith that they might at last yield unassailable truths. Neither, as we shall see in 2.1, do these technologies thwart criminal ingenuity or eliminate tactics of evasion, escape, alterity, and exit on the part of "targeted" populations. But—and here is the point—by raising expectations about the efficacy of policing, they reveal a contradiction at its core: on the one hand, in order to justify their managerial practices, cops must create the impression of rising lawlessness, of immanent disorder, even where it does not exist; yet, on the other, if they are to garner public trust, tax dollars, and a measure of impunity for their excesses, they have to show that they are capable of, and are, "winning the war against crime," even if no such thing is possible. Hence the NYPD ad in the *New York Times* in August 2014 (above, p. 8), in which it sought to persuade the city of an onrushing criminal tide—all this as it inflated and publicized the huge numbers of its arrests. Put another way, by its own account, it was failing and succeeding in the same space-time. Other police departments do the same thing, often, as we shall see in 2.3, playing on the fine line between actively provoking fear, thus to legitimize their recourse to counterviolence and mass incarceration, while simultaneously professing, for political and other reasons, to be turning back the tide (Comaroff and Comaroff 2004a). From the perspective of a public phenomenology, this merely adds another layer to the (race- and class-inflected) dialectic of desire for, and dread of, effective enforcement; the dialectic, that is, of im/possibility, dis/trust, un/decidability that, in the shadow of the criminal specter, attends upon the morphing relationship of governance, capital, and criminal justice.

In short, despite the ubiquity of hyperpolicing, of penality, of cost-efficient outsourcing to the private sector and "the community," these turn out to be aspirations of chronically uncertain accomplishment, ideologies-in-search-of-ever-greater-realization. To wit, one silent assumption of the enforcement model of the moment, despite police rhetoric to the contrary, is that crime can no longer be eliminated, only managed (see, e.g., Super 2013, 88–89; also 2.3); echoes, again, of Peter Manning's "impossible mandate" (e.g., 2003, 63; 1977), itself anticipated by Donald Cressey ([1969] 2008, 282–83). The more the clamor on the part of the state for zero tolerance and the policing of order, the more it concedes to a metaphysic of disorder, the more it provokes anxious ambivalence, the more it makes crime-and-policing into race-and-class war by other means. Remember what we said of the polite, multipoliced precincts around the University of Chicago: how the locals—many of whom had experienced violent attack at firsthand, all of whom regularly did so at secondhand—lived in apprehension of assault on themselves and their property. Just across the heavily patrolled cordon sanitaire between them and the predominantly poor hoods to their north, south, and west, black Americans berated the cops for not protecting them either, for preferring to treat them as, well, a "targeted population." The im/possibilities and dis/trust, in short, transect the very race-class frontier that public order policing has sought to sustain. No wonder that the officer who killed Michael Brown received more cash donations in support of his legal defense—unrequired as it turned out, since he was cleared of any offense—than did the family of the deceased. The white citizens of Ferguson continue to want more policing of the poor black "community" from which came Michael Brown, while that black "community" demands from those same police the "service" that attends the (neighbor)hood from which came the killer-cop. Both mobilized rapidly around their outrage, both building internal solidarity in a quest for security. As (then) US Attorney for the Eastern District of New York, later US Attorney General, Loretta Lynch, said to the Association of Black Women Attorneys in 2000, in paraphrase: "We live in a time where people fear the police. But . . . as bad as that is, they [also] fear that, when they are confronted with the criminal element in our society, they will have no one else to call upon to protect them" (Davidson 2014, 22). Alike for white and black, for rich and poor, desire and impossibility run up uneasily against each other.

So much for the United States. We have dealt with it at length precisely because it is the vortex whence globally expansive models of crime-and-policing have emanated in recent times. As such, it inflects *The Truth about Crime* everywhere. With this is mind, let us turn from the USA back to the RSA, the Republic of South Africa, where our focal interest in the rest of this volume lies.

. . . Then in the RSA

The Republic of South Africa is often taken, alike by its citizens and by the world at large, to be a petri dish in which contemporary patterns of crime-and-policing are to be observed in magnified proportions. This is due, in major measure, to its global reputation for a historically wrought culture of violence, rampant lawlessness, and the deficiencies of its police service. None of these things is as simple as it may seem. But South Africa *does* provide some instructive insights into the ways in which the mutation of the state form, and of the relationship between capital and governance, has affected criminal justice across the globe—partly because of its differences from, partly because of its similarities with, the United States.

Crime, the Phenomenology of Fear, and the Metaphysics of Disorder

The public fixation on crime in South Africa, on its singularity, belies the fact that its "citizens are not much more likely to become victims . . . than those of other countries" (du Preez 2013, 187; above, 1.1),[18] a point underscored, and nuanced, by the statistics interrogated in 2.3. It also belies the fact, mentioned earlier, that lawlessness has long been concentrated unevenly across the country (e.g., Schönteich 2001, 4–5; Shaw and Gastrow 2001, 243)—and disproportionately to the incidence of fear (e.g., Baghel 2010, 71ff.)—with most of it occurring in a few very poor, racially marked police districts. Du Preez (2013, 187) does go on to note, though, that the sheer brutality of violent crime here *is* remarkable; so, too, is the deep, historically honed anger to which it appears to give vent (Bundy 2014, 126–27, 131; after Jansen 2011; see 2.4). Not only are rates of homicide, aggravated robbery, and rape high by any standards, but what many perpetrators, white and black, do physically to their victims appears excessive to a point beyond explanation—although many attempts have been made to explain it with reference to the brutality of the ancien régime and the struggle to overthrow it, the poverty and inequality that afflict much of the population, and the lingering resentment of the oppressed. The search for a single, comprehensive answer, however, is an exercise in futility. Lawlessness, violent and nonviolent alike, is self-evidently not all of a kind. The minor breaches of *les miserables*, driven by necessity, are of different cause-and-effect from the extravagant white-collar transgressions of the wealthy or the racially motivated assaults of angry, hate-filled whites on people of color and vice versa (Msimang 2014, 202). Or the sorts of glam crime committed by high-end gangsters, who elicit a mix of terror, awe, and fascination (cf. Mpe 2001, 5; see below). In a place where daring, iconoclastic enterprise is extolled, where the lure of new, commodity-fired identities goes along with widespread immiseration, where crime is at once a critical mode of production and redistribution, where the law itself is often in question, its forms will inevitably be protean—and, therefore, resistant to monocausal determinations, let alone to a unified theory.

While South Africans of all races, classes, genders, and ethnicities tell each other that since 1994 an irrepressible criminal economy has taken root (Steinberg 2001), they seldom see it as a local manifestation of the specter that lurks almost everywhere in the shadows of the global economy—in its deregulated zones of alegality, in its forms of il/licit violence, at points where the line between the entrepreneurial and the illegal dissolves. Some have sought to deny that there is a criminal economy at all. A few years ago, Jackie Selebi, the former police chief–turned–felon, did so, quite definitively; he certainly did *not* see his own actions in these terms, merely business-as-usual. And ex-president Thabo Mbeki dismissed concerns about rising lawlessness as a "white people's complaint," which "reflect[s] their 'entrenched racism'" (Durrham, Mtose, and Brown 2011, 59). This had some truth to it—it still does— and may once have persuaded the party faithful of the African National Congress. But, as repeated surveys show, few dissent any longer from the common view that, whatever the numbers may say, the country has a real issue with crime and corruption. Not even those blacks who, for a good while, made relative light of these things, lest they concede to a racially motivated critique of the postcolonial regime, disagree any longer.[19]

However the genesis of the criminal economy is to be theorized, whatever the structural conditions for its growth, the ANC regime is regularly held responsible in South Africa for its failure to bring this economy to heel; indeed, government is deemed to be a major culprit in allowing it to run "out of control." Ranking members of the party accuse one another of crime and corruption, and are accused by others, with astonishing regularity. In their more open moments, they admit that this "war" is far from won, even as they declare their determination to prevail. Not convincingly enough, though, suggested Gareth Newham, of the Institute for Security Studies, as he censured President Jacob Zuma, the so-called "commander-in-thief" (above, 1.1), for having "very little to say" in the State of the Nation Address of 2015 "about the growing levels of violent crime"[20]—and, thereby, for failing to respond to the deep anxiety of many concerned citizens. For Ravi Baghel (2010, 71 et passim), a psychologist, that anxiety is symptomatic of a pathological public sphere: it is "[best] described as hysteria, paranoia, or obsession." Maybe. Justice Malala (2007, 171–76), a well-known black public intellectual, speaks of how, having suffered repeated criminal violations, he is "constantly afraid . . . of everyone and of everything" (174), of how he had been driven "insane" (171) by sheer terror after being shot at in his own home, of how "impotent" he feels in the face of it all (175), this in spite of his knowledge that, relative to the havoc (then) being wrought by AIDS, "[crime] seems almost a minuscule problem" (185). Malala touched a raw nerve: experiences of this sort—*pace* Thabo Mbeki, not merely a "white people's complaint," as Redi Tlhabi also has made clear (above, p. 38)—take on a terrifying phenomenological immediacy that no objective calculus of relative risk can dispel. In the circumstances, it is understandable that South Africans would insist, despite evidence to the contrary, that their national predicament is unique, epic, exceptional. Their certainty is asserted in the persuasive language of numbers, frequently of faux numbers, mythostats that, as they circulate, take on the truth-value of urban legends—a point to which we shall return again, in extenso, in 2.3. Local criminologists have noted that fear of crime is "as old as South Africa itself" (Steinberg 2001, 2); that rape and murder rates have probably been elevated in the country for decades (see, e.g., Shaw 2002, 2–4, 15–21); that, AIDS aside, more people die of malnutrition-related diseases, tuberculosis, and traffic accidents than from criminal violence (Statistics South Africa 2013, 60); that local felony rates—parsed by neighborhood, municipality, and region—resemble closely those in other, structurally similar places (Comaroff and Comaroff 2006a); hence, also, du Preez's (2013, 187) observation to that effect.

Nonetheless, almost every day, headlines affirm the opposite, feeding a desire for details about criminality at once apocalyptic and banal. Which, in turn, reinforces a culture of fear. Mass-mediated narratives of law and disorder captivate an endlessly curious populace. The more dire they are, the better, whether they be the stuff of investigative journalism or avid rumor, pulp fiction or scholarly research, official reports or NGO surveys, or admixtures of any and all of these things. As in narrative, so in life. As darkness falls across the country, a strident symphony strikes up. Police vehicles and ambulances take to the streets, sirens blaring. Car and burglar alarms, many of them tripped by their weary, wary owners, play out a furious fugue. Compounding the confusion of reality and myth, families-at-home, in extensively, often expensively secured living rooms, feed an insatiable appetite for TV crime shows—

local and foreign, fiction and docudrama, soap opera and high theater—in which the law triumphs over criminal violence (below, 1.3). Especially alluring, as we shall see in 2.1, are the exploits of unorthodox cops: investigators, possessed of an inspired ability, who deploy extraordinary means to detect the patterns behind the mysteries of everyday life here. And to address, if only in allegory, the materialities and metaphysics of disorder in contemporary South Africa, whose citizens—as Justice Malala's cri de coeur intimates—tend to see lawlessness as at once predictable yet profligate, cynical yet spectral, enigmatic yet expected. Beyond ordinary understanding. It is no surprise, under these conditions, that there have long been urgent calls for a more punitive, more proactive criminal justice system; in short, for the state to seize back sovereign control over life and death, thereby to restore sublime terror to the law. Its most vocal expression? A rising demand, across all the country's fractured publics, for the return of the death penalty, outlawed by the Constitutional Court in 1995 (see 2.3, 2.4).

Insofar as it provides a lingua franca, then, crime has become *the* discursive medium in which South Africans speak to each other about the limits and excesses of government, about citizenship and the cleavages that sunder the body politic, about material and moral economy, about their nightmares, needs, and insecurities. It is, in other words, a master signifier for the diagnosis of social division, disruption, difference, disorder. Take, for example, intimate violence, domestic and sexual alike, which is an inordinately fraught issue in South Africa—to the extent that the latter, sexual violence, argues Rosalind Morris (2006, 57), is "a metonym [here] for the history of criminality" *en effet.* Intimacy, notoriously, was a pervasive, perennial target of colonial surveillance. The "education of desire," along with the prohibition of sex and marriage across the color line, was critical to the reproductive engineering of segregated societies, a process, incidentally, that bred its own forms of physical and psychic urges, taboos, and brutalities (Stoler 1995). It also imprinted a template of racial domination on the texture of domestic and personal life. In the historical upshot, the gross violation of intimate relations—rape, incest, the killing of spouses, lovers, parents, and children, individually or multiply—and the sheer cruelty that often accompanies it, are seen as both ubiquitous and shameful. It is inscribed, some believe, in the "nation's DNA." Predictably, intimate violence is explored repeatedly in South African literature, past and present, epic and everyday: rape, especially across the chasm of race, is the leitmotif of signature works, from Olive Schreiner's ([1897] 1959) *Trooper Peter*

Halket of Mashonaland, through Achmat Dangor's *Bitter Fruit* (2003), to John Coetzee's *Disgrace* (1999; see Graham 2012).

Mounting levels of intimate violence in recent years make it plain that the postcolonial democracy has been able neither to redress the sources of abuse and transgressive desire nor to contain them within the law (Morris 2006, 58)—which has proven a relatively inept instrument for dealing with this species of criminality everywhere, especially in contexts where long-standing structures of gender inequality remain in place (Baxi 2014). In this respect, South Africa, alas, is no exception (Hornberger 2009). Its media are saturated, almost daily, with shocking accounts: accounts of attacks on women of all ages, from the very young to the very old, women who may be conjugal partners, close kin, and/or neighbors; accounts of violations as "corrective" action against women and men accused of "perverted" sexuality; accounts of victims in communities ostensibly beset by high rates of incest; accounts of multiple perpetrators, typically described as groups of boys and men to whom the words "feral" or "angry white" are attached; accounts of drug-crazed children hacking parents and siblings to death both in up-market estates and in impoverished informal settlements; accounts, too, of men described as "depressed" and bereft of all dignity—often cuckolded husbands, jilted lovers, or desperate, unemployed breadwinners—who wipe out entire families and then themselves. Into this last category of murder-suicides, not incidentally, fall a notable number of police officers. There is a great deal to be said about these things. And a great deal *has* been said. But what is most striking for present purposes is the degree to which intimate violence, as a collective scandal, has become a site of argument about the nation and its (anti)citizens, about (un)civil society, about kinship and the (re)production of sociality, about the law and lawlessness. It also yields evidence of new horrific truths.

For some, the ubiquity and imperviousness of intimate violence to the law "proves" that South Africa remains, for all its constitutional talk about being a nonsexist, nonracist society, deeply patriarchal, jointly the heritage of the authoritarian-familistic ideology of apartheid and of African paternalist cultural practices—the latter embodied by a polygamous president who has been tried for rape, even as the ANC Women's League rallied to his defense. For others, it is a fallout of the emasculation of young black men who, with little prospect of employment in a casualized job market that favors females, find themselves unable to marry or graduate to adulthood and vent their anger through gender violence; "for every woman with a job, there is an angry, devalued, unemployed man walking the streets," an irritated young caller told *Morning Talk* on SAFM, South Africa's public radio, in April 2015. Similarly, the volatile, violent aggression of their older (nonelite) compatriots is put down to the fact that they see the "new" South Africa, its constitution and its economy, as serving everyone but themselves, leaving many of them dependent on favors from their womenfolk, particularly those who receive social grants from the state. Black females, in turn, contest the dominant fixation on African criminality: "[i]n our national psyche," writes journalist Sisonke Msimang (2014, 201–2), "whites (and, of late, middle class people of all races) are always the victims of black male violence." Mainstream media ignore completely the victim of color and *her* characteristic terrors, she adds, confessing that her own fears focus on the figures of the malevolent white male: the "grinning rage-filled frat boy," the white farm-owner, or the master of the house. Or perhaps, she might have added, the fallen hero, like Oscar Pistorius (below, 1.3), no longer master of that house, whose emasculated power and thwarted imperial desire finds outlet in violent, primal passion.[21]

All these perceptions are treated, by those who posit them, as truths about the ethnomoral demography of South Africanity and its ruptured nationhood: about "our scourge" (*Daily Maverick* 2014, 209), a capacity for cruelty passed down via a process of pathological social reproduction; about a history of psychic brutalization that proliferates from top to bottom and side to side, that ruptures nationhood and defies the rule of law. It is a scourge, however, that is made speakable precisely by being talked about as criminality—not, in the first instance, in terms of the unspeakabilities of race or gender or generation or culture or even class. What is more, each truth is validated by the (selective) deployment of mass-mediated knowledge about who does what to whom, where, when, why, and under what conditions. And about why it is that, in a constitutional democracy that celebrates the universal rights of citizenship, the state, civil society, and the criminal justice system are powerless to protect even the most intimate reaches of people's lives. By these means are "respectable fears," to recommission Geoffrey Pearson's (1983) felicitous phrase, translated into social diagnostics and, by turn, into a longer conversation about the metaphysics of disorder.[22]

Those fears, that metaphysics—and the criminal obsessions they have nurtured—have clear historical roots. Broadly speaking, constitutional reform here came hand in hand with economic, political, and ethical deregulation: liberation with liberalization, as it were. As elsewhere at the same juncture, the demise of the social contract and the outsourcing of the functions of state, most of all of the means of enforcement, left many citizens unsure where to turn for protection against the rogue violence and rampant property theft that, in Latin America (e.g., Caldeira 2000) and post-Soviet Europe (e.g., Karstedt 2003), accompanied democratization. Or, at least, appeared to. In South Africa it is not clear whether there was actually a rise in serious crime in the early postapartheid days—it was not counted in black residential areas before 1994 and has dropped since (see 2.3)—or merely its migration into previously enclaved zones of white privilege. In many parts of the world, to be sure, political change *has* ushered in periods of moral ambiguity, legal uncertainty, and social disorder, as it did, for instance, in late eighteenth-century France (Foucault 1995, 275) and America after the Civil War (Abbott 1927), although these periods have often been followed by processes of stabilization. In South Africa, the transition from apartheid has had all these effects—moral ambiguity, legal uncertainty, social disorder—and many more besides; effects, we would argue, that are part of the *late* modern, tectonic shift in the relationship between governance, capital, and the state. And, with it, the transformation in the nature of criminal justice.

Policing the Postcolony

Until its later years, the ancien régime relied on a fusion of two modalities of policing: for whites, a bouquet of conventional operations, founded on criminal detection, uniformed street-and-beat, and specialist functions of the sorts found in most Euro-American constabularies at the time; for people of color, especially blacks, paramilitary and public order enforcement, directed primarily at rooting out political dissidents, taming mass protest and labor unrest, punishing transgressions of the laws of segregation, and disciplining the movement of Africans under pass regulations that yielded notoriously high rates of arrest (see above, 1.1).[23] In the latter instance—in black townships, that is—crime, even violent crime, was paid relatively little heed by the state unless it threatened to burst its racially circumscribed bounds. As this suggests, the policing of high apartheid amounted, in many respects, to an antipodean Jim Crow. During the 1980s, however, it began to undergo a paradigmatic shift toward the managerial model,[24] increased privatization, and the transfer of responsibility to "the community." As in the United States, this occurred in tandem with changes in the global economic order, with "the politics of race and class in [a] neoliberalizing regime," as Gail Super (2013) has put it. We shall return to this in 2.4: it was deeply implicated in, and was to feed, the final rounds of the struggle against apartheid, whose demise was itself a product of the world-historical forces that gave rise to that regime. And it was to spawn the forms of "people's justice," the extrajudicial (vigilante) violence, that have become the most visible—if least intended—spin-off of the outsourcing of the police function in South Africa to the private, corporate, and communal sectors: justice whose origins lay, in major part, in the felt need to establish penal mechanisms, indeed sovereign social order, in the void left by the state; justice in communities that had not merely gone unprotected but many of which were subject to unremitting assault from outside and criminality from within; justice often meted out by partisan purveyors of force, many of whom claimed to be revolutionary cadres, some of whom were not above killing personal enemies under the sign of social control and political rectitude.[25]

When the ANC came to power, one of its first moves in breaking with the past was the attempt to create a racially inclusive, demilitarized police force. Not an easy task, this, when some of its early new black recruits, a proportion of whom were struggle alumni, found themselves in the same uniform as men who had previously shot at and even, in a few cases, tortured them. Not an easy task, either, when the mass defection of officers from the ancien régime left both senior and junior ranks thin in quantity and experience. And made no easier by the determination of the Mandela government to rebuild a national constabulary committed to human rights and the rule of law (Hornberger 2013): when we began our own research on policing in the North West Province in 2000, we were presented, ceremoniously, with copies of an official training manual, complete with instructional video, on the proper practices of human rights policing, in which every cop was supposed to be fully trained. It was in this spirit that the South African Police Force was rechristened the South African Police Service (SAPS): the change from "Force" to "Service" here was meant less to mark the move toward managerial policing, as it did in the United Kingdom and United States, than to serve as a signal to the public of a new ethos of enforcement, one befitting the nobility of the liberation struggle. Above all else, the SAPS had to seek the trust and cooperation of thoroughly alienated, thoroughly violated communities, and to persuade them to desist from "taking the law into their own hands"—a cliché become common practice in urban black South Africa—thus to restore sovereign violence to the state.

As Steinberg (2011, 350) observes, the celebrated postapartheid constitution of 1996 identified crime prevention as a foundational principle of democratic order. But efforts to implement a liberal, rights-based approach to enforcement soon ran up against the postcolonial realities of which we have already spoken. Among these were the difficulties of policing effectively in a climate in which the authority of the law, long regarded as illegitimate by the majority of the population, was, from the first, undermined by the explosive necroviolence of crime, both petty and organized, both local and transnational; the often-unruly privatization of security by both the corporate sector—recall, the largest in the world (above, 1.1)—and "community" mobilization; the continued economic exclusion and criminalization of the black poor; and pervasive government corruption, especially in overseeing the justice system (see, e.g., Pikoli and Wiener 2013). And this is not to mention the effects of the criminal specter in opening zones of il/legality and impunity, thus making crime pay very well, with comparatively little risk. Or the hedging about of the SAPS, already burdened by inexperienced cadres, with a raft of procedural regulations that prevented it from the effective exercise of sovereign force. A story that circulated widely in the late 1990s made the point rather pointedly. It told of a police precinct in a wealthy part of white Cape Town where the cops had a panic button secreted under the front desk of their charge office. The button was said to connect them directly to ADT, the international security company, to which they turned in the slightest emergency. Nobody is quite sure whether or not this story is apocryphal. But it captures the fact that, from early on, few believed the SAPS to be capable of protecting the public at large. Or even themselves. That panic button was both an accusation and a metonymic displacement for the moral panic suffered by many citizens from the early postapartheid years onward.

For postcolonial elites—black, white, Coloured, and Indian—this moral panic is focused on the large, increasingly assertive African underclass that, especially since legal restrictions on its mobility were lifted in 1990, has been perceived as an imminent threat to public order, to proper civility, and to the prospect of investment-led growth (Samara 2011, 6, 17). It is from there, as we have said, that hardened criminals are presumed to come, criminals who elude the cops or kill them or collude with them or recruit them to their ranks, thus to void both their authority and the legitimacy of their violence. It is against this population too, against "those who don't belong" (Steinberg 2008, 168), that the domestic private security sector has grown up, using sophisticated media technologies to sharpen the fears that it charges hefty fees to allay; yet another dimension, this, of Marx's parodic "productivity of crime." It is also against them that anticrime associations and NGOs mobilize, paid for by communities of the propertied (Steinberg 2008, 168; Bloom 2009; see 2.4): citizens, that is, who "use crime to . . . become one another's safety zones" (above, 1.1); citizens who thus reproduce the very segregated inequality from which they see a need to protect themselves; citizens who, in making security and social order a commodity to be bought by those who can afford it, deepen the chasm between the insured-and-secured and the immiserated-and-unprotected—and, with it, the grounds of their own moral panic.

For the latter, for those living on the vulnerable fringes of urbane society—in townships and informal settlements, for instance—moral panic focuses less on the high incidence of violent crime, to which, perforce, they have long been accustomed. Rather, it attaches to the cops themselves, toward whom many poor people of color evince acute suspicion, if not unvarnished antagonism. They point to innumerable instances of SAPS lawlessness and to yet more cases of willful police inactivity, even refusal, in the face of felonies perpetrated within their close reach. These sectors of the population, like most of their wealthier compatriots, also mistrust the justice system, not without justification. It lets serious criminals, including repeat offenders, out on bail too easily, they say. Or it affords them rights far in excess of their just desserts. Or it does not prosecute them at all, usually due to investigative ineptitude, poor forensics,[26] the "loss" of case dockets, the failure of officers to appear in court, or some other manner of dereliction.[27] In the upshot, these communities have often been unwilling to allow the SAPS to arrest suspects even when its cadres show themselves ready to do so: they deliberately obstruct the cops, preferring to take action themselves (below, 2.4), typically less by means that sail silently in the lee of the law than by its flagrant, theatrical transgression, thus to assert their own sovereignty. All of which has made enforcement more or less untenable. Conventional policing is "virtually impossible" in this environment, said an advocate for the state to the Khayelitsha Commission of 2014, set up to investigate the failure of law and order in Cape Town's black and mixed-race residential areas.[28] Here, as elsewhere in South Africa, communities still do not "consent to being policed" or believe even in its real possibility, a precondition of all enforcement, adds Steinberg (2008, 20, 181), following Egon Bittner (1990).

But there is a deeply entrenched tautology here: that lack of consent is itself predicated on the conviction that the SAPS cannot be trusted with its mandate to convict. The bases for this conviction, reiterated interminably in public discourse, lie in the various allegations to which we have already alluded: the inefficiency, ineptitude, and unwillingness of police officers to engage; the high felony rates among them; the fact that many of those who have been convicted remain on active duty; their infiltration by organized crime;

their very visible, sometimes deadly violence against dissidents; repeated disclosures of their corruption and of their complicity in the corruption of the political classes (above, p. 35); and, most recently, the finding, sourced to the SAPS itself, that its officers, 75 percent of whom are held to be clinically obese, are severely stressed and prone to substance abuse,[29] evidence, perhaps, of the impossibility of their mandate. The deputy minister of police of the moment, Maggie Sotyu, admitted that, in the circumstances, "the police [can]not continue to fight crime appropriately." Which is precisely what they are so frequently accused of, precisely what is perpetually asked of them. Oddly, their poor health and extreme stress levels have been blamed by a former provincial police commissioner, Lieutenant General Arno Lamoer of the Western Cape, on "attacks [on them] by community members." This completes the tautology. It makes "the community" responsible for the condition of the SAPS, whose senior echelons then blame them, "the community," for not wanting to be policed—in other words, for not wanting what they want, what they constantly demand. The circle is not merely closed. It is vicious. Little wonder, then, that a recent Bloomberg survey listed South Africa as the second "most stressed-out" country in the world.[30] Little wonder, too, that it has yielded a stream of studies, scholarly and lay alike, of the SAPS, all of them partaking in the fantasy of "the police that we want" (Bruce and Neild 2005), police, it seems, currently suspended in an abyss of impossibility. Perhaps it is symbolically overdetermined that, just days after he blamed the public for the underperformance of the SAPS, Lieutenant General Lamoer suffered a nocturnal home invasion. He slept through it.[31] A month later a banner headline reported that he was about to face charges "that included racketeering, general corruption, money laundering, fraud, firearm offences and defeating or obstructing the cause of justice."[32] Perhaps it is also overdetermined that an internationally released social science fiction film set in contemporary South Africa, *Chappie* (2015, directed by Neill Blomkamp), should replace the nation's police officer corps with fantastical robots: robots, manufactured and managed by a private corporation, that look like thin, athletic versions of their human originals, that have replaceable parts and may be reprogrammed, that wear SAPS paraphernalia—save for badges with the acronym RSAP ("Robotic South African Police"?). These machine-men reduce the crime rate radically. Until, well, things fall apart and the abyss reopens.

It is in the face of this fantasy, of this abyss, that the SAPS has turned its back on human rights policing—indeed, on its earlier "soft," service-based ethos in toto—and has moved toward the other extreme: heavily militarized enforcement. The moment of shift is marked in the public memory (cf. du Preez 2013, 201) by an outburst back in April 2008 from the then deputy minister of safety and security, Susan Shabangu: "Criminals are hell-bent on undermining the law and they must now be . . . killed," she declared, adding that she wanted "no warning shots," no "pathetic excuses" in dealing with law-breakers. "End of story. . . . The constitution says [they] must be kept safe, but I say [to the SAPS] No! . . . You have been given guns, now use them." In the unlikely event that any officer entertained residual concerns about the rule of law, she added tersely, "You must not worry about the regulations."[33] Four years later, the Criminal Procedure Act was altered to extend the powers of police to use lethal force (du Preez 2013, 201; Bundy 2014, 119). In fact, Shabangu was not the first states-person to have spoken out in this manner. In 1999 the late Steve Tshwete, then minister of safety and security, assured the country that felons would be treated "in the same way a dog deals with a bone"; before him, in 1995, even Nelson Mandela, still imbued with the idea that democracy depended on crime pre-vention, spoke of the need to "take off the velvet glove regarding lawlessness" (Shaw 2002, 86). But it was Shabangu's call to arms that presaged the process of remilitarization. In 2010 Minister of Police Nathi Mthethwa announced that officers would no longer hold civilian ranks. Military-style uniforms followed. Mthethwa made it plain that this was not intended as a mere symbolic shift:

> We have taken a stance as this Government of fighting crime and fighting it tough. The rank changes are therefore in line with our transformation of the Force, not only in terms of a name change but change in attitude, think-ing and operational duties—This should not be misinterpreted as merely the militarization of the police but as part of our new approach of being fierce towards criminals, while lenient to citizens' safety and maintaining good discipline within the Force. . . . For us to achieve these and other objectives there are certain steps we have undertaken to ensure we win this war. This is a people's war against criminals. For any Force to discharge its tasks effec-tively there needs to be a commander because wars are led by commanders.[34]

The SAPS may have retained its name, but Force, uppercase, is invoked here three times; Service, not at all. The "war on crime" is transformed, along the way, into "a people's war," although, for critics of the SAPS, it is "the people," the "wider public," who are in fact the enemy;[35] observe the unwitting slip in the minister's statement, where he talks of being "lenient to citizens' safety." Use of the term "people's wars" itself, moreover, inadvertently muddies the difference between the sovereign action of a state and popular vigilantism. Nonetheless, as a declaration of intent, the point is abundantly clear, especially when taken together with Shabangu's directive to cops to break the law, in/judiciously, thereby to blur the line, yet again, between the legal and the illegal, crime-and-policing. Back in the 1990s, when Bill Bratton visited South Africa from New York City to market his model of enforcement, many people, ordinary citizens and government cadres alike, were keen to buy into it, seduced by the uncompromising line it took on all criminality, however minor.[36] A decade later, "zero tolerance" rang impotent, little more than a brave cry in the face of odds that appeared increasingly impossible. It was to be replaced by yet tougher catchphrases, shibboleths like "shoot to kill." And "maximum force." And "command and control." Even "an eye for an eye" and, chillingly, "police death squad."[37]

Note that all this was well before the Khayelitsha Commission, the one that spoke about the untenability of law-enforcement across large swathes of Cape Town and, by extension, much of lumpen South Africa. Patently, the militarization of the SAPS has not done much to "win the war against crime," although the state continues to claim to be doing just that.[38] But it has had a number of implications for the pragmatic culture of policing here, one that brings it into line with the broad global trends of which we spoke earlier.

The most visible has been rising police violence under conditions of virtual impunity (above, p. 36)—violence of just the sort we encountered in the United States. Andrew Brown (2008, 190), a former antiapartheid activist, lawyer, and SAPS reservist, has suggested that even the most callous of South African officers have some empathy for the indigent poor and are reluctant to prosecute them. But in the public imagination—buttressed by televised documentary footage of the sort to be seen in *South Africa's Dirty Cops* (2013, directed by Inigo Gilmore) and endless print media reports—the opposite is the case. This is especially so since the Marikana massacre and two notorious police homicides, each of which became an immediate national scandal. Both of them were committed in front of large, agitated street crowds and both were captured on video,[39] later watched by millions of viewers. The first involved a political dissident, Andries Tatane, shot in Ficksburg, in the Free State Province, while protesting the failure of "service delivery"—the provision by the state, that is, of the basic necessities of life, among them water, sewerage, electricity, healthcare, housing, garbage removal, public transport, and access roads.[40] In the second, a Mozambican taxi driver, Mido Macia, was brutally put to death by being dragged behind a SAPS vehicle after allegedly causing a traffic jam and resisting arrest in Daveyton, near Johannesburg.[41] There have been many other fatalities at the hands of cops—several hundred a year, on average—as well as serious assaults on people and property, some of them attributed to "hit squads." So much so that, according to *Africa Check*, "civil claims lodged against police totaled R20.5-billion by the end of the 2013/14 financial year. Around 16.5-billion . . . related to the broad category of 'police action' with an additional R1.4-billion arising from shooting incidents, R175-million from vehicle accidents and R853-million from allegations of assault."[42] If this is accurate, which seems likely, the SAPS faced a legal bill of almost US$1,782,600,000 for those twelve months alone.

But it was Marikana and the killing of Andries Tatane, more than anything else, that brought into focus what all this violence is about. Tatane, as we said, died at a service delivery protest. These "rebellions of the poor" (P. Alexander 2010) and labor strikes have become very common across the country as the promise of a liberation dividend—the promise of "a better life for all"—has, for most South Africans, gone unfulfilled (see, e.g., D. James 2014). Estimates of mass actions, and the growing number of them that end in violence, fluctuate wildly: the highest being nearly three thousand over ninety days in 2013–14, or more than thirty each day; the lowest, around one a day.[43] Whatever their "true" incidence, they are frequent enough, and frequently violent enough, for a senior ANC leader to refer to them as "seas of anarchy"[44] and for the critical media to suggest that, as a nation, South Africa has come to be "defined by [political] violence. . . . After years of unemployment, poverty and crime reaching endemic proportions, with no relief from those in authority, people are taking matters into their own hands, driven by anger and desperation" and the sense that "nobody is listening and nobody cares."[45] For many of those people, it has been argued, informal justice—that is, vigilantism—offers a more meaningful form of moral public, even citizenship (Oomen 2004; N. Smith 2013).

It is this tsunami of dissent and demand that the police function has been repurposed to address, recalling the dark years of the ancien régime; in its 2011/12 financial year, the SAPS responded to 1,194 "unrest-related incidents"[46]—excluding, that year, outbreaks of mass ("corrective," typically dubbed "xenophobic") violence against mostly African foreign nationals, which are handled "as if [they are] service delivery protest[s] or labor dispute[s] that a heavy police deployment can deal with."[47] Concomitantly, "ordinary" criminal investigation, while it has certainly not disappeared, has receded in relative significance. This foreshadowed the militarization of the SAPS. It came with the disestablishment and decentralization of several of its specialist units after the millennium, including the Serious and Violent Crime Unit, the Narcotics Bureau, and the (internal) Anti-corruption Unit, closed down in 2001—despite having received 20,779 complaints of malpractice in the Service over the previous five years[48]—by none other than National Commissioner Jackie Selebi, who, remember, would go to jail later for . . . corruption. Detective teams and intelligence functions were de-resourced in favor of so-called "visible policing," their personnel transferred to local stations;[49] this in an ostensible campaign to prevent lawlessness—to *manage* it, in other words (above, p. 56)—instead of dealing with it after the fact, a pursuit whose untenability was becoming ever more obvious, ever more politically explosive. What was left of investigative operations was concentrated primarily in the units that deal with organized and commercial crime; the type of crime, not incidentally, that most threatens the interests of the political classes and of capital, interests protected under the sign of social order. In the past couple of years there has been an effort to reverse the process of decentralization, which has proved palpably ineffective, and to reestablish some of the disbanded specialist units. To date, that effort has been less than fully successful, especially in the sphere of criminal detection, whose officers now carry an average of 150 cases ("dockets") each, three times the international average—leading to nostalgic calls for a return to the days when well-trained investigators "lived to . . . build cases that would stand up in court" (du Preez 2013, 192).

In the meantime, the shift to a focus on public order policing (POP) to contain all those "unrest-related incidents" (aka political dissidence)—it had also been undermined, inadvertently, by decentralization—has been the most visible thing about "visible policing" in South Africa recently; to wit, in 2014, the SAPS, on the assumption that enforcing public order might conjure up an ordered public, proposed to double its POP cadres. They have also been buttressed by the creation, since 2001, of Tactical Response Teams, which were originally established to combat heavily armed, highly skilled crimes—like cash-in-transit robberies—but then also mandated with the maintenance of public order; notes Colin Bundy (2014, 118), their excessively forceful operations "blurred the line between policing and warfare" and sometimes "looked startlingly like extra-judicial executions," not least in dispersing service delivery protests. In 2011 they would become a unit in the Operational Service Division of the SAPS, some of whose officers, Bundy reminds us (119), killed Andries Tatane.

Accompanying the turn to POP has been a stress on the dramaturgy of enforcement: on theatrical shows of force against offenders of various sorts,

some of them palpably minor, like illegal "aliens" and small-time drug dealers (Comaroff and Comaroff 2004a), even, recently, against a man who locked
himself into his home with thirteen dogs, one of whom had bitten a neighbor;[50] also, on the deployment of flashy "blue light brigades" that transport
and protect statespeople at a cost last year of R75 million, R30 million of it
diverted from detective services.[51] Accompanying this turn, too, has been considerable expenditure on "education," largely in the form of campaigns to con-
vince the country that the SAPS is making major strides against criminality.
And, conversely and contradictorily, much as in the United States, to provoke
"awareness"—fear, really—of the imminence of lawlessness, thus to legitimize
those forceful "crackdowns" and the immunity of police from prosecution for
their actions. To be sure, the protection of its officers from legal sanction is
a reflex reaction of the criminal justice system. Note that the first instinct of
the state at Marikana was to arrest 270 of the striking miners, six of them in
hospital with bullet wounds, for the murders committed *against them* by the
cops; they were arraigned, under the laws of "common purpose," for being in
the crowd that was said to have attacked the police lines, a staggering piece of
audacity—which, as it would turn out, was a step too far even in this parallel
universe of il/legalities. The fact that it was even thinkable reinforces the point
that, in the topsy-turvy crime-and-policing world that is contemporary South
Africa, the line between the law and its transgression, between protector and
predator, between cops and criminals, appears almost infinitely permeable,
always spectral, constantly open to renegotiation.

These transformations, as we have intimated, have been received in South
Africa itself with a mix of resignation, exasperation, fear, and dismay. As the
editor of the largest-circulation newspaper in the country put it, "people do
not expect the cops to care too deeply when a house gets robbed, someone
gets assaulted, or a car is swiped. In many cases, [they] do not bother reporting property crimes," other than for insurance purposes—thus, we might
add, to leave the restitution to the market—being "aware that the odds of [the
crimes] being investigated are vanishingly small. Even when the cops *do* care
deeply . . . they cannot produce results." This is largely because their criminal
intelligence capacities are severely lacking,[52] because there are "no penalties
for [police] under-performance or misconduct,"[53] because witnesses are easily
scared off from testifying by threats of violence, and because their attentions
lie elsewhere. Successful prosecutions, when they do occur, often rely on con-
fessions, sometimes obtained illicitly by subterfuge or brute force. This, argues
Gareth Newham, is why official statistics for the past year indicate a fall in the

rate of many felonies: it is simply that ever-fewer victims—indeed, almost half of *all* South Africans—see any point in going to the SAPS; as a result, the crimes they suffer never make in onto the books.[54] It may also be why, as we shall see in 2.1, supercops of various sorts, both real and fictional, populate the public imagination, promising to make sense of, and to combat, the unfathomable lawlessness with which, it is commonly said, the SAPS either will not or cannot cope. As a report emanating from the Institute for Security Studies concludes, "only once a crime or social disorder problem threaten[s] established interests are police called in to manage or suppress the problem."[55]

Here, then, lies a critical clue to the move by the SAPS away from conventional crime fighting to the management of public dis/order, broadly defined—a move that, when all is said and done, is counterintuitive in a context in which reducing everyday lawlessness is universally regarded as an urgent necessity, in which that lawlessness is commonly seen as a clear and present danger to both civil society and the fledgling democracy, in which the fear of attacks on persons and property is so rampant, and in which crime-and-policing is such a charged political issue. Christopher McMichael pursues the point further in arguing that enforcement in South Africa is primarily about "maintaining state authority and protecting market forces."[56] Like the apartheid police, he says—and the US cops of the present—the SAPS, whose violence is neither an aberration nor an occasional deviation from its ordinary operations, often seems to be acting as an army of occupation: "Police interventions which fall under the remit of protecting order also ensure that conflicts arising from low pay and other economic arrangements deemed to be unfair can be presented as security issues. . . . [P]olice oppression is not just about securing the interests of specific businesses but is central to the wider maintenance of the distribution of property and power, to the rule of the state and the market." Many would concur with McMichael, who adds that, far from being apolitical—as the state, indeed all states, would like its citizens to believe—the SAPS is a partisan organization, one that uses "'invisible' forms of repression," the criminal justice system, and street policing in the cause of "suppressing dissenting voices."[57] Nor are these voices only those of the street. Public order policing has even entered Parliament—on the occasion of the State of the Nation Address in February 2015, no less—to remove an opposition party, the Economic Freedom Fighters, which sees itself as representing the poor and disempowered. Its spokesmen had invoked the procedural rules of the House to insist repeatedly that the head of state answer questions about the use of public funds to "secure" his private rural residence. Their forcible eviction, seen on prime-time TV, broke several laws. Noted one observer, "the Public Order Police seemed very excited to enter the chamber."[58] Meanwhile, outside on the street, other POP cadres fired a water cannon, also in violation of the constitution, at opposition supporters gathered legally and peacefully. Nobody was under any illusion that the officers involved would be disciplined for their actions, or that those actions, justified in the name of social order, were not commissioned purely to protect the leader of the ANC and his administration—and the powerful interests that, in turn, back them. Which is what the police function, from this vantage, appears to have become in South Africa. And elsewhere.

But this, compelling as it is, is not the whole story. There is an addendum to it, an unaddressed remainder, so to speak.

Much of the time, enforcement in South Africa *does* focus on what it takes to be public order. And much of the time the "war on crime" *does* turn out to be a conflict of class interests: a good deal of what is regarded by the SAPS as illegal in poor black communities, and therefore liable to prosecution and prison, tends to be treated, in white middle-class contexts, as pathological and therefore requiring care or counseling—just as one person's prohibited protest is another's democratic right of expression. But late modern policing has not given up entirely on conventional crime fighting. Its mandate might have become ever more "impossible"; it may well see no option, in the age of the market, other than to re-gear into the mode of the managerial, of population control and administration; and the rising criminal specter of our times might constantly muddy the line between what is and is not legal, opening up large spaces of undecidability between the criminal and the civil. Yet, every day, some cops *do* do "normal" police work: they investigate murders, follow up cases of corruption and fraud, act on reports of rape, try to apprehend thieves and poachers, break up rowdy gatherings, and the like. With limited success, perhaps, and with distinctly different levels of commitment, acumen, fortitude, physical ability, or mobility. But they do it. What is more, South African correctional facilities, of which there are 241, are overfilled (to 137 percent of their capacity) with criminals—162,162 of them at a recent count, 31 percent of whom are awaiting trial—put there by the SAPS; recall that the country has among the highest per capita carceral populations. In 2011, the last year for which the Department of Correctional Services published statistics on its website, 54 percent were in for "aggressive" (i.e., violent) offenses, 23 percent for economic crimes, 16 percent for sexual transgressions, and 2 percent for narcotics-related felonies (Jules-Macquet 2014, 4–5); these numbers include many gang members and some major figures from the world of organized crime. As this makes plain, the SAPS is not *only* policing public order, not *only* protecting the state and capital, despite the fact that, wittingly or not, that is where most of its attention is directed and, whatever the motives of its duty officers, where the primary effect of their work lies.

Coda: The Truth about Crime-and-Policing

This mention of the carceral, and of race-inflected class warfare, brings us back to our comparison between South Africa and the United States—and, by extension, to what are becoming common themes in the changing nature of the police function with the transformation of the state, of its forms of private in/direct governance, and of its relationship to capital.

To summarize, then.

In both the United States and the Republic of South Africa, with the breach of the social contract, the principal emphasis of enforcement has moved, normatively, from crime fighting to public order. Or, more accurately, it has moved from a historically labile mix of the two to a heavy stress on the latter, defined in such a way as to discipline "target" populations and their lifeways; this under a criminal justice regime that combines market-style managerialism with militarization, outsourcing with responsibilization, spinning off much of what once constituted conventional law-and-order operations to the private sector. In both contexts, although we have not dealt with it in detail here, labor indiscipline is left largely to corporate control. It is handled partly by company security, partly through hiring and firing, manipulating the demography of a shrinking labor market and monetary reward-and-punishment—unless it crosses the line into the public sphere, in which case it becomes the object of state intervention; or, rather, of state-corporate collaboration. In short, the police function has trifurcated, allocating the enforcement of order to the state, labor to the business sector, and the everyday protection of persons and property to the private domain, itself divided into the commercial (i.e., domestic security services) and the communal (i.e., neighborhood watches, informal justice, civic associations).

In both the United States and South Africa, moreover, mass incarceration, disproportionately of poor people of color, has become endemic. Strictly speaking, however, despite the size of its population behind bars, South Africa is not a penal state in the sense intended by Löic Wacquant. For all its neoliberal tendencies, it retains elements of modernist welfare governance, both visible and invisible, being given to a rhetoric—if not always to the practice—of etatist paternalism and the protection of its citizenry. Consequently, it does not manage its underclasses primarily by carceral means. Nor has it given up entirely on convict rehabilitation or commodified its inmates in the same manner as has the United States; there are only two privately owned prisons in the country. The SAPS, most of whose officers are themselves black, prefers to conduct its "visible policing" in mass counteractions—by means of "crackdowns" and "operations," by "going tactical," and the like—on the streets, in townships, and at work sites, not by rendering lumpen neighborhoods into heavily patrolled gulags and/or by criminalizing their quotidian practices; note that, as of 21 February 2015, 48.7 percent of all US federal prisoners were in for felonies related to substance use, abuse, or trade,[59] as opposed to 2 percent in South Africa, whose drug economy is no less pervasive. Also, US policing has not given up on criminal investigation to the same extent. These differences notwithstanding, policing strategies of criminalization and control in the two countries, alike justified with reference to the protection of social order and alike prone to deadly violence, are broadly similar. Each has sedimented into a systematic regime designed not just for the preservation of privilege or the interests of state and class; nor just for arresting criminals, imprisoning them, and returning them to polite society reformed. They are purposed, rather, to define and defend the line between citizen and anticitizen, thus to protect civil, propertied order, by necro-means if necessary, against those deemed disposable and/or dangerous. The development of these broadly similar regimes, patently, constitutes the latest chapter in a history of the long run, the history whose earlier moments we spelled out above. For those who suffer that history—those who are policed as the imagined enemies of social order—the "war against crime" is apprehended as an assault not merely on their citizenship but, even more, on their humanity. Traces here of Giorgio Agamben's (1998) *homo sacer*, of life stripped bare of all social recognition. Hence, in the United States, the massing counterassertion that "Black Lives Matter." And, in South Africa, the demand for human dignity at the core of every service delivery protest, every mass action in "the rebellion of the poor." The pathological public sphere is often a fertile ground for germinating a popular politics.

As these things suggest, contemporary regimes of enforcement in both the United States and South Africa harbor internal contradictions. Precisely because of their turn to public order in the face of their "impossible mandate," and because of the translation of that mandate into the argot of warfare, they have little alternative but to fan the sorts of fears, indeed the moral panic, that justify their excesses—and their immunity from criminal responsibility for them. At the same time, though, their legitimacy depends on persuading civil society that they are prevailing over the forces of disorder; anything less is an admission that lawlessness *is* "out of control." In other words, criminal justice has to establish the sublime terror of the law—by contrast, among other things, to the lawlessness of "terror"—as at once sovereign, yet incomplete. After all, if its sovereignty were fully regnant, there would be no war; wars occur where the law runs out, not where its conventional means and ends are beyond question. It is this doubling, this negative, never-quite-resolved interplay between sovereign law-enforcement and the chronic immanence of chaos that underlies the experiential paradox of which we have spoken: on the one hand, a desire for "more police"[60]—or, better still, for "the police we want"—and, on the other, a widespread lack of trust in their capacity ever to deal decisively with the threat of disorder. Or to remain on the right side of the porous, hyphenated line between crime-and-policing, il/legality. This, as Loretta Lynch has reminded us (above, p. 48), is especially true for those perennially "targeted" by the cops, who also retain a residual desire for good-faith enforcement—despite deep skepticism of the role of the law in the proxy race-class conflict at the core of the police function.

The counterpoint of desire and distrust—of the im/possibility of the police function, of the undecidability of crime-and-policing, of the murky, spectral spaces of the il/licit—is, we would argue, inherent in the age of fractured sovereignty: the age in which the auratic authority of the law is compromised by the devolution of so much of its operation to the market and the community; in which, in extremis, as in South Africa and inner-city America—and the United Kingdom and France and many places besides—the erosion of the social contract has eventuated in the impression of a "warre of all against all." Or, at least, of civil society against a shadow population of nightmare anti-citizens. This brings us back, finally, to where we began, to the truth about crime. It reminds us that it is in the metaphysics of disorder, of transgression and malfeasance, that societies make sense of—and, as we have shown, for example, in the instance of rape in South Africa, argue about—the worlds that they have created for themselves, what and who they are, and where, in the process of becoming, their history has taken them. Which is why the meaning of crime, whatever its incidences and its consequences, cannot be reduced to a sociological pathology: why it is a semiosis, a system of meaningful signs, through which truths about social life are apprehended, contested, and acted upon. And through which politics and publics, economy and society, are made and remade.

In the circumstances, it is hardly surprising that in contexts like South Africa, where crime is taken to be an index of a failure of governance, of civil society, of democratic nation building, and of postcolonial social reconstruction, there should be an almost-compulsive tendency—in everyday talk, the media, artistic expression, political discourse, scholarly critique—to return to the scene of the crime, as it were. Or to look there for an ontological ground from which to frame questions about the state, security, citizenship, democracy, law, race, class, and gender; also about productivity and profitability, both legitimate and illegitimate—and the banal everything-in-between of everyday life. These criminal obsessions manifest themselves in a vibrant representational economy, an economy in which life and art both replicate and (re)make each other, in which cops and crooks do all sorts of things that illuminate not just the underworld but also the complex entanglements of law, economy, and ordinary existence in the here and now. It is that representational economy to which we now turn.

CHAPTER 1.3

FORENSIC FANTASY AND THE POLITICAL ECONOMY OF REPRESENTATION

Scenes from the Brave Noir World

Given the almost global preoccupation with it, it is hardly any wonder that crime-and-policing should have become an object of fetishism and fantasy, the ur-motif of so much contemporary cultural production. It goes without saying also that, with the proliferation and personalization of communicative media—and with the intensified volume, velocity, and volatility of the circulation of images—the political economy of representation has itself undergone radical space-time expansion. The all-but-planetary effect of the Digital Revolution has been, at once, to reduce the efficacy of "ideological state apparatuses" (Althusser 1971) and to proliferate free-flowing neural pathways of public consciousness, at once intimate and depersonalized; pathways along which travel expressions of fear, indignation, identification, desire, critique. In the circumstances, crime fiction—in literature, art, film, theater, music, public media of all kinds—has become, to a greater extent than ever before, a global vernacular (Hansen 1999). In addition, as hyperportable recording devices put the means of visual re-presentation and mass dissemination in the hands of "everypersons" across the world, forensic images are ever more avidly mobilized and contested in the cause of revealing in/justice; this in a manner that blurs the line between documentary and fantasy, established forms and "under-genres,"[1] models of and models for reality (Geertz 1973, 93). As Terry Eagleton (2015) says of the relation of the real and the illusory in a globalized world: "If the truth contains an ineradicable admixture of fiction, the imaginary can sometimes reveal the truth more effectively than science or historiography." In a similar spirit, our interest here in mass-mediated representations of crime-and-policing is less to distinguish fact from fabrication—or to track the sociology of its reception as one thing or the other—than to treat it as evidence of a society thinking about, arguing with, itself.

None of this is to scant the deep historical roots of crime as allegory. To the degree that the rule of law is a founding principle of modernity, crime fiction, which narrates its ongoing battle against lawlessness, has featured in cultural production and consumption almost from the first. In fact, the genre has an even deeper archaeology. As Satomi Saito (2007, 255) reminds us, citing Walter Ong (1988), material similar to that used by Edgar Allan Poe is to be found in Chinese detective stories of the seventeenth century, although the latter, Ong argues, never achieved the "climactic concision," or the pyramidal narrative structure, characteristic of later Western writing.[2] Others have also identified precursors in the Arabic literature of the medieval Islamic Golden Age (e.g., Pinault 1992).[3] Nonetheless, crime-as-*modernist*-allegory has its epistemic roots in the enduring Enlightenment trope of detection as the quintessential means by which truths are discovered: truths about transgression and, hence, truths about the normative order from which that transgression departs. Forensic investigation, itself foundational to "the [very] nature of knowing" (Most and Stowe 1983, xv), came to epitomize the empirical method: the techniques, that is, by which surface signs are deciphered in order to arrive at underlying truths (Ginzburg 1989, 87; below, p. 102)—hence Durkheim's point about the semiotics of crime, to which we keep returning.

In its conventional form, detective fiction, as Franco Moretti (2005, 143ff.) observes of nineteenth-century Europe, gave voice to mounting anxieties about the very possibility of authoritative control in a rapidly expanding, labile world (see 2.1), an industrializing world in which civility seemed fragile and property under threat. Its plots addressed those anxieties: they restored order by setting to rights the acts and actors that breached it. Even those who contested the sanctity of the law—who dismissed it as an instrument for the protection of wealth and privilege—often did so in the language of il/legitimacy, criminality, theft. And of forensic critique. Both Carl Schmitt (2007) and Walter Benjamin (1978, 287), to take two celebrated examples, maintained, if in different ways, that the liberal conception of legality was woefully inadequate as the basis of viable political order: it gave rise to forms of society that, demonstrably, were themselves wholly criminal. Benjamin (1969, 226) famously referred to Paris, ultimate capitalist metropolis, as the "scene of the crime" (U. Greenberg 2009, 315–16; Salzani 2007)—a characterization more tragically apt, in the age of late modern terror, than he could have surmised. For conservatives and liberals alike, thinking about modern society was inseparable from thinking about criminality: to contemplate the one was to contemplate the other. During the Weimar years, for example, as Udi Green-berg (2009, 315–16) points out, "crime accumulated a unique symbolic weight" among German thinkers, being symptomatic of perverse political and social structures: it was "a lens through which politicians and intellectuals debated society's failures and their alternatives to the modern socio-political order."[4] And about which literati wrote fiction in whose plotlines those failures could be resolved by (more or less) heroic human intervention.

But this normative tendency also bred its antithesis, an antihistory of crime as a different kind of allegory, one that conjured with the genre to disrupt re-ceived orthodoxies; specifically, to erode the confidence with which the law was set apart from lawlessness, righteousness from corruption, policing from villainy—and the certainty that the former could or should or would always triumph over the latter. This rogue tradition used fiction to question the recti-tude and authority of the established order of things by probing its illicit, un-ruly undersides. More often than not, it emanated from one or another dis-placement from the mainstream: Mark Twain's (1902) satirical novelette on the (socio)logical shortcomings of Sherlock Holmes's "scientific methods," his overreliance on the wrong sorts of rationalist, normative assumptions; or the critical allegories from Weimar Germany that placed the felon, rather than the detective, at their dark core (Herzog 2009); or the writings of William Faulkner (1990) and Richard Wright (1940) on crime, race, and gender in the United States; or the abrasive Depression-era crime fiction of the 1930s, which, as C. L. R. James (1993, 118ff.) pointed out long ago, offered a sardonic critique of the failed promise of liberal-capitalist economy and governance in America; or 1940s wartime noir, both written and filmed (Marling 1998), and, later, the tough, edgy African American detective fiction of the 1990s that wrote blacks back into the national narrative (English 2013, 129, 156–57). These examples, like others to which we shall turn in a moment, give the lie to the thesis that the mainstream thriller, at least in English, was, or is, a "historically white genre," a genre that invariably endorses existing relations of class and race—and, consequently, is not easily decolonized or recommissioned by minority authors (Poll 2014, 183; Klein 1999, 4).

This, however, raises two immediate, closely interconnected questions: What, precisely, is different about crime-and-policing as allegory in the con-tinuing present, the present-incomplete? And how have the recent historical transformations that we have highlighted here—the seismic shift in the artic-ulation of the state, governance, and capital—insinuated themselves into the political economy of representation, into its spaces of contestation, into the shaping of its social knowledge, into its quotidian truths?

Beyond its sheer ubiquity as an ur-motif in so much contemporary cultural production—and its migration into domains into which it has rarely gone before—crime fiction appears to be undergoing a series of transfigurations in its form and meaning, its formulae and its functions, enabling it to engage in a much more ironic, more open-ended, even surreal, exploration of late modern doubts, dreads, and discontents; so much so, that some of the most profound existential explorations of economy and society, citizenship and social being, humanity and its sensibilities are to be found, these days, in forensic fiction. This is not to say that the normcentric modernist genre has disappeared. It certainly has not. Formulaic fantasies of enforcement still abound; in them, mythic supercops, CSI technowizards, intuitively inspired detectives, charismatic profilers, and hardened, streetwise officers continue to wrest law from lawlessness. But these endlessly recycled melodramas are, it appears, gradually being overtaken by a crime fiction wave much more given to exploring the contradictions and conundrums of the present moment: the legal and moral murkiness, indeed illegibility much of the time, of the lines between law-making, law-breaking, and law-enforcement; the con/fusion of politics and crime; the desire for, yet distrust in, policing, the im/possibility of its mandate, and the implications of its outsourcing by the state; and so on and on. This wave, patently, harks back to the antihistory of orthodox crime fiction of which we spoke a moment ago: the one in which the genre is mobilized less in the cause of imagining the established order and the repair of its breaches, more to imploding its ambiguities, its hidden secrets, it incoherences and undecidabilities. While that genre may have had its origins largely in the art house, its productions are increasingly going mainstream in film, literature, and other popular forms of expressive culture, like rap music, online videos, even advertising (Caldeira 2006).

Thus, for example, South Africa. Here, it has been said, "crime fiction has hijacked the . . . imagination and continues to hold it hostage."[5] Literary critical orthodoxy has dismissed its rapid rise as a regrettable retreat from the "multi-layered" complexity of apartheid-era writing, notes Leon de Kock (2015, 28–30), who suggests that the explosion of police procedurals—of noir, nonfiction, and "inside stories"—might be less a turn aside from the great liberal-humanist tradition than an attempt to find new ways in which to pursue its central purpose: to document contradictory social realities, to expose injustice, to take the measure of emerging truths, and to raise awareness of changing conditions.[6] These realities and truths and conditions, which do not fit received teleologies of the passage from then to now, are apprehended with startling insight by a raft of authors—the likes of Deon Meyer, Margie Orford, Mike Nicol, Rob Marsh, Andrew Brown—for whom the "mystery" provides a supple formula for probing the strangeness of the "new normal," with its unsettling fusion of the ordinary and the unreal.[7]

A suggestive parallel comes from Colombia, where the establishment of the Medellín Negro festival in 2009 marked the turn of many noted writers, journalists, and scholars to crime fiction as a means, in the words of renowned writer Laura Restrepo, "to find a way to some kind of future."[8] For Hugo Chaparro, reporter-turned-novelist, it has become a critical vehicle for exploring the "illusion of being able to find an explanation of reality in literature because the confusion about reality [i]s so big." In a context in which crime saturates everyday life, most fiction *is* now crime fiction—although, as *Guardian* columnist Melanie McGrath notes, Colombian writers tend to avoid legal thrillers and police procedurals, insisting that "people tend to believe, from experience, that the authorities are on the side of the bad guys; . . . [that] there is no order or equilibrium to be restored." Adds Laura Restrepo, sardonically, they are "wise enough to know 'the future' is not a very reliable concept."

Much the same thing is true in South Africa, not least in the cohort of poised black authors whose dramatis personae are canny, more-or-less cynical observers of the failure of the liberal narrative: of the limitations of the law to rectify past wrongs, of its corruptibility in service of the postcolonial lust for wealth and power.[9] Notable among them is Sifiso Mzobe, whose bildungsroman, *Young Blood* (2010), is an "almost *noir*" novel.[10] Its teenage antihero takes us on a terrifying trip that eschews steady, middle-class aspiration for the seductions of high-speed, high-octane crime—carjacking, drugs, hyperconsumerism—and the dangerous erotics of the "ultimate driving machine," which transports him from a drear township to gangster glitz in the coastal resort of Umhlanga, bypassing the world of workaday business. His is a journey so empathic, so compelling, that his last-ditch redemption seems barely plausible. Equally notable is Angela Makholwa, whose smoldering *Red Ink* (2007) is said to be the first crime novel by a black South African woman. Its plotline is animated by the insatiable, morally equivocal curiosity of a hot, funky investigator: as Lucy Sibongile Khambule plies the "indifferent world of new bling and cutthroat Jozi [Johannesburg] business,"[11] she discovers just how inextricably, if not always visibly, that world is tied to the postapartheid, poststruggle criminal economy.

This turn to moral cynicism and existential uncertainty, suggests de Kock (2015, 34–42), springs from troubling questions posed by the radical transformation that South Africa is going through: Why the reappearance of "bad difference" amid ruptured nationhood and racially marked inequality? Does its population "still know itself"? What defines a "good citizen"? In this way South African noir, to which we shall return in more detail below, seeks to "recover the plot," to shed light on reconfigurations of color and class, on the difficult alignment of democracy with a fractured civil society, on the growing unsettlement of all identities. In this respect, the darkness of its crime fiction echoes other, similarly vigorous local brands across the world. Hence the late twentieth-century advent of Tartan noir, for instance, said to be especially conducive to a dispassionate exploration of the fraught, late modern politics of "the Scottish condition" (Christie 2013, 9).[12] Or the internationally acclaimed Nordic noir, which gives voice to the fear that, beneath the institutionalized liberalism, equality, and social justice of the "Scandinavian model," lurk deadly hatreds, misogyny, and xenophobia (Peacock 2014).[13] Likewise in Japan, writes Saito (2007, 255), a hybrid brand of ornery detective fantasy, first developed in modernizing urban contexts in the 1920s, has been energetically remastered in multiple media in the effort to return to a "new authentic school" of domestic fiction. This idiom now haunts postmodern consumer space, he says, providing a language for confronting the vexed relation of local to global identities—of which it is itself a prime exemplar.

Ernest Mandel (1984) was among the first to theorize this broad shift from the brave new world of the modernist literary imagination to the brave neo, the brave noir, world that is morphing out of it. Writing in the early 1980s, he anticipated the effects of the Digital Revolution and, more embracingly, the shifting lineaments of economy, society, and the nation-state form in which it was entailed. For him, detective fiction, as a privileged vehicle of bourgeois ideology, had begun, concomitantly, to show significant signs of change. Prominent among them was the return of the criminal as outlaw hero, the *picaro*, a rebellious figure much like that of the picaresque bandit of earlier times (above, 1.1), who expressed frankly defiant skepticism about law, order, and the legitimacy of the state. With the rise of capitalism, this figure had been replaced, in the popular imagination, by the image of the felon as a self-serving, antisocial crook, the quintessential enemy of society, whose nemesis was the upright detective, champion of the right and the good, aka the propertied and the privileged. The late twentieth-century renaissance of the picaresque outlaw, Mandel (1984, 132) goes on to suggest—an altogether more ambiguous character, less clearly antisocial, more creatively entrepreneurial, often the object of ambivalent admiration in both life and art—is a corollary of the erosion of received values and certitudes. Think Tony Soprano, Walter White, or Omar Little (above, p. xii), whom we shall encounter again in a moment. And the cynical cops, private eyes, and vigilantes who pursue this "new criminal type": figures who, alike in fact and fiction, are themselves more cynical about the idea of an "absolute Good," themselves more prone to stretch the law. All these things, Mandel says, have been reinforced by the rising interdependence of big business and criminality—the "specter" of which we have spoken—which frequently makes it hard to distinguish lawlessness from law-enforcement.

It is true that this has always been so to *some* degree. But, Mandel insists, the growing scale, dispersal, and complexity of the underworld economy has rendered authorities reliant on criminals and their "insider" information as never before. Recall an example of that symbiosis, subject of a major feature film that we cited in passing earlier: the sensational court case of megagangster James "Whitey" Bulger in Boston in 2014.[14] The thoroughgoing connivance of politicians and police in Bulger's violent demesne—widely viewed by an outraged public as the greatest offense in the trial, if not *on* trial—served to indict the law itself as criminal (Cullen 2013).[15] But the tight interweaving of criminality, legality, and commerce, captured in the new noir, is not just about high-end, organized mayhem (Mandel 1984, 112, 133). Crime exhibits the same motives, means, and mores, the same purposes and practices—and the same "postideological" pursuit of the good life and personal happiness—that now characterize capital accumulation everywhere. Like all business, both clean and dirty, it seeks out sites of ever fewer restrictions in search of ever greater profit (above, 1.1; Comaroff and Comaroff 2001). In the upshot, lines are drawn less between the licit and the illicit than between value and waste, the effective and the ineffective, the productive and the expendable.

Mandel's general point about the political economy of representation is perhaps best illustrated in television and film, the most popular of popular media and the most global in their circulation; also the most able—being simultaneously aural and visual, realist and surreal, temporal and spatial—to capture the in/visible criminal specter that haunts the contemporary *imaginaire*. There appears to be an affinity between that phantasmic specter and what Siegfried Kracauer (1997, xlix) terms the "distinctive spirit" of the cinematic medium. Let us delve into this further, once again in the United States and South Africa, thus to dig yet deeper into the meaning of crime-and-policing in the early twenty-first century.

Forensic Fantasy and the Criminal Everyman

Once upon a Time, in America

The best place to begin, arguably, is with the multiple award-winning HBO crime series *The Sopranos* (1999–2007, directed by David Chase), held by many critics to be among the greatest television dramas of all time, if not *the* greatest.[16] Set in New Jersey, the show explores the entanglement of the private and professional lives of an everyman-mobster "in the era of diminished expectations,"[17] resonating brilliantly with the zeitgeist of the 2000s in America and beyond, including South Africa. Its impact has been magnified by waves of commentary, critique, and commodification—blogs, books, college courses, video games, soundtrack albums, and merchandise—that have rendered it at once a mythic touchstone and a cultural cliché. Its finely wrought, nervy gangster-hero speaks to a host of late modern social issues, personal anxieties, and existential conundrums arising from the deregulation of capitalism and organized crime, through contemporary tensions surrounding ethnicity, race, and religion, to changing norms of kinship, sex, domesticity, masculinity, gender, generation, and the psychic life of the late modern subject. The range of its uptake has been striking: the Freud Museum in Vienna featured an installation on *The Sopranos* in 2010, while down-class teenage hip-hop aficionados whom we encountered in Cape Town that same year riffed on the names of its cast of characters, whose moves they impersonated endlessly. As this makes plain, popular images of crime-and-punishment—just like branded models of zero-tolerance policing (above, 1.2)—travel widely, with unexpected consequences and unpredictable effects on style, affect, ethical orientation, and everyday dispositions.

Perhaps the fascination with this "great criminal" among so many viewing populations lies in the double play on the *Soprano* family, a family that opens up to the public gaze the merging of crime and kinship, the epic and the commonplace. Tony Soprano may be a big-time hood. But, just like the homebound viewer, he is caught up in a struggle to adapt his domestic life and his line of work to postindustrial times. In these times, he notes sardonically, "the big money goes to Enron,"[18] a once-respected megacompany, mentioned earlier (1.1), that profited hugely in the translucent zones of fiscal il/legality—until it went too far, in counterfeiting reality, even for an America remarkably tolerant of the excesses of finance capital. In these times, too, monopolistic, impersonal corporations do not just drive out small and middle-sized firms. They also make it impossible to shake down those firms, once the bread and butter of the mob-as-franchise, a lesson that the New Jersey wiseguys are forced to learn as they try to extract protection money from a local Starbucks. The decline of older forms of business, Tony Soprano comes to understand, makes hustlers, "waste managers," of all who would survive in this day and age. As the president of HBO said of this thoroughly contemporary suburban godfather: "the only difference between him and everybody I know is he's the don of New Jersey."[19] Like everybody else, he takes his traumas to a therapist and his kid on a college tour—all right, so he kills a former foe along the way, while his innocent daughter is in bed asleep, but that is just business, nothing personal or untoward—all the while trying to hold on to an operation that is forced, by changing conditions, to be ever more creatively entrepreneurial.

What we have here, in other words, is a mobster in midlife crisis serving as the average Joe, the Willy Loman of our age,[20] who embodies the alienation bred by the vain pursuit of the American dream—but who, under the conditions of late modern capitalism, runs up against its neoliberal limits. In this, *The Sopranos* is not alone. Take the celebrated series *Breaking Bad* (2008–13, directed by Vince Gilligan). Walter White, its dark, Nietzschean protagonist, is a struggling, terminally ill, uninsured chemistry teacher who turns into a murderous producer of high-grade crystal meth in order to pay his medical bills. Ironically named for the ambiguity of the character—and for his poetic, Whitmanesque play on boundary breaking—White has been hailed as an embodiment of "neoliberal criminology," according to which crime is "no longer a deviant activity outside the mainstream market, but is rather [merely] one market among others" (Pierson 2014, 21).[21] "Funny how we draw the line between what's legal and what's illegal," Walt says to his policeman brother-in-law. "It's arbitrary . . ."[22] A similar ethical ambivalence colors other creative examples, like the "modestly revolutionary"[23] comedy-drama *Orange Is the New Black* (2013, directed by Jenji Kohan),[24] about a vapid yuppie and occasional drug mule who is sent to a women's prison in Litchfield, Connecticut, there to experience a Rabelaisian world that defies received distinctions between crime and culpability, inside and outside, black and white. The women in orange are a microcosm of the world at large: its raw rectangulation of crime, law, violence, and business, its unstable architecture of power, passion, race, sexuality, and class. The camera neither patronizes nor pities, never relapses into a functionalist morality play. Rather, it invites us to ponder the fact that "we are all prisoners of something, dreaming of escape,"[25] that none of us has any choice but to navigate that often-fine line between the criminal and the legal as we go about our daily enterprise. Says Omar Little of *The Wire* (see below), the deadly, quixotic, queer, and perhaps most compelling of bandit philosophers of the new noir: "I got the shotgun, you got the briefcase. It's all in the game though, right?" Criminology, as we have said, has indeed become the new sociology here, turning Durkheim on his head. The signifying power of crime, especially in the multisensory medium of film, no longer obscures the legitimate, normative order. Instead, it captures the pervasive logic of that dis/order in toto, at once right-and-wrong side up.

In short, to return to Ernest Mandel and Tony Soprano—and Pierre-Joseph Proudhon, this time as much in parody as in tragedy—it is not merely that, in art as in life, business is crime and crime is business, sometimes with murder on the side; after all, notes critic Oliver Farry, the analogy between the two has become a truism.[26] It is, rather, that criminality is a window, a wide-angled lens, into the dark heart of the new Order of Things, into the interior workings of economy and society in the global age of the market. Writing about *The Wire* (2002–8, directed by David Simon)—often, *The Sopranos* notwithstanding, held to be the greatest television drama of all time[27]—Farry credits the series with having managed, in its devastating anatomy of the city of Baltimore, to capture the "protean, miasmic nature of contemporary capital [itself]." David Simon, who cocreated the show, has called it a "rebellion . . . against all the horseshit police procedurals afflicting American television." Above all, it was meant as a critique of the war on drugs that, for Simon as for others, has "mutated into a war on the American underclass" under conditions of "untethered capitalism run amok."[28] As was made dramatically evident by the outbreak of mass protest in the wake of the police murder of Freddie Gray in April 2015, life in Baltimore continues to imitate TV, whose news feeds and theater are sometimes scarcely distinguishable.

The genius of *The Wire* for our purposes, however, lies in the ways in which it mobilizes crime as a signifier: how it rewrites the police procedural to permit grand storytelling in the mode of realist ethnography. Its portrait of "how we live together"[29] in the twenty-first-century United States is entirely unique in the degree to which its center of gravity rests, unapologetically, on the drug-dealing corners, the mean streets, and the projects of the black inner city with minimal condemnation, romance, or righteous redemption. The narrative builds a matter-of-fact world in which law and lawlessness, criminal and legitimate labor, gangs and unions blend seamlessly in the business of everyday life, all of them intersecting fluidly with the grand institutions of the American society: with city hall, the police, education, the media, corporations, and worker organizations. Small wonder that *The Wire* has been compared by high-minded critics to the works of Dickens and Dostoyevsky[30]—or that it has been assigned by professors at elite universities as a core text for the study of race, class, and political economy in postindustrial America.[31] What is more, its mise-en-scène may cleave closely to Rust Belt Baltimore. But it also resonates cogently with the urban ecology of Leeds, Liverpool, Lagos, and Johannesburg.

Talk of Dickens and Dostoyevsky returns us again to the issue of historical singularity. Those writers—and others, like Victor Hugo—also directed scathing commentary at the pitiless inequities of a social order that condemned *les misérables*, the "wretched throng" (Dickens 2009, 17), to lives of "crime and punishment." But Dickensian prose paired righteous indignation with a reformist zeal that turned on a sanctimonious certainty about the difference between right and wrong, law and lawlessness; also about a social contract that *obliged* society, as all too palpable an abstraction, to "do its duty" by its "most miserable and neglected outcasts" (Dickens 2009, 17), thus to recuperate them as productive, dignified citizens. By contrast, *The Sopranos, Breaking Bad, Orange Is the New Black*, and *The Wire* take the "truth about crime, and policing," for the reasons we have spelled out, to be much more inchoate, much less given to decisive normative judgment. Largely indeterminate. In all four of them, the state is a recessive, unpredictable presence, having perforce ceded a good part of its monopoly over legitimate violence, its ultimate authority over life and death, to the private sector and, in particular, to organized crime. In all of them, the police—in the case of *Orange*, prison warders—are thoroughly compromised, regularly break the law, and are deeply implicated in illegal dealings of all sorts. And in all of them, "society" is largely evacuated, leaving little to stand between, on the one hand, the entrepreneurial individual and the family and, on the other, the market and the world—except other sorts of "families," like street gangs and criminal associations, oriented around their interpolation into the criminal economy.

In all four of them, moreover, ethnoracial differences, and violence along its fissures, lie at the sociological core of that economy, of what and whom it treats as valuable or expendable, as worth or as waste. In all of them, the family itself, as an institution, is an aspiration whose normative accomplishment turns out to be impossible, as everyone, in one way or another, is drawn into the tainted, dark-gray spaces of the il/licit. Hence, in *Breaking Bad*, the cop brother-in-law of the protagonist outlaw, unwittingly has his medical bills paid from the profits made from drug manufacture by that very outlaw in-law;

meanwhile, he protects his own wife from prosecution for kleptomania, which she fails to acknowledge as wrong. In all of them, too, the line between politics and crime is intermittently drawn and redrawn, despite their complicity and connivance in one another; crime is often the route to advance in politics, while politics depends for its legitimacy on pitting itself against crime. In all of them, finally, the passage between the legal and the illegal is plied in both directions, this being symbolically underscored as money is laundered: in *The Sopranos* it is through, yes, a waste-management business, in *Breaking Bad*, with ironic literalism, through a car wash operation that passes profits from drugs made in a laboratory *beneath a laundry* into the formal sector. The entanglements are endless.

Rather than reassure their publics that normative order will be restored and criminals caught, these new-wave allegories reinforce the sense of vulnerability and impotence, both personal and communal, that underpins the prevailing paradox of desire and distrust, of im/possibility. At the same time, ironically, they also feed the mass appeal of modernist procedurals, those of an older ideological vintage in which—if only in fiction, not in life—officers of the law actually *do* succeed in "turning it around," in "bringing crime under control." It is in this light that we should understand the continuing popularity of those "horseshit" dramas of which David Simon spoke, dramas in which cops seem uncannily capable of solving the mystery, of getting their wo/man, of securing the citadel. The primary example is the award-winning *Crime Scene Investigation*, named the most watched television show in the world in 2011, which celebrates the triumph of forensic science[32]—and raises the ire of police and district attorneys over what they term the "CSI effect," the unrealistic faith among victims and juries that biometric technologies, deployed by scientific supercops, will produce a "smoking gun" in intractable cases (Schweitzer and Saks 2007). It is precisely the late modern conditions captured in the dark hyperrealism of the new noir, we would suggest, that fuel the anxiety to which this faith in forensics offers an answer. *CSI*, as a futuristic anachronism, recuperates a fetishized reverence for the possibility of effective policing—which, after Lacan, merely deepens the sense of irretrievable loss that it seeks to relieve (2.1).

At work, in all this, in other words, is an intense longing for conviction, again in both senses of that term, a longing sharpened by the mass consumption of new-wave crime fiction. Existential angst may be inherent in modernity. But it has been intensified in the here and now, we argue, by the changing Order of Things. And by the political economy of representation that has emerged out of that order, those things. Perhaps this has manifested itself most dramatically in the aftermath of culturally marked watersheds—post–Cold War, post–Socialist, postcolonial, postapartheid—especially in places where the promise of modernity was long deferred, disfigured, perpetually interrupted. Which takes us back, once more, to South Africa, whose own watershed moment, in 1994, has been followed by a heightened sense of normative instability, of *Unheimlichkeit*, of explosive possibility. As a result, the allegory of crime-and-policing is even more productive than usual here, where it challenges existing truths about the very nature of nationhood, sovereignty, society, and the state (cf. Warnes 2012).

Gangsters' Paradise, South Africa

Neil McCarthy's *The Great Outdoors*, singled out by some literary critics as South Africa's "first post-apartheid play,"[33] begins with a monologue by a white policeman. He addresses the audience from a darkened center stage:

> Why is everyone so obsessed with the truth? . . . I am asked to interview a guy. I am told he is a threat to the state. I do my best to get at the truth. And I find something. He has done things. Instigated certain . . . disruptive actions. . . . Now a few years later, people tell me that was not the truth. This guy was actually some sort of hero. The things he did were great things. . . . But where does that leave me? Must I now say that most of my life was a lie? Because his is now true? . . . So now I think this. I think that what actually happened, the facts of the case, who said what and proceeded to act in the following way; all that is incidental. The real truth is behind all that. The real truth might be swimming in a completely different direction to the way the feet are moving. The real truth might be shivering in a burrow between the roots while it looks as though it is eating the fruit from the top of the tree. And that's what you have to get to. The shivering guy. Forget the appearances.

This hardened officer, formerly of the ancien régime, is now policing the postcolony. How is he to deal with radical changes in the coordinates of truth and justice when reality has been radically relativized and the "indoors" of a closed universe opened up to the world outside (cf. de Kock 2015, 41)? The cop strains to solve the mystery, to read the signs, to rediscover the plot. But his craft, born of an age gone by, fails in postapartheid South Africa, where old evidentiary canons are challenged by new kinds of authority, criminality, clues, convictions, and technologies of policing. As McCarthy's lawman laments, appearances mislead. It takes a different kind of insight, and different means, to police a society in which sovereignty is uncertain, in which the lines between the law and lawlessness, violence and democracy, politics and crime, truth and fiction, are rendered less and less legible. But the turn to new means for establishing that truth is not necessarily effective. Muses Bennie Griessel, dyspeptic anti/hero of Deon Meyer's twenty-first-century novels, set in Cape Town: "Now technology ha[s] to do everything. And when it fail[s]"—which it does repeatedly—detectives say, "this case can't be solved."[34] This is why, as we shall see in 2.1, there has arisen a preoccupation among many South Africans with finding their own supercops, cops of sundry sorts. This is also why South African TV has birthed its own answer to the *X-Files* and *The Walking Dead*: *Room 9* (2012–13, directed by Darrell Roodt) is a popular postapocalyptic show, now gone international, that features a special undercover Police Occult Unit that—like the real-life Occult-Related Crimes Unit that we shall encounter in part 2—investigates uncanny events that haunt New Azania (i.e., future Johannesburg).

Dystopic thoughts of this kind underscore the degree to which the noir of the (neo)present, its fixation on crime-and-policing, has its roots in the colonial history of a "country . . . stitched together with violence" (Steinberg 2001, 2). As Loren Kruger (2001, 224) reminds us, Johannesburg, core of the nation's vibrant urban psyche and the setting for most of its recent movies, has long been portrayed through "variations on the crime story and its theatrical cousins, the melodrama and the gangster show." If, under apartheid, the white popular media pulsed with eroticized fears of black lawlessness, ordinary African life was shaped, in large part, by what Bloke Modisane (1963, 153; cf. Nixon 1994, 31) dubbed "the banditry of the law." As segregation took on ever-greater statutory precision in the 1950s, and organized resistance gained momentum, a vibrant strain of early black crime writing gained a voice. Centered on the fabled *Drum* magazine,[35] the genre blurred the line between fiction and reportage, asserting an insouciant cosmopolitanism that drew on the "New Negro" of the Harlem Renaissance, on gangster films and pulp fiction of the 1930s, and on *cinéma noir* to forge its own gritty realism. It focused on city life, its underworld, the violence of the prison system, and the thuggery of the police (Nkosi 1965, 10; Couzens 1985). Famously skittish about politics per se, *Drum* writers were preoccupied with the luminous figure of the outlaw, or *tsotsi*, a protagonist "who understood with a visceral force the culture of ingenious illegality" (Nixon 1994, 32; Matshikiza 2001, xi).[36] Together with a cadre of gifted black photojournalists, these writers did much to fix the flash of the glamorous urban hood in black public consciousness—by contrast to the stereotypic trope of the rurally based, tribally indexed, tradition-bound "native" fostered and disseminated to the world by the apartheid regime.

Drum's sassy heroes foreshadowed the provocative postcolonial *mapantsula* culture—youthful, black, urban, roguishly chic—canonized in a novel genre of gangster movies set in and around Johannesburg at the century's end. Crime-and-policing has made up a strikingly large proportion of the local cinema, television, and music-video industries that have flourished since fin de siècle alongside the prose fiction noted above, with which it has occasionally intersected.[37] This new wave was announced with the film *Mapantsula*, which was initially banned but then released in 1988 to become a landmark of the crumbling of the old order and its transition to the post-. The nation's "first anti-apartheid feature,"[38] it was made for, about, and largely by black South Africans,[39] a collaboration between an African writer-actor, Thomas Mogotlane, and a white director, Oliver Schmitz. The movie was a lumpen bildungsroman. Shot in Soweto, it pulsed with the urban beat of "township jive" and depicted the life and times of a *mapantsula*, a petty thief called Panic. Despite his name, Panic was a cool, streetwise hustler. Caught up in an antigovernment protest, he was arrested, along with a clutch of political dissidents, the "real" enemies of the state.

But it is precisely the inadequacy of reducing resistance to organized politics that is at issue in the film. Panic was a *picaro*, à la Mandel. For most of his life he disavowed that sort of politics and was not above collaborating with the regime—although he always lived by an iconoclastic ethic of his own, robbing wealthy, white beneficiaries of the racist system—until, in the end, he was swept up in the pervasive violence of the times and had to take sides. Here, however, is the point: in moving beyond the conventional narrative of anticolonial struggle, the film posed open-ended questions about the limits and legitimacy of the law, about un/civil society and self-care, and about the changing shape of power relations. While it harked back to the hyperrealism of the stories published in *Drum*, it also anticipated "criminal life in the global postcolony,"[40] gesturing forward to the bold, edgy Jozi Noir, which would include features like *Tsotsi, Hijack Stories, Avenged,* and *Gangster's Paradise: Jerusalema,* movies that, more than any other expressive media, explored the often-scary freedoms—the "exploded view" (Vladislavić 2004, 24; see 2.1 and 2.2)—of the great new "outdoors."

The best known of them, both at home and abroad, is *Tsotsi* (2005, directed by Gavin Hood), which won the Oscar for Best Foreign Language Film in 2006. Based on a novel published in 1980 by Athol Fugard, it tells of a brutal young thug, the eponymous Tsotsi,[41] who finds unlikely salvation. The fact that Fugard's colonial portrait of the alienated poor could so easily be applied to the present makes grim comment on the limits of liberation. The movie opens with a game of craps: life is determined by a roll of the dice, the odds still heavily stacked against lumpen black youth. The optimistic, redemptive tone of the original story has given way to a more sardonic realism: Tsotsi, abused by his parents and then orphaned by AIDS, has come of age in a colony of street kids. A coldhearted killer, he is a self-seeking loner who ekes out a cutthroat living in an urban ecology in which only survival and money matter. One day he jacks a car from its affluent black owner, only to discover a bright-eyed baby on the back seat. Given what we know of Tsotsi's world, the odds that good will triumph are not favorable. The outcome, perhaps a lingering trace of the liberalism of Fugard's text, appears implausible in a now-disillusioned South Africa: when faced with responsibility for life at its most vulnerable, trusting, innocently demanding, Tsotsi is swayed by an elemental kinship that he himself was denied. At great personal risk, he returns the child. The movie ends with him raising his hands in resignation, presumably to face capture. Or worse.

But maybe not. The director, Hood, produced two other, well-publicized endings. In one, Tsotsi reaches into his pocket for the baby's milk, is shot in the chest, and dies. In the second, although hit by a bullet, he escapes and limps off toward an uncertain freedom.[42] This equivocation may have reflected concern about the film's reception by a less cynical overseas market. But it also points to the impossibility of easy moral resolution to the conundrums of crime, inequality, and in/justice in postapartheid South Africa. The irony is compounded by the confrontation between Tsotsi and the cops. It involved two gestures—"hands up" and the reach into a pocket—that have become iconic everywhere of the failure of underclass subjects to defend themselves against the violence of the law.[43] The communicative power of these images makes plain how, as films draw on a transnational aesthetic argot, they invariably convey more than their makers intend. This is especially so when they rely on "embedded" techniques that tap directly into the flow of everyday life on the streets, as did the *cinéma vérité* or "anthropological cinema" of an earlier era[44]—although those techniques are deployed in contemporary South African noir less in pursuit of unmediated truths than to make a virtue of street cred and low budgets. Shot mostly on location in Alexandra township in the medium of *Tsotsitaal* or *Isicamtho* (literally, "gangster language"), a patois spoken by youth in Johannesburg, *Tsotsi* has the grainy realism of a documentary. In major part, responsibility for its scripting, and for its mise-en-scène, seems to have rested with its black cast and crew. As in *The Wire*, most of its actors are "unknowns." But they are more thoroughly at home as hoods-in-the-hood, and in its deep vernacular, than director Hood, an outsider, could ever have been.

Gangster's Paradise: Jerusalema (2008, directed by Ralph Ziman), described as "*Tsotsi* without the feel-good glow,"[45] is an altogether more charged coming-of-age allegory.[46] Like other so-called Mzansiwood movies (Mzansi, "South Africa," from *uMzantsi*, isiXhosa for "the south"), this one was made on a shoestring, using available locations. Lacking the cachet of large studio backing, it did not circulate as widely. But, being closely spliced into the mythic life of the criminal economy, it has a singular place in the national black imaginary. *Jerusalema*, the New Jerusalem, is Johannesburg, vortex of a "new" South Africa, in which most black citizens now have rights without capital, law without order, desire without means. Lucky Kunene is a sharp township kid who is accepted into an elite business school but cannot raise the necessary funds. So he sets about becoming a wiseguy of another sort. In the free market of ambition, he nurtures a repurposed colonial fantasy: a house by the sea. Kunene hatches a scheme for getting rich by extending the techniques of carjacking into the realm of real estate: his crew seize crime-ridden buildings owned by slumlords who extort whatever they can from their pitiably poor tenants. With a nod to the mantra of empowerment, he calls this "affirmative repossession." Here, once more, illicit enterprise, which also produces new kinds of wealth-in-property, becomes indistinguishable from its legitimate counterpart, from "capitalism run amok." Using a quasi-documentary mise-en-scène, the film draws its plot from life: Lucky Kunene, on whom the story is based, is a real hood, one of Johannesburg's most notorious. He perfected a technique for "kidnapping" apartment blocks from their rapacious inner-city owners in the 1990s (cf. Gevisser 2014, 330), his armed thugs "ridding" them of drug dealers, pimps, and hookers as they collected rents, lowered rates, and won the favor of the residents.[47]

In doing the same thing, the fictive Kunene brandishes the simulacra of high-end business: credit cards, bank account numbers, lawyers' letters, all of them fake. He becomes the proprietor of the Hillbrow People's Housing Trust, an organization ostensibly created to protect those "P/people's" interests. Speaking the language of corporate philanthropy, whose ambiguous ethics now pervade South Africa, he plays on the image of the populist entrepreneur to leverage credit for enterprises that clothe themselves in the trappings of conventional commerce. A hoodlum philosopher, Kunene juggles references to Donald Trump and Karl Marx. Can capitalism be made to yield new forms of 'win-win,' postracial redistribution? This is the question that the film seems to be asking. As the *real* Kunene told the director, Ralph Ziman: "Look this was our country, and then the white man came here and he took everything. Under apartheid, blacks were not allowed to own property or own their own homes, and they were not allowed to live anywhere in inner city Jo'burg, they were forced to live in townships outside the city. . . . I'm now taking back land that was taken away from us by scum landlords, so how can anyone have the gall to call me a criminal? It's not crime, it's justice. It's retribution."[48] Thus is Truth-and-Reconciliation recommissioned as Truth-and-Re(dis)tribution. In this version of history-making, the state is all but absent and the police have no sovereign authority. But neither does anybody or anything else. The fictive Lucky presumes a universe in which everyone is responsible for making their own Luck, uppercase: a universe of unrestrained competition and brute force, in which revenge trumps restitution, in which ethical commitment seldom outlives the most primordial of loyalties. A plaintive isiZulu hymn, the movie's soundtrack, sings out a dream of redemption.[49] But no this-worldly moral order or contract seems sustainable for long in South Africa's capital of capital. At the same time, chaos brings possibility. While the film prompted one critic to say that there is "no land more dangerous than a new democracy,"[50] it also suggests that none is quite as fertile—especially when moved by the neoliberal faith that, left to its own devices, the market might yield value, civility, and, ultimately, trickle-down salvation. Kunene is eventually apprehended, only to outsmart the police: *Gangster's Paradise: Jerusalema* looks for justice beyond the limits of the law. Like *Tsotsi*, it brooks no easy conclusion. As he stands alone on the beach to which he has escaped, the beach of his youthful dreams, the bandit hero returns to Marx: "After every revolution comes a new order," he intones, as the rising tide erases sand patterns on the shoreline. "But before that comes opportunity."

Movies like this are part of an intertextual, multimedia conversation that flows expansively through TV drama, talk radio, stand-up comedy, advertising, investigative journalism, art, literature, theater, dance, and music, especially hip genres like *kwaito*, a Johannesburg strain of house. It pervades social media and public communication of all kinds. This flow creates a pulsing, defiant cultural discourse that marks the black generation "born free" of the authoritative certainties of the ancien régime. A distinct visual aesthetic is part of it, carried by seductive commodity-images that meld look, sound, allure, and cunning. The protagonists of popular crime fiction—particularly the figure of the gangster who taunts, terrorizes, and terrifies—epitomize these qualities, a mix of promise and privation, want and anger, aspiration and impatience. With them comes the incitement to experiment with new identities (see below, 2.2) and to test the margins of the i/licit. It is a quality made flesh by noir actors like Rapulana Seiphemo; Seiphemo is intimately familiar to millions of South Africans as a lead in the mainstream, massively popular soap operas *Isidingo*, *Generations*, and *Muvhango*, whose story lines run in parallel with their own lives. He also starred as Lucky Kunene, had a key supporting role in *Tsotsi*, and featured as a charismatic hood in *Hijack Stories*, a film that focuses more explicitly than any of the others on the ways in which crime fiction informs, and is informed by, ordinary experience in South Africa.

Like other examples of this genre, *Hijack Stories* (2000, directed by Oliver Schmitz, who also made *Mapantsula*) depends heavily on the sensibility of a streetwise black cast. It opens with the archetypical middle-class nightmare, now extended to the "new" African elite: a black man in a sharp business suit leaves a convenience store, sauntering toward his luxury car as he chats on his cell phone in English, only to be set upon by gun-toting thugs, who force him to the ground. They seize his keys and make him do a dance on his knees, a humiliation reminiscent of the *tauza*, a ritual once inflicted on "native" prisoners by apartheid police. At its most terrifying moment, the scene is abruptly cut. We have been watching a different kind of shooting: a show for local TV. *Hijack Stories* is about the interplay of violence and image, method acting and gangsterism, legitimate and criminal labor. The story is assertively postapartheid: it follows the quest of a young, educated black actor, Sox Moraga, who has set his heart on landing a role in a popular gangsta series—the very one being filmed in that first scene of *Hijack Stories*.

Sox is the offspring of the new South Africa, his parents having left the township to raise him in the secured, sequestered, sanitary suburbs of Johannesburg. Street thugs call kids like him "*Mandela se goeters*," Mandela's stuff/playthings. But it is not these cosseted "coconuts"[51] who draw the women, drive fancy cars, and capture the popular imagination. It is flashy hoodlums. Sox is too soft to "do township" with any conviction. "I want horror, I want viciousness, I want terror," the frustrated director barks at him at the TV audition. So he returns to the hood to "learn the moves" from dicey gang leader Zama, played by Rapulana Seiphemo; Zama-Zama is the brand name of the national lottery.[52] Disdainful of Sox's desire to profit and derive vicarious thrills by mimicking a *tsotsi*, Zama goes about giving him a lesson he will never forget. Crime is a skilled performance (see 2.2), one whose glamour cannot be severed from its risks. Dilettantes dabble at their peril. The film explores the dangerous erotics of a criminal mode of production. A profitable hit fuels orgies of consumption in high-end malls and riotous street fetes, in which the value "liberated"—the cash, cars, drugs, designer goods, sex—circulates with abandon. Looking down on the potlatch are enormous billboard images: images of celebrity commodities and commodified celebrities, including TV hoods. Polite claims aside, all is fair in this winner-take-all economy, driven by an endless interplay between incitement and excess, representation and "life itself." Racketeering, once more, is merely an intensified form of *all* risky business, *all* modes of seduction, one performance among many. The only real crime, here, is to misjudge the moves, to miscalculate the stakes. And make mistakes. Drawn into the game as a voyeur, Sox is all but undone by it. Meanwhile Zama, escaping the heat on the street, goes to the TV studio to audition in his stead—and secures the role. It is the robbers, not the cops, who grasp the truth about life in the "great outdoors." The point proved compelling to local viewers, as has this genre of movies at large. As writer-critic Bongani Madondo has noted, "shockingly gritty films," like *Gangster's Paradise: Jerusalema* and *Hijack Stories*, have had "profound resonance with township audiences."[53]

Imaging the Real, Realizing the Image, Refiguring the World

Hijack Stories makes the point that, just as there is little to set criminal off from legitimate labor, or truth from fiction, so there is also little to restrain the re-mediation of lived reality through an unending, unedited flow of images that refigure the world as they re-present it. Of course, the dialogue between, and interpenetration of, life and image has always been with us. In the 1950s, as we noted of *Drum* magazine, the Hollywood gangster fired imaginations among South African blacks, who redeployed his stylish iconoclasm in their own practices. Sixty or so years on in inner-city Johannesburg, Phaswane Mpe (2001, 5) has written, "real-life criminals are portrayed as if they were movie stars," and little boys "emulate their TV heroes," whose screen moves they actually mimic in committing their acts of violence; a middle-aged mother from gang-heavy Manenberg in Cape Town told us the same thing, unprompted, a year ago.[54] Mark Gevisser (2014, 250), in his chilling, firsthand account of a home invasion in Johannesburg in 2012, not far from the site of Mpe's narrative, recalls how the armed assailants insisted that "we are the *heroes*. Why are we the *heroes?* . . . Because *we are the ones with the guns*" (emphasis added). They added, underscoring both the skewed interpenetration of the il/licit economy and the gangsta-melodrama of ordinary violence here, "This is our job. This is how we do our work. You go to your work and we go to our work. . . . You must respect us or we will kill you."

The mimetic interplay of art and life, its reciprocal hijacking, is no less evident in policing: the South African cops have often delighted in playing crooks, quite literally (Comaroff and Comaroff 2004a, 823), and the South African Police Service (SAPS) has produced its own "factual" investigative dramas for prime-time TV, shows that are indistinguishable, in feel and staging, from fiction.[55] So complicated is the crossbreeding of incidence and imagination that the distinction between the two seems misconceived—vide those acclaimed South African novels that draw on recent criminal cases (Meyer's *7 Days*, for instance, or Brown's *Coldsleep Lullaby*) or those works of criminology that read like page-turning novels (Altbeker's *Fruit of a Poison Tree*, Wiener's *Killing Kebble*). This con/fusion, this blurring of the line, has become a common feature of everyday perception. Even of national allegory.

Take the notorious case of Oscar Pistorius, Paralympian athlete, arraigned in 2013 for the murder of his girlfriend, model Reeva Steenkamp, whom he shot in his upscale Pretoria home. The judicial process that followed was one of a string of national melodramas. These murder trials, quintessential morality plays, have opened up a mythic realm in which the public at large bears collective witness not just to the prosecution, or just to the dangers and seductions of the criminal economy, but also to questions of life and death that plague the country: Is deadly violence—the violence of predatory passions, of uncontained sexual appetites, racial paranoia, and material greed—part of the South African DNA? Of its inescapably malignant history? Of its signature modes of production, consumption, and circulation? Are acts of life-taking, of defensive counterviolence, justified by mounting fears of assault on persons and property? Are we witness to a crisis of identity, of sexuality, of masculinity? If so, who are its victims? How do we "read" whiteness after its fall from grace? What, at heart, is an Afrikaner, a man, a woman, a South African, an African? How essential are any of these identities and how do they intersect? Are we, in any sense, a moral public, an imaginable community? What does family and kinship mean for us? A safe haven or a site of mortal risk? Is criminality among us driven by the fervid sociology of the present, the dark history of the past, a universal psychology, or a theological propensity for human evil?

Oscar Pistorius's Promethean feats, film star looks, and classy commodity endorsements made him a global celebrity (Scheper-Hughes 2014, 11). In his defense, he claimed to have thought that Steenkamp, locked in the bathroom in the early hours after midnight, was a criminal intruder. In so doing, he evoked a hoary colonial horror, a violent cliché that bleeds into the present: that of the rapacious "native," ever ready to vault the fence in order to assault white domestic propriety (2.5). Thus does Nadine Gordimer's apartheid-era *Something Out There* (1984) return, now as a postapartheid abomination. Wrote crime novelist Margie Orford of the Pistorius case, "the paranoid imaginings of suburban South Africa lurked like a bogeyman at the periphery of this story. . . . It is the threatening body, nameless and faceless, of an armed and dangerous black intruder."[56] The exonerating force of that faceless fear seems to have persuaded the judge of first instance: the defendant's homicidal intent under *dolus eventualis*, she decided, had not been proven "beyond reasonable doubt." In a verdict that shocked much of the nation, Pistorius was cleared of murder and sentenced instead to five years for culpable homicide (i.e., manslaughter), of which he spent less than twelve months in prison. On appeal by the state, however, he was found guilty of the greater charge and, at the time of writing, awaits resentencing.

The trial, which hovered between the forensic and the oracular, played itself out in real-time on South African television. It was the country's melodrama *de l'année* for 2014. According to a local journalist, Pistorius took acting lessons in preparation for his days in court.[57] The claim was denied by the defendant's family but treated as entirely plausible by a public that watched him cry hysterically, throw up repeatedly, and pray fervently in the dock. *Time* ran a cover on him in March 2013. It pictured the blade runner, bare from the waist up, behind the logo "Man, Superman, Gunman," a figure in whom the fabled and the fallen, the real and the representation, fuse in an uneasy narrative, one whose deeper truths remain legally inaccessible, undecidable. Did an all-too-human, defensive reflex drive a vulnerable, legless man to "stand his ground" in sheer terror? Was his an act of predatory violence primed by a personal affront to his manhood? Or did the phantasm of *die swart gevaar*, the black peril at once brutal and erotic, merely mask the passionate violence of a white male, member of the former master race, now constrained to act out its frustrations on its women and children (above, 1.2)?

In 2.1 we visit another iconic case, the gruesome murder in 2005, unsolved to date, of Inge Lotz. She was killed in her apartment, situated in a secure residential complex just off the bucolic campus of the University of Stellenbosch, also an Afrikaner heartland. Young, gifted, and white, Ms. Lotz, still a student at the time of her death, was said to be "an angel" by some who knew her well. She was a born-again Christian, as was her dapper boyfriend, Fred van der Vyver, who was tried for her homicide but acquitted, largely as a result of forensic failure, even alleged malpractice, on the part of the police. Beneath the surface lurked unacknowledged whispers of sex, scandal, sin, race, betrayal, godly wrath, and, yet again, the specter of intruders of color—in this instance, a nest of local drug dealers, one or more of whom, claimed private investigators, were the uncaptured assailants. The story also unleashed a frenzied multimedia flow of narratives and images. It insinuated itself into at least two novels,[58] inspired a gripping work of criminological nonfiction that endorsed the verdict and its indictment of the SAPS (Altbeker 2010), and spawned literally thousands of radio, television, print, and Internet reports and analyses, many of which drift capriciously between the factual and the factitious, rapportage and rumor.[59] Like the Pistorius case, this one has become part of an ongoing, intertextual theater, one in which each court trial is another act, staged before an avaricious, anxious public, in which the criminal justice system itself is in the dock. In which its capacity to bring forth the truth about crime is constantly found wanting. In which the state is indicted for its failure to honor the social contract as inscribed in its Constitution. In which the capacity of the nation to know and live with itself is called into question. Like the Pistorius case too, moreover, this one could well have provided the emplotment for an upmarket, suburban South African noir.

But nowadays these national dramas frequently feature new types of criminal-charismatic. The protagonists who drive their plotlines are less melancholic former rulers than luminous antiheroes of the sort we encounter in Jozie noir: actors impatient to seize their rightful place on the platforms of opportunity that have opened up in deregulated, postapartheid times, actors whose mythic imagination is fired by explosive coming-of-age allegories like *Young Blood*, *Red Ink*, *Gangster's Paradise: Jerusalema*, or *Hijack Stories*. It is here that we meet Molemo "Jub Jub" Maarohanye, protagonist in yet another legal epic at the intersection of life and art, courtroom and cinema, celebrity and violence; yet another instance where criminal justice itself was on trial in a case endlessly dissected in the popular media—and read against those of Pistorius, van der Vyver, and Shrien Dewani, to which we shall shortly turn.[60]

Maarohanye is a rich and famous hip-hop artist, a "hot type" in the new South African pantheon of bling-idols, writes Bongani Madondo.[61] In March 2010, he and a friend, Themba Tshabalala, killed four children while drag racing under the influence of hard drugs along a busy thoroughfare in Soweto, perilously close to a school. Another two survived the incident with permanent brain damage. Initially convicted of murder, attempted murder, and driving under the influence of drugs, the defendants were each sentenced to twenty-five years in jail. The conviction was subsequently reduced, on appeal, to one of culpable homicide, and the sentences were cut to ten years, this being the reverse of what happened to Oscar Pistorius. One of the most insightful among the flood of reporters covering the trial, Madondo described it as a "storybook tragedy starring Soweto's once beloved child star and now its villain," a "mashup [of] ghetto aspiration" as black family values were sacrificed on the "altar of bling." Note the words "storybook tragedy." They evoke the murky line at which fact dissolves into fiction, at which fiction erases fact. The one "hard fact" that was never put on trial in the case, adds Madondo, was class: while the national media endlessly mourned the profane corruption of fame, the tragedy of talent despoiled, the names of the six young victims, and the plight of their grieving families, earned scant mention.

Jub Jub is the local term for a colorful candy that melts in the mouth. Ironically, Maarohanye first impressed himself on public awareness as a child star in TV food ads. Then, as a teenager, he won a place at LaGuardia High School for the Performing Arts in New York City, the school that served as a model for the American television series *Fame*. His experimental mix of hip-hop and gospel, a blend epitomized by the runaway hit "Ndikhokhele" (Lead me), made his voice a virtual sound track of black urban life back home. It was a sound, Madondo astutely observes, that pulsed with "impatience, urgency and the needling anxiety to be seen and adored." In this world, the fastest and the richest reigned, while the poor and powerless "looked on with hardening hearts." Almost an archetype of the argument we are making here, Jub Jub went on to land roles in several South African crime films. They included, most notably, *Hijack Stories*,[62] which brings to light a telling coincidence: just as the parents of the movie's fictional Sox had moved from Soweto to Johannesburg's southern suburbs, so did Jub Jub's nonfictional family, leaving both youths to reenter township hard-life by way of the performative media. But the young artist's most dramatic role of all, the one watched by the South African public as though it *were* a blockbuster about the national condition, was the "storybook" trial itself.

The political economy of representation that stretches from the abrasive streets of Soweto to secure apartment complexes in the Afrikaner heartland does more than just open up zones of indistinction between art and life, the criminal and the legal, rich and poor. Nor is it merely illustrative of patterns of crime-and-policing in the brave noir epoch of a beleaguered country, an epoch reconfigured by transformations in the nature of, and relations among, the state, capital, and governance. It also provides a set of archetypical scripts for entry into the ecology of life and death in South Africa: thus the sad, strange—and yet unnervingly predictable—story of Anni Dewani, a Swedish national of South Asian descent.

Ms. Dewani, by all accounts a woman of striking presence and self-possession, was killed on 13 November 2010 in Gugulethu, a township near Cape Town, while on honeymoon with her British-Indian husband. Shrien Dewani, it was alleged, was gay and had entered into the on-again-off-again marriage to retain his status in a *nouveau riche*, culturally conservative family. The two were together when their vehicle was hijacked; at the time, they were being driven on a nocturnal tour through the township, itself a *very* unusual thing for bourgeois tourists to be doing. He escaped unharmed; she did not. Not thought at first to be a suspect by the SAPS, Dewani returned to the United Kingdom soon after the incident. But on the basis of testimony from a local taxi driver, who admitted to the homicide in a plea bargain, he was accused of having commissioned the hit, which he vehemently denied. After a lengthy legal battle in the United Kingdom, repeatedly deferred on the ground that he was clinically depressed, Dewani was extradited to South Africa to stand trial in 2014, only to have all charges dismissed. Yet again, the investigation had been "botched by [the] police":[63] the prosecution had neither the hard evidence nor reliable enough witnesses to convict him. The South African public at large, which had been talking heatedly about the murder for four years, was convinced of his guilt. So, too, was the National Prosecuting Authority, whose spokesman said, "We can't prove it [before the law], but we know.[64]

The media controversy both before and after the court decision, said Marianne Thamm, "obsessively interrogated the more baffling aspects of this crime."[65] Is it that "we need[ed Shrien Dewani] to be guilty so that we . . . as a country do not bear the burden of shame of how Anni died?" she asked. Or did we "[require him] to be guilty because he deceived Anni about who he really is?" The case became diagnostic, alike in South Africa and the United Kingdom, in significant part because the increasing stress on personal-identity-as-performance has opened up all sorts of apertures for concealment, counterfeiting, and reinvention (see 2.2), not least for those with the means to pay for expert council. So who *was* the inscrutable Shrien Dewani? Upright British businessman or brazen wife killer, loving husband or heartless deceiver?

How was the truth about his character, his sexuality, his *true* identity, to be established? And what about the contract killing itself? Death is to be bought at bargain basement prices in South Africa, as its citizens well know; the media discuss the commerce in violence almost to the point of banalization. But could Dewani *really* have arranged to have his wife disposed of, within hours of his arrival, with the help of a cab driver he had just met? Is the country a poisoned paradise whose citizens prey mercilessly on unknowing innocents, while its rulers fail to enforce any semblance of law and order? Is it a country in which black labor can still be had on the cheap to do the dirty jobs that whites or wealthy foreigners prefer not to do for themselves?[66] Or is it, as a southern democracy, victim of neocolonial defamation on the part of those who would portray it, sometimes for profit, as the very Heart of Darkness? And hence as an ideal setting in which to purchase cold-blooded murder at a discount,[67] a killing staged in such a way as to have it dis/regarded as just another fatal carjacking in a violent township, the sort of *vérité* incident, embedded in every-night street life, that blurs the lines between different notions of "staging"?

Graphic stories like those of Oscar Pistorius, Inge Lotz, Jub Jub Maarohanye, and Anni Dewani—repeatedly retold and dissected, intertextually, alongside narratives of crime fiction—fascinate publics at home and abroad in part because they play on the eternally fascinating themes of sex, gender, lust, revenge, trust, betrayal, and violent death; also, in part, because they throw light on the patriarchal quest of men, old and young, black and white, gay and straight, whole and disabled, to retain mastery of the plot, often casting women as ancillary actors, victims, alibis, mourners, witnesses. But there is more to these stories than this. As we have argued throughout, the semiotic charge of crime-and-policing, its truth-value, lies in its capacity to serve as an especially supple signifier, one whose frame of reference extends to the existential profundities of life itself: to order and chaos, to law, labor, and liberty, to value, property, and personhood, to society and its conditions of possibility. "We are . . . stories within stories within stories," writes litterateur Ivan Vladislavić (2015, 147), whose prose moves seamlessly between fiction and nonfiction, between South Africa and the world outside. "We recede endlessly, framed and reframed, until we are unreadable to ourselves." In this unreadable universe, criminality, about which every South African has stories—indeed, *is* a story, often within a story (see 2.3)—has become the narrative instrument by means of which the nation and its citizens contemplate the truth about themselves, argue about that truth, seek to come to terms with it, seek to frame and reframe it, and seek to remake it in the imaginary spaces of desire and im/possibility.

Not only South Africans. The salience of crime as master signifier, we would argue further, is deeply entailed in global anxieties about social disorder, anxieties arising from the tectonic shift we have described here in the workings of capital, the state, and governance. This shift has sharpened concerns—variously distributed by race, religion, class, ethnicity, generation, gender, and geographical location—about the growing indeterminacy of the distinction between the legal and illegal; about the criminal specter that it has set free; about the nature of nationhood and citizenship; about fissures in the sovereignty of the state and its capture by capital; about the parsing of the police function, specifically, about its focus on public order as it outsources, to a greater or lesser degree, the ordinary protection of persons and property to the private sector; about rising levels of inequality and about the criminalization of those rendered expendable by changes in the global economy—which, to close the circle, makes them yet more dependent for their survival on the criminal netherworld.

Coda: Dramas of Enforcement, Hopes of Order Restored

In 1999 the Johannesburg-based Junction Avenue Theatre Company premiered its first postapartheid production, *Love, Crime and Johannesburg*, a rewrite of Bertolt Brecht's *Threepenny Opera*. Florian Nikolas Becker (2010, 159) argues that, in recasting the play to estrange the historic relations among crime, capitalism, and apartheid, Junction Avenue succeeds in "expos[ing] the discourse of 'lawlessness' that has replaced 'reconciliation' as the near-universal currency for articulating South Africa's post-liberation predicament"; also in "foreground[ing] the accelerating displacement of the biogeography of apartheid by the post-urban topography of spectacular capitalism." Becker puts his finger, here, on one expression of a more ubiquitous forensic vernacular, tailored with precision to the particularities of the South African past. For, as we noted above, it was in confronting its dystopic undersides, its unevenly suppressed tendencies toward fascism, racism, and capitalist crisis, that high modernism first experimented with noir and prefigured its own *late* modern culture.

Junction Avenue, then, was making a point not just about Afropolitan Johannesburg but about much of the world. Almost everywhere, we have argued, criminality has become *the* privileged vehicle for contemplating the labile times-and-places in which we live, for promulgating knowledge about them, for attesting and contesting their received truths. Crime-and-policing mark out, in dialectical asymmetry, the metaphysic of disorder in relation to which the very possibility of society itself is renewed, remade, defended. At the same time, this metaphysic—the terror, desire, im/possibility it conjures— tends to produce a fetishistic ambivalence. On the one hand, it invests dramas of enforcement with the perpetual hope of order restored. On the other, as that hope goes unrealized—the "impossible mandate" again—it reinforces a profound sense of lack, a sense of exile from the very possibility of norma- tive security at the hands of the state, or the law, as decisively sovereign. And yet it also does something else, something that moves beyond the pathologi- cal public sphere. Bearing witness to the drama of disorder, in life as in fic- tion, creates an audience as polis, a "space of appearance" to cite Hannah Ar- endt (1958, 199), in which a vision of social action, a version of social justice, is thinkable.

Let us turn, then, to part 2, to our five uneasy pieces, to bear witness to the drama of disorder. Or, to be more precise, to a number of dramas, each of them arising out of, and illuminating, some of the effects, the aftershocks, of the tec- tonic shift in the triangulation of capital, the state, and governance that we have discussed in part 1.

PART TWO

LAW-MAKING, LAW-BREAKING, AND LAW-ENFORCEMENT: FIVE UNEASY PIECES

CHAPTER 2.1

DIVINE DETECTION

Policing at the Edge

Thinking about crime, we argued in part 1, is inseparable from thinking about truth. And from thinking about the social. Recall Emile Durkheim's (1938, xxviii) observation, serially cited in the part 1, that a society free of lawlessness "would fall into chaos, since it would be bereft of the signs of its own existence as an authoritative order." Functionalist sociology, of course, has long seen criminality as a means of preserving legality. And social order. But our concern here, in the first instance, is less with the sociological than with the semiotic side of Durkheim's observation, with the significance, in the liberal-humanist imagination, of crime-as-sign. The latter was closely tied to the rise, in the nineteenth century, of the practice of detection, a hyperrational mode of producing truth that no less an authority, no less a sociologist, than Sherlock Holmes would call the art of "reasoning backwards" (Block de Behar 1995, 192): of deciphering the hidden meaning of illegal acts, and their signature, from the traces they left behind "in absences, silences" (Summerscale 2008, 83–84). It was an art, as Tom Gunning (2003, 110) reminds us, that fascinated Walter Benjamin, who was persuaded by the possibility of reading from inanimate debris a history of transgression.

Crime detection, says Margie Orford (2011), puts trust in the fact that all violent felonies have a socially recognizable "grammar."[1] It is with reference to this grammar that even the faintest scrap of evidence left by a criminal act may be read and decoded, thus to reveal its perpetrators, their means, their meaning, and their motives. But what of times and places in which the grammar is scrambled, the signs occulted? In which a population loses faith in its ability to explain the violent, transgressive behavior in its midst? In which crime is said, literally, to be "senseless," indeed, "out of control"? In which the drama of enforcement no longer appears capable of conjuring an authoritatively ordered reality—or a legible social world? In which lawlessness is held to exceed the governmental technologies designed to contain it? Where, in such circumstances, are "the signs . . . of normative order" to be found?

The word "clue" derives from "clew," a ball of yarn, this last term also being used of detective stories. Victorians took "clew" to refer, tangibly, to a thread whose unraveling might lead to the light beyond the labyrinth (Summerscale 2008, 68), to a sign on the surface of everyday life, that is, which pointed the way to truths hidden from plain sight. A similar understanding, a sense of indexical connection between observable human actions and invisible social forces, was integral to the episteme of much late nineteenth-century sociology. To be sure, detection and social analysis were the result of a twin birth. Recall, here, Franco Moretti (2005, 143; above, 1.3): detectives were compelling figures in Victorian fiction because they responded to "deep anxiety," in an expanding world, about the very possibility of normative control. The virtuoso investigator embodied the liberal vision of "scrutability": his reassuring gaze was capable of "know[ing], order[ing], and defin[ing] . . . the significant data of individual existence" and of relating them to society as "a unitary and knowable" entity (145). Moretti, here, could well have been describing the founding tenets of social science. Early detectives of note, both real and fictional, displayed a genius for social diagnostics; in this respect they also bore a striking resemblance to Victor Turner's (1967) Ndembu diviner. They had an uncanny, even supernatural (cf. M. Gillespie and Harpham 2011),[2] capacity to unravel the threads, the clews/clues, that link superficial signs to deeper truths, to rules and regularities "inaccessible by other methods" (Ginzburg 1989, 87; cf. Boltanski 2014), by resort to what Carlo Ginzburg dubs "the conjectural paradigm of semiotics" (104). In addition to superior powers of inference and uncommon attention to detail, that capacity required a confident command of cultural knowledge: an ability to read identities and intentions within sometimes-stable, sometimes-labile frameworks of meanings and relations.

As this suggests, legendary nineteenth-century detectives like Inspector Jack Whicher of the London Metropolitan Police[3] or Poe's fictional *le chevalier* C. Auguste Dupin[4] were inspired ethnographers, "criminal anthropologists" if you will, although not in the mode of Darwinians like Lambroso or Francis Galton, who sought to tie criminal types to innate physiological traits.[5] Like modern anthropologists, they relied in large part on firsthand observation of everyday activity, displaying a brilliant facility for reading "tiny details" and "inadvertent" habits (Ginzburg 1989, 87), the nods and winks that, for Clifford Geertz (1973; see above), encode "thick" meaning. In properly anthropological fashion, Sherlock Holmes insisted on the nonobvious significance of obvious facts, on their capacity to disclose elementary truths.[6] Holmes's fondness for the "elementary" was one of many things he shared with Durkheim—and with the social semiotics of Lévi-Strauss (1969).[7] In like manner, Holmes maintained that the bizarre and the mysterious, the magical and the ghostly, could be shown, by a reasoned unraveling, to be the product of very ordinary, everyday human intentions, motivations, and emotions (Highmore 2002, 3). The same thing has been said of the efforts of classic ethnographers to demystify European assumptions about phenomena like witchcraft, totemism, incest, and cannibalism.

But, to restate our question, what do we make of times and places in which public faith in the "conjectural paradigm of semiotics," in what Sherlock Holmes called "systematized common sense" (Conan Doyle 2003, 528), is radically undermined; undermined, that is, to the degree that criminal detection, the quintessential practice of modernist policing, seems no longer possible by ordinary means? Where the failure of criminal intelligence becomes a national obsession, and critical journalists accuse the cops—pun intended—of being "clueless"?[8] Where, in short, lawlessness, and with it social order, appear to have become unfathomable, inexplicable, and, hence, ungovernable?

Of Cops, Crime, and the Uncanny: Tales from the Edge

In July 1997 South African TV aired what it described as "one of the few success stories in a police force that ha[d] almost collapsed under the strain of democracy."[9] It focused on Jackson Gopane, a homicide detective in Limpopo, a northerly province with a high incidence of violent crime, at least by international standards.[10] In South Africa, as we shall see again in 2.3, murder rates are held to be diagnostic of lawlessness run amok, of governance haunted by a brutal legacy that no constitutional reform, no public reconciliation, no rites of restitution, have been able to dispel. In point of fact, those rates have dropped dramatically, almost by half, since the demise of the apartheid regime in 1994 (above, 1.1). Nonetheless, as we noted in 1.1 and 1.2, the South African Police Service (SAPS) is commonly said to be incapable of protecting the populace—let alone winning the "war" between crime and punishment that, with the transition to democracy, has turned the postcolony into a Hobbesian combat zone (e.g., Dixon 2004, xix, xxv–xxvi). A survey undertaken by Plus 94

Research South Africa in 2005, one of the very few that we have not yet cited, indicated that 78 percent of the population of the country believed crime to be "ungovernable," a situation that only 31 percent thought likely to improve any time in the future;[11] this was largely blamed, as we have already seen, on the endemic corruption, criminality, and sheer ineptitude of the police, "facts" confirmed by widely circulated research (e.g., Shaw 2002, 37; Grobler 2013; Faull 2011; Newham and Faull 2011; see part 1). Notwithstanding the extraordinary difficulties cops deal with in their daily dice with death (Altbeker 2005, 9, 43), notwithstanding the fact that they suffer unusually high incidences of mortality and suicide (Shaw 2002, 37; Steinberg 2008), notwithstanding, also, some spirited defenses of the criminal justice system on the part of the state, public discourse continues to dwell, unforgivingly, on the many shortcomings of the SAPS—all the more so since the disestablishment and decentralization of its specialist criminal detection units and the shift to public order policing (above, 1.2).

Compared with most of his colleagues in the Service, Jackson Gopane was said to be almost eerily adept at tracking down killers. Indeed, he was no ordinary cop. In the course of his work, he moved between the forensic and the oracular, between detection and divination, exchanging his uniform and his gun for the dress and demeanor of a traditional healer. In him, scientific investigation met the social diagnostics of the séance. He was, in short, South Africa's first officially recognized diviner-detective. There would soon be others—a fact reflected, interestingly, in African crime fiction, through which occult detection has been spreading, largely on the assumption, it seems, that divination is part and parcel of modern police work (Oed and Matzke 2012, 12).

This is a peculiarly local tale, a tale of the unexpected as a notorious racial state struggles to become a popular democracy. But the story of Gopane plays out something more general: what happens when, as the police function fragments (see 1.1), the protection of property falls to the private sector and state enforcement refocuses itself away from crime fighting toward public order; what happens, in other words, when criminal investigation, effectively vacated by the police, becomes an urgently felt social need, when crimes and misdemeanors trouble everyday life, demanding intervention from authorities who seem no longer willing or able to give it? This question is especially pressing in a South Africa whose geography of apartheid is being undone, a South Africa that now seems to be in riotous motion, driven by a heady mix of enfranchisement, eroding boundaries, consumer desire, and entrepreneurial incitement—all of which have scrambled received signs of identity. The lines between friend and enemy, citizen and alien, propriety and predation, things ordinary and occult, order and disorder, seem hard to draw in a society awash with ever less recognizable others. In these times, writes Achmat Dangor (1999, 33–34), "you never know who [is] innocent and who [is]n't, which bland smile during the day [might] turn into a murderer's smirk at night." And, we would add, who is the cop and who the criminal (below, 2.5). Where, under these conditions, do South Africans look for an answer to the problem of law and disorder that plagues them? And to the metaphysical and practical questions it raises in what, to many of them, appears to be a far-from-legible world, a world of scrambled grammars?

By way of an answer, let us describe a clutch of cases—three stories, really— each in its own way diagnostic of uncertain times. Drawn from the annals of crime-and-policing in contemporary South Africa, all of them express ambivalence about the possibility of setting law apart from lawlessness. Together they bespeak a loss of trust in the will or the capacity of the state, and its criminal justice institutions, to enforce order. But they also gesture toward something more fundamental, more far-reaching: that there may be *no* recoverable grammar to this destabilized world, no way of connecting surface appearances to enduring social facts or trusted truths—at least, and this is our point, not by received, rational means. Extraordinary times, it seems, demand extraordinary measures.

Donker Jonker; or, The Strange Case of God's Detective

The first story goes back to the creation of an Occult-Related Crimes Unit (ORCU)—note, an *Occult*-Related Crimes Unit—by the SAPS in 1992, when the transition to majority rule was in full swing amid rampant violence and public anxiety. While it had roots in both African and Afrikaner supernaturalism, the immediate impetus for its establishment came, in large part, from the United States, where popular concerns about such things as satanic ritual abuse, acutely captured by Lawrence Wright in his *Remembering Satan* (1994), had given rise to the Cult Crime Awareness Network.[12]

While the mandate of the South African unit was to investigate illegal acts "resulting from the practice of any occult science [or] belief system,"[13] it focused on homicides stemming from witchcraft and satanism—echoes, here, of a long colonial struggle to impose the rule of law on the African uncanny. Its founder and moving spirit was Colonel Kobus Jonker, who was widely known by the moniker "Donker," Afrikaans for "dark."[14] A seasoned, dedicated, and highly articulate police officer—he had previously been head of the murder and robbery squad in Port Elizabeth, a major South African city—Colonel Jonker was a born-again Christian and a self-confessed believer in the literal reality of the devil.[15] Dubbed "God's Detective" and "The Hound of God" by the media, he was quick to insist that his role, as a cop, was to track down and arrest killers, not to make judgments about other cultures. He refused to draw a distinction between diabolical beliefs and felonies: satanism and witchcraft, he told us, were, at root, the same phenomenon—and both lead *inevitably* to deadly violence. To close the theologico-legal circle, deadly violence was, to Colonel Jonker, and to those who were later to take over his leadership of the unit, inherently diabolical. His pronouncements, as one might expect, tended toward the apocalyptic: the devil, he once declared, has made a "revolutionary re-appearance" in South Africa, defying the sovereignty of both God and Government.[16] According to a report in the SAPS print media, Jonker should know: "Boldly brav[ing] the world of tangible evil," it said, he has survived many attempts on his life by "occult attackers," a "fact" also reported by the South African press.[17]

Kobus Jonker's fears resonated with rising angst about satanism and witchcraft in both black and white communities in the 1990s (Comaroff and Comaroff 1999a, 292). This, and the avid embrace of born-again faiths in recent times, point to a sense of ontological insecurity in the first decades after the birth of the "new" South Africa. Ivan Vladislavić calls it "the exploded view" (2004), a sense of expansion, implosion, edginess, a loss of known coordinates. On this disrupted terrain, authority is inchoate, identity inscrutable, agency opaque. Mundane communicative acts, Vladislavić says, often take the form of a "sign language from a secret alphabet" (24).

Could Jonker decipher this alphabet? The ORCU worked hard to promote public awareness of the threat of witchcraft and satanism, offering training to organizations concerned to combat the spectral hazards haunting an estranged landscape. It also sought to introduce a new kind of policing, capable of dealing with those hazards. Jonker was preoccupied, above all, with rendering occult-related crimes susceptible to prosecution. Despite the popular view in the 1990s and 2000s that there was an epidemic of mystical evil in the land, very few homicides directly associated with witchcraft, ritual murder, or satanism have actually come to court. It is not merely that South African law has long had a great deal of difficulty in making these things justiceable: the Witchcraft Suppression Act (1957), for example, has never been successfully implemented or superseded by new legislation and, in any case, is of dubious constitutionality in a nation-state that accords substantial recognition to cultural difference (Comaroff and Comaroff 2004b). But even more, said Jonker in the late 1990s, the SAPS is ill-equipped to deal with occult activity: police officers are incapable of recognizing the evidence it leaves behind because they have no knowledge of the beliefs, practices, and motives it entails. In fact, the rationalist assumptions and forensic techniques that underlie modernist detection are inherently insufficient to decipher the clues, or to read the grammar, of the more arcane, enigmatic crimes of our times. This is why the ORCU spent so much time on education. Its personnel believed fervently that, if spectral evil is to be fought effectively, both the police and the public have to be taught to apprehend its signs and traces. Jonker gave us a personal tutorial on these signs, describing hard-to-visualize *materia medica* and showing us objects, ostensibly with the power to do evil, housed in the private museum next to his office on the sixth floor of police headquarters in Pretoria.

A parenthesis here. It could be argued that modernist detection has never been fully separate from the divining arts. Foundational writers, from Poe to Pinkerton, might have emphasized the rational-empiricist basis of their craft. But their prose flirts with something else. The master crime analyst, says Poe (1975, 141), "exhibit[s] in his solutions . . . a degree of *acumen* which appears to the ordinary apprehension praeternatural," especially in contrast to the plodding procedures of the regular police. Anthropologist Hilda Kuper (1984, 139) saw the detective as "the extra-legal superman" who "must accomplish by extraordinary measures" what seems impossible by established means. "Abduction" was the term used by Charles Peirce (1934, 171ff.) to capture these extraordinary measures. Peirce, a semiotician, was an avid reader of Poe and had tried his own hand at detection; abduction, for him, was the mode of conjecture, the flash of insight, the creative guess, that yields testable hypotheses. Here, again, is the parallel with ethnography: Edmund Leach (1961, 5) famously claimed that, at its best, anthropology was "inspired guess-work." Poe and Peirce both mused on what it was that allowed gifted investigators to move beyond the obvious, permitting them, prophetically almost, to arrive at new knowledge by unusual means. It is here that the mystical enters the equation, here that the hyperrational, pushed to its limits in inspired crime detection, enters the realm of the preternatural: Peirce once referred to abduction as a "divine privilege," a "means of communication between man and his Creator," as Sebeok and Umiker-Sebeok (1983, 17) paraphrase his take on the phenomenon. He and Donker Jonker would have understood each other well. So would African diviner-detectives. As one of them, Daniel Moshupa, a charismatic working in the North West Province, took pains to tell us, no detective can divine without the direct intervention of his ancestors (*badimo*).[18]

Kobus Jonker appeared often on television to popularize his work. His website was set out as a public resource. Documentary features about him were filmed by respected network series in the United States and United Kingdom. With the moral panic occasioned by all the talk of satanism and witchcraft before and after the elections of 1994—and with the mainstreaming of mystical discourse across the popular media in South Africa (Fordred-Green 2000)—he and his staff decided, in 1998, to set up a national workshop on the forensics of occult crime scenes. This led to doubts being voiced, both within and beyond the police service, about the constitutionality of the operation, allegedly because it criminalized indigenous cultures.[19] Those doubts persist today and have occasioned regular calls to put an end to occult policing *tout court*.[20] In 2006 the SAPS removed the ORCU from its website, although it has retained a page under the title "Objectives of the Investigation and Prevention of Occult-Related Crime by the *General* Detectives" (emphasis added);[21] also, articles about the ORCU and about the rising threat of felonies spawned by satanism and witchcraft continued to appear in its major publication, *Servamus*. For a while, having been renamed the SAPS Harmful Religious Practices Unit, it seemed to withdraw into the shadows of the world of enforcement, although its officers continued to do their work. Despite the uneasy ambivalence with which his crusade was viewed by many in the SAPS (cf. Teppo 2009, 27), Jonker and his officers were tolerated, precisely because they tackled a problem not resolvable by regular means. Whatever they thought of his enchanted theories, his colleagues needed God's Detective. And not only his colleagues. At the height of his mission, Jonker received some fifty calls a day. Once, while we were in his office, the archbishop of Cape Town telephoned him to arrange an urgent meeting. The divine, it appears, needed the detective.

Although forced by ill health to retire and to hand over the ORCU to a new head in 2001, Jonker remained in the public eye, serving as a consultant on occult crime at home and abroad; he still does.[22] In this capacity he has become something of an icon, "a sanitized Hollywood version of . . . a detective of the Third Dimension," as Mark Gevisser once put it.[23] When the mutilated body of a boy, thought to be African, was pulled from the Thames in 2001, Scotland Yard cited his "expert testimony" to confirm that the child was a victim of ritual murder. This evoked the accusation, especially by Africanist scholars, that, for all its scientific credentials, the Yard remained prone to primitivist stereotypes, succumbing to the racist myths of Satan-hunting "fundamentalists."[24] Similar controversy surrounds the theories promulgated by American "cult cops," whose popular seminars on satanic crime have been offered for continuing-education credit to police in several states. There, too, critics have argued that this recycles reactionary religious views that target "different" cultural practices, among them Mexican American and Afro-Caribbean rituals, like Santeria (Hicks 1991).[25] But those critics make up a minute minority. For much of the public, in both the United States and South Africa, unorthodox policing is not merely acceptable but heroic. Similarly in England, where Scotland Yard employs 132 "Super Recognizers," cops with the special, psychologically patented gift of identifying felons by matching even very poor, fragmentary photo images from crime scenes to faces they memorize. They are described as having "human superpowers. Computers are no match for them."[26]

All this underscores the perception that conventional enforcement is sorely challenged in a world in which causes and motives seem ever more impenetrable. It also dramatizes the occulting of crime and disorder, thus to inflate the fantasy that diviner-detectives—the likes of Jackson Gopane and Kobus Jonker—are able to unravel the mystery, to plumb the murk, that defies ordinary law-enforcement. That fantasy seems to be gaining ground. In South Africa, in November 2010, a team of thirty new specialists were trained to deal with occult-related crimes, and less than two years later, in August 2012, the divisional commissioner of the Detective Service of SAPS instructed each of the nine provinces to have at least two senior officers dedicated to the investigation of felonies "that relate to or emanate primarily from an ostensible belief in the supernatural."[27] Donker Jonker's legacy, his species of policing, pushed for a few years into the gray recesses of law-enforcement, has returned as a national endeavor. And as a national fantasy. In November 2012 SABC 1 broadcast the first episode of *Room 9* (directed by Darrel Roodt; see 1.3), a "post-apocalyptic [TV] series . . . set in the world's only Occult Detective Unit," created to deal with perpetrators of mystical evil and disorder.[28] To the degree that sci-fi crime fiction plays out mortal fears in a parallel space-time, *Room 9* offers the *frisson* that comes with the prospect of doing, by means of militant counterviolence, what Colonel Jonker tried to do in the immediate post-apartheid years: restore order and legibility to a world that seemed to have become unrecognizable, unreal, beset by the arcane.

Of Scorpions and Supercops

Our second story, *Of Scorpions and Supercops*, seems altogether more mundane. But it, too, took on phantasmagoric—eventually, tragicomic—proportions. It is about a special enforcement agency whose cops were to be cast, by an anxious mass public, as superheroes in the struggle for criminal justice, social order, and the moral soul of the nation. Here, yet again, we encounter the essential paradoxes of policing the postcolony, of forensics as fantasy, of detection as fetish.

It all began in the late 1990s, when the idyll of liberation, democratization, and reconciliation was giving way to harsher postcolonial realities. South Africa had become embroiled in a series of scandals that brought charges of crime and corruption into the very heart of the state. The most explosive among them arose out of the so-called Arms Deal—officially, the South African Strategic Defence Procurement Package—a controversial US$4–$5 billion accord[29] contracted by the African National Congress (ANC) government to modernize its defense force.[30] Bitter debate raged across the media, through the corridors of power, on the streets, in sedate sitting rooms and rowdy shebeens, even among some hardcore ANC members: did the country really need this mammoth expenditure, given its huge social welfare deficit, its incapacity to provide clean water, electricity, basic housing, and healthcare to millions of people? Behind the controversy lay widespread suspicions concerning the propriety of the procurement procedures involved in the deal, fueled by rumors that ANC functionaries were enriching themselves, their cadres, and their kin at public expense. Unscrupulous foreign manufacturers, it was whispered loudly, had bribed a shadowy web of local subcontractors, statesmen, and military personnel. Reports also circulated that some ANC leaders had been trying to quash a call by the all-party Public Accounts Committee of Parliament for an inquiry into the simmering scandal (Feinstein 2007).[31]

As tension mounted, the chief whip of the Pan African Congress (PAC), one of the opposition parties, handed a dossier of potentially incriminating documents to Willem Heath, then head of the Special Investigation Unit (SIU), the enforcement agency mandated to tackle high-level crime and corruption; it was also charged with recovering monies lost by the state.[32] At the time, the PAC and other opposition parties were demanding a public hearing into all aspects of the Arms Deal. Heath had been a judge under the apartheid regime and proved fearless in wielding his commission to investigate malfeasance among the rich and powerful. His authority involved an unusual blend of the

investigative and the prosecutorial: the SIU had the right to subpoena witnesses and documents, to search and seize, and also to litigate. A jurist with a
taste for theatrics, Heath was accused by his critics, often those he had crossed,
of a gratuitous overuse of his right to raid and confiscate. Having "swapped
his musty robes for a superman outfit," one respected observer quipped, he
had assumed the role of "rampant cowboy on the frontier."[33] All this proved
immensely popular with those South Africans who longed for an emphatic
demonstration of the rule of law. Yet Heath's autonomy was compromised: despite his mandate, the SIU remained answerable to the executive. As the battle
surged around the Arms Deal, President Thabo Mbeki declined Heath permission to inquire into it and issued a demand on national TV that he hand over
the allegedly incriminating documents. The SIU, he declared, was an organ of
state "out of control," accusing it of precipitating a "situation of ungovernabil-
ity." Faced with a refusal to comply, Mbeki announced plans to reconstitute the
unit, with somebody "other than a judge" at its head.[34]

And so the new, much vaunted Directorate of Special Operations (DSO)
came into being in January 2001. Born amid great public fanfare, it was said to
be a "world-class enforcement agency" made up of "the best police, financial,
forensic and intelligence experts" in the country.[35] Christened the Scorpions,
and "often likened [in the public media] to the US Federal Bureau of Investigation" (Redpath 2004, 7), the unit was charged with combating "national
priority crimes," including high-level corruption, complex financial felonies,
police malfeasance, and organized racketeering.[36] It fell under the National
Prosecuting Authority (NPA), not the police, an arrangement that, from the
start, provoked bitter resentment on the part of the latter, resentment that was
later to degenerate into acrimonious conflict between the two agencies, each
protecting its turf on the murky, politically fraught terrain of intelligence,
investigation, and enforcement in South Africa (see Pikoli and Wiener 2013,
131–279).[37] The DSO retained its predecessor's novel form of prosecutor-led
investigation—and inherited its aura of crusading machismo (Pikoli and Wiener 2013, 133–35): "It sounds like it's been named with a television spin-off in
mind," wrote a bemused BBC correspondent, "perhaps an American series
along the lines of Starsky and Hutch or Serpico."[38] This image was reinforced
by the Scorpions' insignia, a less-than-subtle statement that they intended
to apply the law with deadly dispatch. Multiplying their venomous totems,
their home page featured a hooded cobra, ready to "Strike against Corruption." It also provided a link enabling fans to download ringtones featuring a
menacing heavy-metal band by the same name. A gritty reality-TV video of

young, photogenic, mixed-race Scorpions on a raid drew thousands of hits on YouTube.[39]

The DSO was trained by the FBI and Scotland Yard and was close to Britain's Serious Fraud Office.[40] As it turned out, its agents were no more able than was Judge Heath to resist the popular craving for melodrama. As they set about their high-profile crime-busting mission, they encouraged the media to amplify their image as ace investigators—not least by stressing the contrast between them and the "slipshod South African Police Services." The local press and television channels, as obsessed with criminality as the publics they served, did not need much pushing. They were quick to report, often quite hyperbolically, on the almost "uncanny" capacity of the Scorpions to break into arcane webs of corporate corruption, violence, and money laundering with their novel modes of forensic accountancy—all of which established them as diviner-detectives of finance capital and high-end fraud, in particular the sorts of crimes created by new species of property-as-capital. Admiring stories detailed their putatively preternatural power to outwit felons and fraudsters both at home and abroad,"[41] to recover millions in misappropriated public funds,[42] and to secure mythic conviction rates; 94 percent is the number usually cited,[43] although, like all crime statistics (see 2.3), this figure is to be read with a skeptical eye focused on the manner of its counting. "Drug kingpins, smugglers and racketeers have [all] felt the Scorpions' sting," ran one appreciative account, adding: "A major gang that smuggled platinum, South Africa's biggest foreign exchange earner, to a corrupt English smelting plant has been bust."[44] Crusading detectives, in sum, were portrayed as defending the national patrimony against neocolonial adventurers: foreign dealers in illegal diamonds, interdicted minerals, contraband substances, endangered species. The DSO also played a decisive role in convicting Sir Mark Thatcher for his role in an attempted plot, launched from South Africa, to overthrow the government of Equatorial Guinea.[45]

But what really secured the Scorpions' superhero status for many South Africans, and won them widespread popular acclaim, was the zeal with which they pursued corruption among local political and business elites. In this, again like Judge Heath, they would eventually outrun their mandate; but for a while at least, their brazen exercise of authority was treated with indulgence by those in high public office, who seem to have found it useful for their own ends. Not long after the DSO was constituted, it began aggressively to probe parliamentarians who had falsified official travel expenses; thirty of them entered into plea bargains and ended up paying fines in a scandal that became known as "Travelgate" (Pikoli and Wiener 2013, 183–85). The Scorpions also returned, boldly, to the Arms Deal. As a warm-up, so to speak, they secured the conviction in 2003 of the ANC chief whip, Tony Yengeni, for failing to declare an illicit deal on an expensive motor vehicle arranged by an arms trader; Yengeni was chair of Parliament's joint standing committee on defense, which oversaw the procurement.[46]

Even more audacious action followed, including theatrical raids on the homes of high-ranking ANC leaders, among them the then Deputy President Jacob Zuma, Minister of Transport Mac Maharaj, and Schabir Shaik, a well-known businessman with close connections to the inner reaches of government. Shaik would later be convicted for bribing Zuma on behalf of Thomson-CSF, a French company that was bidding at the time for a share of the Arms Deal (Feinstein 2007, 218). Mbeki, probably fearing a political backlash from some quarters in the ANC (221), refused at first to allow Zuma to be indicted along with Shaik. But he was forced to do an about-face and, in June 2005, fired the deputy president, who was duly charged with corruption; after a long, tortuous, and troubled judicial process, however, the charges against him were dismissed. Famously, Zuma was later tried and found not guilty of rape (above, p. 53), a decision that divided the country. In a spectacular reversal of fortune, helped along by the plummeting popularity of Mbeki, he emerged as a populist hero, leader of the ANC, and widely proclaimed victim of the sitting president's efforts to stifle his succession as the next head of state. For their part, the Scorpions continued to investigate and incriminate Zuma. In a real-life soap opera that enthralled the nation, they conducted televised dawn raids on his private residences in Johannesburg and KwaZulu-Natal, seizing documents and hard drives. According to one account: "There was plenty of drama as a standoff ensued between Zuma's heavily-armed bodyguards and gun-toting Scorpions at Zuma's home. . . . [O]nly a timely intervention by officials saw an amicable resolution. . . . [T]he Scorpions were allowed to complete their search with arms laid down."[47] At one point four officers of the SAPS, wielding automatic weapons and threatening to shoot, also arrived on the scene and had to be persuaded to withdraw.

The splintering of sovereignty is evident here as lawmen, special investigators, and private security struggled to impose order on a potentially explosive situation. That situation became yet more incendiary, and more astonishing, when the Scorpions went on to "cordon . . . off the seat of government in the Union Buildings in Pretoria," bringing its normal business to a halt as they poured portentously over papers they thought might be relevant to their case.[48]

In acting in the name of the law, they subjected the state itself to their authority. While their extravagant exploits thrilled many people and drew considerable public support, they also called forth bitter criticism—and excoriation of their "Hollywood theatrics"—from Zuma's large support base in the ANC, from the Congress of South African Trade Unions, and from the South African Communist Party; from these quarters, too, came furious allegations that the DSO had shown blatant political partisanship.[49] Added to this was yet further resentment among the regular police, who complained that the Scorpions' jurisdiction was unclear and that the unit was high-handed, uncooperative, and surplus to requirements. President Mbeki went so far as to appoint a commission in 2005 to investigate the mandate and efficacy of the DSO. It found the *modus operandi* of the unit to be effective and its hybrid structure constitutional. But it did censure the Scorpions for courting inappropriate publicity, adding that they should be subject to more immediate political oversight.[50]

Undaunted, the Scorpions pursued an equally surreal investigation of Jackie Selebi, head of the SAPS and president of Interpol (above, p. 34). A colorful character, president of the ANC Youth League during the final, halcyon days of the struggle against apartheid (1987–91), and former South African ambassador to the United Nations (1995–98), Selebi had long been rumored to consort with hardened criminals. In early September 2007, unconfirmed reports in the press claimed that, based on the evidence assembled by the DSO, warrants of arrest had been issued against him.[51] The police chief was alleged to have received a great deal of money over a five-year period from a convicted felon suspected in the murder of a flamboyant white mining magnate, who was also an ANC patron with a reputation for racketeering (see 1.1).[52] The process leading up to the issue of those warrants was protracted, contested, and tortuous to say the very least: it became entangled in struggles between the presidency and the National Prosecuting Authority (under whose jurisdiction the DSO fell), in the turf war between the Scorpions and the SAPS, and across lines of power, patronage, protection, and privilege within the ANC. What is more, before the warrants had been officially executed, President Mbeki suspended the head of the NPA, Vusi Pikoli, in an action widely regarded as a bid not merely to shield Selebi from indictment but also to rein in the charisma of the Scorpions.[53] His action failed to have its desired effect, however: on 12 January 2008, in the face of the irrefutable case put together by the DSO, Mbeki had no alternative but to announce, reluctantly, that the police chief was to take an "extended leave of absence." The next day, 13 January, Selebi resigned as head of Interpol. And by 1 February, he was in court facing charges of corruption and defeating the ends of justice (e.g., Basson 2010).[54] As we noted earlier, he was found guilty on 2 July 2010, sentenced to serve fifteen years in prison, died in January 2015 after being released on medical parole and given a heroic funeral arranged by the ANC.[55]

It is remarkable, given all this—and given the political currents that swirled around policing in South Africa at the time—that the Scorpions lasted as long as they did. By the time of Selebi's arraignment there could have been few in high office who did not fear them. The beginning of their end came with the watershed ANC National Conference held at Polokwane in December 2007, where the irrepressible Jacob Zuma was elected party leader and, hence, heir to the presidency of South Africa. For obvious reasons, Zuma's mass following harbored deep hostility toward the DSO and called for its immediate dismantling by act of Parliament. The policing responsibilities of the unit and its authority structure, it was resolved, were to be merged into the regular SAPS. As the minister of safety and security subsequently argued, separating investigative from prosecutorial functions made "for better command and control."[56] Dark allegations began to circulate to the effect that the Scorpions were "sheltering former apartheid security police" and—this was the real rub—had been "acting like an opposition party" with "the aim of fighting the ANC."[57] And so, after the legislature had prepared the way in June 2008, the DSO was formally disestablished by presidential decree in January 2009. It was to be succeeded by another unit, the Hawks, who were placed securely under the suzerainty of the SAPS—and who, despite their predatory name, have never achieved anything like the stature, the almost-preternatural aura, of the supercop Scorpions.

The demise of the DSO provoked an outcry—even more, howls of fury—across much of the nation. The parliamentary opposition accused the ANC of trying to protect its new leader and preempt further investigation of the Arms Deal.[58] Editorials lamented the message sent to the outside world, not least to foreign investors.[59] And blogs decried the lack of a sufficient official explanation for the move: the DSO was being punished for its success, they chorused, which merely served to highlight the mediocrity of regular enforcement.[60] There were even calls for a national referendum on the matter.[61] The "destruction of the Scorpions," wrote respected public intellectual, Mondli Makhanya, "is an issue which civil society, organised business and the silent majority within the ANC's natural support base should use to put the quality of our democracy to the test."[62] Prince Mashele, head of the crime and justice program at the Institute for Security Studies, noted in the *City Press* that "in talking to ordinary South Africans, one gets the impression that the Scorpions had become the trusted saviour of the people." The demise of the DSO, he argued, "sounded a death knell to [the] country's culture of accountability and respect for the rule of law."[63] Pollsters claimed that "almost two-thirds" of South Africans opposed the disbanding.[64] A national online petition, SOS, "Save our Scorpions," gathered thousands of signatures, being hailed as a triumph for civil society. One Johannesburg businessman, Bob Glenister, under the sign of the "concerned citizen," filed an urgent application to the High Court, seeking to stop the government from enacting legislation to dissolve the unit. To do so in this manner, he testified, would violate citizens' rights, using Parliament to indulge a "reckless desire" to destroy a "functioning institution."[65] While sympathizers demonstrated outside the court in Pretoria, bearing aloft a giant model scorpion, a newspaper headline read "Fixation on Scorpions Cramps Real Political Debate."[66] The legal process that followed was too convoluted to recount here, save to say that, after initial reversals, Glenister took his case on appeal to the Constitutional Court. And won. In March 2013 the highest tribunal in the land told the government that it had eighteen months to rewrite its law, that disbanding the Scorpions was invalid, and that the Hawks lacked the autonomy from the SAPS required of a serious corruption-busting enforcement agency.

We have yet to see the final denouement of this epic tale. But the general point is clear. The Scorpions had become a fetish. With their prodigious power to probe the legal and moral murk that surrounds government and business—and with their uncanny capacity to conjure evidence and secure convictions—they were held by many to be the one force that could, and did, draw the line between order and disorder. Mythical supercops, they restored, if only for a while, the fantasy of sovereign justice as South Africa seemed—seems?—to be moving implacably toward a state of Hobbesian unruliness and corruption. As if to affirm the point, and to underline the Scorpions' status as detectives without compare, it was announced, around the time of their demise, that their boss, Leonard McCarthy, was to become head of the World Bank's anticorruption unit.[67]

But here, again, we must ask ourselves: *Why* the excess? Why the uncanny, the preternatural powers attributed to these cops? Why did the Scorpions and the public connive in this particular fantasy? What does this story, and the one before it about Donker Jonker, tell us, more broadly, about crime, policing, and the metaphysics of disorder in this place and time? Before we return to these questions, however, there remains our third story. Let us call it . . .

The Tokoloshe of Matlonyane

This story takes us far from the usual orbit of national melodrama. Drawn from the archive of everyday enforcement in the largely rural North West Province, it illuminates a different face of forensic anxiety: the poignant, popular faith that cops might be able, against all odds, to solve novel mysteries born of perplexing times—a faith to which the now predominantly Africanized police, especially in small, more remote communities, often feel compelled to respond, even when they lack the means.

Early in January 2000, our attention was drawn to a "troubling" case that had been brought to the cops at Lomanyaneng, a village near Mafikeng, capital of the Tshidi-Rolong chiefdom and a regional center of the SAPS in this Setswana-speaking province. The liaison officer there, Captain Patrick Asaneng, first told us about it. A lay leader in the Catholic Church, he was to be deeply involved—as a diviner-detective of sorts—in the effort to solve it. For several weeks, the local newspapers, *The Mail* and *Sepone* (Setswana, "Mirror"),[68] carried the story, with accompanying photographs, several of them quite striking.[69]

The trouble began in the desperately poor homestead of the Sejake family, in the nearby hamlet of Matlonyane, with a series of uncanny events. An intruder had entered the square, mud house in which slept an elderly grandmother and her two grandsons, the first of whom, Tsamaiso, was twelve years old. Their father, Obed, was away seeking work but returned soon after the night in question. The mother of the boys was estranged. She lived "out there," said the old woman, gesturing vaguely across the veld with one wizened hand as she shielded her eyes against the blistering sun with the other. The family had few local ties, living amid the miscellany of migrants who had drifted into the area since the end of apartheid. The invisible assailant had harassed the Sejakes with obvious violence. It (as we shall see, the source of the trouble was not quite human) set upon Tsamaiso, leaving him scratched and sore. It swore volubly at everyone in the quiet household, and destroyed most of their few possessions.

Nor was this to be the only attack. The Sejakes were repeatedly spat at, beaten, pinched, and throttled at night. In one remarkable incident, kin visiting from a nearby village were severely stoned. Another onslaught, even more extraordinary, involved photographs. From *Sepone*, the family had cut out an article about their case, complete with photos—including an unforgettably doleful portrait of the grandmother. This image had been thumbtacked to a picture of the Kaiser Chiefs, the country's most popular soccer team, rudimentarily framed in glass. The attacker had wrenched the whole thing from a shelf and had hurled it against the earthen wall of the front room. It had, it seems, been offended by the effort to frame its uncontained force.

Soon after they were set upon, the Sejake family had gone to lay a charge of assault at the Lomanyaneng Police Station. This in itself is noteworthy: during the apartheid years, black South Africans as a rule did not expect protection or help from the law, which was securely in the hands of whites. The desk officer at Lomanyaneng found it hard to translate the Sejakes' complaint into the language of charges and dockets. Patently, there *had* been an assault at Matlonyane. But who was the assailant? "A *tokoloshe*," said Obed, Tsamaiso's father, who was later to accuse it of trying to strangle him as well. *Tokoloshe*,[70] in/famously, is a squat, hairy witch familiar, whose cultural home was once along the coastal, Nguni-speaking parts of the country to the southeast (M. Wilson 1951), in particular, those inhabited by Xhosa and Zulu, which many Sotho and Tswana speakers see as the centers of traditionalism in the post-colony. But *tokoloshes*, which terrify those who fear attack from them, have also become more mobile since the end of apartheid, having recently migrated northward into the interior. One of them, the Sejake family believed, was the cause of their affliction.

The police at Lomanyaneng, all of them Tswana-speaking, took the case very seriously. For several nights, they allowed Obed and Tsamaiso to take refuge at their station. Apart from all else, young Tsamaiso *had* been hurt and property in the house *had* been destroyed. Nothing was missing, so there was no question of robbery, and the injuries could not, physically, have been inflicted by either the very frail grandmother or Tsamaiso's little brother. Nor was there any evidence that the family, which lived an unusually isolated life, had fallen into conflict with their neighbors, kin, or anyone else. But how could the police track down a *tokoloshe*? Given that they could not arraign the witch familiar—nor knew how to "return" it to its "owner," as local healers are wont to say—what was to be done? How was the spirit of the law to deal with spirits of a very different kind? How was forensic practice to do battle with cultural reason? This, clearly, was a case for the Occult-Related Crimes Unit. But Colonel Jonker was too far away—in all senses.

Instead, the local police called in Captain Asaneng from regional headquarters, summoning the Catholic cop, himself steeped in *Setswana* (Tswana ways and means), to deal with the African uncanny. Asaneng confessed to us that the case had presented him with a conundrum. Technically speaking, a crime had not been committed, since there was no human perpetrator. But the family *did* have cause to complain of assault and the destruction of property. A serious disturbance *had* occurred. Hence, despite the fact that it fell outside their usual purview, narrowly defined, the cops felt called upon to act. They did so by drawing on a synthetic, unconventional repertoire of techniques in the ill-defined zone between policing and healing. Asaneng visited the Sejakes, first with the local media and later with a prophet-healer. He told us that he had taken a TV team and reporters from two newspapers in the hope that the publicity might draw forth assistance from the community. Above all, though, he sought to divine the cause of the trouble by apprehending it on film. But the *tokoloshe* eluded the cameras. Inexplicably, they ran on fast-forward all the time they were inside the haunted house. Out of sync with the force it sought to capture, the footage was unviewable, useless.

There are many ironies here. In his effort to solve the mystery by means of the camera, by producing a pictorial "proof" of its perpetrator, Asaneng evoked the ghost of Walter Benjamin; Benjamin, recall, posited a close allegiance between the space of photography and the scene of a crime. For him, the photographer was a descendant of the augur and the diviner, being able to turn traces invisible to the naked eye into evidence, thus to subject them to the law (Benjamin 1999b, 527; Doane 2002, 152). The fetishism of the photographic as a privileged means of capturing transparent truths has been at the core of modern empiricism, of course, with its commitment to reading the visible "to discover its secrets" (Foucault 1989, 148); this is so, too, for forensic science, despite repeated critique.[71] But with the *tokoloshe*, its alchemy failed, as if to underscore the difficulty, in this time and place, of subjecting inscrutable acts and facts to modern investigation. The Sejakes, for their part, had different expectations. Recalling the widely noted African belief that spirits can be apprehended by the camera, they thought that the photographs might "catch" the intruder and carry it away (Comaroff and Comaroff 1991). They wished, that is, for "abduction" of a rather-literal kind. But the *tokoloshe* had apparently been too canny. Uncannily so. It responded with fury, destroying the image-objects commissioned to capture it.

Asaneng did not rely on the media alone, however. In his effort to stem the assaults, he also engaged the prophet-leader of an African Independent Church, who consulted the scriptures, washed the entire family with holy water, and gave them medicated woolen cords to tie around their bodies as protection. Meanwhile, in the wake of all the publicity, healers and religious adepts of various stripes, from Catholic priests to traditional doctors, also came to Matlonyane to offer their services. There were so many, said the grandmother, that she could not remember them all. They prayed and divined, placed cans of medicine on the roof and buried ritual horns in the ground. All to no avail.

One day in late March, almost three months after the *tokoloshe*'s first attack, we visited the family together with the local beat cop, Sergeant Joseph Monei, who had been keeping a watch on the situation. The old woman was at home, alone and afraid; her grandsons were at the local school, where the teachers had been trying to handle the fear, arising out of the attacks, spreading among the pupils. Obed, she said disconsolately, had been forced to go off again in search of work. Tsamaiso had suffered yet another frightening attack: one evening, when he was using the outdoor deep-pit toilet in the yard, the *tokoloshe* had tried to pull him down into it. And just the night before, it had pushed violently against the door of the house in an effort to get in.

We had to leave the province later that week. On our return, a couple of months later, the officers at Lomanyaneng reported that the matter at Matlonyane had taken a turn for the better. When, again together with Sergeant Monei, we drew up in front of the Sejake homestead, we found Tsamaiso playing happily in the sun. The grandmother ushered us in and told us that, for several weeks, the family had been free from attack. In the end, she herself had found a *ngaka*, a diviner, who had treated the homestead and its occupants. The diviner had used various medicines, which had been hung from the rafters at the corners of the house. Where had she found someone to succeed after all the others had failed? The officiant, it turns out, was a fellow member of the Church of God, one of the many Pentecostal congregations that now offer succor and security in communities like this. The Sejakes had long known of her reputation but could not afford the cost of her treatment. In sheer desperation, however, they had consulted her. The grandmother, who was reluctant to speak of the details of her ministrations for fear of mystical reprisal, insisted that the identity of the assailant who had sent the *tokoloshe* no longer mattered. Patently, though, she suspected her estranged daughter-in-law.

When we discussed the outcome with Captain Asaneng, he remarked, ruefully, that "the solution to peoples' problems is often the one closest to home, the one within their own grasp." But he was acutely aware, in saying this, that he was admitting failure. Despite their often-creative efforts to rein in the assailants invading the intimate reaches of postcolonial life, police regularly stumble over the "grammar" of contemporary crime, crime both ordinary and arcane. Notwithstanding the popular desire for their protection, there remains a crisis of trust in the ability of the SAPS to prevail, a crisis made manifest in the burgeoning resort to unconventional efforts to plumb the mysteries of everyday existence. Divine detection is one such resort. As we shall see in our other uneasy pieces below, there are also others—like the alchemy of reading by numbers (2.3).

Coda: Toward a Criminal Anthropology

As we noted in 1.3, a sensational homicide trial, one of the "most controversial, heated and fascinating in South African legal history" (Mollett and Mollett 2014), came before the Cape High Court in 2007. Recall it: Fred van der Vyver, a young actuary from a wealthy Afrikaner farming family, was accused of murdering his girlfriend, Inge Lotz; Ms. Lotz was a twenty-two-year-old student in mathematical statistics at the University of Stellenbosch, the daughter of a professor there, and, by all accounts, a young woman of talent, intellect, and uncommon attractiveness—details that, no doubt, added to the mass public interest in the case, some of it clearly prurient.[72] The evidence looked overwhelming. Both van der Vyver's fingerprints and a bloody tread from one of his shoes were allegedly found at the scene of the crime. But as the action unfolded, the defense picked the prosecution case apart, clue by painstaking clue, using international experts to challenge the "type, size, place, position and relationship of [the] unique [traces]"—the crimogenic grammar, that is—on which the SAPS relied to try to convict van der Vyver (Altbeker 2010, 257). In the end, the accused was acquitted, although a subsequent study (Mollett and Mollett 2014) argues that he was actually guilty; that the forensic techniques used by the SAPS passed muster and were, in fact, persuasive; that the overseas experts, who "are always [taken to be] honest and infallible" (167), were neither. In his insightful account of the judicial process, Antony Altbeker (2010, 252) remarks that, while never framed as such, the trial was really about "how objects and artefacts . . . are to be read." Not only did it provoke arguments about the truthfulness and the competence of the police involved. More fundamentally, by making it plain that the "hard" facts of forensics are themselves *always* vulnerable to contention and conflicting interpretation, even manipulation, it also shook the authority of evidentiary practice inherited from the colonial past.

Fingerprints were first used in a colonial context, in British India, as a means to authenticate individual identity: in imposing order after the Sepoy

Mutiny of 1858, the Raj turned to body marks to distinguish unruly subjects who "all looked alike" (Cole 2002, 64–65). Ever since, this technology has enjoyed a great deal of legitimacy, especially for purposes of policing and especially among lay publics, despite its professionally acknowledged fallibility; despite, also, the ascent of DNA technology—often itself called, metaphorically, "fingerprinting"—as *the* authoritative means of marking identity. In the postcolonial moment, when, as we have stressed, identities have become markedly less legible, fingerprint technology has come to be more vigorously contested—although reliance on it remains much as before.

The fixation on that technology, and more recently on DNA, points to an enduring ambivalence in the dialectical dance between citizen and state, subject and the law, privacy and publicity, a matter to which we shall return in more detail in 2.2. On the one hand, people in many places evince a strong desire, particularly in uncertain times, for states to have the capacity to know, to recognize, to acknowledge, and to engage with each of them *individually*: the culture of rights, so deeply ingrained in neoliberal citizenship everywhere, is predicated, in part, on this impulse. On the other hand, many of those very same subjects express an equal will to protect their privacy, to escape fixity, and to elude the regulatory eye of governmental authority. This ambivalence plays itself out, in another key, in the tendency, discussed in part 1, of populations both to call for more policing, even as they excoriate its brutality and inefficiency, and to resist it, even as they lament its absences, inadequacies, and impossibilities. One corollary of this ambivalence, of course, is the fantasy that, if a state *did* know all its subjects, it would also know its rogue citizens, thus to make the former safe from the latter. This is why the faith in fingerprinting, and in forensics, was itself on trial along with Fred van der Vyver in the Cape High Court in 2007. South Africans might want both to be recognized by authority and to escape its regulatory reach. But they certainly do *not* want to know that the techniques of identification available to the state are incapable of identifying, arraigning, and incarcerating the violent criminals who threaten them.

In light of this, it is not hard to see why a public anxious about crime, policing, and disorder would have had such an insatiable desire to know who Inge Lotz's murderer "really" was—and how *his* identity might be established. (Gender here was taken for granted, and the matter of sexuality left mute.) Was it the young white man, the embodiment of buttoned-up Afrikaner respectability, a "good young Christian . . . incapable of telling lies" (Mollett and Mollett 2014, 168), or as suggested later, could it have been a local drug dealer, a dark, racially marked outcast from the illicit economy (Altbeker 2010; above, 1.3)? Was this a story about failed romance between intimates, about unrequited sexual lust, about ordinary jealousies? Or was it a visit from that standard South African abomination: the youthful, balaclava-faced killer, who takes life randomly, casually, uncaringly, often in blood lust? Whose "bland smile during the day," to recall Achmat Dangor, "turn[ed] into a murderer's smirk" just before nightfall on that fateful day? Questions, these, that call forth in many South Africans the spectral horrors that haunt their daily—or, rather, nocturnal—imaginings, that challenge their collective knowledge of themselves as a society, that cry out for the truths that violent crime might reveal.

And so, as the prosecution case fell apart, credence in conventional policing and in ordinary forensics fell apart with it. Recall here Durkheim's insight, cited above and several times in part 1: it is in crime that modern society finds the signs of its own existence as a normative, authoritative sociomoral order. Whether this is read as sociology or ideology, it posits the possibility of an inversion: that in the *absence* of a reflexive sense of discernible order, of shared truths and the technical means of producing them, crime appears to become unreadable, mysterious, explosive. And appears to demand creative forms of policing, as much inspirational as technical, as much abductive as deductive. The fact that Inge Lotz's murder remains unsolved[73]—despite the efforts of the SAPS, private investigators, and a host of others—makes the point most potently: unable to plumb the grammar or decipher the secret alphabet, to read the political sociology of violent crime in its midst, South Africa seems to have become less and less legible, as a sociomoral order, with the passing of time.

Could this be one of the reasons why, in the face of the "criminal obsessions" that have gripped the nation (see Comaroff and Comaroff 2004a), the drama of crime and detection carries such inordinate political charge, such extraordinary cultural appeal, such strong, excessive affect? Why the Gopanes, the Jonkers, the Scorpions, the Patrick Asanengs and others[74]—not to mention American "cult cops" and Scotland Yard's "Super Recognizers"—have such magnetic allure? Does that affective excess explain the fetishism, after *both* Marx and Freud, of those uniquely capable, in myth or in reality or in an uneasy fusion of both, of imposing law on lawlessness? Of restoring a knowable, norm-governed world? Could it also be that, in true Freudian fashion, diviner-detectives and supercops of various kinds serve as stand-ins for a sense of profound lack? Given everything that we have said here, the answer clearly appears to be in the affirmative. To be sure, these figures draw attention to feelings of exile from paternalist state protection, to a rupture of the link between cause and effect, and to a sense of deep disillusion with the brutality, corruption, and plodding ineptitude commonly thought to dog conventional enforcement. And thus its incapacity to set apart the law from lawlessness. The gap between a crime and what we know about it, Antony Altbeker (2010, 108–9, 236) observes, has to be filled by evidence whose meaning, in the final analysis, is to be "divined." Or, in our terms here—after the likes of Sherlock Holmes or Edgar Allan Poe or Charles Peirce—arrived at by abduction made all the more urgent as an imagined social world appears to implode, rendering authority in general, and policing in particular, opaque, inscrutable, ghostly.

◆

Diviner-detectives, broadly conceived—with their putatively preternatural, hyperrational capacity for abduction—may be an apt embodiment of the contradictions of law, order, and sovereignty in places and times rapidly outrunning the logos of modernity. But both in life and in art, both in South Africa and elsewhere, they also personify something more abstract: a persisting faith in the possibility of a scrutable world, a world in which person and property are socially anchored and protected, a world in which seemingly random events, pure contingency, may be tamed, situated, explained. As in divination, so too in social analysis; divination, after all, *is* vernacular social analysis, a point long made by anthropologists and archly underscored by the internationally famed *"No. 1 Ladies' Detective Agency"* (McCall Smith 2002), set in Botswana. Carlo Ginzburg (1989, 109) insists that the sheer complexity of the advanced capitalist world might make the idea of systemic knowledge appear fanciful, hence the popular appeal, these days, of *noir*. But the impossibility of forging easy connections between surface and substrate—between, we might add, the incident/al and the social, material, cultural force fields in which it occurs— does not nullify "the existence of a deep connection" between them, he says. "Reality is opaque, but there are . . . clues, symptoms . . . which [still] allow us to decipher it." Clues, again, that draw together the ethnographer and the diviner-detective, that fuel the promise of a criminal anthropology capable of making sense, as we try to do here, of our labile, infinitely ruptured, infinitely involuted world.

CHAPTER 2.2

IMPOSTURE, LAW, AND THE POLICING OF PERSONHOOD

The Return of Khulekani Khumalo, Zombie Captive

Modernist ideas of the self have long been haunted by the image of the *doppelgänger*, the false double. In early European folklore, a *doppelgänger* was usually a paranormal presence, an immanent "evil twin" who portended disaster and death. In its less phantasmic, contemporary form, its traces linger on in the specter of "identity theft," a crime that renders its victims nonexistent, indeed zombified, as legal and social persons. Its perpetrator is the impostor, a con artist who reinvents him- or herself by becoming someone else—typically, if not inevitably, with malicious intent. Like Walter Benjamin's great criminal (1978, 281; above, 1.1, 2.1), this species of charlatan cuts a compelling figure in the popular mind, perhaps because it makes plain the performative, fabricated quality of *all* identity. Marcel Mauss (1985, 17) wrote long ago that modern Western personhood has its roots, at once, in Roman ritual (in the *persona* as mask, artificial "character," and "stranger to the self") and in Roman law (where the *persona* connotes the "true nature of the individual"). These two sides of personhood, the artificial and the authentic, would come together, in tensile copresence, in Enlightenment ideas of consciousness: of the person as a knowing and reasoning subject, that is, a product of a perpetual interplay between self and other. Stephen Greenblatt (2005, 2) notes "an increased self-consciousness about the fashioning of human identity" as an "artful process" already in the sixteenth century. Self-making of this sort implied a doubling: the person both as autonomous construction and as a subject on whom the object forces of the world worked themselves out.

Western thought would play in various ways on this doubling and on some of the anomalies it bequeathed—most notably, that of the person as simultaneously self-possessed, coherent, rational, yet prone to unreason, dissembling, fragmentation at the hands of forces both inside and out. Enlightenment liberalism sought to shape these anomalies into a systematic ideological apparatus, to draw a firm, institutionally regulated line between the "normal" subject and its deviant doubles: the criminal, the insane, the savage, the uncanny. Although hardly homogeneous, this tradition was epitomized by John Locke (1995, 256). For him, personhood was a "forensic term" pertaining only to "intelligent agents" capable of living under law, of being accountable for—of "owning"—their actions, past and present (see Rubin 2015, 272–73). His choice of words implies a view of individuals as moral beings, liable for what they do in the face of blame, criticism, or criminal prosecution (Merrill 1998, 13). While humanity, in liberal thought, might denote inclusive species being, personhood specifically requires jural endorsement.[1] In our own, *late* modern times, however, when that individual is defined not merely as a "proprietor of his own person" but as an entrepreneur-of-the-self (above, 1.1), this ontology is eroding: the line between the person-as-authentic and the person-as-artifice—between the subject and its double, its *doppelgänger*—becomes difficult to sustain. Witness the global rise of what Hillel Schwartz (1996) calls "the culture of the copy," one dimension of which is the increasingly everyday practice of faking, counterfeiting, and plagiarizing others. Witness, also, the emergence of the so-called "Impostor Syndrome," a psychiatric condition whose growing number of sufferers actually see *themselves* as frauds.

Patently, this speaks to a particular genealogy of the self. In South Africa there are many who draw on different cultures of personhood, cultures that interact with this European genealogy in unexpected ways. It goes without saying that the dialectics of self-fashioning here, as everywhere, are anchored in the polymorphous architecture of economy, society, and the state. The *real* sociology of that architecture is highly complex, of course, all the more so given the tectonic shift of which we spoke in part 1. As a result of the globalization of the division of labor, of the spiraling traffic of people, objects, and images, of a burgeoning politics of rights and recognition, nations have been beset from within by assertions of difference, by compromised belonging, and by a con/fusion of private and civic identities; in short, in the age of the protean, when "faking it" seems everywhere possible, by a rising obsession with fixing social identity itself. Bodies both personal *and* public seem ever more threatened by alien, alienating intrusion: by the perfectly ordinary person who turns out to be someone, something, dangerously different from who they say they are, by the counterfeit citizen, the impostor immigrant, the bogus asylum seeker, the respectable rogue, the inscrutable terrorist. In the circumstances, states struggle constantly to deal with the authenticity and artifice of citizens and strangers alike—and tend to do so primarily by recourse to the means and ends of the law. But is the law equal to the task in this, the twenty-first century? Can criminal justice address the paradoxes of personhood born of late modern historical conditions? Do novel forensic techniques resolve the problems to which they give rise? Or do they merely open up new ways of producing selfhood?

Back from the Dead

In late December 2009 one of South Africa's legendary Zulu musicians passed away quite suddenly, victim, it is commonly said, of "medicine" given him by a traditional healer—at the behest of a rival artist. His name was Khulekani Kwakhe Khumalo. Or Khulekani Kwakhe Mseleku, depending on how we translate the niceties of Zulu clanship: the Khumalos are his patrikin; the Mselekus, among whom he grew up, his matrikin. To black South Africans, he was known primarily by his moniker "Mgqumeni." Khulekani was a famed *maskandi*, a singer of *maskanda*, a hip, highly popular folk genre—a genre heavily autobiographical, self-creating, often associated with the migratory road between the country and the city, a genre in which the singer tells stories of life and times in the postcolony, of the living and the dead, of things mundane and mysterious.

The greatest mystery surrounding the man, however, lay not in his music but in a curious turn of events, one that his haunting songs could never have anticipated. Having been interred in 2010, his funeral attended by politicians, public figures, and local celebrities, Khulekani ought to have joined the realm of his ancestors. However, in January 2012, two years later, to the great surprise of his close kin, including his four conjugal partners, "he" returned to the homestead of his family at Nquthu, in KwaZulu-Natal.

The resurrection of Khulekani caused a public furor. Social media in South Africa were abuzz with speculation as an estimated thirty thousand people gathered at Nquthu to welcome their idol back to the preancestral world. So "hysterical" were some of these *maskanda* fans that police officers in riot trucks were dispatched to handle the "frenzy" occasioned by his "official unveiling"—a "frenzy" fanned by the sheer fascination of seeing a recently deceased hero re-create himself, to walk again among the living.[2] The media were out in numbers too, there to bear witness to the mass effervescence—and to hear Khulekani sing. Indeed, the urge to capture and commodify His

Master's Voice would soon launch a vigorous dispute over its authenticity and ownership. Shades, here, of the Lockean idea of the self.

The salutations of the returned *maskandi*, delivered from the turret of a public order police vehicle, were terse and to the point. "I have always been alive," he declared. "I have been held captive by zombies for two years, a victim of witchcraft."[3] Talk of zombies, as we shall see later, evokes a fan of referents here, having to do in large part with the loss of wage labor. "Those who captured me kept me in a cave," he went on. "They shaved my dreadlocks"—one of his celebrated trademarks—"because they wanted to make me tokoloshe";[4] a *tokoloshe*, recall (2.1), is a diminutive, frightening figure used by witches to do their work. "I was forced to sing and eat mud to stay alive. I have lost a lot of weight but it is me." His harrowing experience, he explained, ended when he "escaped,"[5] waking up in a field near Johannesburg, the epicenter of migrant labor and cultural production. From there, a few days later, he returned home.[6] Uncharacteristically for Khulekani, he refused to sing, choosing instead to recite his Zulu clan names and praises, the symbolic substantiation of his "true" identity, his "traditionally" authenticated self. He promised to sing again once he felt stronger.

Many fans were skeptical of the "resurrection." The absence of Khulekani's dreadlocks worried them, as did scarification marks on his face that looked different, more livid. Some said that Khulekani now had a gold tooth, which he had not had before; in parts of central and southern Africa, note, gold teeth have resonances that go back to prophetic, anticolonial figures.[7]

If the fans gathered at Nquthu were divided about the authenticity of the resurrected Khulekani, his family were even more strikingly so. His maternal grandmother, Zintombi Mseleku, greeted his return by declaring, emphatically, "It really is him."[8] She should know, she added tartly, having raised him; her kin told us that the bridewealth owed for his parents' marriage remained unpaid. "He is looking a little worn and his cheeks are less chubby, but it's him." By contrast, his paternal grandfather, Hlalalimanzi Khumalo, was suspicious at first, but he soon decided that "the boy" had indeed come back. As the days passed, Khulekani's two sets of kin began to take opposed sides, however—and to assert them with increasing vehemence. His matrikin, despite Grandmother Zintombi's initial statement, now argued that the returnee was not Khulekani. A maternal cousin, to whom we spoke in 2012, put it thus: "This man is not Mgqumeni. There is nothing about him that indicates this is him. Mgqumeni and I were very close from childhood. It is not him and that is where the Mseleku family stand."[9] He added that the Khumalos would not know him anyway, since Khulekani was raised by the Mselekus. To which the Khumalos responded that, indeed, they had no idea what the *maskanda* singer looked like when he died, since his matrikin had not allowed them to see his body before its burial: a not-so-veiled accusation, this, of bad faith, even perhaps of witchcraft—or, even worse, an effort to conceal the fact that he was not actually dead.

For their part, the Mselekus quickly developed a narrative of what the imposture was all about: money. Another cousin, Nelisani Mseleku, explained that it was a "well-orchestrated plan to steal [Khulekani's] wealth."[10] He had owned two taxis—whose capital value in South Africa is substantial—and was owed an unspecified sum in unpaid royalties; he had released five solo albums, the latest of which had sold more than seventy-eight thousand copies, platinum in the country at the time. Not surprisingly, his "resurrection" resulted in a run on his CDs and DVDs, which were selling in large numbers.[11] As we were told later, there were, are, no hidden assets: the taxis had been repossessed and no royalties were forthcoming, at least to any of his survivors.[12] Nonetheless, allegations of patrilineal greed and hidden wealth continue to circulate.

But what of those who knew Khulekani, or at least his physical person, best of all: his conjugal partners? Here the verdict was split, 2-2. One, Zehlile Xulu, who had a ten-year-old son by Khulekani, was emphatically negative, her "heart broken," she said, as she told of a scar that the singer had not had before.[13] The first reaction of another partner, Nonhlanhla Majola, with whom Khulekani had lived for a time in Johannesburg, was that the returnee was a "bad spirit." But once she had "check[ed] his feet, neck and smile,"[14] she was persuaded that he was not an impostor, loudly denouncing all evidence to the contrary. "I know this is the father of my child,"[15] she said. Her dogged insistence is reminiscent of a similar case of imposture in the United States, now the subject of an acclaimed docu-feature film, *The Imposter*. It tells how a "23-year-old, dark-haired French-Algerian," Frédéric Bourdin, an inveterate trickster, "pass[ed] himself off as a 16-year-old blond, blue-eyed American," the unfortunate Nicholas Barclay, who had disappeared mysteriously from his Texas home in 1994.[16] Despite the obvious differences between the two, Barclay's family, including his mother, fiercely maintained that Bourdin was their son when he turned up three years later—and continued to do so until a chance series of events rendered her insistence implausible.

Well, who *was* the man who appeared at Nquthu in January 2011, the man who claimed to be Khulekani Khumalo, the mythic *maskandi* who would not sing on his "resurrection"? Folk artist or con artist? Record maker or heart breaker? Cultural icon or common criminal? To reiterate our opening questions in another register: what does this story tell us about identity and subjectivity, about its fabrication, performance, and recognition, here and elsewhere?

Many Unhappy Returns

The return of Khulekani Khumalo recalls another, *The Return of Martin Guerre*, subject of a well-known movie,[17] a couple of musicals, at least one historical novel,[18] and an influential scholarly work (N. Davis 1983). The drama began in a sixteenth-century village in southwest France with the arrival of a man claiming to be Guerre, who had abruptly left his wife, child, and kin eight years before. Displaying considerable local knowledge and an appearance not unlike that of the absconder—this in a world without photography, IDs, or fingerprinting—the returnee assumed the latter's conjugal role for three years before his identity was contested in a dispute over family assets, whereupon he was charged with imposture and finally hanged. In her sensitive analysis of the case, Natalie Zemon Davis (1983) argues that the fake Martin Guerre sustained his credibility with the help of intimate others, those invested in the return of a character—a husband, a lover, a nephew, a brother—whom the pretender played *more* effectively than had the original. The drama underlines just how collaborative and culturally nuanced is the production of plausible personhood everywhere, at least personhood in its more capacious sense as an ensemble of social roles. It also demonstrates how struggles over property, when they go to law, require proof of the propriety, the ownership, of one's person, a point that will turn out to be critically relevant to our South African story as well.

But what, to go back to Khulekani Khumalo, was the outcome of *his* return, his resurrection? The brief answer is that the police decided that he, too, was an impostor, one Sibusiso John Gcabashe, a man with a questionable past that included arrests for theft, rape, and perjury; a man who, like Khulekani, is also a teller of stories, albeit of a different sort; a man who, according to his uterine brother Phelelani has reinvented himself many times before, often by means of assuming false identities.[19] At the behest of the Mselekus, the cops arraigned and fingerprinted him soon after his public appearance, which is when his "true" identity was discovered—or, rather, when *five* other identities were discovered, among which the law chose the one that it took to be the most plausible. South Africa might be one of the most biometrically oriented states in the world, one of the most digitally precocious, as Keith Breckenridge (2005, 274–76 *et passim*) has observed, but its efficacy is only as good as the bureaucratic record-keeping on which it depends. And as good as the technology itself: digital fingerprinting, which remains unreliable, has opened up new means of "dissembling, impersonation, and duplication" (276). Identity theft, it turns out, is no less "possible in biometric systems [than in any other]," all the more so in places, like South Africa, where their implementation is outsourced to the private sector.[20]

Palpable, here, is a strange, late modern counterpoint between the fixing and unfixing of identity; between, on the one hand, the effort of the state to profile, panoptically, all its subjects and, on the other, countervailing forces that blur the indices of personhood in new ways. In the face of all this, the man now called Gcabashe continued, continues, to deny all charges before the court; he refuses even to answer to any name but Mgqumeni or Khulekani. Subjected to psychiatric testing, he was declared fit to stand trial, notwithstanding his claim that he was being attacked by witch familiars and other occult forces in prison. Meanwhile, some of those closest to Khulekani—two of his wives and his paternal family—continue to insist that the prodigal is him and would defend his identity before the law. Local musicians, who are keeping a close eye on the case, are also divided. One of them, Siyazi Zulu, told us that few *maskandi* think that the returnee is Khulekani.[21] Another, Maqhinga Radebe, has composed a satirical song about the whole "fiasco." "*Uyimbudane, Gcabashe* [You are a joke, Gcabashe]," he sings.[22] But others are less sure. So, too, is a well-known musicologist of the genre.

At the time of writing, the case is still making its way through the judicial system. At first, nobody seemed to know exactly what to do with it. The magistrate who initially heard it in rural Nquthu in February 2012 handed the docket on to the director of public prosecutions for guidance. By May that year, when the case was moved to a higher court in Vryheid (KwaZulu-Natal), Gcabashe's lawyer, Johan Botha, said that he still was not sure what charges were actually being laid against his client, although the media kept asserting that it was fraud; he also seemed unsure what line of defense to take, since until the matter was resolved legally, it was not really clear whether his client was Gcabashe or Khulekani. And in any event, if the state tried the accused as Gcabashe, it could be said to have prejudiced the outcome of the case, surely grounds for a mistrial. It was equally unclear whether, if indeed Gcabashe was an impostor, he could be found guilty of fraud under South African law[23]—of which more below. The Khumalos, firm in their conviction that the returnee *was* Khulekani, sold some of their cattle to pay his legal fees and slaughtered a cow, in the presence of the ancestors, to "welcome him back into the family."[24]

Some months later, the case was moved again, now to Pietermaritzburg, the provincial capital, where the indictment for fraud was bundled with those earlier charges of rape, theft, and perjury. All the while, the accused has languished in prison, where he has been photographed with his guitar, where he sings *maskanda* and composes new songs, and where warders speak of finding him a strangely compelling charismatic with an extraordinary knowledge of the life and times of Khulekani—echoes here of Martin Guerre. He has grown dreadlocks and, in the view of one correctional officer, looks more and more like the master *maskandi* himself. In fact, prison staff told us that none of them is willing to wager that he is *not* who he claims to be. Note that he has repeatedly called both for DNA testing and for the exhumation of the buried body, thus to prove his authenticity. For reasons unstated—lack of resources or forensic capacity, perhaps—the police have refused. Over three years, hearing after hearing, attended by ever larger publics, ended in deferral. Then, in mid-2016, the man named as Gcabashe was found guilty on all charges, and sentenced to an unexpectedly long twenty-two years; the Khumalos, intending to appeal, say that the case is far from over. The long arm of the law has given way to its *longue durée*. On one thing, however, most *dramatis personae* appear to agree: in contemporary South Africa, there was, is, little alternative but to appeal to courts and to forensics for a resolution to the incommensurate claims over identity being made in this case—even though, for all its promise to do so, the law is not likely to bring closure; most lawyers to whom we have spoken about the case agree that the issue of personhood here is far too complex for the criminal justice system to handle adequately.

For us, we stress, the significance of the story does not depend on its outcome, the assessment of guilt or innocence, authenticity or duplicity. Its significance lies, rather, in what it tells us about the quest, in a time of shifting norms, canons of evidence, and indices of truth, for ways of establishing personhood in postcolonial South Africa—and, perhaps, elsewhere as well.

Postcolonial Personhood and the Culture of the Copy

In writing about the case of Martin Guerre, perhaps *the* archetype of a counterfeit "return," Natalie Davis (1988, 590) notes that in sixteenth-century France, "[i]mposture [was] not an isolated form of behavior, not a disconnected 'monstrosity,' but one extreme on a spectrum" of self-fashioning for "purposes of play, of advantage, [and] of 'attracting benevolence.'"[25] But what might be the spectrum of self-fashioning that frames the drama of Khulekani's return, and

the passion it ignited? How does this strange saga speak of the aspirations, possibilities, and impossibilities of producing a sustainable identity in South Africa today?

As it turns out, postapartheid South Africa is curiously hospitable to im-
personators and impostors of all sorts. The world became aware of this when
the global media reported on the bizarre case of the bogus sign language interpreter at Nelson Mandela's memorial service in December 2013.[26] Thamsanqa
Jantjie, hired by the African National Congress government from South African Interpreters Inc., first attributed his incapacity to transmit the speeches
of the likes of US president Obama—or, more precisely, his rendering of them
into a stream of meaningless signs and inchoate images—to a schizophrenic
episode.[27] Later, he was quoted as saying, "I am the great fake because I expose what is going on in the government and the system,"[28] a point echoed
by one local commentator, who saw the whole event as both singular and yet
an apposite metaphor for "what is happening to us" at a time in South Africa
when "there are no truths at all worth hearing" (Poplak 2014, 267). For his
part, Slavoj Žižek read into the incident another kind of "(non)truth": that the
whole memorial ceremony was nonsense, a fake, a self-congratulatory exercise on the part of dignitaries who pretend to care for the "disabled" but instead
postpone dealing with the explosive crisis of black poverty.[29] Soon after the
event, it became clear that Jantjie was an accused thief, murderer, rapist, and
kidnapper who had not been brought to trial—because he was judged men-
tally unfit,[30] a symptom, this, of the slippage between the normal and the deviant that have become central to the culture of the copy. Yet, for all the attention
that Jantjie received across the planet, his case is not all that exceptional.

The South African public sphere is rife with stories of bogus lawyers,[31]
bogus cops, bogus businessmen, even bogus soccer referees.[32] Some of their
fakery is downright dangerous: like that of the *faux* emergency personnel,
with degrees from a *faux* training college, employed by the Health Authority
of Limpopo Province;[33] or that of phony state physicians, one of whom prac-
ticed, with deadly effect, in the Eastern Cape and served as a standby medic
during the 2010 World Cup.[34] A "qualification verification company," itself a
new kind of institution thriving in this climate, warns that convincingly realistic graduation certificates are now easily purchased,[35] like many other
fake documents. This is not unique to South Africa. It is an industry honed
to perfection, Charles Piot (2010, 79–80) shows, in places where official immigration papers are the magical key to mobility and the prospect of a viable
future; again, where the self-possessed person must be rendered recognizable

before the law. Speaking of mobility, fakery often plays on the distance and displacement between signs and cultures of reference that open up at new conjunctures in expanding worlds. Take, for example, a DJ in Johannesburg who told his radio audience that he was calling in "live from the US," giving fulsome reports—plagiarized from American magazines—of his encounters with Jay Z, Kanye West, Beyoncé, and others. In fact, his broadcasts came from a basement parking lot below his studio, prompting a bemused colleague to remark, "[We] South Africans are especially gullible. [We will] believe anything—especially if someone looks clever . . . [and] claims to have a degree from a US university."[36] Hence Thomas and Calvin Mollett's observation (above, p. 121) that international experts are "always [taken to be] honest and infallible." This is reminiscent of the "frontier fakery" so archly documented by Mark Twain in late nineteenth-century America, a mode of deception that flourishes wherever established canons of verification are challenged by the new and the foreign—as they were in early modern Europe, at a time not merely of Renaissance self-fashioning but of geographical expansion that opened up opportunities for false pretenses, new forms of expertise, and duplicity (Eliav-Feldon 2012).

While hardly devoid of invention, millennial faith, or parody, much of this postcolonial impersonation is a con, desperate and heartless. But *not* always. More benign self-fashioning conjures with similar ideals, a similar resort to performative mimesis in order to breach the gulf between desire and scarcity, reality and fantasy. The Universal Church, for instance, one of the most successful purveyors of the "prosperity gospel" in southern Africa, holds services in which youths come dressed as the professionals they want to be. "Bring them as doctors, bring them as lawyers," the pastor enjoined his congregation in Cape Town in 2011. "If they have faith, God will grant them their wish."[37] Aspiration, the will to self-advancement, surged after the end of apartheid. With liberation came liberalization and its argot of enterprise for all (see also part 1)—even for the indigent, who have been enjoined by *the Big Issue*, a magazine sold by the homeless, to "navigate the streets of entrepreneurship."[38] Chronic unemployment and growing inequality have only spurred the popular obsession with discovering the elixir of upward mobility. Telling in this regard was a narrative in a national news column entitled Young Voices. Ntwisiso Ngobeni, a high school senior from a poor, strife-torn family, shared his dream of becoming a lawyer: "I have a vision of myself as a magistrate," he confessed. "This is a long-standing passion, which used to take me to the courts from a young age, where I could see magistrates in action." There he would observe their practices for hours at a time, vowing that one day he would "sit in their chair."[39]

Note the spirited ambition, the impetus toward mimetic, experimental performance in pursuit of a desired identity. The latter is brilliantly captured in *Hijack Stories*, of which we spoke in 1.3, a film, to reiterate, that centers on the struggle of a middle-class black actor to "learn the moves," the dangerous insouciance, of township gangsters. Criminality, the movie insisted, is *itself* a practice to be learned by copying. It is a performance that has to be convincingly staged. But by the same token, performance is often, also, a kind of crime; we see traces here of the enduring ambivalence between creativity and duplicity in the long history of the modern person.

Not only is imposture especially widespread in South Africa, but fascination with artful self-production seems to be embedded in the national psyche. In his novel *Impostor*, Damon Galgut (2008) probes the unsettling qualities of identity in the South African present, a time of "ferment" (25) when places are renamed, maps reprinted, and landscapes made unreadable. It is a time, Galgut adds, of liberated possibilities and unprecedented deceits, in which conventional signs are suspect and nobody is quite as they appear: flipping false assets, operating under aliases, and peddling simulacral identities are all commonplace. So too, we might add, is plagiarism, the most obvious textual manifestation of the culture of the fraudulent copy: poets, professors, pastors, public intellectuals, scholars, even heads of universities have been accused of it. If liberation unleashed heady new prospects, it also eroded sovereign certitudes and indices of the evidentiary, making it harder to tell truth from deception. But here's the question: Is this antipodean story an exotic exception? Or does it bespeak something more universal about world-making in the current epoch, a time, according to David Graeber (2012), that has seen a "great burst of interest," both theoretical and practical, economic and behavioral, in the notion of "performance" itself.

To be sure, as we noted earlier, modernist self-making has always been dogged by the specter of artifice, fakery, duplicity, the tension between fabrication and authentication. But the South African situation involves something more: not just a concern with the slippage, in a time of flux, between public signs and personal identities or a preoccupation with the semiotics of recognition. What is remarkable here is the sheer profusion of impostors in all walks of life, ordinary *and* elevated. If imposture in early modern France was, according to Natalie Davis, at the "extreme" end of the spectrum of self-making—it was, after all, a capital offense and widely viewed as a satanic act (Eliav-Feldon 2012)—in South Africa it has become a common, everyday practice. As such, it reveals something significant about the disjuncture, in this context, between desire and achievability, ends and means, fact and appearance. Impostors make poignantly plain how precarious is the work of realizing viable personhood, of building the intimate, intersubjective worlds that might sustain it. In this context, fakery—or, at least, creative self-invention—seems hugely productive by comparison to more conventional alternatives, if only in the short term. And who has the luxury or the patience to think about the long term? The pretender serves as a potent parody of the incitement to aspire, to accumulate, to achieve by any and all means.

Let us return, with this in mind, to the case of the impostor *maskandi*. The rebirth of Khulekani Khumalo mobilized a clutch of cultural referents and biographic facts, couched in ties of kinship and affinity, in the traffic between the living and the dead, between occult ill-will, rivalry, and revenge. Although he died in Johannesburg, where he had pursued much of his career, Khulekani "came back" to the homestead in which he was raised, there to present himself to those able to affirm his social identity: his paternal and maternal kin and his conjugal partners. In doing so, the would-be prodigal reenacted an iconic journey, the movement between workplace and rural household that, as Hylton White (2004, 141ff.; 2013) notes, had long linked black wage labor to the trope of return, the building of domestic units, the founding of families, the securing of social personhood, and, with it, ancestral recognition. The alleged imposture of Gcabashe, then, was not merely an effort to usurp a career and the value accruing to it. It was, it is, an attempt to occupy a place in a network of relations—of identity, patrimony, reciprocity—stretching back into the past and reaching forward to the future.

Gcabashe, if it is indeed he, claims, you will recall, that he was snatched from this world by witchcraft, that zombies obliterated his identity, condemning him to a living death. Zombies took on new salience in public life here just as the liberalization of the South African economy was making itself felt in proletarian communities, as labor became increasingly casualized, as large numbers of jobs were lost, and as manufacture and mining were radically restructured (Comaroff and Comaroff 1999a). The popular expectation that, with the end of apartheid, the state would address the problem of rampant inequality soon faded. Instead, the country was caught up in the paradox of "jobless growth."[40] In the 1990s zombies were often associated, explicitly, with the relatively sudden appearance of new wealth in otherwise-unpromising conditions, wealth whose source was obscure. They were held to be phantom workers whose animating spirit had been sucked out of them by the witches who "owned" them—phantom workers who, by "spoiling" the labor market for real, living workers, disrupted the flow of value that once sustained conventional forms of domesticity. Bereft of wages, households now survive on a rough mix of social grants and informal enterprise, both of which foreground women, thus depriving many males of the established means of becoming full adults, of marrying, and of forming families (cf. Dubbeld 2013). Employment remains the *sine qua non* of dignified masculinity here. But, under existing conditions, it is a receding possibility for more and more men, forcing the birth of new economies that capitalize on the detritus of the past.

This is where the *maskanda* tradition comes in.[41] It was a by-product of the migrant labor system, having been incubated in the worker hostels of swelling industrial cities during the 1920s, whence it traveled back to the countryside as men went home with their wages. The music was a dynamic, evolving synthesis, blending diverse influences, from Zulu courting songs to Afrikaans folk *lietjies (ballads)*, using cheap store-bought guitars and concertinas. One of its defining features was Zulu praise poetry (*izibongo*), redeployed to give expression to a new sense of personhood ushered in by the male migrant career. David Coplan (2001) sees *maskanda* as part of a larger category of African identity practices that were born on the road, in the restless journey between country and city, peasantry and proletariat, past and present. As the century progressed, *maskanda* evolved in symbiosis with the cultural mix of urban working-class life. While it would acquire a more formal identity as "Zulu traditional music" during apartheid, in the postcolony it displays renewed vitality, shedding many of its parochial connotations to resonate with consumer-oriented urban audiences and ethnomodern identities.

As such, the genre has acquired intensified heft as heritage capital and as intellectual property in a context in which the sale of culture has, to a greater or lesser extent, replaced the sale of labor. Successful *maskandi*, the ghosts of workers past, can bring in serious money. While his popular CDs and DVDs cover a range of themes more or less standard for the genre (Olsen 2009), Khulekani Khumalo developed a distinctive emotional tone. His wistful sounds and a searing poetics continue to appeal to a wide range of listeners, "traditional" and urbane, in both the country and the city. With pithy irony and disarming directness, he addressed a host of lumpen—chiefly, masculine—concerns. On the signature album, *i Jukebox* (2009), for instance, he returns repeatedly to the arresting image of the title song: the artist as a jukebox, a machine that produces music in exchange for money, and is exploited, in turn, by mercenary women, who make their music for him only as long as the cash keeps flowing, after which they move on to others better able to afford their affections. "You give your love like a loan shark" runs a line on a different track; "you expect to get it back with interest."[42] Other songs draw on classic *izibongo* to extol the dignity of the *maskandi*'s lineage, the strength of his creative powers, and his ability to prevail over rivals who would steal his success or kill him by occult means. One, *"We Belong Together"*—the English title is the original— calls plaintively for tolerance in the face of domestic and ethnic strife. The covers of Khumalo's CDs and DVDs typically splice the urban and the rural. On one of them, the singer is posed against customized, imaginary Zululand landscapes. Often, interestingly, he appears as a double, as two Khulekanis, the man and his *doppelgänger*, each in different clothes.

It was this compelling persona—situated *at once* in Zulu autochthonous and Afro-modern personhood—to which aspired the John Gcabashe identified by the police, the John Gcabashe who would have us recognize him as Khulekani Khumalo. Whether or not he is who he claims to be, he *is* able to play plausibly enough to impersonate the master *maskandi*, as an admiring female prison warder told us. The genre, after all, was integral to everyday existence in many Zulu communities, braided into their kinship reciprocities; performers were often thought to bequeath their gift to successors. Khulekani, for instance, had learned *his* signature style from his mother's brother, a reincarnation of sorts being inherent in *maskanda* itself.

As we have noted, too, the counterpoint between criminal and artistic performance is not all that unusual. Other successful *maskandi*, like some US hip-hop artists, have had prior careers as hoods.[43] What is more, the genre itself seems oddly appropriate to imposture. Kathryn Olsen, an ethnomusicologist at the University of KwaZulu-Natal, observes that "impersonation fits well with *maskanda*." Many musicians, she adds, "put on identities in performance as a way of claiming something lost, giving authenticity not only to the music but to who they actually are"[44]—even, it appears, at the risk of crossing the line, provocatively, between the licit and the illicit. In one remarkable twist to our story, a music producer was accused, in March 2012, of "stealing" a twelve-song CD by one Mpilo Mtungwa. He had, it was said, reissued the disc under the *joint* names of Khulekani and Gcabashe, the deceased and his *doppelgänger*,[45] a highly inventive, profitable counterfeit that depended on a meta-imposture at the intersection of the life, death, and resurrection of Khulekani. The album was reported to be selling widely.[46] Thus does identity imposture become a labyrinthine, layered, recursive practice, woven deeply into the contemporary fabric of South African economy and society. But not only here. As Damon Galgut (2008) suggests, in the age of deregulation, dissembling everywhere becomes the art of the possible. Adds law and economics theorist Richard Posner (1980, 77), speaking more generally, "[c]reative imitation is not just a classical or Renaissance legacy; it is a modern market imperative." All the more so, it seems, in African postcolonies, where perforce the line between the criminal and the creative is gossamer thin. Which is why postcolonial self-fashioning appears to ride so heavily on impostures of various kinds.

Before the Law, After Effects

Laced through our narrative, patently, is the unbidden matter of the law. The postcolonial era, as we have written elsewhere (Comaroff and Comaroff 2006b), has seen a fetishism of legalities: the rule of law and constitutionalism have become a dominant global discourse, to the extent that even in the most remote reaches of the planet, people have learned, through a populist pedagogy of rights, to see themselves as *homo juralis*—and to address their identities, interests, and injuries by recourse to the legal.

In this light, it is little wonder that the case of Khulekani would end up before the courts. But here's the thing. Unlike the colonial peoples of Africa, those governed by a "customary law" invented and enforced by their imperial rulers, postcolonial African populations are constituted as *both* the embodiment of culture *and* as national legal persons, as subjects *and* citizens, as persons *both* ethnic and modern. Had our story been set in colonial times, it would have been dealt with by "native" authorities under the law of patrilineality, inheritance, marriage, genealogy. Those authorities would have had little difficulty with the case. After all, indigenous African societies, according to colonial legal theology and the European anthropology of the time, were governed by ascription, by a principle of replication according to which any person might replace any other person in the same structural position; by the idea, that is, that individuality, in "tribal" society, was everywhere subservient to the normative substance of received social roles. Emile Durkheim famously referred to this as "mechanical solidarity." In practice, as late twentieth-century legal anthropologists of Africa have shown, people rarely just accepted their positions in structures of relations, rank, and status. *Per contra*, rules governing those relations and statuses were always open to contestation and competition. But once an individual succeeded in claiming a status, she or he inhabited it *as if* they were born to it. In that world, once the prodigal son had persuaded "his" patrikin that he was Khulekani—which, of course, he did, a fact marked by the ancestral sacrifice of a beast—he would have *been* Khulekani. There would have been no question of imposture: the question was one of social recognition. Khulekani's matrikin *might* have disputed his patrifiliation on the grounds that *lobola* (bridewealth) had not been paid for his mother, but the Khumalos dismissed this out of hand, asserting that a proper domestic union *had* produced their "son."[47] In any case, for them the pressing question was whether or not the returnee was that man. In this light, they could, and did, claim to have both culture and the law on their side.

But, patently, indigenous South Africa is no longer governed by colonial "native" custom, even though patriliny and chiefship remain significant for many South Africans. It is governed by a constitution that treats every citizen as rights-bearing and gives the state the authority to determine identity and the entitlements that accrue to it. Under these circumstances, Khulekani's matrikin had every right to appeal to the law and to ask for a criminal prosecution; the liberal-modernist conception of personhood at the base of that law, and the values it enshrines, are *also* significant in their lived world.

The moment the law took it upon itself to act, however, it found itself mired in an unholy mess. For one thing, it was faced with claims couched in local cultural terms—witchcraft, sacrifice, kinship—that liberal-democratic states find hard to translate into the language of jurisprudence. But, even more, the justice system here faced technojuridical problems. Just as plagiarism is not typically a criminal offense *sensu stricto*, so imposture raises real difficulties unless a damage can be established, which in this case was anything but clear. Since Gcabashe, if it is he, has not sought any material benefit, the Khumalos' lawyer has asserted that he has no idea what his client is being indicted for in this respect. He also contends that, culturally speaking, he does not know who the man he is representing actually *is*. At one point he intimated that the imposture case should be tried in a Zulu customary court, where a favorable outcome is almost guaranteed; the further corollary is that, once it is found there that his client *is* Khulekani, not Gcabashe, the question of who it is that has been tried for the other crimes becomes irretrievably complicated. Already the defendant has taken to saying that the crimes of which Gcabashe was accused were committed while he was still a zombie captive—which may be one of the more original alibis in South African legal history.

As this suggests, there is also something more profound here than the mere guilt or innocence of a man who may or may not be someone else. It is inherent in a postcolony in which the state is confronted by the demands of cultural difference, which frequently refuses the lingua franca of Eurocentric law; also by Ivan Vladislavić's (2004) *"exploded view."* We alluded to this image above: it evokes a world rendered so inchoate, so difficult to read, that it inculcates a sense of implosion, edginess—and, we would add, infinite possibility. Recall what Vladislavić said about it: that, in this reconfigured world, in which people consistently renegotiate their identities, authority has a great deal of difficulty asserting itself. And mundane communicative acts often take the form of a "sign language from a secret alphabet" (24).

The courts have great difficulty deciphering that alphabet; they are often immobilized in the face of the forms of personhood and cultural practices that are presented to them, frequently being unsure of what is "real" and what is not. Who is really the artist on that CD credited to Khulekani and his *doppelgänger*? And who is the man who is caught up in the judicial process under the name of Sibusiso John Gcabashe, given that his patrikin, validated by lineage authority, regard him as their son, Khulekani Khumalo? How, finally, is the state to deal with the growing problem of impostures of all sorts? Note that already, in 1999, in the Cape Province, the second-largest category of felonies, according to police statistics, were *counterfeit* crimes, crimes that are reported but that never actually happened—which brings us to the curious denouement of our narrative.

Coda: The Strange Case of Musa Khumalo, Brigadier

One of the cops involved in the arrest of the alleged Sibusiso John Gcabashe was Brigadier Musa Khumalo—note the name, shared with the deceased *maskandi*. This Khumalo was a member of the Hawks, the country's elite crime-busting force (above, 2.1). He took great pride in his role in the case. He also came with certificates of commendation for his police work, a photo of himself with Ban Ki-moon, and documents attesting to his exceptional record. As you might have guessed, the brigadier was also an impostor. He was a Zimbabwean murderer who had faked his own death in order to become a South African citizen.[48] Having been exposed, he fled and was eventually caught in December 2012. According to an official report issued by the Independent Police Investigative Directorate, he died later the same day by his own hand in a Pretoria prison.[49]

Musa Khumalo is not, of course, the only fake cop in the history of contemporary South Africa, although he may be one of the few to have captured other fakes. But, more to the point, is "fake," or "impostor," even the correct word for human beings constructing themselves-as-others in a world of simulacral citizenship, a world in which self-fashioning by means of impersonation, of playing with personhood, has become commonplace, even encouraged; a world in which the challenge of the law is to deal with life in a liberal democracy, complicated by cultural difference, under conditions that blur the line between the upright entrepreneur-of-the-self and the criminal; a world, paradoxically, in which the biometric state produces ever more sophisticated means of knowing its citizens, of fixing legal identity, only to discover that those citizens find ever more elusive ways of escaping fixity? It is a challenge to which jurists, organic intellectuals, legal anthropologists, and *maskandi* all find themselves having to respond if they are to decode the secret alphabet, to make sense of the exploded view, that renders uncertain the very nature of identity and order at this frontier in the history of the present.

Imposture has been with us from biblical times through the sixteenth century of Martin Guerre; through the seventeenth century of the kabbalist Sabbatai Zvi, the Jewish counterfeit messiah; through the early twentieth century of Princess Anastasia Romanov, whose notorious *doppelgänger*, a Polish factory worker, fooled Manhattan society for decades; through the twentieth century, also, of Ramenda Narayan Roy, who was either the fabled princely Kumar of Bhawal in India or an unnamed, propertyless *sannyasi* (Chatterjee 2002). But it has not been everywhere, nor everywhere the same. Late modern writings on the culture of the copy, read against Africa, raise questions about the degree to which the phenomenon is tied to the long Judeo-Christian history of the self-possessed subject, tied, that is, to a particular idea of authenticity, individuality, indivisibility, property, and the law—all of them subsumed in the propriety of personhood. At the dawn of the twenty-first century, as humans define themselves ever more as capital, entrepreneurs of the self, authenticity becomes at once fetishized and impossible. The "impostor" is a mythic figure of self-making, a figure who mocks the liberal theology of personhood in the age of digital reproduction, a figure who muddies the spaces between the law and its aporias. She or he is the everyperson *in extremis*, at once irredeemably real and a copy. Postcolonial South Africa, and the story of Khulekani Khumalo, zombie captive, merely makes the point in hyperbolic form.

CHAPTER 2.3

FIGURING CRIME

Quantifacts, Mythostats, and the Production of the Un/real

In an address to Parliament in 1999, then president Nelson Mandela voiced an old cliché. "Figures," he said, "are meaningless in the context of people's concrete experiences." But in the late modern world, the opposite seems to be true. When transformations in economy and society, in technology and demography, in politics and culture erode received certainties and sight lines, figures, especially in the form of statistics, promise to make abstract truths concretely intelligible to personal experience. This is because they appear to speak with authority about the connection of human beings to otherwise incomprehensibly complex forces, facts, and phenomena. As signs that label, measure, and count the real—signs granted singular status as objective, transparent indices of truth—they fill the space between the unknowable and the axiomatic, anxiety and imagination. Viewed thus, the statistic is both a figuration and a fact, a medium of communication *and* a unit of knowledge-as-currency, one whose value and veracity accumulate as it circulates. Part fetish, it has also become a register in the ordinary language of everyday life, invested with heightened salience in contexts, such as those that concern us here, where representations of social order are contested. As journalist Darrel Bristow-Bovey once put it, "Nothing rings with more authority to South African ears than a crime statistic. . . . [It is] the music of our spheres."[1]

The rise of modern Western conceptions of society, Ian Hacking (1990, 1–5) has famously argued, was closely tied to the "avalanche of numbers" produced, publicized, and deployed for purposes of governance by nineteenth-century states (cf. Canguilhem 1989). The fixation on counting and calculating probability, he suggests, had profound epistemic effects. For one thing, "society" itself "became statistical," as, of course, did the related concept of "population" (cf., e.g., Foucault 1980, 124–25). For another, the appeal to lawlike regularities began to replace prior forms of causal explanation, such as "human nature," in making sense of, and acting upon, the world, a turn that, as we have noted, made rates of "deviancy" especially salient to the emerging social sciences and ensured that post-Enlightenment ideas of the collective, the moral, the normal, and the rational would owe much to the crime statistic. This is evident in the actuarial underpinnings of early detective fiction. Take, for example, Edgar Allan Poe, a fine organic anthropologist (see 2.1) with an explicit interest in the "public mind." In common with many writers of good mysteries, as Mark Seltzer (2004, 561) observes, Poe often invoked numbers in the interests of sociological realism; for him, "the death of God" left us with mathematics, "the death of Satan," with forensics. The Victorian impulse to quantify deviance, in both realist fiction and social science, presupposed a rule-governed social order whose positive outlines were most visible in the negative: in "social pathologies" that would become the urgent object of sociology, social engineering, and public policy framed under the sign of reform, rehabilitation, and improvement (cf. Hacking 1990, 118; see above, 2.1); also, the object of biometrics—a term first coined in 1893 to denote the "measurement of life" (Magnello 2000, 83)—whose technologies would be used to identify persons for legal, medical, and other civic purposes (Porter 1986; also 1995). And to enumerate them.

So much for the heyday of Euromodernity, in which the very idea of governance became dependent on statistics, aka the "science of [a] state" (Rose and Miller 1992, 185), as did the dominant liberal telos of the time, whose end was a better world, a greater commonweal. But what about today? Wherein lies the significance of crime rates and incidences at the dawn of the twenty-first century? How do they figure, so to speak, in an age in which foundational assumptions about society, citizenship, criminal justice, and order—not to mention the production of the future—can no longer be taken for granted? In an age in which the market and nonstate forces are overwhelmingly held responsible for addressing social issues? In which popular punitiveness has overtaken the liberal ideal of reform and melioration? In which the sovereignty of "the" state—its capacity to enforce the law, to deal with "deviance," and to provide credible information—is deeply in question?

South Africa, like most nation-states today, produces its own avalanche of numbers. The tide of statistics made publically available by the South African Police Service is swelled, in the age of deregulation, by the state-like exertions of nongovernmental organizations and the private sector. Those figures feed a thoroughly modernist "lust for precision" (Hacking 1990, 5), a fervid faith, even amid a growing preoccupation with official corruption and ineptitude, in the panacea of probability and in a populist sense that countering disorder begins with counting it properly. It is hardly surprising, then, that the crime statistic has taken on unprecedented importance here. Not only has it become diagnostic of the national health. It is also a vernacular currency by means of which government speaks to its subjects, citizens speak among themselves, experts speak to everypersons, and everyone speaks back to (and about) government—while the media mediate all the incessant talk, adding their own inventions, inflections, inflations.

Three things are noteworthy about the rising sovereignty of the crime statistic in this context and about the pivotal place of quantifacts—statistical representations that make the world "factual"—in public discourses. All of them are critical to our broader theoretical concerns here.

The *first* is an inflection of the paradox of dis/trust of which we have already spoken at some length: while crime statistics constitute a widely cited measure of the condition of the country, they tend also—as is the case with other aspects of law-enforcement and forensic intelligence—to be *dis*trusted, due largely to their susceptibility to abuse. They are, in short, at once a fetish and the object of a lively hermeneutic of suspicion. The *second* thing has to do with alienation and intimacy: counter to the commonplace that numbers, especially official statistics, displace visceral experience into the abstract realm of pattern and probability—vide Mandela's observation—it is arguable that they do just the opposite here. As they circulate and are mediated in myriad ways, these statistics reduce and translate a mass of faceless felonies, awful incidents that occurred elsewhere, into the objects of first-person feeling: fear, revulsion, revenge, pain. The *third* thing arises out of the phenomenology of figures on crime: for all the ambivalence with which they are regarded, they tend to be treated not as a *representation* of reality—not mere "words," so to speak—but as a reality in themselves, a reality in which is congealed material facts, moral order, collective identities, even the quality of life (cf. Urla 1993).

In this "uneasy piece," then, our criminal anthropology explores *what*, exactly, it is that crime statistics make real, *how* they take on a public life, and by *what* means they convert the abstract into the intimate, tertiary knowledge into primary experience, quantity into quality. *Why* is it that they have become so much more than the tools of criminologists and social reformers, so pervasive a popular passion, so deeply inscribed in narratives of personal being, so vital to the construction of moral community, so integral to debates about the meaning of democracy, freedom, security, human rights? Conventionally framed as value-free information, these numbers appear to be taking on substantial political heft as the late modernist state deregulates the functions of governance; as sovereignty is parsed, privatized, and pluralized; as enforcement focuses increasingly on public order and outsources to the private sector the ordinary protection of persons and property; as investment in criminal detection declines amid rising concerns about the forensic capacities of the police and about its inability to convict—at just the moment when the mythic powers of criminal science have come to saturate the global imagination. As a result, and as citizens shoulder ever more responsibility for their own security, modes of producing and deploying crime statistics are proliferating. This, as we intimated a moment ago and shall see in exquisite detail, has set in train processes whose effects, often unremarked, are significantly implicated in remaking the nation-state, the nature of its governance, and its political life at a time of mounting anxiety about the very possibility of sustainable social order. But, once again, we are running ahead of ourselves.

Sovereign Statistics: The Alchemy of Numbers

Critical readings of the history of the Industrial Revolution, the rise of democracy, and the consolidation of Euro-nationhood return repeatedly to the ambiguous alchemy of numbers. At work in processes of commodification and bureaucratization, they suggest, was the power of arithmetic to abstract and transform value, to facilitate the expansion of capital, to enlarge the scale of governance, to turn human beings into ciphers, and to alienate them as units of production from both their essence and their experience. Lefort (1988, 18–19), for one, argues that the paradox of the modern idea of "society" is that it can never be concretely actualized: far from materializing "the people," institutions like universal suffrage turn citizens into statistics as "[n]umber replaces substance." Simmel (1978, 297–98, 444) thought otherwise. For him, money, as *the* currency of counting, permitted the translation and commensuration of difference—and, hence, the production of a society of morally interdependent, yet self-sufficient individuals, who realize themselves in their relation to an impersonal mass. New modes of accounting, in other words, enable the emergence of new qualities, subjects, sensations. Even under the most rationalizing, alienating conditions, the traffic between quality and quantity occurs constantly in the construction of meaning and value.

The contentious life of the crime statistic in South Africa makes it plain that enumeration *is* never a mere flight from substance: it is always mediated by historical conditions and methodological effects, intended or not. Some of the ways in which numbers are made to construct and signify the world in the idiom of the actuarial state—to concretize abstractions like "publics," "populations," and "communities" or to render part-whole relations, like "the majority"—have long been integral to the fabric of democracy; vide de Tocqueville, Weber, and much of the history of liberalism. Also a *sine qua non* of liberal democracy, and of the forms of contestations intrinsic to it, is the ever-present awareness that "statistics can lie" (Huff 1954) or, rather, that they can be made to: that measurement always involves decisions, benign or calculating, about *what, whom, and how* to count. Those decisions entail subsidiary techniques for configuring, reading, and interpreting raw numbers, whose deployment is foundational to relations of power, to the rights of citizens and the rule of law, to policing populations and to public policy. Apartheid South Africa, notoriously, rationalized minority rule by dis-counting, literally, the majority of the population, dividing them into "separate" ethnic homelands in order to eliminate them *in toto* from the national body demographic and hence the body politic; opponents of the regime used insurgent statistics—land distribution ratios, poverty datum profiles, mortality rates, wage and taxation rates, and the like—to argue against "unrepresentative" rule. More recently, activists striving to persuade the state of its responsibility toward the homeless and HIV/AIDS sufferers have advocated "emancipatory" enumeration as a strategy (Robins 2004, 259–60).[2] In the "risk society" (Beck 1992), where personal destiny is read in percentages, improving one's chances requires improving the numbers (Crawford 2004, 522) or, at least, some numerical justification—just as in postgenomic, market-based medicine, the treatment of personal health, like pharmaceutical venture capital, depends on speculative profiles of future pathology (Sunder Rajan 2005), assessed against the law of large numbers. Even in everyday colloquial terms, the quality of life is suffused, even haunted, by the prospect of being dis/counted: "I want government to provide more security for people like me before I too become a statistic," said an elderly Tswana man to us in Mafikeng-Mmabatho[3] in 1999, as he reflected on the precarity of his existence. A similar sentiment was voiced, in a slightly different register, by Mark Gevisser (2014, 263) after suffering the home invasion cited earlier (1.3): to the police officers at the scene—cops who were "trying hard" but were "far less educated, or worldly" than even the assailants had been—"we," the victims, "could not be anything other than statistics, in the end."

Although the truth-value of numbers has been a focus of bitter debate between the "hard" and "soft" sciences, there have also long been efforts to grasp the statistic as a social construction (e.g., Kitsuse and Cicourel 1963; Poovey 1998). One influential expression of this concern has been inspired by Foucault's analysis of enumeration as a means of governance (e.g., Cohn 1987, 224–25; Anderson 1991, 163–64; Appadurai 1996); another emerges from science studies (Haggerty 2001, 53; cf. Rose 1999), which have examined the production of various modes of calculation as "artifacts" yielded by the interplay of actors, institutions, and technologies (Latour and Woolgar 1979; Deleuze and Guattari 1987). Both approaches offer insights into the nature of crime counts in postapartheid South Africa. And both have limitations. Thus, we might ask, after Foucault, why measures of lawlessness and victimhood *have* become so salient in managing populations here, overlaying class, race, and other received sociological categories. But it is equally necessary to take note of the public criticism and political conflict that have escalated in response to accusations of inadequate criminal accounting, in all senses of the phrase. Similarly, in charting the tortuous life of numbers, there is a great deal to be gained from tracing, in the manner of science studies, the emergence and circulation of statistical artifacts: in this instance, by following the argument that rages about official crime tallies, about their implications for the rights of citizens and the responsibilities of rule. That argument is itself a fractal drama in which government, media, citizen-subjects, and other parties conjure with the meaning of normality and emergency, the average and the aberrant, public information and partisan dissimulation. At the same time, as we shall see, this conflict bears the imprint of historical and structural forces much larger than can be grasped from the science studies perspective, with its stress on contingent outcomes, assemblages, and actor networks.

But let us begin our excursion with the numbers themselves. In doing this, we enter into the concrete world of quantifacts and those who transact them, into the paradox of dis/trust that fuels their production and distribution, and into the intricately scaffolded reality that crime counts make of life here.

Excursions into the *Un*real: Counting Crime in the Postcolony

Both within the country and outside, as we have said repeatedly, South African crime rates are seen as anything from dire to catastrophic. Well, how bad *is* it? What do the numbers indicate? In order to answer this question, we suspend disbelief for a moment, taking those numbers at face value in order to draw a synoptic portrait, synoptic, first, because the relevant statistical data are readily accessible to anyone who might want to scrutinize them and, second, because our concern here is less with rates and incidences for their own sake than with their political, phenomenological, and discursive salience. For the sake of longitudinal comparison, we take as our baseline the year 2002,[4] for which especially detailed information was made available by the state; it also came after a highly controversial moratorium on the publication of *all* official crime statistics, to which we shall return. The official figures for that year were published in two forms: in the *Annual Report of the National Commissioner of Police for 2002/3* and in an online posting by the Criminal Information Analysis Centre of the SAPS; we rely largely on the latter, read against the *National Victims of Crime Survey: South Africa, 2003*, undertaken independently by the Institute for Security Studies ([ISS] 2004). The latest SAPS counts, at the time of writing, are for 2013/14;[5] *Victims of Crime Survey, 2013/4 (VOCS 2013/4)*, published by Statistics South Africa ([SSA] 2014), is also available for the same period.[6]

Recall the general point made in part 1: what is said to mark South Africa out, and what feeds its obsession with its exceptionality, is less its ordinary criminal profiles than its violence; although, as we shall see below, it comes only third in international counts of *total* violent felonies. Almost 22,000 people were murdered in 2002, about 48 per 100,000 of the population. That number, itself down 19 percent since 1994, dropped consistently thereafter— save for a minor increase in 2006/7—until 2011/12, its lowest point, at 15,609. Since then it has gone up again, rising by 5 percent in 2013/14 to 17,068, 32.2 per 100,000, or 47 homicides each day; the global average is usually given as around 6 per 100,000.[7] Add, for 2013/14, 17,110 attempted murders, 183,173 assaults with intent to do grievous bodily harm (GBH), 167,157 common assaults, 119,357 aggravated robberies, and the tally of dead and wounded bodies is considerable in a population of 54 million.[8] And this is not (yet) to mention sexual assault. At the same time, it is to be noted that murder accounts for a relatively small proportion of all mortality: in 2013, the last year for which we have figures, the total was 458,933, of which 3.84 percent were homicides, by comparison to the 19.01 percent caused by major infectious diseases (Statistics South Africa 2013, 27);[9] the rate of road accidents, among the highest in the world here and rising steadily, is only marginally less at present than that of intentional homicide. Nonetheless, the latter instills a much greater measure of fear and trauma.

Especially traumatic, too, for women, is gender violence. Between 2002 and 2013/14, the figures fluctuated a fair bit but, apart from femicide,[10] rose overall from 52,107 rapes to 62,649 sexual offenses, in rough proportion to the growing national population—although down 11.2 percent from a peak of 70,574 in 2008/9. The category shift, rape to sexual offense, is owed to the Criminal Law (Sexual Offences and Related Matters) Amendment Act 32 of 2007, which redefined rape more broadly than before and listed several new sexual offenses. It did so largely because, as we saw in 1.2, this species of felony is the object of particular national anguish. The numbers published by the police every year are contested for being far too low. Also contested is the finding that relatively few cases occur between total strangers, which is also true of murder (SSA 2014, 60, 62); the standardized nightmare, after all, is of the "unknown black male" as perpetrator. The "real" incidence of rape has long been the subject of widely circulating, widely varying mythostats. In 2001, when we began collecting those statistics, a favored mode of stating them was in rapes per second: we collected estimates of 1 in every 4, 11, 17, 35, or 36 seconds.[11] Even if the last and lowest were correct, the official figure for 2002— 52,107, or 1 every 10.8 minutes—would have been out by a factor of 17 or 18 *times*. The SAPS (2003, 36) believed that their own count was two-thirds out, that only one in three cases were brought to them. One independent victim survey—surprisingly, given that this research instrument ought to yield the *highest* rates of underreporting—guessed that "approximately half" of all victims of rape report it (Hirschowitz, Worku, and Orkin 2000, 2). Even more surprising, *VOCS 2013/4* puts the underreporting rate at 27.5 percent (SSA 2014, 60–61), which means that almost three-quarters of all sexual offenses *were* actually counted. Estimates continue to range wildly: recently, for example, the Medical Research Council claimed that just one in nine rapes is reported, a far cry from three in four. Whatever the figure is in fact—it *is*, after all, unknowable—this species of crime *does* remain worryingly prevalent and is often accompanied by horrific violence. Also, by all accounts, it is not decreasing.

Insofar as they are integral to the phenomenology of fear, two other serious crimes of violence are also noteworthy. One is aggravated robbery: in 2004, 266,789 were recorded; a decade later, that number was down, astonishingly, to 119,351, or 225.3 per 100,000. Translated into a percentage, this means that, were it evenly spread, only 0.0225 percent of the population would have suffered it—much less than public discourse might suggest. The other is carjacking. Many South Africans, we have argued (above, 1.3), have a strong psychoaffective tie to their automobiles; Rosalind Morris (2010, 605) refers to it as the "libidinization of the car." They treat them as extensions of the self, as vehicles of social mobility, almost as homes-in-transit: their violent expropriation, under casual threat of death, is an existential assault that leaves victims feeling impotent, angry, afraid, violated. Unlike rape, however, its incidence is not all that high, again *pace* popular belief: it stood at about 15,000 cases a year in the early 2000s, 11,221 in 2013/14. When we asked informants to guesstimate annual counts, they invariably answered in the six-figure range. What is more, very few end in murder, although virtually all respondents thought that most do.

To what does this eye-glazing torrent of stats add up? The total of serious felonies in 2003/4 was a staggering 2,389,653.[12] By 2013/14 it had dropped to 2,172,876, of which 620,366 were contact, and 562,768 property, crimes. The decrease, around 10 percent in a decade, is the basis of SAPS claims that it is "gaining ground" on lawlessness. There are exceptions to the general pattern, however. Among them are commercial and narcotic-related offenses, which have gone up steeply; so, over the past three years and rising, as we have already mentioned, have murder, attempted murder, and aggravated robbery.[13] The police claim of a strong downward trend, moreover, rarely adds that their figures are shown, by victim surveys, regularly to undercount "real" incidences, largely because of the growing reluctance of the public to report violations, which, in turn, is attributed to the perception that the cops either can "do nothing" or "won't do anything" (SSA 2014, 49).[14] In fact, argues Gareth Newham,[15] the recent decline publicized by the SAPS in several categories of crime may be explained by—indeed, is proportional to—emerging patterns of underreporting, especially, we would add, in areas where local populations bypass the cops entirely and resort to the ways and means of informal justice (see 2.4). The belief that their stats systematically undercount is cited by many citizens as proof that the police are losing, not winning, their "war," feeding the paradox of desire and distrust that surrounds them. Vernacular realism here numbers its truths, unsurprisingly, in damaged persons and seized property. And it discounts all claims against those truths.

But we are not finished with the numbers yet. Parsed sociogeographically, these gross figures take on a more nuanced cast. Perhaps the most striking thing about crime in South Africa is how curiously distributed it is. And how counterintuitively. Focusing for now just on 2013/14, the murder rates among the nine provinces are quite unexpected. KwaZulu-Natal (34.7 per 100,000), often thought to be the most violent of regions, did *not* have the highest; it came a distant fourth. Gauteng (26.2), long assumed to be the homicide capital of the nation, came only sixth. The Western Cape (48.3), widely believed to have taken over Gauteng's position in this regard, came second. Top, surprisingly, was the Eastern Cape (52.1), which lacks cities of the scale of Johannesburg, Durban, or Cape Town. The largely rural Northern Cape (37.7) also scored higher than either KwaZulu-Natal or Gauteng, the latter being beaten out, as well, by the semirural Free State (34.4); the other three provinces had relatively low rates, lowest being Limpopo at 13.2, again somewhat curiously, since it is also presumed in South Africa to be home to a great deal of physical conflict. In short, homicide patterns at this level run orthogonally to public perception, which presumes cities to be far more dangerous in these respects than rural or semirural areas and which tends to be conditioned *not* by rates but by raw incidence; note, in this respect, that the order of the latter, of incidence, put KwaZulu-Natal (3,625) first, then the Eastern Cape (3,453), Gauteng (3,333), and the Western Cape (2,909). *Both* rates and incidences, however, point to a very uneven distribution of violence.

As with murder, so with rape, also assumed to be most heavily concentrated in the four provinces with the highest incidences of homicide. If we restrict ourselves to those incidences, this is indeed the case: those four accounted for 40,855 of the official number of 62,649, about two-thirds. But the rates look altogether different. Gauteng, again often taken to have the highest, actually has the lowest (86.6 per 100,000); KwaZulu-Natal (113.3), also thought to be awash in gender violence, comes seventh of the nine, below the national average of 118.2 and two steps below the Western Cape (134.4), at fifth. The highest, remarkably, is that of the Free State (174.9), followed by the Northern Cape (150.8), and the Eastern Cape (149.5). Hijacking, by contrast, is less counterintuitive, although it does have its surprises. Over half, 6,064 cases of 11,221, occurred in Gauteng and a further 2,274 in KwaZulu-Natal. The Western Cape, where fear of this species of felony continues to be acute, had only 961 cases; the remaining provinces had negligible counts. We could continue: there are many other curiosities across the topography of crime at this level, ones that play havoc with popular perception. Few would guess, for instance, that by far the most elevated rate of GBH in the country, with 751 per 100,000 of the population having fallen victim to it, would occur in the comparatively sleepy Northern Cape. As it turns out, the impoverished of the countryside and of isolated small towns seem often to take out their desperation on those closest to hand.

Curiosities aside, while the ecology of serious crime tends to focus on the provincial level in the national conversation, patterns of variance are both more marked, and more relevant to everyday life, at the microsociological. As the commissioner of police put it in his report for 2002/3 (SAPS 2003, 32), the vast majority of serious felonies, proportionately speaking, occur in "a few township precincts": those with "high levels of poverty, large informal settlements, and prolonged unemployment." This remains true. As Ulrich Beck (1992, 41) once noted, "extreme poverty and extreme risk" tend always and everywhere to "attract" each other. Taken across the statistical terrain of South Africa, the incidence of crime and victimhood typically follows lines of race and class. As of 2014, 13 percent of police precincts, most of them white and affluent, had homicide rates well below the *global* average; 10 percent had zero. Conversely, 75 percent of murders were concentrated in less than a quarter of the nation's precincts, all of them poor and black.[16] In the Cape Province the pattern is especially stark. There 40 percent of *all* violent crime occurred in a few closely clustered neighborhoods on the Cape Flats; that high-density, low-income part of Cape Town contains six of the seven worst microzones in the country for both murder and attempted murder. Making the general point yet more strongly is the fact that on lists of the "Worst Ten Precincts" in South Africa for serious felonies, the fall away in incidence between those at the top and those lower down is remarkably steep;[17] even at its most intensely concentrated, lawlessness is *very* unevenly distributed. This is true, too, for white-collar crime—crimes for which whites tend to be collared—although that species of offense, for all the structural violence it inflicts on the material life of the country at large, incites less visceral panic than moral outrage.

Nor are the panic and anxiety allayed by public knowledge of the highly uneven crimogenic map of the country. In 2004, for example, the *Cape Times* wrote that "the incidence of violent crime has long been almost negligible in predominantly white residential areas."[18] At the time, the reported murder *ratio* of predominantly poor, black Khayelitsha to wealthy, white Camps Bay was 358 to 1 (see above, 1.1); hijacking was 126 to 3; rape, 517 to 12; and housebreaking, 1,621 to 132. Or, to take a slightly more mixed, less "white" neighborhood, nearby Sea Point had 4 recorded murders, 22 rapes, 6 hijackings, and 713 domestic burglaries, still much less than parts of the city inhabited primarily by people of color. But this information had little effect on public attitudes, least of all on the inverse correlation, as Ted Leggett (2004a, 6) has put it, between "fear of crime" and the "actual risk of violence." It rarely does, regardless of whether that violence has been experienced personally (Shaw and Louw 1998, 6); *vide* the fact that in the late 1990s, during a major spike in serious offenses, survey research established that, while 80 percent of blacks had suffered attack, only 20 percent thought themselves under threat, while 80–90 percent of whites felt imperiled, even though only 5–10 percent had been victims (de Haas 2000, 319). Those numbers have changed somewhat, as we have seen, but the general point still holds true. When it comes to criminality, there is little relationship between reported fact and public perception.

This is true, too, of the disbelief that surrounds the long-term downward trends in official figures for all offenses. Most South Africans continue to think that lawlessness is on the rise—or, at best, steady (SSA 2014, 52ff.). Perhaps because crime statistics measure a wide range of insecurities in a highly insecure, untrusting world, few accept at face value "facts" that call into question the national trauma: "[crime] figures are received with a morbid fascination," observes Colin Bundy (2014, 124), "strongly laced with suspicion and scepticism"—and, he might have added, with the insistence that underreporting is rife, rising, and risibly ignored by the SAPS in computing its rates, which are *not* independently audited.[19] Every year, their publication is followed by a stream of apoplectic op-ed pieces and letters in the print media. As long ago as 1998, in the still-optimistic Mandela years, *the Star*, a major Johannesburg daily, published a feature entitled "The Surprising Truth about Crime."[20] Foreshadowing the report in the *Cape Times* in 2004 (see above), it pointed to strong evidence that the country had become much *safer*, for most of its citizens, than it had been under apartheid. "People get angry when you say it [though]," noted senior criminologist Benty Naude. "The public perception is wrong. Crime is not really as high as people think." The inflation of mass fear, the feature went on to say, is owed to the media practice of reporting *incidents*, not *incidence*; its stress on sensational acts of violence has the effect of generalizing the singular, thus to feed the impression that criminality has become endemic in South Africa. *The Star* predicted the way in which all this would be read: a host of angry citizens wrote to the paper, all of them asserting that theirs remained the most crime-afflicted country on earth. Run the story seventeen years later and the reactions would not be very different, the numbers notwithstanding. Nor are South Africans alone in this respect. In Britain, where felony rates are also unevenly distributed and falling, "around two thirds of the public believes [they are] rising or, at best, static."[21]

But how, criminally speaking, *does* South Africa measure up to the world?

A parenthetic comment first, though. A "common way of ratifying shared belief," says Mark Seltzer (2004, 560), "is to share in [its] suspension"; Americans, he observes, affirm something by saying the opposite, such as "it's really *un*believable." This is no less true in South Africa, where the terrifying reality of violence is materialized in words like "*un*real." And "*un*imaginable," "*un*-thinkable," "*in*credible." But a collective sense of selfhood in the face of disorder is also conjured up, here, by evoking the argot of exceptionalism, an exceptionalism that, as we have said, demands to be substantially tempered. While international comparisons are notoriously difficult—largely because both categories and methods of counting are only very roughly commensurable, if at all—South Africa *does* have among the worst rates of most violent felonies. By most accounts, not surprisingly, it comes up first in comparative measures of rape, although this, too, is complicated (cf. Leggett 2002), as non-reporting rates vary widely; in Canada in 1993, for instance, it was said to be a staggering 90 percent (Haggerty 2001, 31).[22] But this is South Africa's only top ranking. It comes third, after the United Kingdom and Austria, for total violent felonies. And seventh for total crimes, after five northern nations (the United States, United Kingdom, Germany, France, and Russia) and one Asian (Japan). In comparative counts of robbery victims, it does not even feature in the top twenty, but places to which many white South Africans have emigrated do, however: Australia and the United Kingdom come joint third, and Canada, joint ninth with Sweden.

In fact, South Africa has long been far from exceptional with respect to property offenses. In 2000, according to the Seventh United Nations Survey on Crime Trends,[23] it ranked only eighteenth, for all categories of theft; against its rate of 1,287.21 per 100,000, Australia (3,514.65), New Zealand (3,313.25), England and Wales (3,257.52), and Canada (2,220.77) looked substantially worse, as did the Netherlands (4,580.26), Norway (4,281.34), France (3,963.83), Germany (3,701.56), Denmark (3,633.73), Iceland (2,662.99), and Finland (2,207.71), all of them commonly seen as havens of peace, order, and civility. What is more, on the United Nations "grand total of recorded crimes" for the same year—which *included* violent offenses—South Africa was tenth, after New Zealand, England and Wales, the United States, the Netherlands, and Canada; it might well have been much lower, but several nations thought to be "crime-ridden" did not submit figures to the UN. Again, we could add many more comparative numbers to this, but the general picture will be as clear as needs be.

There is, however, a more general qualification to be made at this juncture, one that ends our temporary suspension of disbelief. In 1994, at the time of transition to democracy, Lorraine Glanz (1994, 10) declared, dismissively, that it is impossible to "know precisely how much crime takes place in South Africa, or anywhere else." Glanz should know. Or, rather, not know. She was to become the director of crime statistics in the postapartheid Department of Justice. What she was pointing to, implicitly, is the fact that police figures *everywhere*—including the United States, where *the Wall Street Journal* recently lamented the lack of any "decent crime statistics"[24]—are erected on an edifice of indeterminacies and impossibilities. The most pervasive of those indeterminacies are pragmatic. Official numbers are composited from cases either brought to the SAPS by the public or turned up by their own investigations—hence, for all the reasons we have given, the inevitability of *under*counting. But felonies may also be *over*reported. This is less remarked upon in South Africa, with its strong public predilection to stress the pathology of victimhood over offenses that *appear* to be victimless, even though they never actually are. Already in the early 2000s, both the SAPS (2003, 41) and the press[25] reported a palpable rise in faux claims (see above, 2.2), largely but not only for financial motives. It has continued ever since: bearing false witness to having suffered crime has itself become a major category of criminality, extending to robbery, hijacking, housebreaking, assault, sexual violation, arson, even attempted murder.[26] The precise extent of either under- or overreporting is, by definition, unknowable. Together, they make the "real" quantifacts of law-breaking literally incalculable. This is exacerbated by ambiguities intrinsic to criminal record–making itself. For example, because felony figures are determined by the way in which episodes are coded at the opening of a police docket—as, say, sexual abuse, domestic violence, or aggravated assault; murder, suicide, culpable homicide, or accidental death—a measure of arbitrariness is unavoidable. Those figures depend on how victims or reporting officers think, at first flush, that the incidents should be classified. Once they have gone through the criminal justice system, however, they are usually not reclassified. Thus, a death listed as murder that turns out to have been suicide or a carjacking that morphs into a fraud case or an assault whose victim later dies will remain where it was originally classified, there to *dis*figure further rates and incidences in ways that are impossible to unravel once they are aggregated.[27]

Yet another species of indeterminacy derives from a quite-different source. Because felony counts *everywhere* are the dual products of police work and public reporting, it follows that they will fluctuate in proportion to the efficacy of the cops and the trust placed in them by citizens. Hence, paradoxically, rising crime rates may be less an indicator of rising crime than they are of increased confidence in and the success of policing less, in other words, a function of law-breaking than of law-enforcement—or, which is most likely, of a complicated dialectic of the two. As we have seen in the case of the South African

public and the SAPS, that dialectic opens up a Pandora's box of truly unfathomable proportions. But the disfiguration of the real lies not only in the production of statistics. It also lies in their circulation. There is, it appears, a proportional relationship between the generality of a quantifact, the sociological
scale to which it refers, and its capacity to travel as knowledge. The more qualified or refined any number, the less likely it is to survive the rigors of movement or mediation. It is only the most gross, the least qualified—those that
erase the differences which make a difference—that become *national* truths.
Thus, to return to our example for all seasons, South African murder figures
are cited constantly as *the* symptom of the country's state of disorder. Rarely is
reference made to the highly inflected geographical clustering of most of the
killing in relatively few, largely enclaved spaces. In this respect, the ecology
of crime here resembles those of countries, like the United States or Brazil or
France, that have lower homicide rates but whose death zones in inner cities
and *favelas* and *banlieues* are not all that dissimilar from those in South Africa. In these and many other places, as we have seen, relative enclaving—the
distended, uneven topology of violence—is a decidedly better key to the calculus of risk than are national aggregates. The perennial reassertion of those
national aggregates in the circulation of quantifacts, however, is a ritual enun-
ciation of the contemporary mythos of a society at risk—and here the racial
archetype returns—overwhelmingly at the hands of young black men; it is
these men who, in an unfortunate metaphor, are often said to be "holding the
country to ransom." Erased, too, is the fact that South Africa has a social history that has freighted its crime statistics with a great deal of meaning as it
moves toward its future.

To the extent, then, that those statistics are a mode of objectification—alike
a means by which realities are realized and a lens through which a nation may
re-present itself—they take on special salience in South Africa. Indeed, it is
perhaps in this, rather than in its criminal economy, that at least a measure
of exceptionalism lies. But why? Most immediately because, under the *ancien
régime*, crime figures did not circulate as a free currency of social knowledge,
being tightly managed by the state as part of its racial politics of security and
legitimation. Besides which, black-on-black crime was undercounted because
blacks did not count. To wit, it has been said that before 1994, "the 'real' state of
crime" was *never* reported (Marsh 1999, 76; Shaw 1997; Emmett 2000, 290).
But something more profound has happened than the mere provision of new,
putatively improved information. It is only with the opening up of a democratic public sphere—or, rather, of variously articulated spheres—that the

"reborn" South Africa has been able to reflect on itself, on its social order, on the nature of its nationhood, on who now is or is not counted. In that process, crime statistics have become a standardized measure of dis/order and mis/rule, marking out, for many, a new emergency to replace those of old. They are, as it were, a medium of populist discourse that congeals, also, into new arguments, and urgent messages, running between civil society and the state.

To say—through the haze of indeterminate numbers—that the "real" extent of lawlessness in South Africa is unknown, that official stats are a fact-making fiction, is not to deny the brutal truths to which those stats speak. That much should be apparent by now. Nor is it to deny that South Africans encounter criminality in visceral, concrete terms, whether it be at firsthand, by anecdotal narration, or by a barrage of mediated events that, in their repeated retelling, take on a perceptual mass of their own. As they do, these encounters morph from incidents to incidence, read in "the public mind" as the state of the nation, as the law in disorder, as a world under threat. Thus it is that quantifacts become a vehicle for the phenomenology of fear, a vehicle that transforms the abstract into the sensate, the general into the particular, the unknowable into the known. All of which serves to conjure up, once more, our reality-producing aphorism: crime in South Africa *is* unreal. Therein lies its truth-value.

The Calculus of Politics, the Politics of Calculation

When, in July 2000, Steve Tshwete, then minister of safety and security, announced a moratorium on all official statistics, he cited, as the reason, "grave doubts" about their accuracy.[28] No more were to be published for the while: the police commissioner had ordered a revision of prevailing procedures of data gathering and calculation. During the hiatus, government would continue to collect figures for its own purposes. But not for public consumption. Then, almost a year later, and just as suddenly, the silence came to an end. On 31 May 2001, Tshwete declared that a retooled technology of number production was in place: the SAPS had a new, computerized Crime Administration System, new manuals, new staff, new training arrangements and equipment, more precise definitions of felonies, even fresh crime statistics.[29] A New Era of Enumeration had dawned. The flow of figures began again. Once more, South Africa was awash in a stream of stats.

In announcing the moratorium, the minister seems to have sensed what was to come. The ban, he insisted, was "not an attempt at secrecy."[30] Few believed him. The announcement was greeted with outrage. Opposition politicians accused the African National Congress of "an absolute abuse of power . . . outrageous in . . . a democratic country."[31] Martin Schönteich, noting that South African figures were the best on the continent, said that the withholding of crime information would "foster mistrust between the rulers and the ruled." Could it simply be, he asked, "that the police . . . do not like what the statistics say?"[32] The late 1990s, as we mentioned earlier, had witnessed a sharp rise in many categories of felony.

Perhaps the loudest protest came from the print media, however, for whom the febrile fluctuations in the nation's crime figures are a daily staple. In the void left by the blackout, reporters set about doing their own counts "in the public interest." The *Cape Times* called on its readers in Cape Town for reports of violent incidents on the notorious N2 highway, a vital artery that has long been a corridor of conflict between the dispossessed and the prosperous who drive to and from the city. By compiling "an accurate picture" of risk, the paper hoped to "goad" the SAPS into action.[33] Soon after, *Independent Newspapers*, arguing that the moratorium violated the Constitution, took legal action against the minister of safety and security.[34] Joining the chorus, the opposition Democratic Alliance alleged that, in the absence of proper statistics, it was impossible to "evaluate the performance of government" in discharging one of its most fundamental duties: ensuring the security of citizens. Public opinion was as vociferous: "Surely one of the best ways to counter the negative impact of crime . . . is the greatest possible degree of transparency from our public representatives?" wrote a typically angry correspondent to the *Cape Times*, indignantly offering a tally of his own recent encounters with crime.[35]

The argument continued as long as the ban itself. Nor did it abate when the moratorium ended. The SAPS still treats its quantifacts "like national security secrets," complained Ted Leggett (2003: 1–6).[36] Since then, as we have seen, their annual publication has evinced "suspicion and scepticism" about their truth-value (above, p. 154). "Who owns crime statistics?" Gareth Newham asked a decade later, in 2013.[37] The numbers routinely released are far too limited and too out of date to be either informative or useful, he charged. What is more, those numbers are seen by the police to belong to themselves exclusively. Despite their acknowledgment "that [the SAPS] cannot reduce crime alone," they share their data with the public and other government departments only reluctantly and intermittently, which severely undermines the ability of communities, business, NGOs, and even other agencies of state to identify and respond to emerging threats.

As these recurring accusations make clear, crime statistics have become ob-jects of intense struggle. They crystallize arguments about the limits of law-enforcement and the transparency of government, about the reinstatement of the death penalty and the justification for various forms of popular justice, about the efficacy of the new regime and the inalienable right of citizens to information. Small wonder, then, that the ANC should feel compelled to pro-duce credible crime counts and, even more, to put a favorable spin on them for public consumption. Small wonder, concomitantly, that scholars, commen-tators, and the population at large should distrust those counts or that they suspect the SAPS of misrepresentation, misinformation, and bad faith. This is not a specifically South African problem. In September 2002 criminal justice experts in the United States worried that the attorney general was "exerting political control" over independent agencies responsible for collecting crime statistics.[38] Six years later, research revealed that high-ranking New York po-lice officers, recently retired, had been heavily pressured to make "ethically in-appropriate" changes to the total of "index crimes" measured by CompStat, the signature program introduced by William Bratton and now widely fran-chised (Eterno and Silverman 2012, 34; see part 1).[39] Similarly, the Chicago Po-lice Department was accused in 2015 of using statistical "sleights of hand" and creative "new tricks" to lower the city's crime numbers.[40] And one of Scotland Yard's former commissioners admitted to a government committee in 2014 that fiddling crime figures, aka "good housekeeping," was common practice.[41] So-called "gaming" techniques—like "cuffing" (making incidents disappear from official records by downgrading their seriousness), "stitching" (listing charges lacking sufficient evidence as solved), "skewing" (boosting detection rates by directing police activity toward more tractable offenses), and "nod-ding" (raising clear-up rates with false charges)—were all tacitly accepted by the powers that be.[42]

To count crime, in short, is to produce the stuff of politics (cf. Dixon 2002). This, for present purposes, has three dimensions. The first is *epistemic*. It lies in the nature of measurement itself. As we have seen, "true" rates of lawless-ness are unknowable; comparisons in space and time, all but incommensu-rable; and felony figures, an indeterminate product of the counterpoint of law-breaking and law-enforcement. All of which, in turn, lays the ground for a more calculating play on quantifacts, one that seeks to make them signify in different ways for different ends. Here lies the second dimension of the poli-tics of crime statistics, the *strategic*. It was much in evidence in the controversy over the moratorium of 2000, when all parties to that controversy "argued with numbers": opponents of the regime to censure the withholding of data that reflected poorly on the state, victims to highlight statistical aporias and subterfuges, and government to accuse the media and middle-class malcontents of a lack of patriotism. Likewise the national murder count. Where critics of the state cite the standing of South Africa on global tables of ignominy, conjuring with the obscenity of a country wallowing in its own blood, the ANC answers with its own quantifacts. In 2001, for example, the SAPS pointed out that Washington, DC, had a homicide rate of 69.34 per 100,000 for January–June 1998, while Pretoria's was 41.12 (Comaroff and Comaroff 2006a, 223). The logic at work here may not be *totally* arbitrary, both being capitals, but it ignores the fact that although DC was the city with the worst numbers in the United States, Pretoria was far from that in South Africa (Leggett 2003). It also leaves aside the comparative reliability of computation, a "mounting controversy" into which the Institute for Security Studies was to wade in September 2013, asserting that the SAPS had used old population estimates to calculate changes in crime over the prior two years, thus to deflate the rising murder rate from 2.6 to 0.6 percent—although no direct allegation was made of gaming.[43] Undeterred by this kind of critique, the police have continued "playing the numbers game" (Louw and Schönteich 2001): over the years, they have deployed their statistics, tactically, to show that housebreaking and assault are more frequent in Australia, car theft more prevalent in Canada, personal safety levels lower in the United Kingdom, and so on. At issue in these counterfactual comparisons is the production of a state of normality—and, hence, a "normal" state. To claim, for both domestic and foreign consumption, that felony rates are declining, or at worst "stabilizing," and that the police are "winning the war," is to assert that state, to assert *the* state.

As this suggests, crime statistics have become inflated political tender. In addition to all the ways in which they enter into public discourse, social activism, and partisan argument within the country, they are also an index of national worth in a global marketplace in which southern polities must meet northern scrutiny regarding democratization, security, stability, law-and-orderlinesss, creditworthiness, and the like. In contention are such prizes as investment, foreign aid, tourism, and world sports events. Shadowing the public argument about numbers, both within and outside South Africa, is the sense that what is "really" at issue here are unspoken and unspeakable matters of race. As we have noted (1.1), African politicians and cultural commentators often suggest that the exaggeration-by-numbers of violent criminality in white media at home and abroad is an insidious form of racism, disparaging the ability of a black government to maintain order, of black police to enforce the law, of black youth to behave with civility. Conversely, many whites feel themselves to be the victims of a system in which violent crime is a form of racial revenge (van Rooyen 2000) and continue to call upon quantifacts and quantifictions of one sort or another to "prove" it.[44]

Tangible in all this is the paradox of dis/trust to which we keep returning. Allegations about the abuses of enumeration seem only to affirm the faith in its revelatory potential, raising its value and intensifying the quest for ever more rigorous, ever more disinterested measurement. Thus it is that, despite endemic suspicions about their distorting effects, especially in the service of a calculating, defensive government, hope remains in the redemptive power of more "accurate" numbers—unmediated numbers, that is, with the capacity to translate reality both accurately and immaculately. Herein lies their quality as fetish. The statistical practices currently in use may be prone to bias or abuse, but technoscientific advance promises a corrective. Note, in this respect, the long-growing enthusiasm for two internationally acclaimed techniques of enumeration, introduced in South Africa at *fin de siècle*: victim surveys, which we have already encountered, and geographical information systems (GIS). Both have been widely embraced in the belief that they offer a more exact purchase on levels of disorder. As we shall see, however, they are no less open than is any other measuring instrument to the possibility of epistemic, strategic, or contextual distortion. But their use *has* had a palpable effect on the ways in which crime is conceived and counted—and on how it is made to signify in public discourse.[45]

It is precisely to the level of discourse that we turn for the third, the *constitutive*, dimension of crime statistics. Because of the way they circulate, these numbers translate large vectors of danger into personal and collective markers of risk, subjectivity, and identity. In so doing, they render numinous forces of disorder into concrete, communicable "facts," conjuring up citizens, moral communities, the nation. Herein lies their politics (lowercase): their capacity to shape and reproduce meaningful social categories. Nor is this merely a matter of official figures, victim surveys, or geographical information systems. Vernacular statistics, everyday forms of counting crime, are also key tropes of popular communication: they feature centrally in the narratives of lawlessness that are so viral a register of public culture, so vital in the quest to recover a legible world. The semiotics of popular accounting, in short, turn out to be integral to the figuration of self, community, and society. It is to this, their constitutive dimension—focusing on the citizen-victim, criminal geography, and vernacular accounting—that we devote the rest of our excursion into Statistics, South Africa.

Statistics, South Africa, in Three Dimensions:

Constituting the Citizen-Victim

The currency accrued by victim surveys across the world over the past decades, it has been said, is symptomatic of a shift of attention in criminology from perpetrators to those whom they harm (Fattah 1986; Maguire and Pointing 1988). In 1987 an International Crime Victims Survey was proposed by the Council of Europe; its standardized version, now regularly carried out in over fifty countries, is the basis for the South African one on which we drew earlier (SSA 2014), itself the latest in a series that began in 1998[46] in the wake of the Truth and Reconciliation Commission. The method, which involves questioning a large sample of respondents about their experience of a range of felonies over a stipulated time period, is said by its advocates to enhance official statistics, especially by casting light on the "dark figure of crime": offenses, like sexual abuse and assault, routinely underreported, most of all by the poor and the powerless (Banks 1997, 11). These claims have been given wide credence, although some critics have insisted that subjective recollection is *always* unreliable, that this instrument is *"not* ideally suited" for collecting incidents of an intimate sort, and that it may actually register lower rates than do police statistics with respect to such things as rape (ISS 2004, 126; see above, p. 150). Methodology aside, victim surveys also raise philosophical and political issues for those who resist being cast in the passive voice, even when they suffer violence. Witness the protagonist in Njabulo Ndebele's remarkable *The Cry of Winnie Mandela* (2003): "I want to reclaim my right to be wounded," she insists, "without my pain having to turn me into an example of woman as victim."

For those who *do* espouse them, however, these surveys are much more than merely an improved technology of measurement. They are part of a worldwide politics of pain and suffering, a politics around which a global movement has grown up: it lobbies for victims against an international "establishment" that allegedly discriminates against them, excluding them from the criminal justice process for being "emotional and vindictive" (van Dijk 1996, 1; Camerer 1997, 1).[47] The instrument itself owes a great deal to market research, which it closely resembles. To the degree that the cultural practices of late modernity define citizens as consumers, casualties of crime seem most aptly depicted as customers ill-served by government *qua* service provider. For advocates of "victimology," this consumer perspective is crucial to rethinking received, *etatist* approaches to law and disorder. "Get tough" policies have had little success in curbing lawlessness, they note; evidence from across the world suggests that police resources are better spent protecting those at risk (Camerer 1997, 1; Farrell and Pease 2001). But even more than addressing state policy, these surveys aim to be vehicles of popular empowerment. "By shifting the focus of the inquiry from the offender," say Camerer *et al.* (1998, 1), they "provide information which enables victims themselves to take preventive action against further victimization." *Victims themselves* turns out to be the key phrase here.

Displaying a generically neoliberal suspicion of government, the victim movement has been wary, from the first, of having its cause hijacked as an alibi for ever-harsher "law and order" legislation. It accuses the state of "stealing" crime from those who suffer it and of redefining it as an offense against itself. "Victims," proponents maintain, "are victims in their own right, . . . an end in themselves" (Camerer *et al.* 1998, 2). Activists seek to mobilize civil society behind "victims' charters," demanding restitution from ruling regimes for their failure to ensure the safety of citizens.[48] This stress on self-advocacy resonates with a more general tendency to displace politics into the domain of the law, to reduce it to redress and punishment (W. Brown 1995, 27), and to mobilize it for purposes of "class actions," itself a term with considerable semantic overload (Comaroff and Comaroff 2006b, 2003). Victim surveys, then, are themselves caught up in broader historical forces that are reshaping governance, public culture, and politics at a point, critically, where the risk-bearing subject meets the right-bearing citizen.

In the epistemic vision that underlies victim surveys, "each member of society," whether or not they have been attacked, "is an indirect or vicarious victim of crime" (Glanz 1989, 1)—either a past victim, a present victim, or a potential victim, but, one way or another, always-already interpolated as victim. While their results may inform prevention strategies, these surveys, unlike most official crime counts, are directed primarily at the public, being widely circulated, often in sensationalist form, by the print, electronic, and digital media. As such, they have become one of many mechanisms—from community safety associations, through online websites and listservs, to graphic ads for home security—that encourage citizens to see themselves as prey. In this manner, too, they create what they purport to measure. As a wealth of evidence confirms, South Africans tend to identify themselves ever more in terms of vulnerability to violation. And they organize on this basis too, coming together to "become one another's safety zones" (above, 1.1). Support groups mobilize around rape victims, neighborhood watches form in the wake of attacks, petitions circulate in the name of the injured, street justice acts on behalf of the unprotected; AfriForum, a conservative Afrikaner civic action group, for example, has organized a national campaign to have the murder of white farmers prioritized as a "unique crime," claiming—against all evidence to the contrary—that they are victims of a racially motivated "genocide" (du Preez 2013, 188–89). Even felons see themselves as casualties: "Criminality, you have made me your victim!" declared an inmate at a spirited hip-hop-and-poetry performance inside Cape Town's Pollsmoor prison in 2004.[49] Similarly, an article in *The Big Issue*, organ of the city's "marginalized and unemployed" (see above, 2.2), described youths in custody as "helpless animals, dumb and resigned behind their bars" (Kretzmann 2004, 17).

Victim surveys published and publicized in South Africa to date offer insight into the unintended ways in which enumeration tacitly implies evaluation. The results of the national survey of 2003, for example, were released so as to have maximum impact on public discussion in the run-up to the general election of 2004, in which crime was a highly emotive issue. They received prominent coverage. The media stressed that, although lawlessness had *not* gone up since 1998, the population at large felt less safe than it had five years earlier.[50] But not equally so. Their reports gave graphic, color-coded accounts of different people living with different levels of fear: "Race Groups' Views on Safety Differ," declared a typical headline.[51] Surveys of this sort, in contrast to official statistics, describe victimization, and the anxieties to which it gives rise, in terms of hard-lined categories of race, gender, age, and location, thereby obscuring the endemic ambiguities and intersections along their many edges. While they reveal persisting inequities in risk, these measures also reify long-standing signs of difference at just the time when identities, and relations among them, appear to be under reconstruction. A widely reported study by Ted Leggett (2004b), for example, asserted that "Coloureds [in Cape Town were] twice as likely to be murdered" and were much more likely to be jailed than were blacks, whites, and Indians; his evidence was based on numbers from the Cape Flats, a terrain on which subjectivities and identities tend to be more or less labile, being heavily inflected by shifting patterns of class distinction. The director general of labor in the Western Cape, who found the study "disturbing," remarked that it lent itself to the "demoniz[ation] and isolat[ion] of a whole group of South Africans."[52] Not just one group, either:

victim surveys, in South Africa, refigure the racial landscape in the crimo-genic language of predator and prey.

Undoubtedly, victim surveys expand received understandings of criminal-ity. Undoubtedly, too, they offer useful commentary on official counts, some-times by confirming them, sometimes by pointing to important patterns of variance, sometimes by calling them into question. But sometimes too, being complex *discursive* formations, they have effects quite opposite to those they intend. As Wendy Brown (1995, 21) argues, efforts to protect those with injury-forming identities may entrench the very thing they seek to counter: by showing who is most susceptible to attack, profiling *reinforces* risk by reify-ing and reproducing categories of victim—and, *ipso facto,* their vulnerability to violation. In so doing, moreover, such efforts are as likely to instill fear and heighten insecurity as to meliorate it, this being an ironic underside of liberal-ization, of the "responsibilization" of citizens for their own safety. This is why politics, nowadays, hinges so centrally on recognition, through civil action and claims to entitlement, for the relatively disadvantaged; why the disempowered are less a class in or for themselves than claimants in class actions; why social movements, formed out of shared disability or pain, pursue rights to reverse wrongs. Citizenship here is defined as a *process* of personal fulfilment, in which the rational avoidance of danger, resting on incessant calculation, looms large (Rose and Miller 1992, 201). It is this, in major part, that accounts for the fixa-tion on crime stats. But there is a contradiction here. While victim movements seek to prevent the state from "hijacking" crime, they also hold it accountable for the safety of citizens and for securing the sort of society in which self-care and freedom of choice might flourish—while, at the same time, casting doubt both on the efficacy of "get tough" enforcement strategies and on the right of government to a monopoly over the management of criminal justice.

In South Africa, this contradiction takes on a particularly acute local flavor. In regularly calling for more effective policing, its citizens insist that the state make good on its mandate to ensure the security of persons, property, and publics—a mandate, many would argue, rightly or wrongly, that it has failed to fulfill. Hence the mantra that the fledgling democracy, indeed the nation it-self, is mortally endangered by disorder; that it is time to bring back the death penalty; that the administration ought to come down much harder, much more punitively, on crime and corruption; that the flirtation with human rights and community policing has proven a dismal failure. Hence, simulta-neously, the widespread resort to extralegal protection and popular justice on the part of those who see themselves as always-already victims. Small wonder, then, that the state oscillates between outsourcing responsibility for law and order to its subjects and turning to increasingly militarized enforcement and public order policing in the name of emergency, under whose legitimating cloak executive authority easily overrides civil liberties. The line everywhere between neoliberal governance and fascism-lite is paper thin.

In this indelicate balance, the victim has a double valence. She or he is claimed both by government as it conducts its "war on crime" and by civil activists who seek self-determination and recompense, mainly from the state, for the injured (van Dijk 1996, 123); also by "vigilantes," who mete out informal justice to protect those left to fend for themselves. The public, meanwhile, becomes an aggregate of the imperiled, among whom identity and difference are defined largely in terms of pain and trauma. And entities like community and neighborhood—constructs with overrated power and underspecified social content (1.1, 1.2, 2.4)—are given fresh life in the pursuit of order, safety, and personal well-being, the stand-in, in the brave neo world, for a social contract.

Criminal Geography

If victim surveys reduce lawlessness to the social demographics of injury, geographical information systems, or GIS, map its coordinates onto a virtual sociology of space. In essence, GIS uses shifting areal imaging to overlay one slice of data onto another, thus to make visible a composite picture of previously unseen associations. Focusing primarily on the profiling of "targets" by documenting criminal incidents and offenders' patterns of movement, it has increasingly incorporated "the victim" as a category of analysis, reading the significance of *location*, for instance, from repeat cases of assault. As this implies, the two techniques may complement one another: one charts patterns from an "objective," external vantage, the other from subjective experience. For Rose and Miller (1992, 202), this sort of complementarity is an outworking of the regulated autonomy of neoliberal polities, in which a stress on self-assertive citizenship exists alongside mechanisms for "governing at a distance." But victim surveys and GIS may also be seen as potentially contradictory, offsetting modes of reduction: the former, claim their critics, ignore structural determinations by privileging personal hurt; the latter, goes the counter, fetishizes a method that generates depersonalized information whose explanatory powers are often overvalued.

In an era of "intelligence-led" policing (Read 2001, xxi; above, 1.2), the expansive use of GIS underlines the prominence of quantifacts not just in smart forensics and criminal investigation. They are also critical lexemes in the flow of communication about law-making, law-breaking, and law-enforcement across the dispersed agencies—state, public, private, corporate, academic—whose collaborative "partnerships" oversee the administration of everyday life. In addition to the data they carry, numbers circulate as indices of the nature and efficacy of criminal justice—and, even more, of governance itself. Where victim surveys have been called upon as much to challenge state institutions as to aid and abet them, GIS is a synoptic instrument (Obermeyer 1995, 81) most useful in the centralized management of disorder. It has also been deployed in the development of techniques of surveillance-from-a-distance, like CCTV, the advent of which has raised questions across the world about privacy and its violation (Cho 1998, 162). In 2004, for example, the announcement that new British crime-fighting initiatives would include the satellite tracking of serial offenders prompted at least one journalist to remind the prime minister of the Human Rights Act;[53] post-WikiLeaks and Edward Snowden, tapping into personal lives and communications at the behest of government has become a major object of public concern. In South Africa, the use of GIS was largely limited, at first, to mapping incidents reported to the SAPS; but enthusiasm for it has always been marked. When, in 2001, the minister of safety and security told the country that it had been introduced at 340 police stations, he spoke passionately of how it would "greatly enhance . . . operational planning."[54] Since then, it has been variously deployed in other domains, including service delivery—which, as we saw in 1.2, is a critical site of both political struggle and public order policing.

A virtue of GIS, it has been said, is its ability to "influence people" by translating statistical analysis into accessible visual displays (Hirschfield and Bowers 2001, 6). It is also held to reveal otherwise-undetectable patterns of risk for various species of offense by situating crimogenic hot spots within their wider physical locale/s. But how exactly *does* an elaborate mapping of the distribution of lawlessness advance our understanding of its rates and incidences? Ken Pease (2000, 228–29), reflecting on the British scene, has expressed concern that the ready legibility and aesthetic seductiveness of GIS, plus a measure of technophilia, might have inflated its presumptive utility at the expense of other ways of approaching crime. Mapping belies the fact that victimization is *not* always structured along spatial lines, he argues. Nor does it capture the multidimensional characteristics of those who share anything *other* than location: students and immigrant populations, for example, and those resident in sheltered accommodation and mobile homes all share elevated risk but tend not to cluster geographically (229). In short, the assertion that GIS enables information to be "seen at a glance" is misleading. Victimization and the experience of injury remain the naked truth that GIS *ought* to be able to reveal and explain. But it has distinct limitations in respect of both.

Pease has hit on a critical problem here. The manner in which GIS treats space, tacitly attributing causality to it, does *not* derive from a principled criminological theory, statistical or otherwise. Nor does it grow out of hypotheses about the forces and factors, the underlying conditions or proximate circumstances, that produce lawlessness. Methodologically driven, it is a repertoire of *techniques* whose object is to make crimogenic patterns so plain to see as to appear self-explanatory. But space is *always*, in the first instance, an effect of human practice, both material and meaningful. As Merleau-Ponty (1962) and others (e.g., Soja 1989) have argued, it does not exist, in unmediated form, as a phenomenon with determinations of its own. Consequently, spatial configurations cannot, in themselves, reveal hidden causes, however well they are mapped; hence, despite the optimism that surrounds GIS, and the inordinate explanatory weight that it has been accorded (see, e.g., Robertshaw *et al.* 2001, 68; Louw *et al.* 1998, 20–21), police in the United Kingdom and elsewhere have been disappointed with the insights and intelligence it has actually yielded (Pease 2000, 228). Still, both it and victim surveys continue to be deployed widely by police, who *presume* their utility, perhaps because they translate their data into categories that render microsociological complexity into a logos of legible zones—inner cities, suburbs, exurbs, townships, informal settlements, slums, and the like—that are easily identified, labeled, and rationally managed, zones whose aesthetico-moral attributes are readily differentiated, tautologically, by their crime stats. Recalibrating these zones by reducing their ratio of violence and vulnerability, of waste and value, has become central to enforcement strategies; *vide* the forms of hyperpolicing mobilized to protect high-status urban enclaves from invasion by the uncouth and unruly (above, 1.2; cf. Caldeira 2000, 213ff., on São Paulo). These managerial strategies *appear* to yield results—which accounts for the enthusiastic claims made for them—but they tend less to *reduce* criminality than to *redistribute* it, quietly pushing it away from "hot spots" in high-status city-center and suburban loci to poorer, less-protected places, precisely those whose populations are "dis-counted."

If maps of state mark out the space of the nation, GIS "hot spots" plot the limits of its sovereign reach, making visible the criminal specter, the counternation, lurking within. But the panoptic eye here is ambiguous. It is *not* simply that of regulatory authority or ruling regimes. A technology that indicts as it reveals, its dispassionate gaze may also be deployed by private interests for purposes of policing, scientific research, commerce, critique, insurgent politics, and much else. It is as available to organized crime as it is to the more or less dis/organized agencies that fight it. Therein, arguably, lies the persuasiveness of GIS data and victim surveys as politico-aesthetic, evidentiary, and/or didactic statements for those who conjure with them. This makes a broader theoretical point: if these technologies are taken to be instruments of "government at a distance," which they have been, what exactly is *meant* by government? Foucauldians, eager to avoid reifying the state, gloss it as the "shifting alliances between diverse authorities in projects to govern a multitude of facts of economic activity, social life and individual conduct" (Rose and Miller 1992, 174). But surely this fudges the effects of technicization and privatization on the *limits* of that governance, on *misalliance* among those diverse authorities. Technicization and privatization also force open wedges, and reveal contradictions, in fields of power and projects of regulation. In the upshot, the concept of "governmentality," as we have said before, seems less than adequate in disclosing how technologies like GIS serve as—polymorphous, often antipodal—instruments of politics and world-making.

Take an instance of the deployment of GIS cartography in the South African media just before the millennium—years, recall, that witnessed a panic-inducing spike in violent lawlessness. The double-page spread published by the *Saturday Star* in late 1999 under the banner headline "Pinpointing Our Crime Hotspots"[55] featured a large map of Gauteng Province, which centers on Johannesburg, which, as we have noted, has long been associated with terrifying criminality, recently reprised in nonfictional reminiscences of life in the postapartheid city (e.g., Cohen 2004; Gevisser 2014). The *Saturday Star* spread was embellished with graphics of a gun, prone bodies, an abandoned infant, and a pair of cuffed hands. Box inserts tabulated figures for the "top-ten hit parade": the policing areas with the highest concentration of serious felonies. The text began by situating—if, as we have seen, erroneously—the reader on this chart of terror: "Tourists and locals alike are familiar with Gauteng's reputation as South Africa's crime capital. . . . But there are certain areas where you are more likely to be the victim of a specific type of crime than others."

Here it becomes clear how statistical renderings of "real-life" lawlessness intersect with other genres of representation, giving rise to the total crime fact. The communicative powers of GIS are extended for maximum impact, being overlaid by a montage of melodramatic pictorial images drawn from a standard repertoire. The visuals are framed by captions that sport the grit-and-flash of classic crime reporting, leaving the text to reinforce the effect by spelling out the implications of the map for the reader-as-potential-target. Together, they illuminate how so-called risk-reducing data triggers fear by tying victimhood to identity. "Women living in Johannesburg, Soweto, and Vaalrand should exercise extra caution because in these areas between 43 and 216 women are raped for every 100,000," declared the text. "If you live in Pretoria or Johannesburg, ensure you have a good security system or a fierce dog, because the two cities are equally susceptible to housebreaking." Finally, "[i]f you are able to dodge hijackers, be careful where you park your car: avoid Pretoria and Johannesburg's city center . . ." and so on. The report garnered considerable attention. In Mmabatho, in the North West Province—where we were doing research at the time and where the *Saturday Star* has a large readership—it prompted one Tswana family to consider bringing their daughter back from college in Gauteng. This sort of "authoritative" intervention, like terror alerts issued by the US Department of Homeland Security after 9/11, is a common feature of official communication in the risk society. It announces a serious and probable threat that, while graphically highlighting vulnerable people and places, remains agonizingly vague. Risk, as the word itself suggests, is *terminally* uncertain, "both real and unreal" (cf. Beck 1992, 29). Like the criminal specter that haunts the global economy, it is everywhere imminent yet nowhere easily pinned down.

Filtered through the technical aura of GIS maps, as in the *Saturday Star*, risk avoidance is written in a register calculated, literally, to induce permanent dread: the hapless addressee is asked to ponder the odds of survival in a city like Johannesburg, where, it is asserted, simply being female is to be chronically endangered, where owning property requires a fierce dog, where driving a car invites a joust with jackers. But the value that accrues to these maps as they circulate, as they invoke apprehensive subjects and publics, is also configured by a wider social context: one in which violence has become a currency of politics and of economic enterprise; in which government both abhors disorder, yet uses it for its own ends; in which citizens are at once repelled and fascinated by brute lawlessness; in which other urgent social issues, like poverty and ill health, are eclipsed, making it more likely that law-breaking serves as a routine mode of production, circulation, representation, mobilization. The publication of evocative cartographies of crime also owes much to efforts to devolve the business of policing, efforts that aim—in the commonplace cliché of our times, here uttered by a community-policing spokesman—to get individuals and neighborhoods "to take responsibility."[56] Yet as we have said, these efforts seem to achieve precisely the opposite. They fuel insistent calls on government to act with sovereign authority in treating crime "like the national emergency it is," calls that constantly return to statistics to substantiate their cause.[57] Either this, or they persuade cynical citizens to take the state at its word and cut to the chase: to set up their own means of enforcement (see 2.4).

Trauma Testimonies and Mythostats; or, Figuring Popular Experience

Whatever else they might be, crime rates, we have argued, are a psychic barometer, a gauge of new truths in the "great outdoors" of the postcolony (1.3). They measure the fall of old lines of separation, old securities, old geographies. And the rise of new patterns of engagement, integration, circulation, redistribution, and insecurity—legitimate and otherwise. But how exactly *do* they feature in popular discourse? What prompted us to contradict Nelson Mandela in asserting that, far from rendering it alien, numbers give substance to experience?

A telling statistic from South Africa circa 2004 was that 58 percent of its metropolitan population—49 percent overall—had discussed crime in the prior two weeks (ISS 2004, 49–50). Narratives of lawlessness rival other topics of everyday talk, cutting across lines of difference: testimonies to transcendent truths, they root credibility in the heft of personal experience. This endless retailing of mundane melodramas seems part of an ongoing effort to find the general in particular events, to wrest some kind of order from cacophony and chaos. Tokens of a type, they evince several common features. One notable technique is to distill circumstantial evidence into recognizable "fact" by enumerating incidences. Not only does this signal plausibility through the appearance of precision, but it also imparts primary value to second- or thirdhand happenings, translating a multiplicity of accounts into a shared subjective currency. The play between quantity and quality involves a humdrum hermeneutic that spells out the social proportions of risk and uncertainty, like in this story, told us in June 2000 by a Tswana woman in her midseventies:

> Taxis have become very dangerous here in Mafikeng.[58] My daughter had a terrifying experience last November: she hailed a [minibus] taxi that was traveling to town. By the time it got to the main road, she was the only passenger. . . . The driver, who was drunk, turned sharply in the wrong direction and picked up speed. When L. called out to him, he pointed a gun over

his shoulder and kept going. Luckily, he was forced to slow down behind a donkey cart, and she leapt out, rolling down a bank at the side of the road. She was badly bruised and lost her purse. This is now the third case I have heard of recently in which women have had trouble in taxis. We really can't travel around the way we used to in this town, even to wakes or funerals.

This testimonial evokes the complicity of the listener by invoking several recognizable tropes. It begins with a fact for which the tale is evidence: the danger of traveling in taxis, itself iconic of the heightened mobility of black South Africans since liberation—and liberalization. Then come the indices of identification-by-intimate-association: the credibility of the speaker as witness and the veracity of the account derive from the relationship between the narrator and the victim, in this case mother and daughter. In the process of detailing events encountered at one degree of separation, reported speech enters the realm of shared experience. "We"—black, petit-bourgeois, peri-urban women—are meant to feel terror as an ordinary ride becomes a nightmare journey, calamity just the flick of a drunken trigger finger away. And so the story produces its own subjects and sensations of the real, its own culture and sociology of vicarious victimhood. Her experience is *our* experience: "we" are *all* at risk in an inadequately secured public sphere; we are *all* victims of taxi assault; we have *all* lost our freedom to violence.

Tales of this kind are less about uniquely horrifying events than about the "fact" that such things have become commonplace. The incident in the taxi invoked other instances. Comparability overrides singularity. "This is now the third case I have heard of recently" turns a random occurrence into a condition of *public* being and suffering. A letter to the *Cape Times* from a returned émigré, written during the moratorium on statistics, deploys a similar semiotics of (ac)counting: "In the 12 weeks I have been back . . . I have personally 'encountered' 10 criminal acts against friends and acquaintances. . . . At nearly one incident per week these statistics are mind-bending. If this is happening in my relatively affluent and sheltered life, I can only imagine what life must be like in less protected areas."[59] Again we see how the idiom of calculation makes visible the putative limits of order, and thereby gains purchase on a population united in its sense of vulnerability. Street statistics are a means of embracing otherwise-unimaginable sectors of society ("less protected") into a people in search of security. The writer computes a homemade victim count, multiplying his "personal encounters" tenfold, thus assimilating thirdhand incidents to firsthand experience. The numbers here are mobilized to make evident a hidden truth—the "real" pervasiveness of the criminal specter—about which "the public" has a right to know. But the manner of its manufacture merely inflates the menace. Here, as in the taxi story, quantity turns into a qualifact: that the nation is deeply at risk. In this day and age, the most fungible evidence, about criminality or anything else, comes from victims. "How many more innocent people have to die before the government will admit that its so-called law and order is a sick joke?" wrote Patsy Tyler to the *Cape Argus* in July 2003.[60] "Stand up and be counted," she urged the public. Let all who had suffered crimes submit their accounts. Were the media then to publish them simultaneously, such that "every story [was] told," the "comprehensive list" of offenses would be so large—by contrast to the dodgy official statistics—that it would "shame [the] government in the eyes of the world." And, perhaps, shame it into action.

But the popular calculus of crime also works by magnifying single, epic events into mythostats. These are events that, in their singularity, come to signify collective being and trauma—and, in turn, give rise to the most terrifying statistic of all, namely, that *everyone* has intimate familiarity with one or more persons who have suffered brutal attack. Norm-defying violence tends to be a necessary condition for an incident to have this sovereign effect. Other social considerations also add uncommon sign value to particular episodes, such as their occurrence, for example, in relatively enclosed, relatively crime-free populations. One such example is the slaying of fifty-two-year-old Motlhabane Makolomakwa in the village of Matlonyane, home of the *tokoloshe*-affiliated Sejakes (2.2). Known as "Ten-Ten" after a famed soccer star, he was the most prominent resident of his impoverished community. A successful farmer, former government employee, and chair of the local "tribal council," Ten-Ten had also sponsored a football team. In 1994 five youths hacked and burned him to death in his own truck. They insisted that he had killed their fathers and turned them into zombies, this having become a common explanation for why some prospered while others, especially young males, remained jobless. Found guilty, the "boys" were each sentenced to twenty years.[61] The murder and High Court trial, which were avidly covered by local media, riveted the Tswana-speaking population of the province. They made plain just how much the division between young and old had been exacerbated by fears of escalating crime. Older citizens returned repeatedly to the incident as evidence of a loss of communal order and, predictably, respect for authority, on the part of "the children." For them, it underlined the virtues of "traditional" discipline. Young men, on the other hand, took the case to illustrate the negative effects of the monopolization, by their seniors, of the means of producing wealth, often by dangerous, illegitimate means. Among both, it hardened lines of distrust and inscrutability across generations and fed into intergenerational conflict.

A similarly singular, epic incident, also productive of wounded identities, occurred in January 2003, when nine men were murdered at Sizzlers, a male massage parlor in Sea Point, on Cape Town's salubrious Atlantic seaboard. This neighborhood is as sociologically, culturally, and geographically distant from Matlonyane as it is possible to imagine. Again, the violence was terrifying. The victims had their throats cut before they were shot in the head.[62] The site, scale, and bloodiness of the killing pointed to a hate crime. The Gay and Lesbian Equality Project of South Africa quickly became involved, its representatives meeting with the assistant national police commissioner. The SAPS reported a huge response to the request for leads, and unusually, sex workers and gay organizations "joined hands" with the ANC in a memorial service.[63] While the case remained uniquely distressing for the sheer scale of its brutality, its meaning grew murky as the cops came to be convinced that the motives for the crime were more routine: that it was drug related, perhaps, or the aggravated consequence of a robbery.[64] Yet the atrocity retained its mythic proportions, entering public discourse as an index of heightened risk to *all* gays in post-apartheid South Africa. Just how such episodes generate terrors of their own became clear in June 2004, when the Gay and Lesbian Alliance lodged a complaint against a website that, among other offensive statements, said—with obvious reference to the massacre—that homosexuals should be "Sizzled."[65]

This case makes plain how epic crimes may intensify a sense of citizenship, even humanity, by playing on vectors of identification and antipathy. Mass mediation is integral to the process, converting extraordinary incidents into a *generic* perception of vulnerability. Those incidents, as they are narrated over and over again, come to appear *at once* utterly unusual and horrifically commonplace: you, I, anyone, could be next. As Derrida (2002, 248) once observed, each murder may be *"singular, thus infinite and incommensurable"* (original emphasis). But ironically, its capacity to bespeak the general, to instill a feeling of common predicament, derives from that very singularity. At the same time, mythic crimes signify by means that go beyond mere identification or transference. In his or her slaying, the socially marked victim is rendered sacrificial. She or he stands metonymically for other members of existing or emergent categories, categories that take on (re)new(ed) sociological salience and affective solidarity in response to the violation: women, children, gays, youth, blacks, whites, farmers, property owners, the homeless, the nation. As it opens up new channels of communication, moreover, the forfeiture of life serves as a game-changing indictment of the powers that be, one that wills acknowledgment. And more. While the anguished rhetoric that surrounds such acts of slaughter often depicts them as "senseless," it tends also to cast them as somehow meaningful and salvific: with their innocent blood, the dead redeem their kind, making evident the inequities of protection, privilege, care, and humanity that they continue to suffer.

Particularly galvanizing in this regard was the kidnaping of Leigh Matthews, twenty-one-year-old daughter of Sharon and Rob Matthews, a Johannesburg businessman, in July 2004. In South Africa, many persons, young and old, male and female, go missing each year. Yet this case mobilized an "overwhelming" reaction from people across the land.[66] Why?

What made this incident so compelling was not merely the media melodrama or the voyeuristic curiosity aroused by the private suffering of the attractive and the affluent. Neither was it the just appeal of its blond victim, pictured again and again in a satin ball gown, on the poignant brink of womanhood. It was the way in which these things, occurring at the intersection of race and class, came together to make the case seem at once exceptional yet indicative of the state of the nation-as-trauma. Ms. Matthews—like Inge Lotz (p. 93), "touched by an angel"[67]—was singled out by social circumstance: experts opined that her kidnappers had probably researched her father's income.[68] Yet, as *You* magazine noted on its cover, "not only [the] rich" are targets. "*You* could be a victim."[69] The dialectic between the singular and the ordinary at work in the image of Leigh Matthews is evident, too, from an account in a national weekly: "Hundreds of South African families," like the Matthews, "are tormented by the anguish of not knowing when their missing loved one might be found," it read. "More than 1800 adults and nearly 1300 children were reported missing . . . last year."[70] Missing, but not kidnaped. There is a wealth of difference between abductions, runaways, and kidnappings. A wealth of difference and a difference of wealth. Child abductions have long been prevalent in poor communities all over the country. They seldom merit media attention, a point forcibly made by several black callers to talk shows in Cape Town at the time; one community network, Bush Radio, refused to cover the event for this reason. As Rebecca Davis recently put it, speaking more generally of the relative value of life in South Africa, where murderers are "instantly presum[ed to be] black strangers" and "middle-class white bodies are routinely granted more reverence and dignity in death."[71] The discrepancy is underscored in Michael Williams's perspicacious detective thriller *The Eighth*

Man (2002), which follows the parallel destinies and deaths, in the Western Cape, of two young people separated by race and class. By contrast to those of affluent white youths, Williams's story tells us—again, in a context in which crime fiction and everyday reality intersect (see 1.3)—the bodies of impoverished young blacks often still do not count. In the United States, which has seen a disturbing number of African Americans killed by police, this point is powerfully echoed nowadays under the sign "Black Lives Matter."

Leigh Matthews was immediately set apart from those faceless victims. Her case had proved a challenge, said the head of the Missing Persons Bureau, "because kidnaping for ransom [i]s not . . . common" in South Africa.[72] Of course, this depends on what, precisely, "common" is taken to mean. SAPS figures indicate that in 2004, the year in which Ms. Matthews was seized, there were 3,004 kidnappings across the country; in 2014 there were 4,117, the total for the past eleven years being 34,017.[73] Relative to, say, carjacking (itself *not* a high-incidence crime, as we saw earlier, with 11,221 cases nationwide in 2014), its rate has always been low. Nonetheless, a spokesman for a corporation that markets "risk assessment" and "crisis management" across the world, and so has an interest in inflating fear, suggests that it has become a "brazen industry" in search of quick turnover.[74] This corporation, which trains wealthy, nervous South Africans in "pre-incident" and anti-kidnap techniques—its courses are covered by ransom insurance—insists that the vast majority of those taken are returned alive.

Not in this case. A cash ransom was delivered by Mr. Matthews,[75] but his daughter was not returned. As the days went by, a public coalesced visibly around the incident. Police set up a twenty-four-hour hotline to deal with the "flood of information" coming in; hundreds of South Africans, including many abroad, posted messages of support on a special website.[76] Strangers in the street, in elevators, and in taxis exchanged information across the lines of gender, generation, class, color. The tragic discovery of her body eleven days later drew forth an outpouring of emotion: "Country mourns for Leigh," intoned a typical headline, above a photograph of a diverse group of fellow students signing a book of sympathy on the private university campus from which she was snatched.[77] A petition was launched on the Internet calling on government to reinstate the death penalty: "Do it for Leigh Matthews," it read,[78] this being one of several "landmark" murders, especially femicides,[79] to have elicited demands for capital punishment in the name of the victim (see 2.4). Nelson Mandela, the state president, and representatives of all major political parties offered public condolences. "Leigh Matthews was a flower, the lifeblood of the nation," said an ANC spokesman. "We can't unite . . . if these sick elements are in our midst."[80] But it is precisely around events like these that the nation *does* unite: hyperreal, dehumanizing events that become the measure of a traumatized citizenry transcending its differences, if only for an instant. "Something like this could happen to any of us," wrote the Matthews family to the *Sunday Times;* "we need to come together as a community, as a nation, and take a stand against such wickedness."[81] Obscured here is the place of this tragedy in a larger pattern of lawlessness, one heavily inflected by difference and inequality, one in which, as we have seen, rates of injury remain heavily concentrated among the black urban poor. The fact that the perpetrator, Donovan Moodley, was a young fellow student and son of a Baptist minister—not, as widely anticipated in the media, a Nigerian gangster—merely adds to the irony.[82]

Crime statistics, then, count and discount the quality of life, and the state of the nation, in a less-than-legible world. In making the singular into the plural and *vice versa*, they give the lie to the conventional, bloodless sociology of dis/order. Therein lies their alchemy: in that and, concomitantly, in the capacity to turn the abstract into the affect laden, thereby to mobilize and rationalize collective action.[83] And, also, to fuel a politics of indignation. "It is our country and our right to be able to live free of fear," said that same Internet petition in the name of Ms. Matthews. This species of politics, filtered through and magnified by social media, does little in and of itself to address the structural conditions that underlie the criminal economy. Or the ecology of risk to which it gives rise. Or the passions that drive it. *Per contra*, in reproducing a culture of fear, and a sense of incipient, sacrificial victimhood, it tends to draw attention away from those conditions, focusing instead on the alarming immediacy of their effects.

Coda: On the Quality of Quantity

In Lewis Nkosi's play *The Rhythm of Violence* (1964), the main action takes place in a makeshift police station in the Johannesburg City Hall, overlooking a square in which a mass protest meeting is in progress. The crowd yells,

"Freedom in our lifetime!"
Jan ([a young, white policeman] nervously): "How many of us are here?"
Piet (his senior): "Two hundred men at the ready to shoot . . ."

Jan (more nervous still): "You think that number is enough?"
A voice from the square, across the dialogue: "Can they rule by the gun for-
ever?" (3)

In this brilliant cameo, Nkosi captures a telling moment in the tortured history
of numbers in South Africa. Critical episodes in that history were, are still, fig-
ured in stark fractions, the proportions of which have not changed very much.
The brutal percentages of apartheid—13 percent of the people with 87 percent
of the land—have morphed into new, but still racialized, metrics of inequality: grossly uneven rates of victimization, a close correlation of poverty with
violence and disease, and the like. Now, as before, politics crystallizes in ratios,
and not just with respect to crime. Few issues loomed as large in the national
debate over the gravity of AIDS than the statistics that purported to measure
the pandemic; similar arguments have surrounded assessments of the extent,
and the implications, of unemployment. This, too, is evidence for one of our
central contentions: that, in their very abstraction, numbers make real phenomena otherwise beyond the grasp of human experience. But in so doing,
they produce new indeterminacies. And P/politics in both the upper- and the
lowercase.

These politics, we have argued, are more complex than is implied by sociological theory of the sort that sees numbers as autonomic agents of abstraction
and extraction, commensuration and regulation, or of the conversion, without remainder, of qualities into quantities. Neither are they illuminated by the
brute association of statistics with biopolitics or governmentality. Quantifacts
are polymorphous constructions that yield meaning, value, and the stuff of
contestation in diverse ways precisely *because* they enjoy privileged status as a
presumptive means of producing objective, value-free knowledge. When they
fail over and over again to do this, they are seen as having been corrupted—by
virtue of either venality or ineptitude—and hence as falling short of being the
transparent, truth-bearing media that they *ought* to be, *can* be, were *intended*
to be. As governance is reduced largely to service delivery, and as citizenship
comes to hinge on the recognition of rights and the provision of security, crime
rates become the prime currency of the realm: a prime index of dis/order
and in/effective administration, a prime measure of the rule of law and the
il/legitimacy of the state, a prime symptom of progress in redressing the legacy
of colonialism, and a prime suspect in efforts to detect a politics of bad faith.
Whatever they may or may not actually measure, those numbers are the con-

stitutive elements of a mundane communicative practice across more or less dispersed sites of governance, politics, civic life, and sociality. They provide a lexicon with which to traffic between the unknowable and the explicable, the coincidental and the calculable, contingency and causality.

As this makes plain, crime statistics are uncommonly good to think with, which, in part, is why enumeration is not limited to state bureaucracies or even to those who count in the public interest. But as we have seen, they are no more capable of eliminating uncertainty than is any other form of calculation. No forensic advance—or, for that matter, honest arithmetic—can dispel the paradox of distrust that clings to these numbers; neither will the avid telling and retelling of horror stories. By making thirdhand happenings into first-person sensations, popular criminal quantifacts both define and multiply the perception of vulnerability, reiterating the algorithms of risk and apprehension that make trauma hard to transcend. This, we reiterate, may explain why such anger is evinced by evidence that South Africa is *not* as exceptional in its crimogenic profile as it may seem. At the same time, numbers do not mean the same, experientially, everywhere across the social spectrum: recall one last time that, statistically speaking, fear of crime and the risk of falling victim to it do not correlate, that they tend toward the inverse. It is also the case that the victims who count most, who escape "becoming a statistic" by attaining mythic status, are seldom those for whom suffering is part of their ordinary existence. But it is such epic felonies, like the Makolomakwa murder, the Leigh Matthews kidnapping, and the Sizzlers massacre, that become iconic of collective identities, of publics, of a nation said to be sinking into a sea of violent incivility. Therein lies the horror from which social order is to be wrested. Therein lie the perverse politics and the peculiar productivity of lawlessness. Therein lies the criminal anthropology of the neoliberated South Africa.

CHAPTER 2.4

OUTSOURCING JUSTICE, PRIVATIZING PROTECTION
Practices of Popular Sovereignty

The transition to democracy in South Africa, as we have seen, opened up a social and moral vacuum in the national consciousness, a vacuum into which the fear of violent disorder, real and imagined, seeded itself deeply. Many scared, scarred citizens, as they lost faith in the ability or the will of government to enforce the law (Ballard and Muntingh 2012), came increasingly to essay the need for alternative modes of enforcement. Wealthy whites, who felt imprisoned in their heavily secured homes and abandoned by a police force that had previously made their protection a high priority, were especially quick to arrive at this view. But residents of poor, largely black neighborhoods, which had even less police coverage, began steadily to share it. For them, community justice seemed the only way to achieve a measure of the security that, for all the talk of their new constitutional rights, was still denied them. Reports suggested that street executions were becoming a regular occurrence in some parts of the country. "Necklacing," a "particularly South African" institution (Minnaar 2001, 18) that emerged in the 1980s to deal with political renegades, was increasingly deployed to strike back at alleged criminals (see Harris 2001). Elsewhere, in rural and semirural areas, there was a (re)turn to "the African way of stopping crime," this being the slogan of Monhle John Magolego, charismatic founder of *Mapogo a Mathamaga*, the nation's largest indigenous vendor of private policing. To its critics, that "African way" amounted to brute vigilantism. But, for others, its harsh corporeal discipline was an entirely appropriate means of punishing known offenders. Counterviolence, ran the rationale, was the only effective means of restoring order in a world run amok.

Recourse to private protection and alternative justice was hardly new in South Africa. White business and some householders had long purchased the services of security firms, later to be rebranded as "armed response." But alternative justice also has deep roots in African juridical practices that survived in the colonial countryside and traveled to urban areas along with migrant workers in the late nineteenth century (Buur 2010, 35). Under apartheid, urban blacks, acutely distrustful of the police and the criminal justice system, had little option but to rely on "informal" providers of protection and dispute settlement (Nina 2000; Steinberg 2008), from *mabangalala* (right-wing gang enforcers, who often enjoyed state support; Haysom 1986, 1989)[1] to *makgotla* (people's courts, derived from Sotho-Tswana adjudicatory institutions; Gerhart and Glaser 2010, 84). In the later years of the *ancien régime*, as it began to unravel, extralegal enforcement multiplied on all sides: while informal tribunals, civic organizations, and street committees expanded their hold in the townships, Afrikaner militias and shadowy, government-sponsored operatives meted out their own forms of disciplinary violence, much of it intended to undermine the liberation struggle. The state, in other words, had no simple monopoly over the means of enforcement.

Contrary to expectation, the end of apartheid did little to lessen the appeal of informal justice. As it has elsewhere across the world, especially in peripheral urban neighborhoods in the Global South (Sen and Pratten 2008; K. Gillespie, forthcoming), the attractiveness of alternative policing has intensified, giving rise to a bewildering array of security, investigative, and quasi-judicial services. Those services, in a country in which the term "service delivery" carries mythic resonance (see above, 1.2), are offered by private companies, civic and nongovernmental organizations, religious fraternities, traditional authorities, gangs, even taxi associations. Each has its own approach to crime, and most of them collaborate to some degree with the cops, albeit more or less un/easily, in/formally, and il/legally. A subtle, unresolved dialectic is clearly at work here between the state and civil society, one in which the legal and the extralegal, the official and the unofficial, constantly interact with each other across an inchoate, labile boundary.

This dialectic has long been intrinsic to modernist governance, of course. But its marked intensification is part of the tectonic shift, of which we spoke earlier, from vertical, relatively integrated structures of sovereign authority toward lateral patchworks of partial sovereignties (see 1.1; Comaroff and Comaroff 2006b, 35): sovereignties of different durations and temporalities; sovereignties with jurisdiction over variably scaled terrains, populations, property, moral projects, and behavioral conventions; sovereignties buttressed to a greater or lesser degree by coercion, direct and indirect. For von

Schnitzler *et al.* (2001, 15), the raison d'être of alternative enforcement in the postapartheid era has been marked by a shift from "politics to crime." Superficially speaking, this is true, as we just noted with respect to "necklacing," but only insofar as the two—politics and crime—can be cleanly separated, either for practical or for analytical purposes. We have argued that they cannot be, that the line between politics and crime is always provisional, historical, contingent, contested; all the more so since the capacity of the modernist state to hold that line—itself *the* supreme aspiration of sovereignty—has been seriously eroded.

As this suggests, the escalation of informal justice since 1994 has been triggered by more than just heightened feelings of vulnerability, of risk in the face of rising criminality, significant though these things obviously are. It also expresses a deep suspicion of established authority. That suspicion, patently, is rooted in local conditions. But it also taps into a pervasive late modern *angst*: the haunting fear that—as the state form itself morphs, as the criminal specter rises in the murk of the "new" global economy (again, see 1.1)—lawlessness might simply be impossible to bring permanently under control; that, being immanent everywhere, it invades previously protected spaces and bypasses previously policed boundaries. In the event, calls for ever more punitive responses, ever more cogent counterviolence, are a plea for the kind of action that wrests back a legible, predictable, and manageable lifeworld: action that might set politics and the body politic apart from crime and the criminal economy, citizen from anticitizen, moral public from a society of strangers. It is a plea, moreover, for a nation with the capacity to know itself, to command the means to make truth distinguishable from deception. And social order from ethical entropy.

We are, we repeat, *not* saying that the threat of criminal violence has been unimportant in the resort to popular justice. Reports of murderers at large and escaped prisoners, of unsolved dockets and uninvestigated sexual assaults, of sheer ineptitude, forensic incapacity, and malfeasance in the overstretched police service continue to flood the news media almost daily.[2] These things, perhaps, are inevitable in a rapidly changing social world in which the downsides of the neoliberal turn—themselves now widely documented for the world at large (e.g., Gray 1998; Stiglitz 2002; United Nations 2005) and for South Africa in particular (e.g., Sharp 1998; Habib and Padayachee 2000; McDonald and Pape 2002; Bond 2003)—have been so acutely felt. What we *are* suggesting is that the manner in which South Africans have framed the problem, and proposed to solve it, has been driven not merely by instrumentalities. It has also been shaped by considerations of history and ideology: by the aspiration for a form of constitutional sovereignty, long deferred and still to be fully accomplished, that is at once authoritative yet committed to the rule of law—a sovereignty capable of strong governance in the cause of an open, more equal, postracist society, yet in step with the spirit of global liberalization. While the former (state sovereignty) remains a work in progress, the latter (liberalization) has proceeded apace; here as elsewhere, they have proven to be uneasy bedfellows. Taken together, they have exacerbated the appeal of alternative policing: while the postapartheid state has not shown itself capable of ensuring the safety of the population at large or of containing rogue violence, its commitment to liberalization has encouraged a wide array of actors and organizations, both authorized and unauthorized, to claim the right to protect one or another segment of the population.

Let us look, then, into the various elements that make up the terrain of enforcement beyond the domain of the state in South Africa. We start with the efforts of the SAPS itself to disperse policing, or some of its functions, into the "community" and the private sector. Its efforts say a good deal about the ideological scaffolding of law and order in neoliberal times here and elsewhere—and about the ground on which alternative justice has spread its roots.

The Fall, and the Fall of Community Policing

It has been argued that North American models of policing, which have had a profound impact on the rest of the world, have gone through three broad phases (Martin 2000): the first stressed order, the second, law-enforcement, and the third, service and prevention, as exemplified by the shift toward managerialism and community policing (CP). In point of fact, this telos refers more to the ideological substrate of official *policy* than to actual practice; it also glosses over the latter-day parsing and privatization of much of the police function (see part 1). The latter, as we have stressed throughout this volume, is always more complex than its public branding allows, always an unstable ratio of coercion to criminal investigation, punishment to protection, enforcement to education. In South Africa, as elsewhere, the last phase, the one that stresses CP, began with the move toward liberalization in the 1970s. But it would be more fulsomely espoused during the transition to democracy, when its rhetoric of rights and popular empowerment was devoted to the task of restoring the nation's confidence in the criminal justice system; this is also when the South African Police Force morphed into the South African Police

Service and its precinct stations renamed "community service centers." CP was not meant to replace the earlier models. It was, to cite a refrain of SAPS itself, to build upon existing commitments to the maintenance of order and law-enforcement by newly collaborative means.[3]

But CP was, above all, about making virtue of necessity in dauntingly difficult circumstances. Speaking of the formidable challenges facing law-enforcement in the countryside in the late 1990s, for instance, Antoinette Louw of the Institute for Security Studies told *Business Day* that the SAPS had no alternative but to rely on this model. Without it, she intimated, few people would be arrested or convicted even for serious crimes.[4] This reflected two things: a lack of capacity and commitment on the part of the early postapartheid criminal justice system and the continuing reluctance of many communities to be policed (Steinberg 2008; see above). Left undefined in all this, however, was what, exactly, was *meant* by "community policing." Did it refer to policing of, in, or by communities? Counterintuitively, perhaps, we would argue that the oft-noted vagueness of the term has actually been crucial to the efficacy of its deployment by various parties in various ways. But its lack of specification also points to something else, something deeper and as significant.

The concept of community, or more precisely "*the* community," has had an ambivalent history in South Africa and elsewhere since the 1980s. Once used without critical reflection in sociology and anthropology to describe a group with shared values, it now calls forth almost universal suspicion. Nevertheless, and in spite of scholarly skepticism, the "imprecise aura of vacuous virtue" implicit in the term (Reiner and Cross 1991, 10) has made it a panacea for states everywhere in the era of liberalization. Institutions—the clinic, the prison, the school, bureaucracy—were, as Foucault noted, the hallmark of modernity, the disciplinary tools with which it upheld the natural order of things. Now, with the neoliberal turn, the forms of care and social management once provided by government are deinstitutionalized and "returned" to "the community." The latter, a cipher with no intrinsic substance, has become *the* signifier of the private sphere collectivized. It is an abstraction that denotes, on the one hand, aggregated self-interest, its "stakeholders" expected to take initiative for effecting social ends; and, on the other, a "responsibilized" civic space, where ethically awakened subjects volunteer their service in schools, hospitals, homes, libraries, police forums, and the like, from which state provision has been retracted (Muehlebach 2012). Within that liberated space, an unorchestrated bouquet of enterprises—from long-established religious associations to an ever-expanding sector of NGOs and philanthropic organizations—is presumed to give texture to social life. And to animate "civil society," another elusive abstraction with a putative capacity for sustained collective action (Comaroff and Comaroff 1999b).[5]

In late twentieth-century South Africa, the growth of "civics," the in/famous associations that operated in the townships in the 1980s, had a different but not unrelated genealogy. The apartheid regime might have been isolated from the international order in many respects, but it was not immune to global forces. In the 1970s, it began to shed some of its governmental functions, including a number of its policing operations. While this was in line with ideological shifts elsewhere at the time (see 1.1, 1.2), it was also a tacit acknowledgment that lawlessness had become an intractable problem, one to be "managed" rather than solved (Super 2013, 88–89)—especially in already-underserved townships, which were now being run by locally elected Black Legal Authorities. Needless to say, the South African Police Force retained firm control over public order. But "communities" were called upon to "take responsibility," in their own cultural idiom, for dealing with the "crime risk" in their midst (Super 2013, 88–89). Which they did, although not in the manner that had been envisaged in Pretoria. The townships in the 1980s were critical sites of apartheid's endgame: young men, many of them affiliated with the liberation movements, organized among themselves at once to make urban black areas ungovernable by the state or its proxies and, within them, to provide civil protection, "people's justice," and political resistance in the face of growing paramilitary repression—hence the proliferation of "civics." Both here and in the countryside, however, youth power was contested, often with the clandestine connivance of the state, by older community representatives, who spoke for more conservative values and traditional authority. Extrajudicial violence was glorified on all sides (Ndebele 1991; du Preez 2013, 189), bequeathing a legacy of distrust, division, and generational strife; also, a will to popular sovereignty (Buur 2010, 38; Thornton 1999, 95) that lives on in postapartheid times—all the more as the promise of democracy dims and the disadvantaged remain deprived, for the most part, of safety, security, and inclusion.

It is the legacy of this fractious history, this conflict-laden sociology, that fills the contested space of "community" in many parts of South Africa today. The state tried to tame it after 1994, as we said earlier, by appealing to the model of CP in order to build legitimacy for the SAPS (Super 2013, 92; Minnaar 2013, 63). Community Police Forums (CPFs) were set up and Community Police Officers appointed. The African National Congress (ANC) government aimed thereby to establish a nonauthoritarian authority, striving to draw a sharp distinction between "people's power" and rogue sovereignty (Buur 2010, 41–42). The informal courts, flowers of grassroots democracy during the struggle years, were now deemed undisciplined, out of control, and destructive of civil society. In putting in place its new regime of crime management, the SAPS envisaged a national network of CPFs as a platform for local-level prevention, one that would also provide a mechanism to "domesticate and diffuse" the lingering threat of popular justice (cf. Buur 2010, 43). Their members were meant to meet regularly with police officers to discuss strategies for combating lawlessness and for making communities safer. CPFs were specifically *not* created to apprehend suspects or patrol neighborhoods: permitting them to do these things would have officially authorized the kinds of action that blur the line between legitimate and vigilante violence. But, in practice, that line has proven to be indistinct and, as often as not, flatly illegible. Almost from the first, CP has served as cover for a messy interdependence of legal and extralegal enforcement, some of it conducive to state control, a lot of it quite antithetical.

CP, as a construct, in other words, is often a working fiction that complicates the distinction between law and lawlessness, il/legal coercion, crime-and-policing, drawing a veil over the uneasy articulation of state and extralegal force. As such, it is many things. At one end of the spectrum, CPFs have remained empty ciphers, despite active efforts to give them life. In 2001, for example, at Lomanyaneng Police Station in the North West, we encountered Inspector Irene Lefenyo; *this* "community service center" was still called a "station" by everyone. The young police officer, optimistic and energetic, reveled in her crime prevention work. Put in charge of CP, she visited the villages around Mafikeng-Mmabatho, the provincial capital, urging their residents to establish CPFs, with a view, eventually, to securing their own communities. She targeted schools, prime sites of drug dealing, rape, violence, and gang activity, encouraging them to "adopt a cop" (Department of Law and Order 1994, 83). But, she said, "people do not seem . . . interested. They are not ready to take us as friends." Not surprising, this. The apartheid-era distrust of black police endures in many places. Scheduled meetings of the "community policing committee" at the station went unattended. Joe Leteane, a local Tshidi-Rolong royal, said to know everything and everybody in the district, was blunt about the whole thing: a forum existed in Mafikeng, he said dismissively, but he "knew nothing of it"—except that no one took it seriously. Those associated with it, he added, were *bampimpi* (informers), a notoriously dangerous thing to be. Not too long ago, a suspected *mpimpi* was likely to killed by necklacing.

This last remark is telling. Critical to the collaboration between cops and citizens under the rubric of CP was the expectation, on the part of the SAPS, that it would yield useful criminal information. The efficacy of detection, notes Steffan Riebe, former East German lawman and public intellectual, has *always* been proportional to the availability of local *social* knowledge.[6] But gathering this sort of information, Holy Grail in policing everywhere—and not just for purposes of detection—rests on a measure of trust in the criminal justice system. In the North West, as in many rural and semirural areas, a good portion of enforcement and conflict management is handled beyond the purview of the state, or, as we shall see, by traditional authorities, whose relationship to government is ambivalent at best. The kind of confidence in the SAPS presumed and required by CP is simply not there.

Elsewhere, CP or, rather, the cover it offers, has been deployed to traffic between the state and extralegal enforcement. Jonny Steinberg (2008, 55) describes how veterans of the Civic Associations and Youth Congress formed a Patrol Group that, in the late 1990s, helped "bring the police back" to Alexandra, a township in Gauteng that had long spurned them. Having responded to the call to found a CPF in 1994, the men—who, as alumni of the 1980s, enjoyed considerable moral authority—were officially formed into an armed Safety and Security Patrol five years later. With and without the cops, the patrol took to searching for illegal activity and weapons, making citizen's arrests, delivering suspects to the SAPS, and writing witness statements—all activities that far exceed the formal charge of the CPF. The latter had been toothless here until it mobilized a more robust mandate, one recuperated from the archives of struggles past. Do these enforcers embody democratic people's power, asks Steinberg (62), or are they merely one among many groups that have come together, bearing arms, to protect themselves and sell security to others? This question, put in more general terms, does not yield a straightforward answer. But, under the alibi of CP, some civic associations seem to have enjoyed renewed life as wellsprings of insurgent activism "from below," putting pressure on government to fulfill its commission with respect to justice, housing, health, schooling, and service delivery—only, at times, to find themselves criminalized by the ANC regime.

Lars Buur (2010, 30–31) provides rich illustration of the ambiguous role of so-called "Safety and Security" (S&S) units that have emerged in some crime-ridden urban areas, enabling CPFs to appear effective in assisting the SAPS. In KwaZakele township outside Port Elizabeth, he writes, S&S activists are preoccupied with how they might "discipline criminals and young people" without being sent to prison or "kicked out of the CPF." Buur (43) says that, *de facto*, these young warriors are "everyday sovereigns." Sporting CP IDs, they extract information about felons by violent means, like the use of whips, which are the signature weapon of the most notorious of "vigilantes" (see below), all this while the cops and CPFs turn a blind eye. But sometimes those CPFs *do* act on their own account, and do so in ways that test the law. Thus, for example, anger flared in the Western Cape town of Worcester in 2015 when the local white CPF issued green cards to local gardeners and handymen—and to known, "legitimate" job seekers—who regularly frequent affluent neighborhoods in the town; the point, it was claimed, was to prevent crime by keeping out persons with no business to be in those polite neighborhoods. The cards, with pictures and personal details of their bearers, were issued *only* to people of color. Anyone who did not have one, allegedly, was treated as suspect and closely monitored. Black residents of Worcester, who observed that their unprotected communities were much more crime-ridden than were wealthy white ones, were outraged. They accused the CPF of reinstating the apartheid-era "pass system."[7]

In light of such evidence, it is something of an overstatement—or, at least, a simplification—to argue, as some have, that CP was "abandoned" or "at best . . . ignored or disregarded" by the SAPS within a few years of its official launch (Bundy 2014, 122; cf. Minnaar 2013, 64). It might seldom have worked as claimed. But, as a necessary fiction, it has been invoked again and again when the impossibility of maintaining order by established means has erupted into crisis. In the event, it seems more accurate to suggest, as we do, that CP has sustained itself largely to the extent that it has served as a cover for something else: for the reliance of the SAPS and local authorities on "private" actors and contractors who provide strong-arm protection and alternative justice at the indeterminate edges of the law, edges that the state cannot, and does not, reach. For some, and from some perspectives, this form of justice—inasmuch as it invokes "the people" and/or "the community"—may seem appealingly "domesticated" (Buur 2010). But even as it projects the *appearance* of control, it appropriates sovereign power over life and death unto itself.

In neighborhoods where rates of violent crime are especially high, where the police have long been repudiated, and where brutal justice prevails, CP is a pipe dream. But as such, as a present-absence, an impossibility, it is the cipher against which arguments about law and disorder proceed. Such is the case in Khayelitsha, on the Cape Flats in Cape Town (see 2.3), where an independent *Commission of Inquiry into Allegations of Police Inefficiency and a Breakdown in*

Relations between the SAPS and the Community, appointed by the premier of the Western Cape in 2012, reported gross failures of enforcement and a total "breakdown in relations" between cops and community.[8] Residents complained of a lack of any visible policing, a chronic failure to respond to emergency calls, and a spate of brazen executions performed under the full gaze of CCTV cameras in the notorious "Killing Field"[9] situated in a nearby informal settlement.[10] "We don't see the police here, so we basically have to fight for ourselves," a single mother told the commission. "They only come when the crimes are finished and done, so what is the use of them?"[11] Locals have formed street committees to patrol the area, making "community arrests," holding public "prosecutions," and carrying out sentences with dispatch: sometimes beatings or banishment, but mostly death by necklacing or stoning.[12] Large crowds gather to watch these penal spectacles. Recall: it is precisely this with which we began the book, with the theatrics of the public execution that, for Foucault, embodied the will of the sovereign and the force of the law in the prebourgeois world. In Khayelitsha, the drama takes place on ground effectively vacated by the state, deserted by a regime that no longer seems willing to enforce the law, to monopolize the means of violence, or to ensure the protection of the persons or property of its subjects.

This, then, is CP of a rather-different kind: it evokes the era of "state making as organized crime" that Tilly (1985) described for Europe before the consolidation of the modern nation-state form (1.1). While cops told the commission that Khayelitsha was well-nigh impossible to police, its residents insisted that, although they abhorred vigilante violence, they had no choice but to rely on strong-arm protection in the face of rampant gangsterism.[13] Wrote one reader to the *Mail & Guardian* at the time: "It is the prime responsibility of Government and the police to maintain law and order. It is also the prerogative of people that they may defend themselves. If the police and the Government abrogate their responsibility, then how can vigilantism be wrong?"[14] The pressure to appoint the commission in the first place, against stiff ANC opposition,[15] had come from various civil society organizations, most of them operating on the national level, beyond the strife-torn areas that were its focus.[16] Ironically, the first of its practical recommendations was that "each police station should adopt a Community Policing Commitment in consultation with members of the community." The responsiveness of the cops would be improved, it advised, if neighborhood watches, CPFs, and Street Committees were adopted; these, of course, are precisely the kinds of platforms that suc-

ceed only as the *outcome* of collective trust, of the kind of reciprocal legitimation lacking under the social conditions the commission had itself laid bare.
In fact, its report acknowledged that existing CPFs had floundered due to lack
of funding and "police responsiveness,"[17] a point that has also been made all
over the Cape Flats by community and neighborhood watch organizations.[18] It
should be noted that, at the time that these recommendations were being prof-
fered, the provincial police commissioner and four of his senior officers were
charged with corruption and racketeering (above, 1.2),[19] underlining yet again
the difficulty, here, of setting law-enforcement apart from (especially organized) crime. Within a year, local residents were again protesting against what
they described as an ongoing, "low-intensity war" among unpoliced criminal
gangs. At least one CPF supported their call for the army to be brought in to effect a complete lockdown of the most afflicted neighborhoods.[20]

The case of Khayelitsha makes plain that, even *in extremis*, CP remains central to the discourse of social dis/order in South Africa and to the fractious
conversation between the state and its citizens. It also remains integral to the
imagined landscape of a less crime-ridden, less violent society. This is despite
the government's failure to give "meaningful and systematic support" (Pelser,
Schnetler, and Louw 2002, 83) to CP, which rides a set of contradictions, and
not only in South Africa (Ellison 2006; Olutola 2013; Nalla and Newman
2013). As we have noted, criminologists have long insisted that the burden
of dealing with crime has become an "impossible mandate" for police everywhere (above, 1.1, 1.2; also Burger 2006): the complex causes and effects of
lawlessness extend way beyond the purview of criminal justice into the social
and material structures of the world at large. The gangs that so afflict the Cape
Flats, for instance, have extensive connections with civic and political elites,
as well as strong underworld partners in Nigeria, China, Pakistan, India, Russia, and Britain (Goga 2014). The economy that they operate, aka "Gangland
(Pty) Ltd" or "Gangland, Inc.," bears all the marks of neoliberal business at its
most contemporary, and most difficult to police.[21]

What is more, in polities governed through the management of crime, the
ever-present threat of disorder, its "insurmountable" challenge,[22] must be sustained in public consciousness as the very condition of rule. The persistent
crime *kampf* legitimates—indeed, appears to demand—paramilitary enforcement and peacekeeping, particularly in the face of the audible anger of the
alienated, the excluded, the criminalized. Also the libertarian. How realistic is
it, then, to expect state-mandated CP to operate effectively on such a terrain?

And yet, at the same time, this is precisely the ground on which alternative policing and informal justice of various sorts flourish—largely because they present themselves to the unprotected, the unpoliced, and the uninsured as an everyday necessity.

Of Death, Vengeance, and Sovereignty

In their mounting dissatisfaction with the failure of the criminal justice system to curb lawlessness, South Africans—as we have already noted several times (see 1.2, 2.3)—return repeatedly to argue about the death penalty. By abolishing it in June 1995,[23] the Constitutional Court drew the curtain on a long, shameful history of politically motivated executions. But popular sympathy for capital punishment has remained strong; calls for its reintroduction have grown over the years. A survey conducted by the Human Sciences Research Council in 2003 reported that 75 percent of its large adult sample agreed, 50 percent of them "strongly," that convicted murderers should be killed; 72 percent of the blacks counted were among those who concurred, as were 76 percent of the Coloureds, 86 percent of the Indians, and 92 percent of the whites.[24] Follow-up studies have shown a hardening of support,[25] especially among blacks (Ambrosio 2005). In line with conservative movements elsewhere, several South African political parties, one of them actually called the Pro–Death Penalty Party, have campaigned for a national referendum, their cause intermittently emboldened by public outrage at epic homicides, like that of kidnap victim Leigh Matthews in 2004 (above, 2.3), of Senzo Meyiwa, celebrity goalkeeper and captain of the national football team, in 2014,[26] and of a prominent dermatologist in 2012—this last a murder that persuaded the head of the South African Medical Association, no less, to say that in a "country under siege," criminals have to be shown that "if they kill they will be killed."[27] Activists have been known to turn up to courts trying murder cases with rope nooses in hand.[28]

Criminologists have testified repeatedly that capital punishment has little deterrent effect. To almost no avail, however. What is most often at issue, says legal scholar Pierre de Vos, is a brute desire for vengeance; while understandable, he adds, the focus on penality merely deflects attention from the root causes of violent crime.[29] But there is also something more fundamental involved in the call for the death penalty: an effort—an exercise of the general will?—to goad the state into acting like a true sovereign, one that enforces the law with deadly dispatch, without delay, debate, deferral, preferment. It is the perceived absence of that sort of sovereignty in South Africa, we argue, that has persuaded so many of its citizens to turn to alternative policing and informal justice: to a species of social action that takes upon itself *precisely* that kind of sovereignty, the immanent capacity to stage dramas that decree death, or graphic violence just short of it, to assert the finality of its authority. And to rewrite a social contract that, in a Schmittian world of friend and enemy, proffers protection to the right and the good—and ensures punishment to those who transgress.

South Africans with the necessary capital, both cultural and material, purchase protection in the private sector. What they buy extends from elaborate domestic security systems, monitored by commercial firms, to the services of whitened, company-registered versions of the "vigilante" organizations that operate in black residential areas. Many of them also make collective arrangements to police community space. These vary from orthodox neighborhood watches, through the paramilitary patrolling of ethnic enclaves in Johannesburg by former soldiers (Steinberg 2008, 160ff.; Bloom 2009, 55), to more unconventional enterprises, like that of the so-called Mountain Men who guard Cape Town's southern suburbs from the slopes of Devil's Peak.[30] For present purposes, however, we are less concerned with capitalized, commercial private security than with the forms of alternative policing and informal justice that occur at the edges of, or beyond, the market and the law. These, as we shall see, range widely in their organizational elaboration, in the nature of their practices, and in the ways in which they do or do not go about exercising sovereignty.

The Anatomy of Informal Justice (1): From Lone Rangers to the Sovereignty of the Street

Let us begin, then, at one extreme: individuals who patrol the meaner streets of South Africa's cities, flying solo as guardian angels of the vulnerable. We refer to them as Lone Rangers.

Lone Rangers

One such man, a token of the type, was Tutu Mgulwa, who provided an escort service for abused young women in Gauteng during the late 1990s. Mgulwa claimed to have begun his anticrime crusade after a close friend was sexually assaulted by a policeman.[31] Dubbed the "sex vigilante" by the press, he special-ized in tracking down offenders, whom he sought to have tried and convicted. Mgulwa also founded the South African Stop Child Abuse organization, although it seems chiefly to have been a cover for his solo activities. In 1998 he paraded a youth accused of rape naked through the streets of Atteridgeville, a large township outside Pretoria. Carnivalesque displays of this sort led women to seek his services, as a result of which he often landed in court, along with his clients, as a witness for the prosecution—or, conversely, as a defendant against charges of having assaulted suspects. Mgulwa was seen as a saint by many people, his exploits covered in the national media; a hint here, perhaps, of the return of the early modern outlaw (see 1.3 above), although to the SAPS this Lone Ranger was less a people's bandit than a violent, habitual felon. His career was derailed in 2000 when he was jailed. For? Rape, of course.[32] Mgulwa cried conspiracy on the part of corrupt lawmen whom he had exposed. The judge decided otherwise. But if there *was* a covert effort to neutralize this Lone Ranger, it showed a fine sense of the symbolic, showcasing yet again the ironies that attend the tenuous distinction between cops and criminals.

Another case of an individual taking the law into his own hands casts sharp light on the complex counterpoint of race and authority in the domain of popular justice, an issue to which we shall return in our discussion of *Mapogo a Mathamaga* below. It involved a white farmer in Vryheid, KwaZulu-Natal, who decided, in 2005, to hunt down two men suspected of housebreaking on his property. Except that he did not do so himself. Instead, he ordered three of his black employees to find and dispose of the (alleged) felons;[33] the labor economy of apartheid, its racialized dirty work, remains alive and well in many parts of the country. Farmers, especially in isolated locales, see themselves as particularly vulnerable to violent attack; recall that AfriForum, the conservative civil rights organization, has launched a campaign to have farm murders classified as a "unique," racially motivated priority crime (see 2.3), a point argued passionately, if provocatively, in the melodrama *Treurgrond* (2015, directed by Darrell Roodt; Afrikaans *treur*, "mourn" or "grieve"; *grond*, "ground" or "soil"), whose afflicted protagonist is played by Steve Hofmeyr, an Afrikaner activist who has claimed that whites are being "killed like flies."[34] Specifically targeted or not, many of those farmers, lone ranchers of sorts, take it upon themselves to deal with assaults on their persons or property. Or they charge their hired hands to do so. Those dispatched by Johan Els, chief accused in this case, duly apprehended the two suspects and attacked them with a hunting knife, one fatally. The father of Mduduzi Mkhize, the accused who had wielded the weapon, testified that Els had "told him that his son [should] take the blame and not implicate him." In return, he would buy the father "a car or a cow." Els was sentenced to five years as an accessory to murder and attempted murder; Mkhize, to ten. The difference reflects the legal distinction between commissioning and committing murder, to be sure. However, it also points to the effects of enduring structures of inequality on the workings of justice, both formal and informal. In general, rogue violence tends to reinforce existing inequities of race, ethnicity, gender, sexuality, and age.

But sometimes not. Sometimes lone rangers emerge as unambivalently heroic, even to the cops. Jasmine Harris, a fifty-six-year-old woman of color on the Cape Flats, has been described by *the Daily Voice* (a peoples' tabloid that, for all practical purposes, is the newspaper of record for exo-city, down-class Cape Town) as "the aunty who *skriks vir niks*,"[35] which translates, roughly, as "is scared by nothing." We first heard of Aunty Jasmine in July 2015. At the time, she was on a mission to "clean up the streets of Mitchell's Plain," taking on local criminals and drug dealers, "breaking down" their places of business, and assaulting them physically; she once, it is reported, "beat a suspected Tanzanian drug dealer with a crate until he bled." Said the *Daily Voice*, "[we have] seen grown men running away in fear as she approaches them," grown men who have included "hardcore gangsters that . . . make police officers hesitate." The senior police officer tasked with antigang operations in the area, Major General Jeremy Veary, has commended Aunty Jasmine for her "indomitable spirit." He has called her "a vigilante" but, like his colleagues in the SAPS, seems not at all to mind what she does. Once a founder member of the local CPF, whose efforts she found inadequate, she confesses to being proud of the label and proud of what she is doing to bring safety and security to those around her—which brings us to our next form of popular justice.

Rogue Justice and the Sovereignty of the Street

By far the most common forms of popular justice involve groups of people coming together to "take care of themselves." While typically described in middle-class and mass-media discourse as "mobs" or "kangaroo courts"—as unorganized crowds, that is, driven by spontaneous rage and bloodlust—they are anything but all alike. Still, they *do* evince a predictable *mise-en-scène* in many respects. Often, though *not* invariably, they are unplanned, appearing to materialize as the result of a triggering incident and a public call to arms like the infamous cry of "*Nal'iSela*" (There's a thief).[36] This expresses the shared moral outrage occasioned, in the residents of poor communities, by demonstrations of their insecure ownership of their bodies and their hard-won property; the fact that the loss of relatively small items—a cell phone, a handbag—can spark death-dealing rage underscores how marginal are these lives, how deep can be this desperation.

While ranging widely in scale and composition, these disciplinary gatherings have several common features: their rapidly escalating affective energy, their propensity for quick-fire, uncompromising violence, their single-minded sense of legitimate grievance.[37] They often generate an atmosphere of arousal, akin to Lacan's *jouissance* (Harari 2004, 212), an impulse toward transgression that is itself at once painful and pleasurable, deadly yet somehow transformative, even transcendent. An observer, waiting in a minibus, witnessed one such incident in Khayelitsha in 2014.[38] Out of nowhere a man came stumbling toward him, covered in blood, chased by a crowd of some forty to fifty people: "[T]here was a lot of commotion in general, but when he fell down . . . members of the community in the mob continued to assault him and there was one weapon that I saw. It was a big piece of wood and one of the guys kept on just smashing [him] . . . on the head . . . and there was [*sic*] some more people as well kicking him in the head and just stomping him in the stomach . . . [And] as they were beating him there was a police car parked . . . only a few metres away." As they assailed their victim, he said, the attackers made two kinds of noises. "When they smashed him in the head with a piece of wood, you would hear that the crowd would cheer, and it wasn't only cheers of joy and laughter, it was also like people who were actually really upset and afraid." Eventually another cop car arrived, and the man, still able to walk, was rescued. He was fortunate. Often those subjected to street justice are less so. Sometimes the police are actively prevented from intervening, on the suspicion that the criminal will be freed on bail and/or will escape punishment. Nor is this suspicion ungrounded, as the records of the Khayelitsha Commission prove. The cops and the crowd are caught up in a tangled, unpredictable choreography of engagement-and-refusal. It is a choreography rendered yet more complicated by the fact that, in their public order operations—as we saw in the cases of Andries Tatane, Mido Macia, and others (above, 1.2)—the police resort to methods that are often indistinguishable from those of street justice. And some of them, we discovered ourselves, are not averse to encouraging extralegal ("community") enforcement. Or even, off duty, to take part in it.

The fact that these incidents of street justice share so many common features gives the lie to their ostensibly impromptu, formless character. Apart from all else, they invoke a historic archive of mass action, carried in embodied memories and ritual practices that reenact past anger, and recurrent conflict, exemplified in the harsh community discipline meted out during the struggle years, alluded to above. But these incidents also recall an older debate about the nature of popular mobilization and the architecture of "crowd psychology": Are they upsurges of primordial passion, contagious outbreaks that overwhelm civilized selfhood and legal responsibility, as suggested, classically, by Le Bon (1896)? Or are they liminal moments of "communitas," of suspension, which allow influential political actors to fashion and foster new kinds of legitimacy, new social arrangements, (re)new(ed) norms (R. Turner 1996)? These days, as Mazzarella (2010, 697) observes, to speak of crowds is to imply "hothead savagery," especially if race and class are at issue. This is the case in South Africa, most of all when mass action involves passionately angry young black men. Hence, Pumla Gobodo-Madikizela admonishes against seeing vigilantism as senseless violence or as a reflex reaction to the absence of policing.[39] It ought to be read in its broader context, she insists: it expresses a shared grievance, a desire for social justice long postponed, a feeling of enduring humiliation, *anomie*. As such, it flows from an existential fragility bred of existence in dumping grounds, where livelihoods are precarious and supportive networks are ever in flux.

But there is a further point, a corollary, that flows from this. Group violence, destructive as it may be, is also productive of immediate, intense sociality. It has many of the features of the ritually orchestrated "collective effervescence" that Durkheim saw as generative of social life *sui generis*—indeed, of society itself, of its transcendent reality. Bill Buford's (1991, 219) account of the "seduction" of crowd violence among football fans ("thugs") in the United Kingdom adds yet another layer to Durkheim's elementary formulation. These "thugs," Buford says, turned out to be surprisingly diverse in class background; he was alarmed at how pleasurable he found their rough company. He discovered, though, that their collective violence resisted easy explanation. On the surface, it looked like one of among many "antisocial kicks," an adrenaline-rich spur to a mind-altering, euphoric empowerment. At the same time, while it created a frenzied crowd high, it appeared to be surplus to requirement, at least for a supporters' club, *except*, perhaps, for the fact that it has the ability like little else to engender a potent sensation of sociality in times and places—and here he cites Susan Sontag (2009, 264) on "the pornographic imagination"—where "the need to transcend [the] personal" is very poorly served (268). In some circumstances, in other words, violence that seems excessive becomes its own affirmation, its own originary force. In the cruel drama of "mob" justice, acts of killing may be exhilarating, and not only to the poor or the powerless, precisely because they give transient reality to the vacuous notion of community, to the social in society, and thereby assert its sovereignty—a sovereignty born of righteous life-and-death violence. This is all the more so in a context, arguably, that compels individuals, *qua* individuals, constantly to confront their own precarity, their self-responsibility, the fact that, however right-bearing they are said to be, they are always a great deal more risk-bearing.

Many who live within the arc of street justice decry its brutality.[40] But they depend on its protection and respond readily to its call. Listen to a woman from Khayelitsha as she describes the reaction to cries of "thief" in her neighborhood early one morning: "In no time, and I mean, *no* time, everybody was coming out, slamming doors behind them. . . . It was as if they were waiting, ready all night for exactly this kind of thing to happen. Then they descended upon this man . . . *in no time*—they had finished him."[41] The effectiveness of this sort of common purpose, its shocking defiance, affirms the power and the values that it enacts. Such after all, is the brilliant tautology of collective ritual action. Its dramaturgy, here, consolidates the authority of "street sovereigns" (Buur 2010, 43), complicating further the counterpoint between community justice and law-enforcement, cooperation and insurgence, by seizing initiative away from the state and the SAPS. Accounts are legion in South African townships of the refusal of their residents to yield to the cops. For example, an "enraged mob" dragged an alleged serial rapist and his accomplice *from a police car* in KwaMashu in KwaZulu-Natal in 2006, summarily executing them both.[42] And a crowd in Tafelsig, Mitchell's Plain, outside Cape Town, attacked SAPS officers after charges were dropped against a man accused of killing his mother and dumping her body in a garbage bin; some five hundred people gathered at the man's home to force him "to admit guilt" and hurled stones at the lawmen when they arrived.[43] Acting upon the bodies of offenders, "fighting fire with fire," though, is more than just a rebuke to government, more than just a rite of rebellion marking the failure of the state to discipline the forces of disorder. It also asserts sovereign control over the streets against the rogue rule of criminals and "gangsters," whose burning serves as a rather-literal kind of exorcism, unifying a community of affliction by eliminating a malign influence at its core (cf. Buur and Jensen 2004).

The Anatomy of Informal Justice (2): Moralizing, Indicting, Punishing

Witch-Finding, Profiling, and the Demonization of Difference

Popular sovereignty of the sort we have been discussing asserts collective agency almost of necessity. As we and others have stressed, those who enforce street justice are typically spoken of as crowds or mobs, ostensibly undifferentiated and leaderless—although some congeal into informal associations, like *Southern Eye* and *Supreme* in Lavender Hill, Cape Town, that, in part, mimic neighborhood watches but, more or less often, also resort to their own means of penality.[44] The legitimacy of their actions stems from *shared* outrage that, by its very nature, "transcends the personal." As such, they resist the delegation or assumption of individual responsibility, and/or guilt, essential to ordinary criminal prosecution; which is why, in response, ruling regimes appeal to the legal doctrine of common purpose in their efforts to bring this sort of action under the purview of the law.[45] While usually said to be made up of young men, described as black and poor, these groups are often quite diverse in gender, age, and ethnolinguistic composition. Women and children, who are disproportionately vulnerable to predation and sexual abuse,[46] tend, as all our examples show, to be overwhelmingly supportive of their activities (Meth 2013, 75; Posel 2004, 235). It has been claimed that their direct involvement is less common (Meth 2013, 86). Not infrequently, however, women *are* accused of dealing out lethal punishment, as were a mother and daughter who took the initiative in beating to death a young man for alleged theft in the rural North West in 2015;[47] as, too, was Angy Peter,[48] a well-known social activist, who testified on police corruption before the Khayelitsha Commission, and who was arraigned, along with her husband, for necklacing a neighbor said to have stolen their television in 2012. Time and again, it is women who raise the alarm that a crime has been committed ("My bag!" "There's a thief"). It is also they who often point out suspects—and provide the kind of eyewitness testimony, the intimate social intelligence, that establishes guilt in street prosecutions.

But women also engage in concerted, collective action *as* women. One group, Women of Vision, was established in Westbury, a Coloured township in Johannesburg, where employment has long been scarce and criminal violence endemic. Reacting to a spate of sexual attacks on elderly females, its first act, avidly reported by the *Mail & Guardian* on 17 February 2000, was to march on the home of a suspected rapist, apprehend him, and turn him over to the police. A similar group, formed in Soweto in 2000, was more prone to punitive violence on its own account. Its traumatized, elderly members were reported to sleep with pangas, large machetes, under their pillows. Shalo Mbatha, a reporter from *the Sunday Independent* who interviewed fifteen of these women in March 2001,[49] said that they knew well who were the miscreants in their midst: "We were dumped here in 1968 and we are a close-knit community," one remarked. Most of the younger people had moved, leaving behind them households headed by aged pensioners, people especially vulnerable to attack. But these "grandmothers" did not concede to being easy or willing targets. They spoke of killing suspected robbers as if it were commonplace. "Why all the media hype about the death of this particular motherless criminal?" one asked, referring to their most recent victim. "We nearly killed another [last] week." The group lacked a name or any formal structure, but its actions followed a clearly grooved pattern: the victim was dragged into the open and, in front of whoever wished to watch, was laid into by everyone present with whatever came to hand. Women of this ilk are no less ready to engage in direct, brutal enforcement than are their male counterparts. Members of the Soweto sisterhood described rituals of violent justice that had "a festive mood to [them]. It was payback time. We all agreed that this is the ultimate deterrent." One remarked that "it [feels] good to strike back." She said that the police "seemed relieved that one of the thugs was dead when they arrived." Another noted that the SAPS had been invited to a forum to discuss local anxieties about crime. "But they never came," she said, bitterly. "They really do not care."

While women participate, variously, in street justice, they are less frequently its targets. But they *are* prime objects of other kinds of normative enforcement that are no less brutal. Nor are they any less infused with the aura of righteous outrage. Take, for example, "corrective rape," a particularly marked form of punitive action in a land in which, as we saw in 1.2, intimate violence is a singularly troubled issue. Despite being the first African state to legalize same-sex marriage, South Africa has a mounting record of aggression against gay, bi-, and transsexual women and men.[50] Attacks on them—some involving sexual violation, others not—have been perpetrated by larger or smaller groups, including women, under the sign of moral policing: of "teaching" them how to be proper citizens, proper human beings, proper Africans. Such, notoriously, was the fate, in Khayelitsha, of nineteen-year-old Zoliswa Nkonyana, murdered for being a lesbian.[51] An argument broke out in a tavern between her and another female patron about the right of "tom boys" to use the ladies' toilet. Ms. Nkonyana and a friend then left the establishment, to be followed into the street by a number of men and women, who, joined by a swelling crowd, pursued her and stabbed her to death. Six years later, after numerous postponements, four men, less than a quarter of those alleged to have participated in the killing, were finally sentenced.[52] There have been many such incidents across the country. Significantly, they have much in common with attacks on accused witches, mounted to purge rural communities of the sociomoral evil that afflicts them.

The study of African witch-finding, a historic form of popular justice, has long alerted us to the psychosocial logic underlying mass accusations of moral culpability. Drawing on intimate circumstantial evidence, prosecutions reveal nonrandom patterns of suspicion. They follow culturally attuned theories of causality (profiling, in modern forensic parlance) shaped in large part by existing lines of friction manifest within proximate worlds and the relations that compose them. But, to a greater or lesser degree, they are conditioned by structural forces that extend beyond their purview. Witches may be directly tied to parochial misfortunes, conflicts, deaths, catastrophes. But they are often also seized upon as the would-be perpetrators of more diffuse sorts of malaise, like AIDS, ecological disaster, joblessness, or social disorder.

While accusations of occult evil are hardly new in these contexts, mass attacks on alleged witches began to rise, especially in the largely rural North West, Limpopo, and Mpumalanga Provinces,[53] in the mid-1980s, reaching a crescendo in the mid-1990s at the time of the *Commission of Inquiry into Witchcraft Violence and Ritual Murders* (Ralushai *et al.* 1996; see Comaroff and Comaroff 1999a). Those who did the purging were mainly young men—the "majority of the youth," noted an eyewitness account of the necklacing of an elderly woman in the hamlet of Ha-Madura in Limpopo[54]—almost all of them unmarried and unemployed. Often, these firebrands were referred to as *comtsotsis*, a "new criminal type" (Siegel 1998; see above), named after the *enfants terribles* of the turbulent urban struggles of the 1980s, part comrade and part criminal. Their victims were usually called "old women," although men, often quite well-to-do men, were also accused (Comaroff and Comaroff 1999a).[55] Affect-laden indignation seemed to unify such crusades: those attacked were said to have subverted communal prosperity by means both immoral and uncanny—just as, some years later, immigrants, especially traders from elsewhere in Africa, were to be attacked amid allegations that they steal wealth and jobs, foster crime, spread AIDS, and deprive South Africans of the fruits of citizenship (Comaroff and Comaroff 2012, 90). In the widening gap between promise and impossibility, popular indignation acts to reclaim a sense of determination, to draw lines between friend and enemy, insider and outsider, prosperity and impropriety, the lawful and the lawless.

Faith-Based Enforcement

Communities of outrage have also turned to organized religion as a basis of social mobilization, both in pursuit of people's justice and as a source of popular sovereignty. Most faith-based initiatives start with efforts at "moral rearmament," campaigns to counter crime by solidifying the collective *conscience*. But divine protection has also been more directly invoked. Already in the late 1960s, Catholic clergy, at least in parishes in the rural North West, had adapted Christian rites of prophylaxis to traditional Setswana techniques for securing domestic space against invasion (*go thaya motse*); each year, they visited the homesteads of congregants to sprinkle their boundaries with holy water.[56] The police have also sought godly assistance: the Spiritual Services Division of SAPS has long held a National Prayer Day against crime.[57] As public anxiety became ever more fixated on lawlessness, local civic associations followed suit. The Mafikeng Development Forum organized its first interdenominational Crime Prevention through Prayer campaign in 1997. In Atteridgeville, Pretoria, the Concerned Residents Association initiated a yearly Anti-crime Prayer Day in June 2000.[58] Political leaders at both national and provincial levels have repeatedly urged churches, mainstream and independent alike, to involve themselves actively in building communal resolve against corruption and crime. Also, to support CPFs[59] and persuade their members to cooperate with the work of law-enforcement.

An altogether more proactive, forceful approach has been taken by the Muslim organization People against Gangsterism and Drugs, or Pagad, formed in 1995 on the Cape Flats. The product of an anticrime initiative in Cape Islamic circles (Botha 2001), it came to national attention in 1996 by virtue of its role in a gruesome murder, broadcast live on prime-time television. Rashaad Staggie, an infamous gang leader, was doused with petrol, set alight, and shot outside his home. His fiery demise replayed, on the one hand, the necklacing of informers and witches and, on the other, the summary killings carried out in the name of street justice discussed a moment ago. Pagad's purely crimefighting activities, however, were relatively short-lived: the movement was absorbed into the increasingly influential, militant politics of Qibla,[60] a Shi'a group founded in the 1980s that espoused *jihad* and aspired to the establishment of an Islamic state in the country. Under its influence, Pagad's tactics became more incendiary. The advocacy organization *Democracy Watch* linked it to almost seven hundred acts of violence in the first forty-two months of its existence. These included assassinations of gangsters, drive-by shootings, neighborhood gun battles, and the bombing in downtown Cape Town of US-owned franchises and of gay, moderate Muslim, and Jewish sites.[61] South African state functionaries also came under attack: in September 2000 Magistrate Pieter Theron, who was presiding in a case involving Pagad members, was murdered.[62] Pagad denied involvement in this or any other of these incidents. Nonetheless, an ANC news briefing in 2000 observed that while "Pagad was initially welcomed by ordinary citizens, . . . opinion has turned firmly against it after police linked it to ongoing urban terrorism."[63]

Despite this mayhem, the state was initially careful in its dealings with the organization. Although Pagad could be expected to arouse public antipathy, both within and beyond the Muslim community, groups of this kind also resonated with the popular view that community justice in crime-ridden neighborhoods was warranted by the failure of government to ensure civic order[64]— especially when they framed their actions in overtly moral terms, promising to make the world both safe *and* spiritually clean. At the same time, a chain of ever more audacious and bloody attacks led to the arrest, in 2002, of a number of Pagad activists. These included Abdus-Salaam Ebrahim, a prominent leader who was convicted of public violence and sentenced to seven years behind bars. No one was actually found guilty of the bombings, but the incidents, and the attribution of acts of terror to Pagad, subsided dramatically in the years that followed. Talk on the streets and in the media had it that the organization had "gone underground."[65]

And then, suddenly, it returned. "[U]nbelievable as it is, Pagad has managed a comeback," wrote Khadija Patel in April 2011, as public anxiety over gang and vigilante violence on the Cape Flats reached a new high.[66] "Not only has it reemerged from the doldrums of obscurity to the cheers of Lavender Hill residents," she went on, but "it has also returned emboldened with an endorsement from the authorities." A cautious city official is credited with having said that "Pagad has a voice and represents a very frustrated and irritated people; to ignore them is completely counter-productive so we must make a positive solution." But he was quick to insist that the organization would be required to "stick to the law." Meanwhile, its representatives insisted, on record, that the "new" Pagad had purged itself of "political Islam" and that it was committed to fighting gangsterism and drugs by legitimate means. A sedate website and Facebook presence, along with a street-level office in the heart of the Cape

Flats, suggested the profile of a regular, law-abiding Muslim fraternity, albeit one dedicated to curbing the murderous vice that afflicts its members: "We call upon communities to stand up against any form of injustice," urged a message on its home page. "[W]e must feel the pain of those suffering and eradicate the evils in our communities."[67] Chief among these evils were the trade in drugs (*smokkel*, in local parlance), above all in *tik*, or crystal methamphetamine. But this was merely symptomatic, reenacting the script that gave rise to Pagad in the first place: the widely perceived failure of ordinary law-enforcement, and of the state, to fulfill its sovereign mandate, leading to its dialectical antithesis, community policing that sees no option but to prevail by dint of brute force.

Sure enough, amid the upsurge of criminal violence that led to the Khayelitsha Commission, incidents of arson and pipe-bombing began again, targeting the homes of known drug lords.[68] This upsurge seems to have been fueled by three factors: a worsening local economy, rising meth sales, and the parole of key gang leaders.[69] Coincident with it, by all accounts, was a revived Pagad presence in the most blighted areas. Reports spoke of well-orchestrated nighttime motorcades that drove by drug dens in provocative shows of strength. In the run-up to the 2014 South African elections, Pagad activities were said to be attracting ever more popular support. A couple of its mass marches on the Flats were enthusiastically endorsed by the Economic Freedom Fighters, one of the country's more radical opposition parties.[70] They were also accompanied by an official contingent of police, although the motives for their participation may well have been mixed. The SAPS was keeping closer than usual tabs on the organization at the time. It had detained several of its members, including Abdus-Salaam Ebrahim, who, having been released from prison in 2009, had become national coordinator. Arrested for the murder of three Tanzanians rumored to be drug traders, Ebrahim claimed that he was the victim of a witch hunt. No evidence connected him to the crime, he insisted; the charges were later "temporarily withdrawn." Upright in posture and unbending in spirit, Ebrahim refused to retreat from the fight. "Our people [are] dying in this country, being raped and robbed, and sodomised," he declared.[71]

The affect that fuels such statements, often reinforced by ethnic solidarity ("our people"),[72] is widely shared in communities in which Pagad has been reborn. Certainly, there is some public uneasiness about its means and motives, especially among non-Muslims. But here, again, an assertion of moral authority helps. Pagad's rank and file are passionate about their crusade. A fifty-year-old hairdresser, devoted single mother, and member of a local school council in Mitchell's Plain is an ardent advocate of the movement. "I am with Pagad," she told us recently. "They take charge. I work hard to raise my children and I won't have gangsters imprison us in our home." After repeated efforts to elicit a response from the police to a rowdy drug den (*pella pos*) opposite her house—she even provided them with video evidence of round-the-clock mayhem—she called Pagad. "Already, they have been effective," she said. With a telling change of pronoun, she explained: "Our motto is 'One drug merchant, one bullet.'" On being summoned to a place of *smokkel*, Pagad members hold loud, condemnatory gatherings outside its doors. "We caution them," she went on. "Sometimes, we organize a drive-by, sometimes we light a fire right there as a warning. If there is no response, we strike." She then listed several renowned gangland figures who had been "dealt with" in this manner. And so the struggle continues. Action here might deal with symptoms, not causes. But it enacts a form of communal justice that is quick and sure, exerting a cathartic force that the state is unable either fully to endorse or finally to deny, appropriate, or quell.

The Anatomy of Informal Justice (3): Organized Anticrime

The Respectable Face of the Nongovernmental

The summary character of popular enforcement, its signature lack of due process, has led to the entry of a few NGOs—organizations that promote civic order beyond the arc of the state—on to the terrain of alternative policing and community justice. In many ways heirs to the great nineteenth-century projects of civilizing humanism, these initiatives, whether transnational or local or a blend of both, have had a limited impact on violence in South Africa. Precisely because they pursue social order through mechanisms like mediation and restorative justice that presuppose a modicum of trust and security, they depend, like CPFs, on what is *absent* in most strife-torn neighborhoods. They also offer scant means of producing that trust or security. One well-meaning example that has persevered against the odds is Conquest for Life, originally founded in 1995 in Westbury, the same Coloured township that produced Women of Vision (above, p. 199). It now extends its mission to three other working-class suburbs on the outskirts of Johannesburg.[73] With funding from the Open Society Foundation, the British High Commission, and other sources, the organization established its Victim Offender Conferencing Pilot Project with the lofty goal of leading the way to sustainable alternative justice in South Africa.[74] By 2015 it had qualified its aims, now describing itself as a nonprofit social enterprise, devoting its efforts to "strengthening" selfhood and family structures and to abetting crime prevention by offering empowering life-skill programs to youth at risk in troubled environments. The Victim Offender Conferencing Project still exists, but its objectives now sound more tentative, focusing on "human issues of crime through a face-to-face interaction between the offender(s), their respective families and to some extent appointed support persons from the community."[75] This is valuable work to be sure, but—like the Ceasefire project in Cape Town, which, in facilitating conflict mediation led by ex-gangsters, seeks to pathologize, and hence prevent, the "disease" of violence[76]—is unlikely to make deep inroads into the situations to which full-blooded street justice responds.

A second project began by focusing more directly on alternative policing than on mediation. Called the Peace Corps in Gauteng and the Peace and Development Project Western Cape on the Flats, it was funded initially by Danish, German, and US sources; the Cape chapter was run by a German NGO with backing from the University of the Western Cape. Its recruits, known as Community Peace Workers, had to be eighteen, have no prison record, be politically "independent," and have ten years of schooling. After a four-week training course, the workers patrolled the streets by day, unarmed and in fairly large groups, gaining information about criminal activities and intervening in unarmed conflicts and family disputes. They also monitored pension payouts and such other potential sites of violence as funerals and marches, administered first aid, helped people lost or under the influence of drugs and alcohol, and so on. Twice a month, on payday, when people carry home their wages, they also did night rounds. Like Conquest for Life, they claimed to have had considerable success at first, if nothing else as a model for community self-regulation. Certainly, the recruits with whom we walked the streets of Crossroads in 2000 took their work very earnestly. At the same time, they confessed that their impact on the troubled cityscapes of Cape Town remained small indeed. And sure enough, in recent, more explosive times, the organization, now part of a larger Peace and Development network,[77] has had to shift attention to prophylactic interventions aimed at communal empowerment and at "protecting refugees and migrants to prevent conflict and enhance social cohesion." In that domain, as well, they have been ineffective as agents of triage in the face of explosive outbreaks of xenophobia.

NGOs dedicated to combating crime have their tragicomic side too. One, the Ithutheng (or Student) Trust—or, rather, its coordinator, Jackie Maarohanye—held a ritual one Sunday in 1999. Some 2,500 "juvenile delinquents," largely schoolchildren, were persuaded to throw their illegal weapons, mainly fire-arms, into the Klip River in Soweto during an inspirational ceremony, which, oddly, included the sound of gunshots. The next day, police divers searched the river and found a handful of knives, axes, and spears—but nothing capable of shooting a bullet. The guns had all disappeared. A local newspaper photo-graphed one man searching in the water. Another confessed happily that he was about to fetch a large magnet to catch himself a pistol. What started out as an effort to rid the town of the means of violence turned out to be an elabo-rate exercise in its redistribution.[78] In fact, the story is a perfect allegory for a state in which the Hobbesian compact—by which citizens abandon their right to self-help in exchange for protection—gives way to a Hobbesian nightmare. It is a nightmare in which the failure of Leviathan to meet its side of the bar-gain yields to a world in which individuals and groups feel compelled to rely on the partisan, partial protection of competing sovereigns, those who, after Charles Tilly (1985; see 1.1), take hold of the instruments of force and mimic a state-in-formation.[79] In such a world, there are no privileged political or moral monopolies, merely divisive, fractious, and violent loci of power all seeking to extend their legitimacy.

African Redux: Mapogo, or Bicolored Leopards

This takes us, finally, to *Mapogo a Mathamaga*, perhaps the most distinctive, controversial, and ambitious self-policing operation to have emerged in South Africa. Long a force to be reckoned with in Limpopo and Mpumalanga, where it has dispensed its "African way of stopping crime" (above, p. 181) for almost twenty years, it had expanded, by the turn of the century, into the suburbs surrounding Johannesburg and Pretoria. *Mapogo* has since moved into the North West, Free State, and KwaZulu-Natal Midlands. At its height, it was probably the largest organization of its kind in the country and, as we have already noted, the nation's largest indigenous vendor of private justice. Its *modus operandi* has evolved, over the years, to subsume all the various forms of alternative policing and popular justice discussed above. *Mapogo* has, at times, taken on features of a CPF, resembled an NGO, acted as a moral police force, consorted with traditional authority and religious groups, and morphed, in some peri-urban locales, into a private security company. Consequently, it of-fers a living summation of our arguments about all these phenomena. Monhle John Magolego, charismatic postal-worker-turned-entrepreneur, founded it in 1996, at age fifty. Magolego is a veteran of the conflicts that beset the countryside after the end of apartheid. His biography has put him at the epicenter of the new configurations of class, generation, and gender that began to trouble the northerly provinces as expectant, largely unemployed youth ran head on into an older generation of rising black businessmen intent on consolidating their position (Delius 1996; Oomen 2005, 152).

Magolego is a seriously gifted publicist, skilled at promoting both himself and his cause. "My movement emerged as a response to a real need," he told us solemnly in 2000. "Democratization [had failed] to ensure a 'better life for all' and to protect the property of honest, hardworking citizens."[80] As he later said to the Afrikaans press in its own language, "We are sick to death of the soft-handed techniques of democracy. . . . Crime knows no color. If [criminals] won't listen, their arses must burn."[81] From the start, Magolego has understood the niceties of branding. He has packaged his "African" approach to enforcement in such a way as to appeal to a broad array of postapartheid discontents. He rejects the term "vigilantism" but holds to its underlying logic: *Mapogo* presents itself as a necessary response on the part of ordinary people entitled to enjoy the fruits of their labor, upright citizens who deserve better than to live in a society run out of control. But he trades, too, on a barely suppressed nostalgia for patriarchal authority and gerontocratic discipline. Magolego understands well the *angst* of South Africa's small-business owners, which cuts across the lines of color and gender. He set out initially to serve a hundred small black entrepreneurs in Limpopo, but *Mapogo* spread like wildfire, drawing in shopkeepers of all races—even isolated white farmers, who posted its logo, the heads of two snarling tigers, on their gates (image 3). As the organization grew, Magolego faced a number of challenges to his control but appears to have faced them down. In 1998 there were reports of a split among the leadership over the wisdom of its signature methods. According to the founder, his view—that "criminals should get a taste of their own medicine"— prevailed. As did he.

By 2000 Monhle John Magolego took credit for a network of ninety branches, with some seventy thousand members[82] and its central office in downtown Pretoria, a mere three hundred meters from police headquarters. That same year, there were rumors that a white member, building contractor Pieter Oosthuizen, was "restructuring and even computerizing" *Mapogo*'s activities and taking over its financial management, leaving Magolego to concentrate on "being the leader." Magolego denied this to us and others. He repudiated Oosthuizen's claim to authority and implied that some Afrikaner cadres had tried to usurp his control.[83]

IMAGE 3. Logo of *Mapogo a Mathamaga* as displayed on residential signage

Clearly, however, the structure of the organization was becoming more complex, and Magolego was losing his monopoly over the brand. He still claimed, to Nicholas Smith (2013, 152) in 2010, that he was life president of the organization. But the expanding commercial security operations that now were conducted under its name sported a very different, airbrushed, all-white image. The founding of its predominantly white chapter in downtown Nelspruit, Mpumalanga, for instance, was held at the local civic center and conducted almost entirely in Afrikaans.[84] On its family-oriented websites, smiling suburban managers offered high-tech domestic installations and armed response. And yet, listed on one of the largest of those sites are services that unabashedly invoke the movement's earlier, more robust image: "[We] include locals as information source," reads one bullet point. Another adds that "[we] hand suspects and criminals over to police after suitably disciplining them."[85] Included, too, is a chronicle of the organization, a lengthy mélange of quotations both from sponsors and from critics that make its extralegal history and its violent methods all too plain. Obviously, *Mapogo*, as brand, still trades in terror. Its security coverage, signaled by its fierce logo, is often listed as a desirable feature of homes on the suburban real estate market. At the same time, at least on the white side of the color line, it is now one among many firms in the competitive business of private policing and community protection. In small, dusty Afrikaans towns, the crime-fighting teams of *Mapogo Security* sport an Aryan paramilitary look, treating the public to weekend picnics with clowns and balloons. This face of the franchise has shifted a good deal, in other words, away from the Afrocentric image of Monhle John Magolego. The movement has indeed become a thing of many colors.[86]

In the northern countryside, however, *Mapogo is* still associated with the patriarchal authority personified by the man himself. Here, in place of clowns and balloons, untrammeled by the presence of the state, are the famously elaborate rituals through which Magolego sets up new branches, bearing *Mapogo's* claws for all to see. Like others who have expressed interest in the movement, we were invited to witness its triumphal entry on to virgin terrain, in this case a desolate village in the Bushbuckridge district, Mpumalanga. The daylong ceremony accords well with other accounts of similar events (e.g., Soggot and Ngobeni 1999, 136; N. Smith 2013, 171ff.). Its syntax opens a window on to *Mapogo's* political sociology. Magolego led the advance, traveling in a large, well-maintained BMW. He was flanked by loyal supporters—including, on this occasion, white farmers—clad in *Mapogo* T-shirts. Some of them wielded *sjamboks (whips)*, a weapon long associated with rough, racist discipline on Afrikaner farms. Led by a pickup with a huge banner, a motley procession of cars driven by signed-up and would-be members made its way to the house of the local chief, horns blaring. He, like several other traditional authorities, according to Magolego, had requested *Mapogo's* presence. The long audience that followed left no doubt that Magolego's convoy bore royal *imprimatur*. In fact, the entire ceremonial progress pointed to the promise of a return to old-time discipline, to another sovereignty.

For the opening in Bushbuckridge, a cross section of the village had gathered at the dilapidated community center. It included small businessmen, cell phones in hand, and a band of elderly churchwomen garbed in blankets, piously intoning Methodist hymns. Technology and tradition, business and godliness, complement each other at these moments. As Magolego's assistants set up a stall against one wall to sell bumper stickers, placards, and shirts, a crew of younger local women prepared meat donated by grateful residents. No *rites de passage* here are complete without the assembled company consuming a slaughtered beast in a show of moral resolve—and communal order remade. As these cultural trappings suggest, *Mapogo* invokes alternative sources of authority to speak truth to the sovereign power of the state: as its legitimacy and hegemony are in question, as its police function is parsed and privatized, the organization offers another sort of contract. It is one that appeals both to the customary, the ever-present underbelly of liberal "modern" law and institutions of governance (Obarrio 2014), and to various idioms of transcendence.

After some time, having ended his audience with the chief, Magolego himself, attired in a stylish suit,[87] swept into the room. He was accompanied by armed bodyguards and a video technician. All subsequent proceedings—the prayers, Magolego's address, the enrolling of new members, even our interview—were captured on video. Magolego always carries a gun, a cell phone, and a Bible, to which he sometimes turns in describing his mission. Like the great "fisher of men" in Luke, he says, he has been enjoined to "fish people" wherever he can through his movement. In March 2000, near White River, a reporter observed two signs outside an Afrikaans Christian camp. "Jesus Christ is our Lord," one proclaimed. "This property is protected by *Mapogo a Mathamaga*," declared the other. Magolego claims to be an active Catholic and defends rural Catholic establishments free of charge. A week after the Bushbuckridge event, he was to visit one in a distant town that needed help with repeated theft and vandalism.

Magolego has described his founding of *Mapogo* as the product of a conversion experience. The crime wave that attended the birth of the "new" South Africa, especially the killing of businessmen, "dissatisfied" him deeply. "What we were suffering was not merely theft," he told us. "It was war." In August 1996 an incident involving an elderly shopkeeper in Jane Furse, a town in Limpopo, made a lasting impression. Taken from his shop one night, the victim was found dead in the morning under a bridge, naked and bereft of his private parts. To Magolego, enough was enough. The killing had to be stopped. Local criminals acted with impunity, the state was nowhere to be seen, and political leaders lacked the will to make the police act effectively. He and colleagues called a meeting of almost a hundred black businessmen from that part of the country on 25 August. It was here that *Mapogo* was born. Magolego addressed the gathering. Everyone present, he said, felt motivated to "engage in the struggle" on behalf of the nation. Note the appropriation of both liberation movement lingo and imagined community. Note also that the atrocity that finally moved Magolego to action had the hallmarks not only of a robbery but of the ritual killing of a man of venerable age—and hence total disregard for the authority of elders. In a more recent recounting to Nicholas Smith (2013, 167), Magolego struck an updated evangelical chord: corporal punishment forces criminals to "repent and leave their dirty activities" so that they can be "born again." It was "not only good for the soul of the suspected criminal but also good for the soul of the nation."

Not only was Magolego the movement's founding visionary, but he also gave it its name and translated it into a striking visual image that, while Afro-traditional in idiom, communicates its intimidating message unambiguously across cultural and linguistic boundaries. *Mapogo a Mathamaga* derives from a Sesotho saying: "*Ge ole ngkwe ke lepogo o beli radithamaga*" (If you are a leopard, remember I am a tiger, we are both of the same color).[88] Magolego claims that the proverb warned people inclined to violence that they "are not the most powerful beings on earth." It tells them that "your force will be met by my force." He translates *Mapogo a Mathamaga* literally as "brown-spotted [i.e., bicolored] leopards." What it connotes for the organization is captured clearly by the logo: the heads of two face-to-face tigers (image 3). Magolego also has a more personal version of his *beroef*, his "vocation." He recounts that, on or around 22 August 1996—just four days after he called for the fateful meeting on the 25th, and likely as a consequence—he was attacked. He was driving home when he suddenly decided to visit a friend. Outside her house, he was confronted by armed youth, who took his Bible, his bag, and his keys but then withdrew, leaving a cache of liquor untouched on the back seat. Magolego said that the "uncanny" timing of the incident produced a "trauma" in him. Clearly, this was a warning not to establish the organization. He had never been robbed before. But he went ahead and now calls this experience a kind of "baptism." He has not, he insists, been attacked since then.

As the founders of *Mapogo* tell its history, the organization began with the intention to assist the work of the law. At first, it kept in communication with government and the SAPS. It also drew up a constitution and sent a memorandum to the provincial member of the Executive Council for Safety and Security, laying out its grievances and demands (von Schnitzler *et al.* 2001, 15). In the early years, it does appear to have handed over suspects, but it changed tactics when the police failed to take action (Minnaar 2001, 25). *Mapogo* very soon developed a reputation for its distinctive modes of extending protection and meting out punishment. Although concerned largely with property crimes, it also provided personal security and, on occasion, dealt with cases of assault and murder. Members paid a joining fee and a means-related annual assessment and were expected to volunteer for specific "operations" on behalf of the organization.[89] Some paid with their labor. In urban areas, "reaction units" drew on the unemployed, who were appropriately "rewarded."

All the available evidence suggests that, at root, *Mapogo's* signature methods have remained unchanged. When an attack occurs, its units visit the victim and his or her kin and neighbors to gather information. They then go to find the "right people," as Magolego puts it, demand to know the whereabouts of the stolen goods, and punish the perpetrator(s) severely enough to prevent any repeat offending. It is often said of the organization that it scants on investigation and gives little opportunity for those accused to defend themselves. Unsurprisingly, the police authorities have been skeptical from the start: "The notion that *Mapogo* has a sophisticated intelligence network is nonsense," Seth Nthai, then a safety and security official for the Northern Province, told Jonny Steinberg. "If a crime is committed [they] will not try to get to the bottom of it. They will go to a known criminal and beat him up."[90] Senior officers said the same thing to us; some of their juniors, however, condoned *Mapogo* to us and claimed that a number of their colleagues participated in its activities. Their take on Magolego and his cadres was distinctly ambivalent, an unstable mix of recognition and condemnation, opprobrium and admiration. But none of this has had much effect on *Mapogo*'s style of operation or their business model. In 2015 the website for the commercial security arm of the organization prefaced its menu of services with the following statement, alongside a picture to two cute, vulnerable-looking blond girls: "Criminal cases are investigated and dealt with by our agents the real African way. People who are found in possession of our customer's goods do not have the luxury of long-lasting court cases and being found innocent on a technical point. They will immediately be dealt with in a traditional way."[91] Magolego has long insisted, with some justification, that the cops will never get the help they need from the public to catch criminals successfully—even if they "really" wanted to. People simply deny all knowledge and avoid testifying in court. CP is an abject failure for the same reason, he insists. We are back, here, to the point that criminal intelligence is next to impossible without the kind of trust and recognition essential to the social contract and the sovereignty of the state, now largely fractured—the kind of trust and recognition that *Mapogo claims* to draw on in countering crime. "We rely on community knowledge to do this," Magolego told us. "People used to be afraid to provide information. But they were not once they joined us." They could "punish the disrespectful boy next door without fear" because they had the organization behind them. As Oomen (2004, 161) has suggested, *Mapogo* has established a moral community of sorts, even a facsimile of citizenship, albeit one ring-fenced by a shield of fee-for-service terror.

That shield is crucial to *Mapogo*'s strategy, not least to the many women who join the organization.[92] Few of them participate in its coercive operations, although they *do* contribute greatly to *its* criminal intelligence. But most seem persuaded that displaying its logo reduces the chances of rape, abuse, theft, and, especially in the case of the elderly, attacks by young "thugs" with designs on their pensions. Given the fearsome name of *Mapogo*—and the emphatic manner in which it reminds offenders of the consequences of their actions—this faith has some foundation in fact. It is little wonder that Monhle John Magolego has been received into poor rural communities as a redemptive force, albeit one who arrives in a souped-up BMW, with videographer and sundry sidekicks in tow.

But how exactly did his organization establish its singular reputation? Other providers of alternative justice have not succeeded to nearly the same extent. Effective marketing is one answer. As soon as it was established, *Mapogo* set about making the brute seriousness of its intentions widely known. When it attacked known criminals with *sjamboks*, "television, radio, and newspaper reporters rushed to the hospitals to take pictures, showing the entire country the backsides of [our] victims." The tough talk that accompanied some of the more theatrical acts of discipline underwrote its punch in popular perception. And perception was what counted. Once, in Nelspruit, *Mapogo* members were accused of plunging a man suspected of concealing evidence into a crocodile-filled river. "I asked my local members if it was true, and they denied it," says Magolego. But, he added, "it's wonderful that people think that it happened. That's exactly what we want."[93] Not all was bluff and hype, however. *Mapogo's* reputation was backed, as its motto declares, by graphic displays of its ways and means. Informants told us, in some detail, how its units had administered electric shocks to the genitals of suspects and to have dragged others behind vehicles; this last method, beloved of apartheid-era lynch mobs and lately revived by the cops (see 1.2), underscores the parallels between *Mapogo* and the SAPS. It also invokes visceral memories of violence past.

This point is important. As the movement gained momentum in the 1990s, observers, some black police officers among them, expressed concern that it would encourage "a racist-backlash among white right-wingers."[94] It has given them "a legitimate discourse," said Seth Nthai, the former safety and security official quoted earlier: "They can now call [all] blacks criminals and feel they have reason to beat people."[95] Almost from the start, as we have intimated, *Mapogo's* rough justice—and, symbolically, its use of the *sjambok*—appealed to pistol-packing farmers in Afrikaner strongholds; for them, it recalled the heyday of the *ancien régime*. Moreover, the nostalgic appeal to "traditional" African justice, in a world putatively bereft of order and respect for authority, fostered an alliance across the lines of race between those most threatened by the new order of things after 1994: conservative whites, the older black petty bourgeoisie of the countryside, chiefs dissatisfied with the limited recognition granted them under the democratic constitution, and a good proportion of their subjects (cf. Oomen 2004, 159).

This alliance fed a culture of patriarchal populism in opposition to those ostensibly entitled by the new dispensation: youth, women, and agricultural workers. A white farmer in Limpopo put it like this: "The only thing black people understand is violence and authority. They don't understand democracy, they need a chief. That's their tradition, their culture. They can't help it. *Mapogo* is the best invention since the wheel, because they beat the hell out of them, and that's all they understand" (von Schnitzler *et al.* 2001, 33). For the likes of this farmer, as for chiefs, Magolego's men offer violence-by-proxy, violence on the cheap, protecting them and their property against those whom they would discipline, those whom they wish to bring to heel. In the process, they reinforce racial divides. As an ANC report from the Northern Province noted in 2000, "it is inconceivable that an Afrikaner will ever suffer the wrath of *Mapogo*" (von Schnitzler *et al.* 2001, 34). At the heart of Magolego's crusade, too, is an uncivil war between generations. He frequently harps on the youthfulness of the criminals, who, he alleges, have always opposed his movement and the moral order that it secures: young men who struggled against elders accused of "selling out"—traditional authorities notably among them—in the late apartheid years; young men who now, like their urban counterparts, dispute the legitimacy of a regime that is selling *them* short.

Already in the late 1990s it was clear that *Mapogo* had come to mean different things to different people. Its legendary charter had evolved into an ideology with a momentum of its own, one that reached beyond the control of Magolego himself. By the early 2000s, as he struggled to rein in the rogue force he had created, it was not always clear that his network even knew about incidents that occurred in its name. The state itself, like some of the police to whom we spoke (above, p. 213), had thus far displayed a decided ambivalence toward the organization. It had, after all, curbed crime in areas where law-enforcement was ineffectual. As *Mapogo* grew in strength, however, government began sporadically to clamp down on it. But Oomen (2004, 164) suggests that this may have been driven more by concerns over Magolego's partisan allegiances than by his alleged criminal activities: opponents of the ANC who were sympathetic to him, like the United Democratic Movement,[96] courted him to run for office, seeing his movement, perhaps, as a potential voting bloc. Although he came quite close to winning a seat in the provincial legislature in 1999, his ambitions in this direction never went any further. Nor did his open political opposition to the regime.

In the end, however, *Mapogo* seems to have been overtaken by something else: Magolego's loss of control over his brand to competitors in a rapidly expanding security market that allowed any methods the trade would bear.

In June 2000, ostensibly to bolster an image of respectability, Magolego declared that *Mapogo* was "going mainstream";[97] this announcement came in the midst of his battle with white partners like Pieter Oosthuizen, who were already "restructuring" the organization along commercial lines. He claimed that he himself had started a "professional security firm" in Limpopo, one that refrained from flogging suspects, used marked patrol vehicles, and was registered with the national Security Officers' Board. But it is unclear how far this venture was ever taken. Meanwhile, clones, like *Mabogo* Securities, sporting a clearly derivative tiger image, began to advertise their services. What *is* sure, though, is that, in its guise as corporate franchise, *Mapogo's* twin-headed logo began to travel to polite suburban places it had not been before, having become one among many in the private protection industry. Had the leopards changed their spots? Magolego's enterprise continues to ply its own signature trade alongside the various spin-offs. Each side of the Janus-faced or, rather, tiger-faced operation—the "Afro-traditional" original and its commercial counterpart—has become an alibi for the other in the delivery of il/licit strong-arm justice. Both hover at the edges of the law as South Africa, like the rest of the world, drifts ever more in the direction of market and moral, executive and juridical, deregulation.

Coda: The End(s) of Justice?

As we noted at the start of this chapter, neither alternative policing nor informal justice are new in South Africa. Both were a feature of life on the colonial frontier. And both flourished under apartheid, which drew an especially sharp line between those shielded by the law and those disciplined by it, leaving the latter to look beyond the purview of the state for security and the management of conflict. In the late years of the *ancien régime*, as enforcement began to be liberalized and privatized—a process that, we have seen, preceded 1994 and has gathered pace ever since—alternative policing and informal justice multiplied on all sides. They continue to do so. In South Africa, as elsewhere in the world, this has given, is giving, rise to a vibrant array of processes, practices, and platforms in and beyond the marketplace, in and beyond "the community." Taken together, they point to an open secret: that the late modern, liberal state is less and less able to secure social order or to "control" crime. Whether this is true or not—how does one actually measure such things?—much of the *angst* of contemporary social life is dogged by the specter of criminality, by a metaphysic of disorder.

We have argued that the latter-day explosion of alternative justice is part of an unfolding, open-ended, largely underdetermined dialectic between the state and civil society. Born of shifts in the nature of sovereignty with the morphing of the state form under the impact of the global economy, it is a dialectic that has rendered murky, often illegible, the line between the legal and the illegal, ordinary enterprise and malfeasance, crime-and-policing. With their increasing corporate capture, states have ceded to the market control over many of their signature functions, most of all their monopoly of force. As a result, vertical structures of authority are giving way to a lateral montage of partial, overlapping sovereignties, making it ever more difficult to separate government from business and business from criminality (cf. Roitman 2005, 2006, on the Chad Basin). These processes are inevitably inflected by particular historical circumstances: in South Africa, they have been more than usually acute, which may be why, in this respect as in many others, this country appears as a harbinger of futures elsewhere. Here, anxieties about the regime's capacity to secure its population and their property against the criminal specter, or to prevail over disorder, came just as the majority of its population won the long-deferred right to full citizenship. In these times, the image of the vigilante appears irresistible: unrestrained by the law, plying the zone between the licit and the illicit, s/he promises to restore a sharp line between law and lawlessness, friend and enemy, citizen and anticitizen. With lethal certainty, s/he appropriates the awful, awesome violence on which the sovereignty of the liberal state has always depended, the authorized violence that underwrites the social contract. Or at least is meant to, but scarcely does any longer, having been fractured and dispersed and privatized. The promise of that sovereign violence is not merely to harness rogue lawlessness or to lay to rest the threat of criminal disorder. It is also to redress the effects wrought by an amoral economy, one that, in fostering savage appetites and unfulfilled desires, undermines the very possibility of a legible, habitable, and socially viable world.

CHAPTER 2.5

SHARP ENDINGS
A Pointed Afterimage

Crime, as we have shown throughout this volume, compels us to think through—and with—it about the ways in which it has become constitutive of our world: of its micro- and macrogeographies, its visible and invisible dimensions, its politics both large and intimate. Like horror, it "prods the bounds of the unthinkable," of "that which cannot be said under normal circumstances," that which "we simply *know* . . . to be true" (Comaroff and Ong 2013, 8). A saturating signifier, it has colonized our imaginations both abstract and concrete, our social habits and habitats. It pervades our storytelling, our public conversations and private thoughts, our theory work and aesthetic impulses, the way we see and hear, the way we inhabit the spaces in which we live, our traffic with others, the walls that we erect around ourselves. And it does all these things in ways far in excess of the instrumental. To be sure, quite ordinary objects bear witness to the status of crime as a total social fact. Thus, we come finally to the story of *Eina*, a uniquely postcolonial contribution to the technology used to "burglarproof" homes in the "war against crime."

◆

Even the most practical of things engage us in ways that exceed their given purposes, their obdurate, single-minded materiality. It is not merely that they bear within them the value—use value, exchange value, sign value—with which they have been invested, wittingly or otherwise. Nor even is it that they "matter" as embodiments of the social worlds, of the ecologies of power, production, passion, and panic whence they come and/or in which they circulate (Butler 1993a). It is also that, as things, they are always-already "scripted," entreating us to engage in further interactions with them (Bernstein 2011, 11–12), if in ways we never fully control. They call out to us in a culturally specific manner, issuing solicitations to action that enlist us as subjects. Scripted objects invite us, dare us, seduce us, compel us to engage with them, making us complicit in what appear to be their designs. Yet for all this, they do not have agency in and of themselves, even in a qualified sense. To the contrary, agency—along with identity, affect, and value—is produced in the process of our traffic with things, in our ongoing, historically shaped encounter with the very stuff of existence (Bernstein 2011, 11–12), in the counterpoint, willed or unwilled, of subjects and objects, sharp edges and blunt truths.

Let us return, then, to the thing that its makers call *Eina*.

Eina is, literally, a cutting-edge South African device designed to protect property and people from intruders.[1] A singular fusion of the menacing and the comely, the brutal and the beautiful, it consists of rows of galvanized "metal fingers, twisted over 1.5m lengths [of barbed wire] to simulate branches and twigs" (see image 4). Those metal fingers are "serious, razor sharp security spikes" that are said nonetheless to be "very pleasing to the eye." Most often coated in green, they are covered with synthetic leaves, "available in variegated ivy or solid vine." The wire is laid in such a way as to snake along the tops and sides of walls, fences, and gateways—"domestic, commercial, or industrial"—marking out the contours of private property with the aesthetic of the colonial estate. Part devils' teeth, part *faux* horticulture, *Eina* is billed as a cunning camouflage. "Beauty can be deceptive," its manufacturers tell us. While "environmentally safe"—"it will not harm the birds"—their product is also "extremely dangerous and not easily seen at night time."

Eina's artful foliage, then, entwines a crude, thinly veiled threat. Despite the claims to the contrary made for it, there is something disturbingly unnatural about those regimented leaves. They unsettle the viewer, compelling a second look. It is as if the contrivance itself gives a knowing wink: "Don't even think of it!" "*Eina*" is Afrikaans for "Ouch!" It is an exclamation of pain, an infantile onomatopoeic; some say that it derives etymologically from the San of the Kalahari, from *é* + *ná*, which captures the reaction to a sudden sting, a sharp hurt. It may also evoke a bluff, a playful truth-or-dare. But what *is* the game here? What thorny encounter is being anticipated along those fault lines, those beguiling leafy borders that mark off private property from public space in contemporary South Africa?

In answer to these questions, allow us just a little repetition.

The final days of apartheid, its death throes, were not lacking in violence.

IMAGE 4. *Eina*: floral home protection

But they also did not occasion the apocalyptic bloodbath grimly anticipated by generations of South Africans who had lived under the "banditry" of its law (Modisane1963, 153). Being part of the planetary geopolitical shift that brought the end of the Cold War, and the formal triumph of the global capitalist economy, liberation here, as we have noted before, came hand in hand with liberalization, truth-and-reconciliation with a hardening commitment to market-led development. Political transformation—in this case, the rise of constitutional democracy—was not accompanied by a significant restructuring of the economy. Postapartheid empowerment, aka the reallocation of assets, might have yielded the emergence of a class of very wealthy "black diamonds." But for the majority, things remained the same, or worse. The nation at large was soon beset by new challenges: like other industrial societies across the world, it suffered a drastic reduction of the workforce, growing casualization of labor, sharply rising unemployment, and a widening gulf between rich and poor—even by the grotesque standards of the apartheid years. The heightened visibility of the destitute and homeless in a putatively desegregated landscape mocked expectations of entitlement and inclusion, fostering frustration, especially among those most dramatically disadvantaged. Left stranded, above all, were young African men, who were less able than their female counterparts to draw on social grants or ply informal trade. Upsurges of anger and youthful impatience were manifest in urgent street politics and expressive culture, in flagrantly macho populism, brutality against women, xenophobic attacks, and witch purges, and in the vibrant criminal economy that flourished under newly deregulated conditions. Plying the space between expectation and fulfilment, that economy served both as a mundane mode of production—"affirmative redistribution," as the protagonist in *Hijack Stories* called it (above, 1.3)—and as a curt riposte to the rule of law, which appeared, as before, to protect the powerful and the privileged. In the upshot, as have seen, talk of a society in disarray, of endemic violence, of justice stretched to breaking point gained traction across the social spectrum of a nation not yet worthy of the name.

Old elites, and some new fellow travelers, have depicted the high incidence of violent criminality here as a necropolitics (cf. Mbembe 2006) or a stifled civil war (cf. Steinberg 2001, 5; above, part 1). It has also been read as an expression of racial revenge, a settling of scores left unrequited by the advent of constitutional democracy. This is despite compelling evidence to the contrary, including the fact, cited more than once above, that the black poor suffer predation more than any other segment of the population; also the fact that white women are much more likely to be killed or hurt by their partners or husbands than by a random black assailant, a revelation that some conservative Afrikaners refuse to believe and rail against.[2] Whatever the statistics show (2.3), most whites and many blacks, especially among the middle classes of the faded rainbow nation, feel themselves uniquely vulnerable to rage, attack, and immanent disorder. A number of them have left the country for what they take to be safer havens. But most have stayed on, despite their feelings of ambivalence, being deeply attached to the land, its history, and its modes of life. The whites among them regard themselves as African. They regularly hark back to the avuncular figure of Nelson Mandela and to the transition agreement that guaranteed both their citizenship in South Africa and their right to retain their assets—all the spoils of apartheid. Yet their terror and their suppressed feelings of guilt remain palpable despite their bluff resolve. They are haunted not merely by the expectation of assault on their persons and possessions but by a stifled sense that crime is the product of an inequality that indicts their own wealth, itself still so visible on the divided landscape. They suffer, too, from a gnawing awareness that, to the vocal majority—among whom the mantra "one settler, one bullet" is increasingly audible—their property is nothing more than theft. For new black elites, there is also apprehension, but it takes a different form: "We understand that . . . crime comes from the pathological need for historical vengeance. . . . [But we abhor] violence because we fear that ours will be the next throat to be slit."[3]

It is this environment that has given birth to *Eina*, a darkly comic afterimage to the rise of a mighty criminal economy, an inventive security industry, and a spirited "war on crime," itself an allegory for continuing struggle along lines of class, race, gender, and generation. *Eina*'s menacing foliage expresses an unresolved ambivalence between the right to private property and the inevitability of invasion, between enclaved security and an impending incursion on privilege. It anticipates the defiant vault over the fence, the mundane seizure, by the multitude, of the means of survival. We are *"waiting for the barbarians"* (Coetzee 1982), says *Eina*. In paraphrase, "We stand our ground, defy efforts to intimidate us. Our final displacement might be inevitable. But in the meantime, we will defend our well-earned assets, own homes and gardens. We defy the view that we live under siege. Our defenses might not in the end be effective, but they are ornamental, refined, civilized."

Thus does the metaphysic of disorder, the sublimity of crime, script the everyday aesthetics of contemporary South Africa, a land of searing beauty and barely concealed violence, a land of energetic aspiration and cold-eyed cynicism, a nation-in-becoming not yet at one with, at home with, itself.

In the words of Sisonke Msimang:

> The question [is] why, regardless of this decline [in crime], so many South Africans, across race and class lines, continue to feel so physically insecure.
>
> The obvious answer is that violence in South Africa signifies a deeper malaise. It operates as a stand in for declining levels of trust. . . . [T]o a large degree it serves as a foil. . . . In contemporary South Africa rage is our lingua franca. . . . We are a nation beholden to criminals; we hate them and yet we cannot ignore the contexts that create them.[4]

The nation is also beholden to criminality as a touchstone of things that "we simply know to be true," at a time when received forms of certainty and authority are deeply in question. As we have argued throughout this volume—in confronting the big picture and in our five uneasy pieces—crime-and-policing has become a, perhaps *the*, critical medium for contemplating sovereign authority anew, for recalibrating our understanding of the law, for retooling our conceptions of property, personhood, citizenship, and the social contract. Also the nature of the "real" itself—in South Africa and in much of the world at large.

ACKNOWLEDGMENTS

We have been working on *The Truth about Crime* for quite some time now and, along the way, have benefited from the generosity of many institutions and individuals. Our research in South Africa—at times more participatory than we might have wished—has been variously supported by the National Science Foundation, the American Bar Foundation, the Lichtstern Fund for Anthropological Research at the University of Chicago, and our Oppenheimer Fellowships at Harvard University. The ideas explored in this book began life as the Jensen Memorial Lectures at the Johann Wolfgang Goethe-Universität Frankfurt am Main and were expanded and taken in new directions during fruitful spells at the Radcliffe Institute for Advanced Study at Harvard and the Stellenbosch Institute for Advanced Study in South Africa. Our thinking has been immensely enriched, too, by our ongoing engagement with colleagues in a range of intellectual contexts: in the Department of Anthropology, the African Studies Workshop, and the Center for Contemporary Theory at the University of Chicago; in the Department of African and African American Studies, the Department of Anthropology, and the African Studies Workshop at Harvard; at the American Bar Foundation in Chicago; and at WISER, the Wits Institute for the Study of Social and Economic Research, University of the Witwatersrand. We are also indebted to countless participants in seminars and conferences across the world, scholars who have responded—more or less patiently, more or less enthusiastically—to our particular criminal obsessions. Over the years, these interlocutors have given us more than they could possibly imagine.

A few people warrant special mention. Janet Legalatlhadi, Elizabeth Tlhoaele, Mhengwa Letsholo, and Joe Leteane were among those who first introduced us, with tact and insight, to the community in Mafikeng, in the North

West Province of South Africa, where we have worked, on and off, for over forty years. We owe them a lifelong debt of gratitude. Of the many officers of the South African Police Service who assisted us during the course of our ethnographic research in that province, three were especially generous with their time and forbearance: Patrick Aseneng, Jacob Monei, and Irene Lefenyo. We learned a great deal from each of them. Steven Robins, Sarah Nuttall, Bernard Dubbeld, Fernanda Pinto de Almeida, Theresa Alfaro-Velcamp, Darja Djordjevic, Achille Mbembe, Dennis Davis, Stephen Clingman, and William Julius Wilson, all close friends and colleagues, consented—or, more accurately, were drafted—to do battle with this volume in manuscript form, an assignment they undertook with uncommonly good humor and consummate thoughtfulness. Our many conversations with them have been critical in shaping our understanding of crime-and-policing in South Africa and the United States—and much else besides. So, too, have the many extraordinary cartoons on the topic by Jonathan Shapiro, aka Zapiro, South Africa's most inspired satirist, who has graciously consented to our reproducing one of his classic images.

Alma Medina, our research and administrative assistant, has been unfailingly cheerful and resourceful in supporting all our endeavors, as has the remarkable staff in the West Wing, aka the offices of the Department of African and African American Studies at Harvard University. Finally, the two reviewers for the University of Chicago Press, Peter Geschiere and Teresa Caldeira—the first an Africanist of immense accomplishment; the second, the author of a pathbreaking anthropology of crime, policing, and citizenship in Brazil that precedes ours in a number of respects—gifted us with unusually acute and generous readings of the text. This book has been greatly enriched by their criticisms and suggestions. Its remaining shortcomings, as always, are our own.

A concluding word of appreciation is due to Joe Leteane, whom we have already mentioned. Joe was our first Setswana teacher, way back in 1969–70; we, and now our children, have remained in contact ever since. A social analyst by proclivity, Joe was a frequent companion as we did our research in the North West during the late 1990s. Together we frequented police stations and taxiranks, courts and coffee shops, haunted houses and family gatherings. Like us, he has lived to see the birth, in South Africa, of a fraught, contradictory new order, one that has unleashed not only a newfound liberal democracy but a dangerously lawless *doppelgänger*. Every bit as challenged as we have been by these new realities, he has posed his own questions about them, developing his own take on the problem of crime and culture in the wake of apartheid.

We might not have always seen things in quite the same light, but his unusually acute insights have certainly helped us to hone many of the arguments we make in this book. His lively curiosity, like those of so many colleagues and compatriots, has continued to sustain us in an inquiry and a shared history that are still unfolding.

NOTES

Preface

1. Zapiro [Jonathan Shapiro], *Mail & Guardian*, 4 July 2002; reprinted in Zapiro (2002, 125).
2. Pieces 2.3, 2.4, and 2.5 are heavily revised versions of essays that we have published before (Comaroff and Comaroff 2006a, 2007, 2013). In the case of the first (2.3), the statistical material is completely different and our commentary has been rewritten accordingly; the second (2.4) is almost twice the length of its predecessor and, again, is situated in a much-refined analytical frame; and the third (2.5), the short endpiece, has been substantially reshaped as a closing coda for this volume. Piece 2.1 was first presented by Jean Comaroff as the Ryerson Lecture at the University of Chicago in 2011.

Chapter 1.1

1. Kim Hjelmgaard, "Cameron: U.K. Riots Result of 'Pure Criminality,'" *MarketWatch*, Market Pulse Archives, 9 August 2011, www.marketwatch.com/story/cameron -uk, accessed 5 October 2011.
2. Glen Ford, "Ferguson Unmasks the War on Black America," *Common Dreams*, from the *Black Agenda Report*, 20 August 2014, http://www.commondreams.org/views /2014/08/20/ferguson-unmasks-war-black-america, accessed 27 August 2014.
3. "Map-Based Crime Reporting for South Africa," mailto:info@mypetition.co.za, received 3 October 2011, original (bold) emphasis. The URL of the Turn It Around, South Africa, website is http://turnitaround.co.za/, accessed 27 August 2014.

4. An overview of Capita, plc, a company to which many functions of state are outsourced by the British government, is to be found at http://m.capita.co.uk/who-we
-are.aspx. The cited passages (with original, capitalized emphases) are from the page entitled "Police and Justice" under the hypertext "What We Do," http://m.capita
.co.uk/what-we-do/sectors/police-and-justice.aspx, accessed 29 August 2014.

5. Johannes Leithäuser, "Crime Groups Become an Increasing Security Threat, Officials Assert," *Frankfurter Allgemeine Zeitung*, 22 May 2001, English edition, 2.

6. Henning Mankell, Sweden's celebrated crime novelist, quoted in Sarah Lyall, "Brightening Thrillers with a Gloomy Swedish Detective," *The New York Times*, 13 November 2003, B1, 5.

7. Paul Foot, "Above the Law," *Guardian* (UK), 29 May 2001, 8.

8. Sarah Lyall, "Soggy Pastures Where All Things Crash and Burn," *New York Times*, 7 April 2001, A4. The quotation is attributed to social critic Polly Toynbee.

9. Nigel Morris, "The Mysterious Case of Why Crime Is Falling in Britain," *Independent* (UK), 24 January 2014, 19.

10. This slogan appears in, among other places, a posting by Crime Busters of South Africa, http://www.100megspop2.com/crimebusters/AboutUs.html, accessed 11 December 2003.

11. "Contact crimes" include the following official categories of felony: murder, attempted murder, grievous bodily harm, common assault, aggravated robbery, and sexual offenses. See below, 2.1, for the evidence for the drop in these rates.

12. The rather-curious inclusion of Adelaide derives from a BBC TV Channel 4 documentary, *The Trials of Joanne Lees*, screened in July 2002. The accusation drew loud denials from the Australian government and media sources. It is also especially ironic since Adelaide is the sort of "safe" place to which white South Africans, fearful of crime, have fled. The notion of "crime capital of the world" ought, anyway, to be regarded with skepticism. Not only does it depend on how criminality is counted, which, as we shall see in 2.3, is rather less than an exact science, but rates may also fluctuate wildly over time. For example, the homicide rate in Ciudad Juárez was comfortably the highest in the world in 2010 but dropped remarkably over the next three years—and, since then, appears to be on the rise again. See Patrick Corcoran, "Is Violence Returning to Ciudad Juárez?," *In Sight Crime*, 23 August 2013, http://www.insightcrime.org/news-analysis/is-violence-returning-to
-ciudad-juarez, accessed 3 July 2015.

13. South African geography, by contrast to that of the United States, refers to predominantly white neighborhoods that fall within urban municipalities as "suburbs." Urban black residential areas are known as "townships." White communities outside urban municipalities (i.e., suburbs or exurbs in the United States) are

called "villages" or "towns," depending on size; their rural black counterparts are almost always referred to as villages, whatever their population.

14. Matt Apuzzo and Michael S. Schmidt, "In Washington, Second Thoughts on Arming the Police," *New York Times*, 24 August 2014, A1, 16. Apuzzo and Smith also observe that despite fears of terrorism, it too remains relatively rare on US soil. And yet, they add, "any effort to cut police funding would be met with sharp opposition." On the NYPD claim to the contrary, see the full-page "Open Letter to the Chairperson of the Democratic National Convention," from the Sergeants Benevolent Association, Police Department, City of New York, in *New York Times*, 26 August 2014, A5; it asserts that shootings in the city had increased by 13 percent since 2013.

15. For a counterargument, see Matthews (2005).

16. Excerpted from Sergeants Benevolent Association, Police Department, City of New York, "An Open Letter to the Chairperson of the Democratic National Convention," *New York Times*, 26 August 2014, A5. See n. 14 above.

17. Kate Zernike, "Camden Turns Around with New Police Force," *New York Times*, 1 September 2014, A1, A12.

18. See, e.g., Devlin Barrett, "Wanted: Decent Crime Stats," *Wall Street Journal*, 9 October 2015, A3.

19. An analysis that argues for dropping global crime rates is to be found in "Where Have All the Burglars Gone?," *Economist*, 20 July 2013, www.economist .com/news/briefing/21582041-rich-world-seeing-less-and-less-crime-even-face -high-unemployment-and-economic, accessed 1 July 2014. To complicate matters, however, a simple Google search, done in August 2014, indicated that numbers in the Global North have fluctuated both up and down over relatively short periods during the past decade—as indeed they are doing at the time of writing. See also Garland 2001, 207–9. It scarcely needs pointing out that these numbers are inflected by many things, including, most of all, (1) policing strategies and legitimacy, (2) levels of public reporting of breaches, and (3) law-making that expands or contracts what is defined, officially, as criminal.

20. Dardot and Laval (2014) approach "the new way of the world" in a manner that owes much to Foucault (2008), much more than does our own analysis.

21. Schneider and Schneider (2008, 352) cite the 1764 edition. The earliest translation that we could locate is listed in our bibliography under its translator, Farrer (1880).

22. This, of course, is a play on a commonly cited phrase in Hobbes's *Leviathan* (chap. 13, "Of The Naturall Condition Of Mankind, As Concerning Their Felicity, And Misery"): "that condition which is called Warre . . . is of every man, against every man." Hobbes was referring here to the absence of government ("a com-

mon Power"), not specifically to the violation of the social contract, although, for Locke, the effect of criminality was much the same.

23. Sullivan (2001, 31) cites Locke's notion that the (criminal) effort of one person to exercise absolute power over another is akin to entering a state of war. Perhaps as significant is Locke's statement in *The Second Treatise*, sec. 11, that one who commits "violence and slaughter" has, in effect, "declared war against all mankind."

24. Many police forces produce their own "actuality" television shows. In South Africa, for example, the police service aired *Crime Watch* for many years; its reruns are still shown. Others cooperate closely in the making of both fictional and documentary programs. A few even have their own TV channels and news services.

25. The source of this very apt term appears to be Mark Kennedy, to whom it is attributed, without further citation, by Greenberg (1993, 39).

26. See Linebaugh (1991) on the frequency of hanging in eighteenth-century London, which he ties to the rising salience of private property, its effect on the laboring poor, and the "contention between the classes" (xvii); this as part of an exploration of the dialectical relationship between crime and capitalism. His analysis, however, has been called into question; see K. Thomas (1992), from whose review of Linebaugh's study our next sentence in the text, the one about crime and capitalism, is paraphrased.

27. This quotation from "The Usefulness of Crime" is from D. Greenberg (1993). It first appeared in *Theories of Surplus Value*, vol. 1 (1963; see Marx 1993). A slightly different translation of the same passage is to be found in Mandel (1984, 11).

28. It has often been pointed out that Marx himself did not have much to say, specifically, about policing, violence, criminality, or criminal justice (e.g., Emsley 2007, 124). But it hardly needs saying that a well-established criminology has arisen on the scaffolding of his theory work in political economy.

29. The origin of modern policing, as Garriott (2013) notes, is usually dated—not altogether accurately—to the late 1820s.

30. The phrase "the body of corporate nations" is quoted from the missionary David Livingstone (1857, 34).

31. Except, that is, among expatriate colonizers, settlers who remained citizens of empire (Mamdani 1996) and were subject to legal regimes fashioned along the same lines as those "at home."

32. Within their own jurisdictions, indigenous courts dealt with a wide array of breaches and conflicts arising out of property relations. But these were treated as civil, not criminal, matters and did not, in any case, hinge upon ownership in the same terms as those understood in Europe (see Comaroff and Roberts 1981). Furthermore, "native" courts, according to their official mandates, were not permit-

ted to try a wide range of serious offenses, including such things as homicide and rape, or those that involved "traditional" practices deemed repugnant by colonial authorities; they were dealt with by the state (see e.g., Moore 1986).

33. By 1846, of course, the United States was no longer a colony. But what was said of slavery in postindependent, antebellum America applied to various forms of "captured" labor throughout much of the colonial world. Besides, for black Americans, the United States might as well have remained a settler colony for all that autonomy from Britain affected their status as subjects.

34. Historians have pointed out that harsh exploitation of convict labor in the late nineteenth century was not confined to the South alone; see, e.g., H. Thompson (2011, 17).

35. The term "crooked ladder," as Gladwell (2014, 37) notes, is owed to sociologist James O'Kane (1992).

36. Cf. Sally Engel Merry's (1998) account of the role of "work violations" on British and US sugar plantations in nineteenth-century Hawaii.

37. In South Africa, master-and-servant acts date back to the 1850s in the Cape Colony and Natal and to somewhat later in the Boer Republics. They remained in force, renamed the Native Labour Regulation Act, after Union in 1910. Subsequent legislation further tightened the control of "native labor" over the course of the twentieth century. In addition to the scholarly studies noted in the text above, see, for a readily accessible popular history, *South African History Online: Towards a People's History*, chap. 9, http://www.sahistory.org.za/archive/chapter-9-struggle-against-sweating, accessed 7 July 2014.

38. Although their origin dates back to the late eighteenth century, the "pass laws" were put in place in the Union of South Africa in 1923 under the Natives (Urban Areas) Act, later replaced by the (very similar) Natives (Urban Areas) Consolidation Act of 1945; both applied to (most) black men over the age of sixteen in urban areas. Despite major protests in 1950 against their extension to women, the 1945 statute was replaced, in 1952, by the yet more draconian Pass Laws Act. There is a very large literature on the legal infrastructure of apartheid, particularly on the pass laws, which were repealed in 1986, and on their carceral effects. The *Annual Reports* of the South African Institute of Race Relations, for example, published a running commentary on the latter throughout much of the life of the regime. But for one accessible source on the pass system itself, see Helen Suzman Foundation, "Key Legislation in the Formation of Apartheid," http://www.cortland.edy/cgis/suzman/apartheid.html, accessed 15 August 2014.

39. For one account in the South African press, see Mogomotsi Magome, "Ramaphosa Set to Step into the Firing Line," *IOL News*, 10 August 2014, http://www

.iol.co.za/news/politics/ramaphosa-set-to-step-into-the-firing-line-1.1733035#
.U-deiU10w5s, accessed 10 August 2014. The e-mails written by Ramaphosa to the
former South African police chief and to other mining company executives, in
which these statements were made, were widely published in the local media. At
the same time, it is important to note that a direct *causal* connection cannot, and
should not, be drawn between Ramaphosa's communications and the command
to shoot at the miners. Our concern here, rather, is the fact that the vice president
of the country was so quick to deem the protest "criminal" and to recommend that,
as such, it be dealt with appropriately—and forcefully—by the police.

40. See Greg Marinovich and Greg Nicolson, "Marikana Commission: Police's Defence Collapsing," *Daily Maverick*, 9 September 2014, http://www.dailymaverick
.co.za/article/2014-09-09-marikana-commission-polices-defence-collapsing
/#.VBQ5zE10w5s, accessed 11 September 2014. While it was heavily critical of the
police commissioner, the Marikana Commission of Inquiry into the massacre,
presided over by Judge Ian Gordon Farlam, held nobody in the executive responsible for the shootings. On Ramaphosa it chose its words very carefully: "The Commission has found that it cannot be said of Mr. Ramaphosa [that he] was *the* cause
of the massacre" (emphasis added). It did not, however, say that his actions were
not *a* contributory factor.

41. There is a huge mass-mediated literature, and a growing scholarly one, on Marikana. Its causes and effects, both proximate and longer term, have been debated
ad infinitum; so, too, have the actions of all those involved. But about one thing
there is no dispute: that the mass protest of the striking miners was treated from
the first as a criminal threat to public order; to wit, the government tried, in the
days immediately after, to indict the strikers themselves for the killings, not the
police who shot them. Whether their criminalization was justifiable, of course, is
another matter, one that hinges on the way in which the line is drawn between illegality and the (political) right to collective freedom of expression.

42. Jon Swaine, "'This Is a Revolution, Plain and Simple," *Guardian* (UK), 21 August
2014, 4–7.

43. Jon Swaine and Chris Campbell, "National Guard Moves into Ferguson as Violence
over Shooting Intensifies: Autopsy Confirms Officer Shot Teenager Six Times,
Washington Investigates Civil Rights Aspect of Case," *Guardian* (UK), 19 August
2014, 3.

44. Apuzzo and Schmidt, "In Washington, Second Thoughts on Arming Police." As
this article notes, the supply of surplus military ordnance to the police is sanctioned under a Pentagon program put in place by the US Congress in the 1990s; it
has been ramped up after 9/11, ostensibly to support the fight against terrorism.

Since the events in Ferguson, however, the wisdom of arming cops in this manner has been called into question.

45. As is well known to anthropologists, Turner used the term to describe collective rituals among the Ndembu of Zambia that were intended to reverse misfortunes of various sorts.

46. See *PAIA Civil Society Network (PAIA CSN) Shadow Report: 2013,* 29 October 2013, prepared by Catherine Kennedy and the Freedom of Information Programme Team at the South African History Archive (SAHA) for the PAIA Civil Society Network, http://cer.org.za/wp-content/uploads/2013/11/PCSN_ShadowRep2013 _final_20131029.pdf, accessed 5 February 2015.

47. Jane Duncan, "Are Secrecy-Obsessed Spooks Putting the State before Citizens," *Sunday Times* (RSA), 8 February 2015, 21.

48. These laws permit citizens to kill in the ostensible name of self-defense or, more precisely, under the rule that a citizen has "no duty to retreat from a place where she or he has the right to be."

49. See n. 4.

50. Russell Fraser, "In the Future Our Police, Lawyers and Jails Will Be Run by G4S," *New Statesman,* 22 April 2013, http://www.newstatesman.com/politics/2013/04 /future-our-police-lawyers-and-jails-will-be-run-g4s, accessed 20 July 2014. In 2014 G4S plc operated in 125 countries and had 620,000 employees.

51. This quotation is from Jill Lepore (2014, 101), summarizing one of the central arguments of Elizabeth Warren (2014).

52. These figures are for 2014, when the country had 163,000 police officers (see Bundy 2014, 120); note that the figure given in the text for security guards, 411,000, does not include the many who are unregistered. The Private Security Industry Regulatory Authority (Psira) listed 9,000 registered security companies in the same year; see Nabeelah Shaikh, "Our R140bn Crime Rip-Off," *IOL News,* 21 September 2014, http://www.iol.co.za/news/crime-courts/our-r140bn-crime -rip-off-1.1754080#.VOxIEE10yRQ, accessed 22 September 2014.

53. See Russell Nichols, "The Pros and Cons of Privatizing Government Functions," *Governing.com,* December 2010, http://www.governing.com/topics/mgmt/pros-cons -privatizing-government-functions.html, accessed 6 September 2014. Patently, there have been towns created by the private sector before (most famously in recent US history, Celebration, Florida, established by the Disney Development Company in 1996), but this speaks to a different political-economic sociology from the privatization of existing municipalities.

54. Says Lomnitz (2014, 85), "the representation of political opponents as bandits was a salient practice of the Mexican revolution."

55. According to Richard Wilson (2013, 450), speaking of Africa, the global promotion of human rights jurisprudence has "enlarged the category of criminality"— typically mobilized by incumbent regimes against their enemies but also sometimes mobilized against them—to include new forms of felony, like crimes against humanity, war crimes, and genocide. Echoing others, he adds that public order on the continent is now pursued more through "the idiom of criminal justice than by way of political and legislative processes." In all this, one might add, Africa, its states and statesmen, have themselves been criminalized anew (cf. Bayart, Ellis, and Hibou 1999, 1ff.).

56. There are several online points of access to the video. See, e.g., Lisa de Moraes, "John Oliver: Shut Down 'F**k Barrel' of Municipal Fines Targeting Poor," 23 March 2015, *Deadline Hollywood*, http://deadline.com/2015/03/john-oliver -fuck-barrel-municipal-fines-1201396977/, accessed 28 March 2015. We should like to thank our colleague, Harvard sociologist Lawrence Bobo, for alerting us to this video clip.

57. See n. 44 and, e.g., Rand Paul, "We Must Demilitarize the Police," *Time*, 14 August 2014, http://time.com/3111474/rand-paul-ferguson-police/, accessed 27 January 2015; Radley Balko, "Rise of the Warrior Cop: Is It Time to Reconsider the Militarization of American Policing?," *Wall Street Journal*, 7 August 2013, http://www .wsj.com/articles/SB10001424127887323848804578608040780519904, accessed 27 January 2015; and Paul D. Shinkman, "Ferguson and the Militarization of Police," *US News*, 14 August 2014, http://www.usnews.com/news/articles/2014 /08/14/ferguson-and-the-shocking-nature-of-us-police-militarization, accessed 27 January 2015.

58. Goffman's (2014) portrayal of everyday life in inner-city Philadelphia has been the object of both extravagant praise and resounding critique. For examples of the latter, see Dwayne Betts, "The Stoop Isn't the Jungle," *Slate*, 10 July 2014, http://www.slate .com/articles/news_and_politics/jurisprudence/2014/07/alice_goffman_s_on _the_run_she_is_wrong_about_black_urban_life.html, accessed 25 October 2014; Christina Sharpe, "Black Life, Annotated," *New Inquiry*, 8 August 2014, accessed 25 October 2014; and Steven Lubet, "Ethics on the Run," *New Rambler*, 26 May 2015, http://newramblerreview.com/book-reviews/law/ethics-on-the-run, accessed 26 May 2015. These critiques notwithstanding, the experience of confinement on the part of poor black communities, and of the police as an invading force, is hardly contentious.

59. Tom Nolan, "Stop Arming the Police like a Military," *DefenceOne*, 24 June 2014, http://www.defenseone.com/ideas/2014/06/stop-arming-police-military/87163

/?oref=d-river, accessed 28 January 2015. In addition to being a twenty-seven-year veteran of the Boston Police Department, Nolan is an associate professor of criminal justice at the State University of New York, Plattsburgh.

60. This is according to the World Bank's Global Financial Inclusion Index (Findex) for 2014. See http://databank.worldbank.org/data/reports-aspx?source=1228#, accessed 4 April 2016.

61. See http://beta2.statssa.gov.za/?page_id=737&id=1, accessed 5 February 2015.

62. See Daniel R. Amerman, "Making 9 Million Jobless 'Vanish': How the Government Manipulates Unemployment Statistics," http://danielamerman.com/articles/2012/WorkC.html, accessed 4 July 2014.

63. In June 2014 the *IMF Survey Magazine* carried an interview entitled "Rise of Inequality at the Center of Global Crisis," www.imf.org/external/pubs/ft/survey/so/2012/INT061412A.htm, accessed 2 July 2014.

64. The literature explicitly linking rising inequality to "global crisis" is growing very quickly; see, e.g., Dowd (2009) and, on the United States, Johnson (2014). For an account of the pungent "satirical activism" provoked by the yawning wealth gap in the United States, see Haugerud (2013).

65. Thamm (2014b, 89), in discussing Piketty's (2014) invocation of Marikana, speaks of the "unholy trinity of capital, politics and security . . . pitted against labour."

66. See, e.g., http://en.wikipedia.org/wiki/Death_of_Eric_Garner, accessed 24 February 2015. The police officer who killed Garner—by means of a choke hold maneuver actually banned by the NYPD itself—was not indicted after a Grand Jury hearing, despite the fact that the coroner had declared the killing a homicide.

67. A substantial critical literature has grown up on the failure of the US legal system to provide adequate legal defense services for indigent and immigrant defendants. For just two examples, see Hadfield (2014); and Katzmann (2014). In the United Kingdom the situation is probably worse. There the serving Lord Chancellor, Chris Grayling, "does not believe prisoners should have access to free legal advice" at all. See Fraser, "In the Future Our Police, Lawyers and Jails Will Be Run by G4S."

68. Large international corporations' movement of their profits into offshore havens in order to avoid taxes, and to claim financial stress to avoid raising workers' wages, seems to be occurring on an unprecedented scale. For the allegation that this has been true of Lonmin, the mining company involved in the Marikana massacre—which refused to raise the pitiful monthly pay of its rock drill operators in 2012 to R12,500 (approximately US$1,250 at the time)—see Loni Prinsloo, "'So You've Taken Billions, Lonmin? Give Us Just R1m,'" *Sunday Times* (RSA), sec. Business Times, 1 February 2015, 5.

69. For just one press report, see David Jolly, "I.M.F. Chief Is under Scrutiny in Corruption Inquiry by French Court," *New York Times*, 28 August 2014, B3.

70. "SA Slang Enters the Oxford Dictionary," *Big Issue*, no. 233 (24 July–24 August 2015): 6.

71. Elizabeth Olson, "Despite Exposure of Madoff Fraud, New Schemes Emerge," *New York Times*, 11 July 2014, B4. These shell games have many precedents, of course. The late 1990s saw an explosion of pyramid schemes across the world (Comaroff and Comaroff 1999a).

72. This is not to mention those "private contractors" who, while conducting "operations" on behalf of (or, in the case of insurgent movements, against) states, have escaped indictment for the killing and torture of innocent people. Nor does it include military and intelligence personnel who have perpetrated—or given the order to perpetrate—similar atrocities, and who are rarely held to account for their actions. But that is another topic, with its own literature, and is beyond our present scope.

73. The latest and largest of these in the United States, at the time of writing, involved BNP Paribas, France's biggest bank. BNP agreed to plead guilty to criminal charges and to pay a fine of $8.9 billion for doing business in New York with clients from countries under US trade sanctions by means of falsifying those clients' names. It was "the seventh bank to settle a criminal sanctions violation case," according to one contemporary press report. See Ben Protess and Jessica Silver-Greenberg, "BNP Admits Guilt and Agrees to Pay $8.9 Billion Fine to US," *New York Times*, 1 July 2014, B1, 4.

74. For a technical account of the murky practices involved in the Enron scandal—on the part of both the company itself and its auditors, Arthur Andersen LLP—see C. Thomas (2002).

75. Human Rights Watch, *Illusion of Justice: Human Rights Abuses in US Terrorism Prosecutions*, 21 July 2014, http://www.hrw.org/reports/2014/07/21/illusion-justice, accessed 22 July 2014. For the quotation from the Newburgh Four case, see http://www.hrw.org/node/126100/section/2, accessed 22 July 2014.

76. We were reminded of this by a comment in the *New Yorker* by Margaret Talbot (2014).

77. See, e.g., Vikram Dodd, "Manchester Chief of Police under Criminal Investigation," *Guardian* (UK), 13 August 2014, 4.

78. "No State Funeral for Selebi, ANC to Pay," *Times Live* (RSA), 27 January 2015, http://www.timeslive.co.za/politics/2015/01/27/no-state-funeral-for-selebi-anc-to-pay, accessed 28 January 2015.

79. See, e.g., Eusebius McKaiser, "It's Wrong to Pass Judgement on Selebi Simply Being either a Hero or a Villain," *Cape Times*, 2 February 2015, 9.

80. But not only in South Africa and the United States: the comparative literature on corruption and criminality among police is very large, too large to cite here. For a telling example, however, one that provides a direct parallel to South Africa, see Jauregui (2013a) on India.

81. In 2013 an authoritative report, based on SAPS figures, noted that, of 157,470 serving officers, 1,148 were convicted of serious crimes in 2013; another 8,846 criminal charges were pending against police. See "South Africa's Criminal Cops: Is the Rot Far Worse Than We Have Been Told?," *Africa Check*, 27 August 2013, http://africacheck.org/reports/south-africas-criminal-cops-is-the-rot-far-worse -than-we-have-been-told/, accessed 30 January 2015.

82. The SAPS—and especially its then commissioner, Riah Phiyega, who comes in for harsh censure—contested the content of the report, calling it "malicious." However, at the time of writing, no official rebuttal of its substance has been forthcoming, merely quibbles with its methodology. See Sarah Evans, "Police Commissioner Rejects SAIRR Report on SAPS Criminality," *Mail & Guardian*, 28 January 2015, http://mg.co.za/article/2015-01-28-police-commissioner-rejects-sairr-report-on -saps-as-malicious, accessed 31 January 2015.

83. These data are from a survey of 3,048 adults in South Africa undertaken by FutureFact. See "Three Quarters of South Africans Believe that a Lot of Police Are Criminals," 3 February 2015, http://www.futurefact.co.za/futurefact-finds /futurefact-finds-three-quarters-south-africans-believe-lot-police-are-criminals, accessed 4 February 2015.

84. Carlo Petersen, "17 Cases of Police Corruption Reported in Cape," *Cape Times*, 9 February 2015, 1.

85. Ilya Somin, "We Should Condemn Both Crimes against Police and Crimes Committed by the Police Themselves," *Washington Post*, 23 December 2014, http:// www.washingtonpost.com/news/volokh-conspiracy/wp/2014/12/23/we-should -condemn-both-crimes-against-police-and-crimes-committed-by-the-police -themselves/, accessed 28 January 2015.

86. See "Occupations More Dangerous Than a Police Officer," *PoliceCrimes.Com*, http:// police crimes.com/police_job.html, accessed 7 July 2015. See also Wildavsky and Wildavsky (2008), who list farming but not the other occupations noted by *Police Crimes.Com*. In addition, they place the figure for police fatalities "per 1000 Persons at Risk" far below the category "US population—all causes 2003"; the former is 20, and the latter is 840.

87. See www.stolenlives.org and www.october22.org, respectively.

88. Redditt Hudson, "Being a Cop Showed Me Just How Racist and Violent the Police Are: There's Only One Fix," *Washington Post*, 6 December 2014, http://www.washingtonpost.com/posteverything/wp/2014/12/06/I-was-a-st-louis-cop-my-peers-were-racist-and-violent-and-theres-only-one-fix/, accessed 10 February 2015.

89. Siyabonga Mkhwanazi, "Foreigners Not Targeted—Minister," *Cape Times*, 18 May 2015, 4.

90. Redi Tlhabi, "A Toxic Mix Gives Criminals the Upper Hand," *Sunday Times* (RSA), 5 April 2015, 17.

91. Although Reiner (2010, 141) is careful to stress that while popular police and public culture alike see them largely as crime fighters, in practice cops spend a considerable proportion of their time on record keeping, dispensing advice, and maintaining the peace. This last, "maintaining the peace" (aka public order), is a matter to which we shall return.

92. In some places, companies have been accused of depressing wages—in order to make their employees more dependent on holding their jobs and, thereby, to ensure their quiescence—by engaging in "wage theft." For an account from the United States, where the practice seems fairly widespread, see Steven Greenhouse, "More Workers Are Claiming 'Wage Theft,'" *New York Times*, 1 September 2014, A1, B1.

93. The speech was given, just before the British national election of 1983, as a warning of what was likely to happen to the United Kingdom were Margaret Thatcher to win, which she did; Labour lost badly. A video recording of the speech, made in Bridgend, Glamorgan (Wales), on 7 June 1983, is available on several Internet sites; see, e.g., https://www.youtube.com/watch?v=-QPhMVbleU0&feature=player_embedded, accessed 10 May 2015. It is sometimes said to be one of the greatest speeches in modern British political history.

94. It has been argued, as Caldeira (2000, passim) points out, that recent changes in law-enforcement regimes in countries like Brazil—and, by extension, South Africa—may be explained with reference to processes of democratization: that, following Lefort (1988, 19), those processes tend to be accompanied by "the dissolution of the markers of certainty" and, therefore, by anxieties about social order, by increasingly violent forms of policing, and by public ambivalence about the management of crime. In our own view, democratization—especially in its late fin de siècle form, itself rather different from its high-modernist predecessors—is itself a symptom of the tectonic shift of which we have spoken: a product, that is, of the changing triangulation between capital, the state, and governance. As such, it can-

not be taken to explain, independently, transformations in patterns of crime-and-policing: it is an entailed effect, not a cause. In South Africa, to be sure, democracy, as we note in the text, is widely seen to be under siege *because* of rampant crime and ineffective policing, not the other way around, as the democratization thesis would posit.

Chapter 1.2

1. Roy Walmsley, "World Prison Population List (9th Edition)," International Center for Prison Studies, University of Essex, 2011, www.idcr.org.uk/wp-content /uploads/2010/09/WPPL-9-22.pdf, accessed 9 January 2014. See also Joshua Holland, "Land of the Free? US Has 25 Percent of the World's Prisoners," *What Matters Today*, 16 December 2013, http://billmoyers.com/2013/12/16/land-of-the-free -us-has-5-of-the-worlds-population-and-25-of-its-prisoners/, accessed 9 January 2014.

2. See Nicholas Kristof, "When Whites Just Don't Get It," *New York Times*, 31 August 2014, A11. The basis of Kristof's claim is a report published by the National Bureau of Economic Research, according to which "nearly 70% of black men who never graduated from high school have been imprisoned."

3. The broken-windows theory, first introduced in 1982 by James Q. Wilson and George L. Kelling, holds that the strict policing of minor offenses and vandalism helps prevent escalation to more serious crimes. It served as motivation for significant reforms in criminal policy, including the controversial mass use of "stop, question, and frisk" by the New York Police Department. See George L. Kelling and James Q. Wilson, "'Broken Windows': The Police and Neighborhood Safety," *Atlantic*, March 1982, www.theatlantic.com/magazine/archive/1982/03/broken-windows /304465/, accessed 9 January 2014. See also Sampson and Raudenbusch 2004.

4. These data, based on FBI and Department of Justice figures for 2006–10, are cited by the Rape, Abuse, and Incest National Network. See Rape, Abuse, and Incest National Network, "Reporting Rates," https://rainn.org/get-information/statistics /reporting-rates, accessed 18 February 2014.

5. Again, the literature to this effect is substantial. For just a few examples, see, for the United Kingdom, Waddington (1999); for the United States, Conlon (2004); and for France, again, Fassin (2013). Our own fieldwork in South Africa made the point to us repeatedly, as will become clear in the account below.

6. See "Private Prison Companies Want You Locked Up," *Justice Policy Institute*, 22 June 2011, http://www.justicepolicy.org/news/2615, accessed 6 July 2014.

7. There has also been research that paints them in more positive light, most notably

a study by Simon Hakim and Erwin Blackstone, funded by three of the companies in question, which was reported widely in the media. The report, entitled "Cost Analysis of Public and Contractor-Operated Prisons," 29 April 2013, is a working paper issued by the Center for Competitive Government (formerly the Privatization Research Center)—note "competitive government"—at Temple University, where Hakim and Blackstone are professors of economics. For a copy of the report, see http://www.google.com/url?sa=t&rct=j&q=&esrc=s&source=web&cd=1&ved= 0CB0QFjAA&url=http%3A%2F%2Fwww.researchgate.net%2Fprofile%2FSimon _Hakim%2Fpublication%2F257780985_Cost-Analysis-of-Public-and-Contractor -Operated-Prisons-FINAL3%2Ffile%2F60b7d525d89b12cebb.pdf&ei=BwPAU _qYOMGNyAT92YHYDg&usg=AFQjCNG3vBflWnsTtQd6ZCr1k1yPjr2Xng&bvm =bv.70810081,d.aWw, accessed 12 July 2014.

8. Stephanie Clifford and Jessica Silver-Greenberg, "Orange Is the New Green: In Prison, Facing Exorbitant Fees to Communicate," *New York Times*, 27 June 2014, B1.

9. New York City, birthplace of zero-tolerance policing, has also led the way in reforms aimed at curbing its excesses. It has reined in the "stop-and-frisk" tactics and profiling that have proved so racially divisive—although none of these things appear to have reduced police violence, as the killing of Eric Garner on 17 July 2014 has made plain. See Benjamin Weiser and Joseph Goldstein, "New York to End Frisk Legislation with Settlement," *New York Times*, 31 January 2014, A1.

10. Bill Keller, "America on Probation," *New York Times*, 27 January 2014, A17.

11. Steven Fraser and Joshua Freeman, "Creating a Prison-Corporate Complex," *TomDispatch.com*, 19 April 2012, http://www.tomdispatch.com/blog/175531/, accessed 9 January 2013.

12. James Kilgore, "The Myth of Prison Slave Labor Camps in the US," *Counterpunch*, 9–11 August 2013, http://www.counterpunch.org/2013/08/09/the-myth-of-prison -slave-labor-camps-in-the-u-s/, accessed 9 January 2014.

13. Of course, the Foucault of governmentality (1991) and biopolitics (2008) placed greater stress, under neoliberalism, on a regime of power that, for him, subsumed and eclipsed disciplinary force, operating at a much more comprehensive scale as it took hold of life itself; although it is not always clear, especially from the extensive, often-opaque commentary literature on these concepts, whether Foucault intended this as a teleological progression of cumulative degree or a categorical transformation in kind.

14. See Joseph Goldstein, "Safer Era Tests Wisdom of 'Broken Windows' Focus on Minor Crime," *New York Times*, 25 July 2014, A1, 21.

15. This echoes Wacquant's (2009a, 114) observation of an *inverse* relationship, at fin

de siècle and after, between rates of crime (which were flat or falling) and rates of imprisonment (which rose dramatically), coupled with the fact that, while the proportion of African Americans in the criminal population decreased, "their share of the carceral population rose rapidly."

16. As Baltimore police lieutenant Terry McLarney (2009, 644)—the officer on whom a famous TV cop in the United States was based—put it in David Simon's *Homicide*, "We police are obsessed with describing our fellow man, . . . everyone categorically defined."

17. See http://crimestoppers-conference2014.com/ for the first words quoted and https://www.crimeline.co.za/tipoff.asp for the second. Both were accessed on 27 July 2104. The first URL is an announcement for a conference, in October 2014, of Crime Stoppers International, whose deliberately chosen acronym is CSI.

18. Du Preez (2013, 187) adds that, in their "obsess[ion] with crime"—"the one topic that you're guaranteed to see on the front pages of . . . newspapers every week"— South Africans treat it as "a barometer of how the country is doing" and, in the process, get "the picture . . . completely distorted."

19. Middle-class blacks who made light of crime on this ground were, are, not wrong. Much talk among whites—who, despite all the evidence to the contrary, see themselves as victims and blacks as perpetrators—does carry heavy racist overtones (cf. Msimang 2014, 201–3).

20. Gareth Newham, "President Zuma Ignores Increasing Violent Crime in His State of the Nation Address," *ISS Today*, 23 February 2015, http://www.issafrica.org /iss-today/president-zuma-ignores-increasing-violent-crime-in-his-state-of-the -nation-address, accessed 25 February 2015. Newham is head of the Governance, Crime and Justice Division of the Institute for Security Studies.

21. Sisonke Msimang mentions Oscar Pistorius elsewhere, but in less specific terms; see "I Told You So: The Return of Angry White Men," *Daily Maverick*, 10 November 2014, http://www.dailymaverick.co.za/opinionista/2014-11-10-i-told-you-so -the-return-of-angry-white-men/#.VUM0_U10wnM, accessed 1 May 2015. In that column, she adds that "the contours of male rage aren't particularly different across colour lines and so all male violence (not only the transgressions of black men) deserves careful scrutiny."

22. Much the same thing might be said of other felonies, of the sorts of information revealed about and through them in the course of their coming to public light, of the truths to which they are made to speak. Thus, corruption, self-evidently, is the discursive frame in terms of which the rights and wrongs of government are subjected to truth-finding. It is, above all else, about the ways in which a ruling regime deals with the fiscus—specifically, about how its personnel outsource its functions

and distribute the commonweal into private hands; about its technologies of regulation, including enforcement and criminal justice; about the differences between rule-of-law, rule-by-law, and rule-above-the-law; about the properly hyphenated relationship between state-and-nation, nation-and-state; and, of course, about its management of public anxieties concerning, among other things, crime and corruption, including its own.

23. As we note in the preface, the history of South African policing during and after the apartheid years has accumulated a large and informative scholarly literature. There is no reason to annotate it again here.

24. Cf. Super 2013, 88–89, which we cite again in this respect in 2.4.

25. Fink [Nicholas] Haysom, "Policing the Transition: Transforming the Police," African National Congress Discussion Document, undated, http://www.anc.org.za/show.php ?id=252, accessed 20 January 2014. See also Haysom (1986, 1989); below, 2.4.

26. For a damning recent report on forensic inefficiency in the SAPS, see Gareth van Onselin and Monica Laganparsad, "Forensic Backlogs Drag Out Pain of the Bereaved," *Sunday Times* (RSA), 8 March 2015, 12; also Klatzow (2014).

27. For just one summary statement of these indictments against the criminal justice system, see Robin Carlisle, "There IS Something Wrong with Crime Rate," *IOL News*, 30 May 2014, http://www.iol.co.za/news/there-is-something-wrong-with -crime-rate-1.1696533, accessed 11 June 2014. Robin Carlisle is a former member of the Executive Council (MEC) of the Western Cape Province for Transport and Public Works. For non–South African readers, the Executive Council is akin to a cabinet, and its members to government ministers, at the provincial (rather than the national) level; MECs are appointed by the premier of each province in the country.

28. On the statement to the Khayelitsha Commission, see Xolani Koyana and SAPA, "Informal Areas Can't Be Policed," *Cape Times*, 24 January 2014, 1. On the closure of public facilities as a result of criminal violence, see Francesca Villette, "Gangs Jeopardising Health Care to Thousands," *Cape Times*, 13 April 2015, 3.

29. Sipokazi Fokazi, "SA Cops Are 'Fat, Sick and Stressed,'" *IOL News*, 12 March 2015, http://www.iol.co.za/news/crime-courts/sa-cops-are-fat-sick-and-stressed-1 .1830856, accessed 12 March 2015. The data derive from a screening of 53,000 officers, almost a third of the SAPS, undertaken by Polmed, the police medical aid scheme. The quotation from Maggie Sotyu in the following sentence is reported in the same article; so is, a little further on in the paragraph, the attribution of blame for poor health and stress in the SAPS by Lieutenant General Lamoer to "the community."

30. See "Most Stressed-Out Countries—Bloomberg Best (and Worst)," http://www

.bloomberg.com/visual-data/best-and-worst//most-stressed-out-countries, accessed 10 March 2015. Nigeria (70.1 out of 100 on a complex scoring system) topped South Africa (70), but only just; these two nations were a long way ahead of the third, El Salvador (57.6). Norway (5.4) came out lowest of the seventy-four countries in the survey. The United States (25.7) was listed as fifty-fourth.

31. Kieran Legg, "Robbers Hit Cape Police Boss's Home," *IOL News*, 17 March 2015, http://www.iol.co.za/news/crime-courts/robbers-hit-cape-police-boss-s-home-1 .1833186#.VRL9Ik10xQc, accessed 18 March 2015.

32. Aziz Hartley and Ashfak Mohamed, "Lamoer Hauled to Court," *Cape Times*, 17 April 2015, 1.

33. Graeme Hosken, "Kill the Bastards, Minister Tells Police," *IOL News*, 10 April 2008, www.int.iol.co.za/index.php?set_id=1&click_id=79&art_id=vn200804100546 46122C815080&newslett=1&em=177481a1a20080410ah, accessed 10 April 2008.

34. Johan Burger, "To What Extent Has the South African Police Service Become Militarised?" *ISS Today*, 6 December 2012, http://www.issafrica.org/iss-today/to -what-extent-has-the-south-african-police-service-become-militarised, accessed 3 March 2015.

35. Christopher McMichael, "The South African Police Service and the Public Order War," *Think Africa Press*, 3 September 2012, http://thinkafricapress.com/south-africa /police-service-and-public-order-war-saps-marikana-lonmin, accessed 22 February 2015.

36. Angella Johnson, "Bill Bratton Sets His Sights on South Africa," *Mail & Guardian*, 2 August 1996, http://mg.co.za/article/1996-08-02-bill-bratton-sets-his-sights-on-south -africa/, accessed 15 January 2014.

37. For the first and last phrases, as they are associated with the SAPS, see, e.g., Stephan Hofstatter, Mzilikazi wa Afrika, and Rob Rose, "Shoot to Kill: Inside a South African Police Death Squad," *Times Live* (RSA), 11 December 2011, http://www.times live.co.za/local/2011/12/11/shoot-to-kill-inside-a-south-african-police-death -squad, accessed 30 October 2014. For an example of the second and third (and, again, the first as well), see Dominic Farrel, "South Africa's Police Shoot to Kill," *Think Africa Press*, 22 July 2011, http://thinkafricapress.com/south-africas-police -shoot-kill, accessed 12 February 2015. On the fourth, "an eye for an eye," see Karima Brown, "Why Police Brutality Became Inevitable," *Sunday Independent* (RSA), 10 March 2013, http://www.iol.co.za/sundayindependent/why-police-bru tality-became-inevitable-1.1483742#.VQyEX010xEo, accessed 26 February 2015. The national police commissioner at the time, General Bheki Cele, seems to have been especially fond of "maximum force."

38. John Jeffery, "We're Winning War against Crime," *IOL News*, 10 June 2014, http://www.iol.co.za/news/we-re-winning-war-against-crime-1.1701342, accessed 11 June 2014. John Jeffery is deputy minister of justice and constitutional development.

39. The killing of Andries Tatane may be seen on a CNN video clip, posted on YouTube, at https://www.youtube.com/watch?v=oL-FuBGioHw, accessed 3 June 2014. Footage of the Macia incident is to be found at https://www.youtube.com/watch?v=CO_Hej_Vw2g, accessed 15 December 2014.

40. There is a large literature on service delivery protests in South Africa. For three very different examples, see Booysen (2007), Hough (2008), and P. Alexander (2010). Sarah Lockwood (n.d.), a Harvard doctoral student, observes in her dissertation proposal on the topic that, while there have been many efforts to account for their occurrence, none offers a comprehensive explanation for why some but not other publics turn to this mode of mass action. We should like to thank Ms. Lockwood for sharing her literature review with us.

41. See the Wikipedia entry "Death of Mido Macia" for a brief but accurate summary of the reports of the incident; http://en.wikipedia.org/wiki/Death_of_Mido_Macia, accessed 2 March 2015.

42. Julian Rademeyer, "SA Police Face R14 Billion in Civil Lawsuits, Not R7 Billion as Reported," *Africa Check*, 18 November 2014 (updated from 22 April 2013, hence the difference in numbers between the headline and the passage we quote in the text), http://africacheck.org/reports/sa-police-face-r14-billion-in-civil-lawsuits-not-r7-billion-as-reported/, accessed 12 December 2014. See also du Preez 2013, 202. Africa Check is a nonpartisan organization dedicated to fact-checking and accurate news gathering across the continent. Its website is hosted in partnership with the University of Witwatersrand School of Journalism. Africa Check is a project of the AFP Foundation, based in Paris, whose aim is the global support of free, independent, and responsible media.

43. For the first figure, see Max du Preez, "Our Protest Culture Is Far from Dead," *Pretoria News*, 11 February 2014, http://www.iol.co.za/pretoria-news/opinion/our-protest-culture-is-far-from-dead-1.1645081#.VRMgtU10xQc, accessed 15 January 2015. The Social Change Research Unit of the University of Johannesburg, which defines "community protests" more narrowly, reports the lowest numbers, although it does note an upward trend over the long run. See Laura Grant, "Research Shows Sharp Increase in Service Delivery Protests," *Mail & Guardian*, 12 February 2014, http://mg.co.za/article/2014-02-12-research-shows-sharp-increase-in-service-delivery-protests, accessed 15 February 2015.

44. Johan Burger, "Between a Rock and a Hard Place: Policing Public Violence in South Africa," *ISS Today*, 14 February 2013, http://www.issafrica.org/iss-today/between-a

-rock-and-a-hard-place-policing-public-violence-in-south-africa, accessed 12 January 2015. The ANC leader was Ngoako Ramatlhodi, head of the important ANC Elections Committee, whose name is misspelled in the article.

45. Ranjeni Munusamy, "South Africa: The Place of Shame, Violence and Disconnect," *Daily Maverick*, 17 April 2015, http://www.dailymaverick.co.za/article/2015-04-17 -south-africa-the-place-of-shame-violence-and-disconnect/#.VTDInU10wnM, accessed 17 April 2015.

46. Burger, "Between a Rock and a Hard Place: Policing Public Violence in South Africa."

47. Munusamy, "South Africa: The Place of Shame, Violence and Disconnect."

48. See Julian Rademeyer and Kate Wilkinson, "South Africa's Criminal Cops: Is the Rot Far Worse Than We Have Been Told?," *Africa Check*, 27 August 2013, http:// africacheck.org/reports/south-africas-criminal-cops-is-the-rot-far-worse-than -we-have-been-told/, accessed 30 January 2015. This report offers fairly comprehensive figures on malfeasance in the SAPS over the previous fifteen or so years.

49. For a brief but comprehensive summary of these transformations, see Johan Burger, "The South African Police Service Must Renew Its Focus on Specialised Units," *ISS Today*, 31 March 2014, http://www.issafrica.org/iss-today/the-south -african-police-service-must-renew-its-focus-on-specialised-units, accessed 27 March 2015.

50. See Yazeed Kamaldien, "Siege Man's Death Diary," *Weekend Argus*, 16 May 2015, 1. The man, who committed suicide, Michael Volkwyn, kept a diary in which he described the last moments of his life. In it, he told of the arrival of "riot police" in large numbers, guns drawn, accompanied by an armored vehicle.

51. This was widely reported in the South African press. For just one example, see Charl du Plessis, "Cops Lose R30 Million to VIPs," *City Press*, 26 October 2014, http://www.citypress.co.za/politics/police-lose-r30%E2%80%89million-vips/, accessed 30 March 2015. At the time, US$1.00 = ZAR 11.60.

52. Editorial, "Senzo Case Shows Police Can't Do Their Job Even if They Want To," *Sunday Times* (RSA), 25 January 2015, 20. Senzo Meyiwa, the popular captain of the national soccer team, was murdered in October 2014; at the time of writing, his killer(s) has not been apprehended. We have condensed this passage to cut redundant phrases, but without altering its content.

53. Gareth Newham (interviewed by Chris Barron), "So Many Questions," *Sunday Times* (RSA), 22 February 2015, 19.

54. Newham, "President Zuma Ignores Increasing Violent Crime in His State of the Nation Address."

55. See Burger, "Between a Rock and a Hard Place: Policing Public Violence in South Africa."

56. See Christopher McMichael, "SAPS: South Africa's Wrong Arm of the Law," *Think Africa Press*, 31 May 2013, http://thinkafricapress.com/south-africa/wrong-arm -law, accessed 22 February 2015. The following quotation is extracted from this article. In order to render it as tersely yet coherently—but as faithfully to the orig-inal—as possible, we have excised some sentences and phrases and elided the rest.

57. The quoted phrases in this paragraph are from McMichael, "The South African Police Service and the Public Order War." In this article—specifically in speak-ing of "suppressing dissenting voices"—McMichael quotes Jane Duncan, "On the Marikana Massacre and Intellectual Self-Defence," *Perspective* (Rhodes University), 30 August 2012, http://www.ru.ac.za/perspective/perspectivearticles/perspective archive/onthe marikanamassacreandintellectualself-defence.html, accessed 4 April 2015. Duncan's piece first appeared in the *Sunday Independent* (RSA).

58. See Bongani Mahlangu, "Alarming to What Level Oppressive ANC Is Willing to Sink to Protect One Man," *Cape Times*, 17 February 2015, 9. There were literally thousands of accounts in the local media and copious video footage of this inci-dent, which caused a storm of public debate across the country. There is much too much of both to annotate here. It is also clear from other rapportage that the public order police took great pleasure in their action in the parliament. See e.g., Carlo Petersen, "Silence on the Officer Who Allegedly Targeted Malema," *Cape Times*, 17 February 2015, 4.

59. This figure is provided by the US Federal Bureau of Prisons; see http://www.bop .gov/about/ statistics/statistics_inmate_offenses.jsp, accessed 14 April 2015.

60. The call for "more police" has been common in South Africa; it even featured, in 2003, as a double entendre—the other reference being the band The Police— in billboard advertisements for a local music radio station. In the United States, it has appeared recently in media discussion of a report from the Brennan Center for Justice at the New York University School of Law, entitled *What Caused the Crime Decline?* (Roeder, Eisen, and Bowling 2015). An increase in the number of police officers is given as a major reason for the decrease in crime; see, e.g., Inimai M. Chettiar, "More Police, Managed More Effectively, Really Can Reduce Crime," *At-lantic*, 11 February 2015, http://www.theatlantic.com/national/archive/2015/02 /more-police-managed-more-effectively-really-can-reduce-crime/385390/, ac-cessed 4 April 2015.

Chapter 1.3

1. We are indebted to Teresa Caldeira for underlining the importance of "under-genres" produced outside the mainstream media and artistic world—such as videos, blogs, and underground publications—although these, of course, also partake, to a greater or lesser extent, of more mainstream vernacular registers.

2. Saito (2007, 255) points out that Ong (1988, 146) linked this difference to the effects of print culture and private reading, by contrast to public storytelling.

3. An example offered by Pinault (1992, 86–91) is taken from "The Three Apples," a tale in *One Thousand and One Nights*. In it, the Abbasid caliph purchases a chest that turns out to contain the dismembered body of a young woman and orders his vizier to solve the crime on pain of death.

4. It was their shared embeddedness in this dialogue that enabled Benjamin to express similar views of criminality to those of Carl Schmitt, despite his diametrically opposed political position.

5. See Lynda Gilfillan, review of *Young Blood*, by Sifiso Mzobe, Gorry Bowes Taylor Extraordinary Literary Events, April 2012, http://www.gorrybowestaylor.co.za/reviews/151/young-blood-sifizo-mzobe, accessed 23 May 2015.

6. Scholars of contemporary crime fiction in Africa at large have noted its penchant for social engagement: "more than any genre in African literatures," write Anja Oed and Christine Matzke (2012, 11), "crime fiction seems to effortlessly combine elements of entertainment and social commentary."

7. Speaking of the "new normal," Deon Meyer remarked in a radio interview in 2006 that "it would have been totally impossible to write a book about policemen or former policemen in the old South Africa under the apartheid regime. I don't think it is possible to have a protagonist in a police state as a hero" (Matzke 2012, 227).

8. Melanie McGrath, "Colombia Clean-Up: Will the Newly Laundered Image of the Country's Second City Medellín Do Crime-Writers Any Favors?," *Guardian* (UK), 11 November 2015, 21. All quoted passages in this paragraph are from this source.

9. In 1991 Eugene Schleh (1991, 3) observed that Africans across the continent—not just in South Africa—were beginning to write detective fiction in growing numbers.

10. See Gilfillan, review of *Young Blood*.

11. See Mike Nicol, "*Red Ink*: Angela Makholwa's Page-Turning Debut Reviewed," *Crime Beat*, 25 July 2007, http://crimebeat.bookslive.co.za/blog/2007/07/25/red-ink-angela-makholwas-page-turning-debut-reviewed/, accessed 23 July 2014. Another strain of black writing in South Africa seeks to address unresolved ten-

sions between vernacular custom and Western jurisprudence—and the normative complexities that occur as a result of their coexistence. It is exemplified by the late Meshack Masondo (e.g., 2008), who wrote crime fiction both in isiZulu and in English, mixing the traits of "traditional" trickster figures (La Hausse 1990) with those of a deadpan detective.

12. See also Guilty Conscience, "Scottish Crime Fiction: Writers to Watch," *Crime Fiction Lover*, 13 March 2012, http://www.crimefictionlover.com/2012/03/scottish -crime-fiction-writers-to-watch/, accessed 14 July 2014.

13. "Scandinavian Crime Fiction: Inspector Norse," *Economist*, 11 May 2010, http:// www. economist.com/node/15660846, accessed 14 July 2014.

14. *Whitey: United States of America v. James J. Bulger* (2014, directed by Joe Berlinger).

15. The point has also been made in any number of recent fictional portrayals of organized crime. For an especially graphic South African example, see *iNumber Number* (2013, directed by Donovan Marsh), released in dubbed form as *Avenged* (2013).

16. Tim Lusher, "The *Guardian*'s Top 50 Television Dramas of All Time," 12 January 2010, http://www.theguardian.com/tv-and-radio/tvandradioblog/2010/jan/12 /guardian-50-television-dramas, accessed 7 July 2014. See also "TV Critics Call: Here Are the Decade's 10 Best," *Huff Post Entertainment*, 14 December 2009, http:// www.huffingtonpost.com/bill-mann/tv-critics-call-here-are_b_391101.html, accessed 7 July 2009; and Bruce Fretts and Matt Roush, "TV Guide Magazine's 60 Best Series of All Time," *TV Guide*, 23 December 2013, http://www.tvguide.com /news/tv-guide-magazine-60-best-series-1074962.aspx, accessed 7 July 2014.

17. Peter Biskind, "An American Family," *Vanity Fair*, April 2007, www.vanityfair.com /culture/features/2007/04/sopranos200704, accessed 27 October 2011.

18. Ibid.

19. Chris Albrecht, cited in ibid.

20. Willy Loman is the protagonist of Arthur Miller's classic play *Death of a Salesman* (1949). A strikingly similar sentiment was expressed by Scott Cooper, director of *Black Mass* (2015), a movie based on the best-selling book by the same name about the unsavory alliance—mentioned a few pages back—between the notorious Boston mobster Whitey Bulger and the FBI: "I didn't want to make a film about criminals who happen to have a human side," he said. "I wanted to make a film about humans who just happen to be criminals." See Michael Cieply and Brooks Barnes, "In a Callous Killer, One Soft Spot," *New York Times*, 2 September 2015, C1.

21. See also Erica Wagner, "The Capitalist Nightmare at the Heart of *Breaking Bad*," *New Statesman*, 22 December 2014, http://www.newstatesman.com/culture/2014 /12/capitalist-nightmare-heart-breaking-bad, accessed 19 January 2015.

22. *Breaking Bad*, season 1, episode 7, "A 'No-Rough-Stuff'-Type Deal."

23. Matt Zoller Seitz, "Seitz: A Rewarding TV Year Continues with Netflix's *Orange Is the New Black*," *Vulture*, 11 July 2013, http://www.vulture.com/2013/07/tv-review -orange-is-the-new-black.html, accessed 9 July 2014.

24. The series is based on Piper Kerman's (2011) memoir, *Orange Is the New Black: My Year in a Women's Prison*.

25. Seitz, "Seitz: A Rewarding TV Year Continues with Netflix's *Orange Is the New Black*."

26. Oliver Farry, "*The Wire*—'Every Villain Has Their Reasons,'" *Irish Left Review*, 12 March 2009, http://www.irishleftreview.org/2009/03/12/wire-every-villain -reasons/, accessed 19 January 2015. The quotation immediately below about *The Wire* is taken from the same source.

27. "When television history is written, little else will rival 'The Wire,'" wrote Brian Lowry in a review of the show. See *Variety*, 7 September 2006, http://variety.com/2006 /film/reviews/the-wire-2-1200513665/, accessed 8 July 2014. See also "*The Wire*: Arguably the Greatest Television Programme Ever Made," *Telegraph* (UK), 2 April 2009, http://www.telegraph.co.uk/news/uknews/5095500/The-Wire-arguably-the -greatest-television-programme-ever-made.html, accessed 8 July 2014.

28. "My Standard for Verisimilitude Is Simple and I Came to It When I Started to Write Prose Narrative: Fuck the Average Reader; David Simon Talks with Nick Hornby," *Believer*, August 2007, http://www.believermag.com/issues/200708/?read=inter view_simon, accessed 7 July 2014.

29. David Simon, "The Target," Audio Commentary Track, *The Wire*, season 1, episode 1 (HBO Video / Warner Home Video, 2005).

30. "*The Wire*: Arguably the Greatest Television Programme Ever Made."

31. Anmol Chaddha and William Julius Wilson, "Why We're Teaching 'The Wire' at Harvard," Washington Post, 12 September 2010, http:www.washingtonpost.com /wp-dyn/content/article/2010/09/10/AR2010091002676.html, accessed 27 July 2016.

32. Bill Gorman, "'CSI: Crime Scene Investigation' Is the Most-Watched Drama Series in the World!," *TV by the Numbers: Network TV Press Releases*, 13 June 2011, http:// tvbythenumbers.zap2it.com/2011/06/13/csi-crime-scene-investigation-is-the -most-watched-drama-series-in-the-world/95460/, accessed 19 February 2012.

33. "The Great Outdoors," *Artsmart*, 13 March 2002, http://www.artsmart.co.za /drama/archive/534. html, accessed 18 July 2014. The play, which premiered at the Standard Bank National Arts Festival on 30 June 2000, had not been published at the time of writing. We thank Neil McCarthy for generously making the script available to us.

34. The quotation is taken from *Cobra* (Meyer 2014, 248–49). Meyer's novels, writ-

252 ◆ *Notes to Pages 84–86*

ten originally in Afrikaans, have a global following and have been translated into more than twenty languages.

35. First established in Cape Town as *The African Drum* in 1951 with capital provided by the Abe Bailey mining fortune, the magazine had a national circulation of seventy thousand in its heyday, with editions in Ghana, Nigeria, and Kenya. Run by a series of white editors and an African Advisory Board, *Drum* was one of the few vehicles available to black creative writers at the time. By the early 1960s the publication was increasingly besieged by government restriction and bans, its staff suffering repeated threats and harassment. In April 1965 it ceased to appear as an independent monthly, becoming a fortnightly supplement to the *Golden City Post*. It was revived again in 1968 and remains a widely circulating black lifestyle magazine (Woodson 1988; Switzer 1997; Chapman 2001).

36. There is, of course, a related literature on the history of the "heroic criminal," or *picaro*, in colonial Africa more generally (see, e.g., Austen 1986; La Hausse 1990).

37. For example, widely published crime novelist Deon Meyer (see n. 34 above) has also written several movie and TV scripts and has sold film rights to some of his novels, at least one, *Heart of the Hunter* (2003), to a South African company. In addition, he has directed his own local production, *Die Laaste Tango* (2013), set in the small Karoo town of Loxton. While deeply engaged with the complex diversity of the postcolony, the center of gravity of these works remains more with cops— albeit, pretty hard-boiled ones—than with criminals or the black street. See *Die Laaste Tango*, http://www.imdb.com/title/tt2980650/plotsummary?ref_=tt_ov_pl, accessed 31 July 2014.

38. *Mapantsula*, Southern Africa Media Center, 1989–90, http://kora.matrix.msu.edu/files /50/304/32-130-1447-84-calif%20mapan2%20opt.pdf, accessed 21 July 2014.

39. "*Mapantsula*," *California Newsreel*, http://newsreel.org/video/MAPANTSULA, accessed 18 July 2014.

40. Wikipedia, s.v. "*Mapantsula*," http://en.wikipedia.org/wiki/Mapantsula, accessed 16 July 2014.

41. The name of the protagonist, Tsotsi, is also a generic term for "young, urban black gangster." It rose to prominence in the 1940s and 1950s, but its derivation is disputed. Some claim that it is a Sesotho corruption of "zoot suit"; others, that it is from the Nguni word *tsotsa*, "to dress flashily." For a relatively early discussion in the scholarly literature, see M. Wilson and Mafeje (1963, 15); also Nkosi (1971).

42. Both alternative endings can be seen on the *Tsotsi* DVD. Mumbletree, Tim Steele, "Tsotsi and the Open-Ended Conclusion," *SPU: South Africa Program Weblog*, 7 May 2013, https://kwsegall.wordpress.com/2013/05/07/tsotsi-and-the-open-ended-con clusion/, accessed 20 January 2015.

43. "Hands up, don't shoot" became a unifying chant in the demonstrations that followed the killing of Michael Brown in Ferguson, Missouri (see above). This chant, and the accompanying gesture, has become iconic, more generally, of resistance to police violence. In many cases, the shooting of black men by cops has allegedly been triggered by the victim reaching into his pocket, interpreted as intent to retrieve a firearm.

44. *Cinéma vérité* was pioneered by, among others, Jean Rouch, filmmaker and anthropologist, who developed his style of "direct cinema" in West Africa. The prolific Nollywood tradition of direct-to-video filming that burgeoned in the 1990s also draws on real-world locations to produce popular low-budget features.

45. Joe Morgenstern, "Gangster's Paradise," *Wall Street Journal*, 10 June 2010, http://online.wsj.com/news/articles/SB10001424052748704312104575298250480 097456, accessed 25 July 2014. This review appears as part of a longer column under the title "Film Review: 'Bone' Knits Poor Girl's Quest into Classic."

46. Many local black viewers preferred this movie to its predecessor, largely because it was "[a] mirror of Jozi and what our lives are really like." See Kudos Mzansi, "An Ace in the Hole for the Home Team," *User Reviews: IMDb*, 8 September 2008, http://www.imdb.com/title/tt0783532/, accessed 25 July 2014.

47. The practice continues. In May 2015, the Office of the Presidency announced the intention of the SAPS to "go for criminals involved in hijacking buildings." See Siyabonga Mkhwanazi, "Foreigners Not Targeted—Minister," *Cape Times*, 18 May 2015, 4. The minister in question is Jeff Radebe, whose official portfolio is minister in the presidency.

48. Tom Seymour, "Ralph Ziman," *Little White Lies*, 21 July 2010, http://www.little whitelies.co.uk/features/articles/ralph-ziman-11785, accessed 25 July 2014.

49. Both the United Congregational Church of South Africa and the Evangelical Lutheran Church objected to the movie, the first for associating the Holy City with the criminal underworld, and the second for naming one of the principal hoods "Nazareth." See Nkosana Lekotjolo, "Churches Slam 'Jerusalema,'" *Times* (RSA), 23 September 2008, http://www.timeslive.co.za/thetimes/article23881.ece, accessed 3 October 2009.

50. See Alex K., "Jerusalema: Gangster's Paradise," *Ruthless Reviews*, 26 July 2011, http://www.ruthlessreviews.com/11865/jerusalema-gangsters-paradise/, accessed 2 August 2014.

51. "Coconut" in South Africa has the same connotation as "Oreo" in the United States. It refers to a person said to be black outside but white within.

52. Presumably from isiZulu *ukuzama*, "attempt," "test," or "try." In the film, Zama claims explicitly to have taken his name from Zama-Zama.

53. See Bongani Madondo, "Jub Jub: The Life and Trial of a South African Child Star," *Mail & Guardian*, 21 December 2012, http://mg.co.za/article/2012-12-21-00-jub-jub-the-life-and-trial-of-south-african-child-star, accessed 18 December 2015.

54. Similar things have been reported from time to time in the South African press. For just one example, see Caryn Dolley, "Raids Fail to Stop Gang Warfare," *Weekend Argus*, 23 May 2015, 4.

55. Show like *Behind the Badge* (SABC 1) and *Duty Calls* (SABC 2) aired in the early 2000s. Another, *When Duty Calls*, debuted on SABC 2 in 2009. Billed as a flagship SAPS program that would be a "nemesis to criminals," it profiled missing persons and aimed at encouraging audiences not to be "passive viewers, but active participants in working with police to apprehend some of the scoundrels who torment society"; http://www.sanews.gov.za/south-africa/saps-tv-programme-deals-blow-criminals, accessed 28 May 2015.

56. Margie Orford, "Oscar Pistorius Trial: The Imaginary Black Stranger at Heart of the Defence," *Guardian African Network*, 4 March 2014, http://www.theguardian.com/world/2014/mar/04/oscar-pistorius-trial-black-stranger-defence, accessed 30 July 2014.

57. Jani Allan, "Letter to Oscar," *Daily Maverick*, 15 April 2014, http://www.dailymaverick.co.za/opinionista/2014-04-15-letter-to-oscar/#.VUyHQE10wdV, accessed 5 May 2015. The letter was reprinted from Ms. Allan's blog, where it appeared the day before. Her actual words, addressed to Pistorius, were "I have it from a reliable source that you are taking acting lessons for your days in court."

58. The case is referred to, with the names of the protagonists changed, in Deon Meyer's *7 Days* (2012, 14–15). It also appears to be the inspiration, at least in part, for one of the plotlines in Andrew Brown's *Coldsleep Lullaby* (2005).

59. It also yielded a book by two amateur sleuths, Mollett and Mollett (2014), who argue in exquisite scientific detail that the evidence assembled by the prosecution was wrongly dismissed by the judge. More recently, it was reported that yet another volume is to be published that will show the motive for the murder to have been "a dark family secret," eliciting a threat of suit on the part of the victim's parents; see Caryn Dolly, "Lotz's Father: We'll Go to Court over Claim," *IOL News*, 21 March 2015, http://www.iol.co.za/news/crime-courts/lotz-s-father-we-ll-go-to-court-over-claim-1.1835335#.VUzH4010wdU, accessed 8 May 2015.

60. See "Oscar, Dewani on Everyone's Lips after Jub Jub Ruling," *eNCA* (RSA), 8 October 2014, https://www.enca.com/south-africa/oscar-dewani-everyones-lips-after-jub-jub-ruling, accessed 18 December 2015. See also Alan Cameron, "Top Cases of 2010," *iAfrica.com*, 13 December 2010. http://news.iafrica.com/features/693250.html, accessed 18 December 2015.

61. Madondo, "Jub Jub: The Life and Trial of a South African Child Star." Our account of the case is heavily indebted to Madondo's acute analysis of its broader social and historical implications; all our citations of his words are taken from this article.

62. "Promising Career Gone Awry," *Sowetan Live*, 17 October 2012, http://m.sowetan live.co.za/news/?articleId=6917468, accessed 19 December 2015.

63. See, e.g., David Smith, "Shrien Dewani Goes Free after a Trial Doomed from Day One," *Guardian* (UK), 8 December 2014, http://www.theguardian.com/world/2014/dec/08 /shrien-dewani-murder-trial-collapse-anni-south-africa, accessed 4 May 2015.

64. "'It was the husband who planned all of this! We can't prove it, but we know,' said the NPA's [National Prosecuting Authority] spokesperson Nathi Ncube after last week's ruling that set Shrien free"; see Marianne Thamm, "The Killing of Anni, Afterthoughts: So Did Shrien Dewani Do It?," *Daily Maverick*, 14 December 2014, http://www.dailymaverick.co.za/article/2014-12-14-the-killing-of-anni-after thoughts-did-shrien-do-it/#.VK6J8U0o7IU, accessed 8 January 2015.

65. Ibid.

66. As Rebecca Davis wrote of a later femicide, the contract killing of Jayde Panayiotou in April 2015, "In a country where so much of the dirty work is outsourced by wealthy South Africans to blacks, why not murder too?" See Rebecca Davis, "Pana-yiotou, Patel, and Trevor Noah's 'Cousin': The Relative Value of South African Life," *Daily Maverick*, 26 May 2015, http://www.dailymaverick.co.za/article/2015 -05-26-panayiotou-patel-and-trevor-noahs-cousin-the-relative-value-of-south -african-life/#.VWRSlU3bInM, accessed 26 May 2015. We return to this essay again in 2.3 below.

67. Margie Orford, "The Grammar of Violence," *International Crime Authors Reality Check*, 17 January 2011, http://www.internationalcrimeauthors.com/?p=1300, ac-cessed 30 July 2014.

Chapter 2.1

1. As Margie Orford puts it, there is "a grammar to violence. It is a language. . . . There is a syntax of pain and fear that is etched into the cells as much as it is etched into our hearts. This grammar . . . is written in the bodies of victims." Signifi-cantly, the protagonist of Orford's detective fiction is a police profiler, one Clare Hart. Orford's novels include *Like Clockwork* (2006), *Blood Rose* (2010), *Daddy's Girl* (2012a), *Gallows Hill* (2012b), and *Water Music* (2013).

2. We were surprised and delighted to read the concordance between the Gillespie and Harpham (2011) essay on the topic and our own take on it, which was summarized in lecture form and presented earlier the same year, on 17 May 2011, by Jean Coma-

roff as the Edward and Nora Ryerson Lecture at the University of Chicago; see www .youtube.com/watch?v=UYngRIzG3Uk. Other lecture versions had been presented at several universities in the United States, South Africa, and Europe in 2010.

3. Jonathan "Jack" Whicher (1814–81) was among the first members of the Detective Branch established by Scotland Yard in 1842, according to the historical records of the Metropolitan Police of the United Kingdom; see www.met.police.uk/history /constance.htm. He is the eponymous figure in Summerscale's account (2008) of the notorious Road Hill House murder of 1860 and, it is said, "one of the inspirations for Charles Dickens's Inspector Bucket, Colin Dexter's Inspector Morse, and R. D. Wingfield's Jack Frost, among other fictional detectives"; see Wikipedia, s.v. *"Jack Whicher,"* http://en.wikipedia.org/wiki/Jack_Whicher.

4. Dupin, famously, has attracted a remarkably large literature, having been the protagonist in Poe's "The Murders in the Rue Morgue," often said to be the first modern detective fiction story. See, for just a very few examples, Eco and Sebeok (1983); Garner (1990); Van Leer (1993); and P. Thomas (2002).

5. As historians of science well know, both Lambroso and Galton actually used the term "criminal anthropology" (see, e.g., Lambroso 1895; Galton 1890). For his major work on crime and physical disposition, see Lambroso 1912; Galton's writings on the topic are discussed in several intellectual biographies; see, e.g., Bulmer (2003).

6. So, later, did G. K. Chesterton's Father Brown, for whom, too, there was "nothing so important as trifles" (Hurley 2012, xxiii)—and for whose literary creator the dramaturgy of detection shared "an essential symmetry with the highest form of revelation" (Hurley 2012, xxi; Chesterton 2012). Father Brown, of course, was both a divine and a detective.

7. On Sherlock Holmes's fondness for the "elementary," see also Gillespie and Harpham (2011).

8. Matthew Savides, "Clueless as List of Cold Cases Grows," *Sunday Times* (RSA), 1 March 2015, 8.

9. *Search for Common Ground*, SABC 3, 17 July 1997. Tellingly, Antony Altbeker's study of policing in postapartheid South Africa (2005) is entitled *The Dirty Work of Democracy*; see esp. 166–67 for a statement to this effect by a senior South African police officer, ca. 2003–4, and, more generally on the topic, Altbeker (1998).

10. To give a very rough idea of comparative figures, in 2002, during one of our periods of field research in the northerly provinces, the homicide rate in Limpopo was 12.7 per 100,000; during the same year, it was 5.6 in the United States, less than half. The rate of aggravated assault in the same year in Limpopo was 382.2 per 100,000.

11. See "Death Penalty: The Last Throw of the Dice for South Africans" (referendum on death penalty research), *Plus 94*, October 2006, www.plus94.co.za/press-releases /2006/10/referendum-on-death-penalty-research, accessed 8 July 2013.

12. A fairly detailed, well-annotated, and largely—though not entirely—accurate historical account of the ORCU is to be found in Wikipedia, s.v. "Satanic Panic (South Africa)," http://en.wikipedia.org/wiki/Satanic_panic_(South_Africa), accessed 7 January 2014.

13. This quotation was taken from the SAPS website, http://saps.org.za/divstat/occult /index.htm, in 2003; the site has been taken down since and replaced with a much-updated one.

14. Our account of the ORCU is based on three lengthy visits to its offices in Pretoria in 2000, extensive interviews with Colonel Kobus Jonker and Gary Prins, a senior member of its staff, and open access to its records. We should like to express our gratitude to both Colonel Jonker and Mr. Prins for their extraordinary openness and willingness to help us.

15. Mark Gevisser, "Donker Jonker's Righteous Crusade," Profile, *Mail & Guardian*, 6 October 1995, http://mg.co.za/article/1995-10-06-donker-jonkers-righteous -crusade-20, accessed 12 December 2003.

16. Ibid.

17. Madaleen Fourie, "God's Detective: Left but Not Lost," *Servamus.online.duty*, www .10111.co.za/servamus/servamus200105/gods1.htm, accessed 29 March, 2008.

18. Interview at Bodibe, his home, on 18 July 2000. Daniel Moshupa was attached to the SAPS at nearby Lichtenburg. We worked with him over a two-month period in 2000 and discussed his work with his station commander and other colleagues, all of them Tswana speakers. They were unanimous in their belief that he was an unusually valuable member of the SAPS.

19. For his part, Kobus Jonker insisted that he was careful not to criminalize satanism or witch beliefs as such and that he merely prosecuted the acts of violence to which they gave rise. But he was wont to say, both publically and privately, that evil beliefs lead inexorably to evil deeds. Given his deep belief in the moral worth of what he was doing, he lived perfectly well within the contradiction. So have many others.

20. There have been several calls to disband the ORCU in recent times. For just one example, see Jacques Rousseau, "South Africa: Occult Crimes Unit Offensive to Common Sense and Morality," *All.Africa.Com*, 13 November 2013, http://allafrica.com /stories/201311140217.html, accessed 8 January 2014.

21. I.e., detectives in general. See http://web.archive.org/web/20040922161210/http:// www.saps.gov.za/youth_desk/occult/occult.htm, accessed 9 January 2014.

22. As recently as May 2015, Kobus Jonker, referred to as an "occult expert," gave evidence at the High Court, Pretoria, in a trial in which a teenager, convicted for killing four members of his family, blamed his actions on "a demonic spirit." Jonker testified that there was no proof of satanic influence. For an accessible press report, see Zelda Venter, "Boy Who Axed Family to Death Gets 80 Years: 'Satanic Forces Made Teenager Kill,'" *Weekend Argus*, 23 May 2015, 5.

23. See Gevisser, "Donker Jonker's Righteous Crusade."

24. Jimmy Lee Shreeve, "Adam 'Sacrifice' Case: Was Scotland Yard Duped?" *Crime Author*, 7 July 2006, www.newsguide.us/art-entertainment/books/Adam-Sacrifice-Case-Was-Scotland-Yard-Duped/, accessed 30 March 2008. See also John Freedom, "Thames Torso Case Heralds Satan Myth Two," *SAFF*, April 2002, www.saff.ukhq.co.uk/ttorso2.html, accessed 30 March 2008.

25. Debbie Nathan, "Inside the 'Satan Scare' Industry: The Devil Makes Them Do It," *In These Times*, 1 January 2003, www.smwane.dk/index2.php?option=com_content&do_pdf=1&id=14, accessed 29 March 2008.

26. There have been several media reports of Scotland Yard's Super Recognizers. The quoted words and phrases here are taken from one of them: Katrin Benhold, "London 'Super Recognizer' Matches Faces to Crimes," *New York Times*, 10 October 2015, A11.

27. The SAPS has not made the memorandum announcing these measures public. However, a copy was leaked and widely circulated by the Pagan Rights Alliance, which has strenuously opposed the existence of the ORCU. See www.paganrightsalliance.org/documents/SAPS%20religious%20crimes%20unit%20Mandate.pdf, accessed 9 January 2014. The lines quoted are from paragraph 4 of the memorandum.

28. See "New TV Series with Muti Murders and Tikoloshe Hits SA Screens," *SA People News*, 8 November 2012, www.sapeople.com/2012/11/08/room9-new-television-series-south-african-screens-359/, accessed 18 January 2014. We should like to thank Jessica Dickson, currently a doctoral student at Harvard University, for drawing our attention to this series.

29. The actual figure in US dollars is difficult to specify. For one thing, it was affected by the labile exchange rate of the South African rand at the time. For another, the cost of the package rose dramatically in the first year after the deal was announced, and it is anything but clear that the numbers admitted by the government were accurate and not significantly downplayed. An eventual amount as high as US$5.5 billion has been alleged.

30. The South African Strategic Defence Procurement Package was the country's larg-

est ever arms deal. It involved the purchase of corvettes, submarines, light utility helicopters, lead-in fighter trainers, and advanced light fighter aircraft from manufacturers in France, Britain, Italy, Germany, and Sweden. See *Arms Deal Virtual Press Office*, www.armsdeal-vpo.co.za/, accessed 29 March 2008. For one detailed scholarly account, see Holden and Van Vuuren (2011).

31. Terry Crawford-Browne, "Good Deal, Bad Deal," *SABC News*, 11 January 2001, www.armsdeal-vpo.co.za/special_items/summary/the_deal.html, accessed 29 March (2008).

32. Barbara Slaughter, "Arms Corruption Scandal Erupts in South Africa," *World Socialist Website*, 20 March 2001, www.wsws.org/en/articles/2001/03/arms-m20.html, accessed 4 April 2008. This feature article offers a well-balanced and fairly comprehensive summary of the events surrounding the Arms Deal up to the time of its posting. On the SIU, see its home page, at www.siu.org.za.

33. Jonny Steinberg, "Far from Being Independent, Unit Head Is Responsible to President," *Business Day*, 6 December 2001, www.businessday.co.za/Articles/Tark Article.aspx?ID=269525, accessed 1 April 2008.

34. Slaughter, "Arms Corruption Scandal Erupts in South Africa."

35. There are many accounts of the origins and history of the DSO. For two examples, written a telling eight years apart, see Redpath (2004) and Berning and Montesh (2012). Another account, interesting insofar as it was a report to government covering some of the controversy surrounding the DSO, is to be found in the *Khampepe Commission of Inquiry into the Mandate and Location of the Directorate of Special Operations ("The DSO")*, February 2006, www.info.gov.za/view/DownloadFileAction ?id=80441, accessed 8 April 2008.

36. The National Prosecuting Authority of South Africa, www.npa.gov.za/ReadContent 424.aspsx, accessed 26 March 2008.

37. Pikoli and Wiener's book (2013) is itself positioned on that terrain: Pikoli was the national director of public prosecutions—and hence head of the NPA, under whose command the DSO fell—between 2005 and 2007. These were to be the most fraught years in the history of the Scorpions, politically speaking, and the years during which the battle between them and the SAPS was at its most bitter, a point to which we shall return. Still, Pikoli's account of the events in question make plain the complex nature of the conflict, the lines of antagonism involved in it, and the positions of the various parties drawn into its purview.

38. Jeremy Vine, "World: Africa—Scorpions Target South African Crime," *BBC News*, 1 September 1999, www.news.bbc.co.uk/2/hi/africa/435550.stm, accessed 4 April 2008.

39. Khadija Magardie, "Tailing the Scorpions," *You Tube* (video made initially for the SABC series *Special Assignment*),www.youtube.com/watch?v=Ih3NpEEPYa0, accessed 5 April 2008.

40. Fred Bridgland, "Wounded Nation," *Free Market Fairy Tales*, undated, www.fmft .net/archives/002963.html, accessed 22 March 2008.

41. Ibid.

42. Wyndham Hartley, "Anti-corruption Unit Saves State R4,5bn," *SIU News*, 10 March 2006, www.siu.org.za/news.asp?show=34, accessed 4 April 2008.

43. This is the number cited in the National Budget by the Minister of Finance, Trevor Manual, in 2009. It is also the one given by the opposition Democratic Alliance during its campaign to prevent the DSO from being disbanded. See Democratic Alliance, "The Case for Retaining the Scorpions," February 2008, www.da.org.za /docs/6647/Scorpions_document.pdf, accessed 1 April 2008. For a press report on the Democratic Alliance campaign, see Cedric Mboyisa, "SA Needs Scorpions: DA," *Citizen*, 6 February 2008, www.citizen.co.za/index/article.aspx?pDesc =57827,1,22, accessed 1 April 2008.

44. Bridgland, "Wounded Nation."

45. Terr-Liza Fortein, "Scorpions Salute Racketeering Judgement," *Cape Argus*, 9 June 2006, www.capeargus.co.za/index.php?fSectionId=49&fArticleId=3284679, accessed 1 April 2008.

46. "Judgement Day for Tony Yengeni," *Mail & Guardian Online*, 11 December 2005, www.mg.co.za/articlePage.aspx?articleid=256241&area=/breaking_news/breaking _news__national/, accessed 4 April 2008.

47. Zenzile Khumalo, "South Africa: Zuma vs. the State," *Bnet*, November 2005, http://findarticles.com/p/articles/mi_qa5391/is_200511/ai_n21383022, accessed 6 April 2008. See also Pikoli and Wiener (2013, 152–56), for an account from the Scorpions' perspective.

48. In doing this, they enlisted the aid of members of the Assets Forfeiture Unit; see Khumalo, "South Africa: Zuma vs. the State."

49. "Cosatu Slams NPA over Zuma," *News 24.com*, 27 November 2007, www.news24 .com/News 24/South_Africa/Politics/0,,2-7-12_2228497,00.html, accessed 4 April 2008.

50. *Khampepe Commission of Inquiry into the Mandate and Location of the Directorate of Special Operations.* See also Mashele (2006).

51. "Row over SA Police Boss 'Warrant,'" *BBC News*, 28 September 2007, www.news .bbc.co.uk/2/hi/africa/7017029.stm, accessed 6 April 2008.

52. Sam Sole, Nic Dawes, and Stefaans Brümmer, "Jackie Selebi's Shady Kebble

Links," *Mail & Guardian Online*, 26 May 2006, http://mg.co.za/article/2006-05-26 -jackie-selebis-shady-kebble-links, accessed 6 April 2008.

53. On the troubled process leading up to the arraignment of Jackie Selebi, see Pikoli and Weiner (2013, 233–79).

54. For one mass-mediated account, see Jeremy Gordin, "Court Makes Exception for a Smiling Selebi," *Independent Online*, 3 February 2008, www.int.iol.co.za/in dex.php?click_id=13&set_id=1&art_id=vn20080203090604973C871555, accessed 6 April 2008.

55. See Thamm (2014c) for a detailed account of the pursuit and arrest of Jackie Selebi, told from the vantage of Paul O'Sullivan, a forensic consultant who was closely involved in the investigation.

56. "SA Moves to Scrap Scorpions Unit," *BBC News*, 12 February 2008, www.news.bbc .co.uk/2/hi/africa/7241164.stm, accessed 10 April 2008.

57. These accusations, made by ANC general secretary Gwede Mantashe, were leveled in particular at the head of the Scorpions in Gauteng, Gerrie Nel. Nel was himself arrested on charges of fraud and perjury by the regular police in January 2008 in what was widely interpreted as a turf battle between the DSO and the SAPS. The charges were subsequently withdrawn. See Boyd Webb, "NPA Stands Up for Scorpions," *IOL.News*, 16 April 2008, www.int.iol.co.za/index.php?set_id=18click_ id 798art_id=vn20080416ah, accessed 26 May 2008.

58. See Democratic Alliance, "Case for Retaining the Scorpions." See also SAPA, "Khampepe Report Raises Political Questions," *IOL.com*, 4 May 2008, www.int.iol .co.za/index.php?set_id=18click_id=798art_=nw20080!, accessed 26 May 2008.

59. Karyn Maughan, "It's Time to Fight Back," *Star*, 22 March 2008, www.int.iol.co .za/index.php?set_id=1&click_id=3045&art_id=vn20080322121754459C933339, accessed 11 April 2008.

60. Bridgland, "Wounded Nation."

61. Response to Khaya Dlanga [PoliticalKhaya], "The Scorpions: No Good Deed Goes Unpunished," *Thought Leader*, *Mail & Guardian Online*, 26 March 2008, www .thoughtleader.co.za/khayadlanga/2008/03/25/the-scorpions-no-good-deed -goes-unpunished/, accessed 10 April 2008.

62. Mondli Makhanya, "Let the People Decide Whether Scorpions Should Be Disbanded," *Times* (RSA), 27 January 2008, www.thetimes.co.za/Columnists/Article .aspx?id=692511, accessed 12 April 2008.

63. Prince Mashele, "Polokwane Is a Festering Sore beneath South Africa's Skin," *City Press*, 29 March 2008, www.news24.com/City_Press/Columnists/0,,186-1695 _2296481,00.html, accessed 12 April 2008.

64. Hans Pienaar, "Save Our Scorpions—Survey," *Daily News*, 24 March 2008, www
    .int.iol.co.za/index.php?set_id=1&click_id=6&art_id=vn20080324111612967
    C709874, accessed 10 April 2008.

65. Wilson Johwa, "South Africa: Private Court Bid to Rescue Scorpions," *Business
    Day*, 18 March 2008, www.allafrica.com/stories/200803190367.html, accessed
    11 April 2008.

66. Chartey Quarcoo, "Fixation on Scorpions Cramps Real Political Debate," *Cape
    Times*, 18 February 2008, 9.

67. "Scorpions Boss Joins World Bank," *IOL.News*, 6 May 2008, www.iol.co.za/news
    /politics/scorpions-boss-joins-world-bank-1.399067, accessed 27 May 2008.

68. *The Mail*, formerly *Mafeking Mail*, is an English-language weekly that has been
    published locally for well over a century. *Sepone*, a vernacular tabloid, is of more
    recent vintage. Both are widely read in the North West Province; the former serves
    as something akin to a regional newspaper of record.

69. Our account of this case is based primarily on field research over fifteen months
    in 1999–2000; at the time we were doing an ethnographic study of policing in the
    North West Province, centered on Mafikeng and Lomanyaneng.

70. *Tokoloshe* is not uniformly pronounced or spelled in South Africa. In histories
    and ethnographies of the peoples of the eastern reaches of the country, it is often
    rendered as *tikolosh* or *tikoloshe*, give or take orthographic variations. We spell the
    word as we do in order to capture the manner of its vernacular utterance in the
    North West Province.

71. See Brad Reagan, "CSI Myths: The Shaky Science behind Forensics," *PM*, 7 Decem-
    ber 2009, http://www.popularmechanics.com/science/health/a4535/4325774/,
    accessed 11 February 2015.

72. This is also true of a case with which we deal in 2.3, the kidnap and murder of Leigh
    Matthews, to whom many of the same adjectives were applied.

73. Fred van der Vyver went on to sue the state for malicious prosecution in the Cape
    High Court in 2011, a case that we attended. He won: the presiding judge, Anton
    Veldhuizen, like the judge in the original murder case, Deon van Zyl, excoriated
    the police for their dishonesty and bad faith in presenting dubious "facts" to the
    court. Veldhuizen held that at least one SAPS officer knowingly presented false
    evidence during the trial, and he awarded van der Vyver hefty damages. But to
    the astonishment of many, the Supreme Court of Appeal, in 2013, overturned that
    judgment, arguing that the claimant had not established malicious intent on the
    part of the police and that its evidentiary bungles could have been a "mistake." For
    a highly critical evaluation of this judgment, see Antony Altbeker, "When the Law
    Is an Ass," *Sunday Times* (RSA), 31 March 2013, 13.

74. Among them are some ex–police detectives, like the legendary Piet Byleveld, who has regularly been hired by wealthy South African families to solve murder cases (for his website, see http://www.pietbylcci.co.za/, accessed 22 February 2015), and Paul O'Sullivan, the private investigator who was involved, entirely on his own account, in the investigation and indictment of police chief Jackie Selebi (Thamm 2014c) and other notorious criminals (see, e.g., Thamm 2014a, 116–24).

Chapter 2.2

1. For example, the linking of personhood to legal rights—as distinct from human species being—emerged in a legal brief presented to the New York State Supreme Court by the Nonhuman Rights Project in 2015. In arguing a case for the legal personhood of two chimpanzees, the brief asserted, "Person is not a synonym for 'human being,' but designates an entity with a capacity for legal rights." See "Judge Grants 'Human Rights' to Chimpanzees in Landmark Case," *Cape Times*, 24 April 2015, 6.

2. Bongani Mthethwa, "Maskandi Artist Back from the Dead," *Sunday World*, 5 February 2012, www.sundayworld.co.za/news/2012/02/05/maskandi-artist-back-from-the-dead, accessed 6 July 2012.

3. See Slindile Maluleka, "Family Support 'Dead Singer,'" *IOL News*, 14 February 2012, www.iol.co.za/news/crime-courts/family-support-dead-singer-1.1234188, accessed 15 July 2012. SABC TV coverage of the event gives vivid evidence of the size and state of the crowd gathered at Nquthu; see www.youtube.com/watch?v=dA-WOkwjqH8, accessed 1 August 2012.

4. See Sean Michaels, "Zulu Singer Claims He Rose from the Dead," *Guardian* (UK), 7 February 2012, www.guardian.co.uk/music/2012/feb/07/zulu-folk-singer-risen-dead, accessed 6 July 2012.

5. Also translated from Zulu as "freed myself."

6. See "Witchcraft Fans Mob Man Claiming to Be Reincarnated Singer Abducted by Zombies," *Independent* (UK), 8 February 2012, www.independent.co.uk/news/world/africa/witchcraft-fans-mob-man-claiming-to-be-reincarnated-singer-abducted-by-zombies-6660309.html, accessed 6 July 2012.

7. The historical roots of "The Native with the Gold Teeth," a rumor spread by migrant laborers in Central Africa, are discussed by Karen Fields (1985, 3–23). She points out that its genealogy may be traced to Marcus Garvey. Interestingly, during Barack Obama's election campaign in 2008, there appeared in South Africa a range of commodities bearing his visage—with a prominently glittering tooth.

8. Michaels, "Zulu Singer Claims He Rose from the Dead."

9. See, e.g., Slindile Maluleka, "Family Split over Maskandi Artist's Claim," *Daily News*, 8 February 2012, www.iol.co.za/dailynews/news/families-split-over-maskandi-artist-claim-1.1229827, accessed 8 July 2012.

10. See Canaan Mdletshe, "I Know This Is the Father of My Child—Mgqumeni's Lady," *Sowetan*, 8 February 2012, www.sowetanlive.co.za/news/2012/02/08/i-know-this-is-the-father-of-my-child-mgqumeni-s-lady, accessed 10 July 2012.

11. "South African 'Back-from-Dead Singer Mgqumeni' Detained," *BBC News*, 6 February 2012, www.bbc.co.uk/news/world-africa-16905521, accessed 6 July 2012.

12. The role of the recording studio/copyright owner in all this remains murky. At the time of his "return," the man who would be Khulekani said that he "suspected a *Maskandi* producer of having hired a hitman to threaten him." See Mdu Ncalane and Kiki Ntuli, "The Chicken Begins to Suspect the Mealies," *Occult Zulu*, 27 March 2012, https://occultzulu.wordpress.com/page/4/, accessed 12 February 2015.

13. "Zombie Singer Turns Out to Be Sibusiso John Gcabashe, Not Late South African Zulu Folk Singer Khulekani 'Mgqumeni' Khumalo," *Huffpost Weird News*, 8 February 2012; www.huffingtonpost.com/2012/01/08/zombie-singer-not-zombie_n_1262481.html, accessed 8 July 2012; and "Man Claiming to Be Zombie-Held Famous Musician to Remain in Jail," *ABC News*, 8 February 2012, http://abcnews.go.com/blogs/headlines/2012/02/zombie-held-famous-musician-to-remain-in-jail/, accessed 11 July 2012.

14. See Mthethwa, "Maskandi Artist Back from the Dead."

15. See Mdletshe, "I Know This Is the Father of My Child—Mgqumeni's Lady." Of the other two partners, Lamulile Ngema believed the returnee to be Khulekani; Nomkhosi Mbatha disagreed. According to the *Daily Sun*, a former fiancée, Thembi Ntombela, also confirmed that the returnee was Khulekani; see Muzi Zincume and Anil Singh, "This Zombie Is a Fake!," *Daily Sun*, 6 February 2012, 1–2.

16. Jeannette Catsoulis, "Missing Child Seems Found, but His Family Is at a Loss," movie review, *New York Times*, 12 July 2012, http://movies.nytimes.com/2012/07/13/movies/the-imposter-about-the-con-artist-frederic-bourdin.html, accessed 30 July 2012.

17. *The Return of Martin Guerre* (1982, directed by Daniel Vigne). A Hollywood film, *Sommersby* (1993, directed by Jon Amiel), later adapted the story to events during and after the American Civil War.

18. Fictionalized versions of the story have appeared in a number of works, dating back to the mid-nineteenth century (Dumas 1896).

19. Slindile Maluleka, "No Way Is He Mgqumeni," *Daily News*, 14 March 2012, www.iol.co.za/dailynews/news/no-way-is-he-mgqumeni-1.1256076, accessed 1 August 2012.

20. See Jane Duncan, "Social Security Debased by the Profit Motive," *Mail & Guardian*, 3–9 January 2014, 10. Duncan holds a chair in the School of Journalism and Media Studies at Rhodes University in South Africa.

21. Personal communication, 6 August 2012.

22. Khosi Biyela, "Take That, You Fake! More Fame for the Zombie," *Daily Sun*, 30 March 2012, 5.

23. We consulted Dennis Davis, a High Court judge and judge president of the Competition Appeal Court of South Africa, and Peter Gastrow, former council to the minister of safety and security, Sydney Mufamadi (personal communication, 8 August 2012). Both were of the opinion that, given its circumstances, this case would be difficult to prosecute for fraud.

24. Anil Singh, "Maskandi Man Back in Court," *Daily Sun*, 8 February 2012, 4.

25. Davis here cites de Vienne (1547, 63).

26. See, e.g., Alexandra Topping, "Mandela Memorial Sign Language Interpreter Accused of Being a Fake," *Guardian* (UK), 11 December 2013, www.theguardian.com /society/2013/dec/11/mandela-memorial-sign-language-interpreter-making-it -up-fake, accessed 30 December 2013.

27. See, e.g., Botho Molosankwe, "Sign Language 'Fake' Blames Illness," *IOL News*, 12 December 2013, www.iol.co.za/news/south-africa/gauteng/sign-language-fake-blames -illness-1.1621044#.UsLTLU2x45s, accessed 30 December 2013.

28. See SAPA, "I Am the Great Fake, Says Bogus Signer from Sterkfontein," *Mail & Guardian*, 27 December 2013, http://mg.co.za/article/2013-12-27-i-am-the-great -fake-says-bogus-signer-from-sterkfontein/, accessed 28 December 2013. Note that Sterkfontein is a psychiatric hospital in Krugersdorp, Gauteng Province.

29. See Slavoj Žižek, "The 'Fake' Mandela Memorial Interpreter Said It All," *Guardian* (UK), 16 December 2013, www.theguardian.com/commentisfree/2013/dec/16 /fake-mandela-memorial-interpreter-schizophrenia-signing, accessed 4 January 2014.

30. See e.g., Karyn Maughan, "Exclusive: Mandela Deaf Interpreter Accused of Murder," *ENCA*, 13 December 2013, www.enca.com/south-africa/interpreter, accessed 14 December 2013. See also Taylor Berman, "Fake Mandela Interpreter Helped Burn Two Men to Death," *Gawker.com*, 16 December 2013, http://gawker.com/fake -mandela-interpreter-helped-burn-two-men-to-death-1484081850, accessed 16 December 2013.

31. Ruth Hopkins and Grethe Koen, "Who Is Watching the Lawyers," *Saturday Star*, 26 June 2012, www.iol.com.za/Saturday-star/who-is-watching-the-laywers-1.132 8182, accessed 7 August 2012.

32. See SAPA, "Interpol Roped into SAFA Investigation," *IOL News*, 20 December 2012,

www.iol.co.za/sport/soccer/interpol-roped-into-safa-investigation-1.1443476, accessed 21 December 2012.

33. Moloko Moloto, "Fake Degrees: 1000 Health Workers Deregistered," *Star*, 24 July 2012, www.iol.co.za/the-star/fake-degrees-1-000-health-workers-deregistered-1.1347685, accessed 7 August 2012.

34. Lynn Williams, "Fake Doctor Killed Patients," *Herald*, 14 February 2011.

35. Slindile Maluleka, "Concern at Rise in Number of People Faking Qualifications," *Daily News*, 18 June 2012, www.iol.co.za/dailynews/news/concern-at-rise-in-number-of-people-faking-qualifications-1.1321067, accessed 7 August 2012.

36. Japhet Ncube, "Why Fikile Mbalula Wants to Be an American," *Independent* (RSA), 25 June 2012, www.iol.co.za/sundayindependent/why-fikile-mbalula-wants-to-be-american-1.1326643, accessed August 7 2012.

37. Sunday morning service at the Universal Church of the Kingdom of God, 7 February 2011.

38. "Navigating the Streets of Entrepreneurship," *Big Issue*, no. 200 (August 2012): 16–17.

39. Ntwisiso Ngobeni, "The Truth Can Set Us Free," *Sunday Times*, Review 2, 5 August 2012, 1–2.

40. "Jobless Growth: The Economy Is Doing Nicely—but at Least One Person in Three Is Out of Work," *Economist*, 3 June 2010, www.economist.com/node/16248641, accessed 13 August 2013.

41. *Maskanda* is thought to derive originally from *musikant*, the Afrikaans word for musician (Coplan 2001, 109).

42. This is from the song *"Owami Lomama"* (This mother of mine). A fuller discussion of these and other lyrics will be provided in our forthcoming book on the life and work of Khulekani Khumalo.

43. See Olsen (2009, 151), on the Shwi Nomtekhala duo, whose style is quite close to that of the late Khulekani. One of their popular songs declares, "I was another one who had believed in guns, then my father came to me in a dream."

44. Kathryn Olsen, personal communication, 6 August 2012.

45. See Lerato Matsoso, "Fake Zombie Stole My Songs!," *Daily News*, 29 March 2012, 6. The music producer in question was Enoch Nondala, of Enoch Nondala Music Production. Mtungwa's CD, according to this report, was allegedly made for Nondala's company in the absence of a contract.

46. Canaan Mdletshe, "Fake Maskandi CD Is Hot," *Sowetan*, 30 March 2012, www.sowetanlive.co.za/entertainment/article4468159.ece, accessed 14 September 2012.

47. Countering this argument might not have been easy, or even possible, for the Mselekus. For one thing, the primary *dramatis personae* were either dead or long

departed from Nquthu and hence not available to give evidence. For another, they would, in this highly conservative part of rural KwaZulu, have had to answer the question of why they had allowed their daughter to enter a domestic union if bridewealth had *not* been negotiated.

48. Mandla Zulu, Matthew Savides, and Bongani Mthethwa, "'Fake' Hawk Had Police at His Beck and Call: Khumalo Exposed as Zimbabwean National," *Sunday Times* (RSA), 5 August 2012, 5.

49. See "IPID Is Investigating the Death in Police Custody of Musa Muzi Khumalo, Pretoria Moot CAS 12/12/2012," 3 December 2012, www.ipid.gov.za/media_state ments/03122012.asp, accessed 30 December 2013. See also "Fake Hawk Dead in Police Cell," *Witness*, 4 December 2012, www.witness.co.za/index.php?showcontent &global%5B_id%5D=92153, accessed 30 December 2013.

Chapter 2.3

1. Darrel Bristow-Bovey, "Metamorphosis a Painless Escape from Mind-Numbing Questions," *Sunday Independent* (RSA), 6 August 2000, 12.

2. Robins (2004, 93) cites a document circulated by the People's Dialogue, a South African NGO that "services" a local grassroots housing organization connected to the global slum dwellers' network. Entitled "Some Notes on Enumeration," it questions Foucauldian notions of governmentality—in particular, the idea that counting inevitably buttresses state surveillance and bureaucratic control. Enumeration, it argues, can also be used to make dispossessed people, who otherwise remain invisible, "more legible to the state in order to lobby for access to . . . resources."

3. Mafikeng-Mmabatho is the capital of the North West Province. Mafikeng (now known as Mahikeng), one-half of the hyphenated town, has been the chiefly seat of the Tshidi-Barolong, a Tswana people, since the mid- to late nineteenth century. Mmabatho, the other half, was established by the apartheid regime as the headquarters of the ethnic homeland of Bophuthatswana, which was formally given "self-rule" in 1971. Mahikeng, known in English historically as Mafeking, was the site of the famous—or notorious, depending on historical perspective—Siege of Mafeking during the Second South African War (1899–1902).

4. The statistics posted by the Criminal Information Analysis Centre, no longer available online to our knowledge, also came in two versions, one for the financial year (ending 31 March 2003) and the other for the calendar year (to 31 December 2002). As they are the most detailed of the official counts, we use the second version of the Criminal Information Analysis Centre figures, those for the calendar year 2002.

5. These figures are available at http://www.saps.gov.za/resource_centre/publica
tions/statistics/ crimestats/2014/crime_stats.php, last accessed 20 May 2015. Unless otherwise specified, all numbers are sourced from this site.

6. In its methods, categories, and reporting, this *VOCS* follows the International
Crime Victims Survey. For purposes of economy in the text, we shall refer to it as
SSA (2014) and to the earlier one by the Institute for Security Studies as ISS (2004).

7. For a summary of these comparative numbers, see "Fact Sheet: South Africa's
Official Crime Statistics for 2013/4," *Africa Check*, undated, http://africacheck.org
/factsheets/factsheet-south-africas-official-crime-statistics-for-201314/, accessed
25 May 2015.

8. Note that this is much lower than it had been in 2002, when, for example, there
were over double the attempted murders and 80,000 or so more GBH cases in a
population of approximately 45.81 million, almost 10 million fewer than today.

9. *The Lancet* (Global Burden of Disease Study 2015) gives a different rank order of
medical causes of death from that published by Statistics South Africa (2013) for
roughly the same period. We have no empirical basis for evaluating either set of
counts, but the contrast between them has no impact on our general point, which
is to compare so-called "natural" with "nonnatural" deaths, especially those resulting from criminal violence.

10. Overall, femicide has declined substantially since 1999, although the subcategory
of intimate femicide seems to have remained at much the same levels. See Lisa
Vetten, "Racial Scare-Mongering in South Africa Makes Light of Women's Murders," *Africa Check*, 17 July 2013, https://africacheck.org/2013/07/17/racial-scare
-mongering-makes-light-of-womens-murders-2/, accessed 3 August 2014.

11. For mass-mediated mythostats of this sort, see, e.g., J. Standley, "South Africa
Targets Domestic Violence," *BBC News Online*, 15 December 1999, http://news.bbc
.co.uk/1/hi/world/africa/566160.stm; and K. L. Caxton, "Shock Male Rape Stats,"
South Africa Online, 25 October 1999, http://www.southafrica.co.za/dailynews/Oc
tober1999/october25-2999/news 261019991.html; both accessed 30 June 2000.
The numbers are usually derived by multiplying police counts by the imagined
proportion of unreported cases.

12. We use 2003/4 rather than 2002 here, as it is the first year for which the longer-
term SAPS figures are (almost) fully comparable.

13. Between 2012/13 and 2013/14, recorded murders went up by 3.5 percent, attempted murder by 3.2 percent, and aggravated robbery by 11.2 percent. Sexual
offenses are said to have dropped by 6.9 percent and GBH by 2.8 percent.

14. This increasing reluctance to report crimes to the SAPS—along with the causes

given for it—contradicts the one curious finding in the *VOCS 2013/4* (SSA 2014, 2), namely, that "more than 60 percent of households were satisfied with the way in which police and courts were doing their work." There is plenty of evidence to the contrary presented later in the document (41ff., esp. 49).

15. Newham, "President Zuma Ignores Increasing Violent Crime in His State of the Nation Address."

16. See Lizette Lancaster, "Where Murder Happens in South Africa," *Africa Check*, 19 September 2013, http://africacheck.org/2013/09/19/where-murder-happens -in-sa/, accessed 3 August 2014.

17. See "Worst Ten Precincts: Largest Number of Reported Crimes," *Crime Stats SA*, 2014, http://www.crimestatssa.com/topten.php, accessed 4 June 2015.

18. Tony Weaver, "City Crime: How It Affects You: Figures Illustrate Stark Disparities between Black and White Areas," *Cape Times*, 23 September 2004, 1, 3. The same point is made in an editorial the next day; see "Figuring Out Crime," *Cape Times*, 24 September 2004, 10.

19. See, e.g., "Understanding Crime Statistics in South Africa: What You Need to Know," researched by Nechama Brodie, edited by Peter Cunliffe-Jones, *Africa Check*, undated, http://africacheck.org/factsheet/sa-guide-to-crime-statistics-in-south -africa-what-you-need-to-know/, accessed 3 August 2014.

20. R. Brand, "The Surprising Truth about Crime," *Star*, 28 January 1998, 19. All quotations in the remainder of the paragraph are taken from this source.

21. See Nigel Morris, "The Mysterious Case of Why Crime Is Falling in Britain," *Independent* (UK), 24 January 2014, 19. This report is based on the Crime Survey for England and Wales, 2014. The one for the following year, *Crime in England and Wales, Year Ending September 2014* (United Kingdom, Office for National Statistics, 2015), shows the same trajectory; see http://www.ons.gov.uk/ons/dcp171778_392380.pdf, accessed 31 May 2015.

22. See, e.g., http://www.nationmaster.com/country-info/stats/Crime/Rape-rate, accessed 31 May 2015. Nation Master is a website that tabulates statistics from a large number of origin points. In comparing its figures—which are updated regularly— we have found it to be a very useful and largely representative megasource. The reliability of the data, of course, is subject to all the caveats that apply to crime counts *sui generis*. For convenience and easy reference, we cite all our information here from it.

23. See *Seventh United Nations Survey on Crime Trends*, http://www.unodc.org/pdf /crime/seventh_survey/7sc.pdf, accessed 2 June 2002. For the older numbers, we also rely on a study summarizing the UK Home Office and Council of Europe data

for the early 2000s (Barclay and Tavares 2003, 10); cf. also Masuku (2001, 19). Note, too, that, at the time, South Africans reported crime as often as did citizens of other countries (Louw 1998).

24. Devlin Barrett, "Wanted: Decent Crime Statistics," *Wall Street Journal*, 9 October 2015, A3.

25. See, e.g., "Lying about Crime," editorial, *Cape Argus*, 10 January 2002, 13.

26. So grave was the problem in the late 1990s that a Zero Tolerance Action Task Group was set up in the Western Cape to deal with it. Note that overreporting does not only result from malicious intent. In the North West in 1999–2000, we learned of many incidents first thought to be felonies that turned out not to be: gift exchanges gone awry that, in the heat of a moment, were said to be stock theft, domestic violence reported by wives who wanted to "teach their husbands a lesson" for philandering, and so on.

27. Those figures are also affected by demographic indeterminacies. In order to arrive at any felony rate from a raw incidence, patently, the size of the population has to be taken into account. This, in South Africa, is hard to assess accurately: the country's many informal settlements resist easy enumeration, partly because of their mobile social ecology but also because they are home to a fluctuating population of "foreigners" whose numbers, although often wildly guessed at, are difficult to verify with certainty.

28. See, e.g., Martin Schönteich, "Moratorium on Crime Figures," *Focus 19*, September 2000, http://www.hsf.org.za/focus19crime.html, accessed 5 January 2001. This URL is no longer accessible. It has been replaced by http://hsf.org.za/resource -centre/focus/issue-19-third-quarter-2000/moratorium-on-crime-figures, dated 1 October 2009.

29. Mr. S. V. Tshwete, "Media Statement by the Minister for Safety and Security," 31 May 2001, http://www.saps.gov.za/ 8_crimeinfo/bulletin/crime2001.htm, accessed 17 June 2001.

30. "Crime Statistics Inaccurate: Request for Moratorium Not Attempt at Secrecy or Gagging, says Commissioner," *Star*, 17 July 2000, 2.

31. M. Power, "Year-Long Blackout on Crime Statistics Angers Analysts and Politicians," *Sunday Independent* (RSA), 13 August 2000, 3.

32. Schönteich, "Moratorium on Crime Figures."

33. J. Smetherham, "Call to Make Dangerous N2 Safer," *Cape Times*, 31 January 2001, 9.

34. SAPA, "Legal Challenge to Crime-Stats Moratorium," *IOL News*, 7 February 2001, http://www.iol.co.za/news/politics/legal-challenge-to-crime-stats-moratorium -1.60427#.VXAjvU3bInM, accessed 17 June 2001. The allegation on the part of

the Democratic Alliance, cited in the following sentence, is documented in the same report.

35. C. van der Spuy, "Came Back to Crime," *Cape Times*, 16 June 2003, 8.

36. See also A. Leithead, "SA Gets Tough on Crime," *BBC News*, 7 October 2003, http:// news.bbc.co.uk/1/ hi/world/africa/3168688.stm, accessed 16 December 2003.

37. Gareth Newham, "The Politics of Crime Statistics," *Africa Check*, 22 September 2013, https://africacheck.org/2013/09/22/the-politics-of-crime-statistics-2/, accessed 18 May 2015.

38. F. Butterfield, "Some Experts Fear Political Influence on Crime Data Agencies," *New York Times*, 22 September 2002, 23.

39. Eterno is himself a retired police captain. See William K. Rashbaum, "Retired Officers Raise Questions on Crime Data," *New York Times*, 6 February 2010, http:// www.nytimes.com/2010/02/07/nyregion/07crime.html?_r=0, accessed 18 May 2015. The report noted that the NYPD disputed the findings of the study but that similar concerns about tampering with crime statistics had also been raised in Atlanta, Baltimore, Dallas, New Orleans, and Washington, DC.

40. David Bernstein and Noah Isackson, "New Tricks," *Chicago Magazine*, 11 May 2015, 4, http://www.chicagomag.com/Chicago-Magazine/June-2015/Chicago-crime-stats/, accessed 19 May 2015.

41. David Barrett, "Lord Stevens Admits Police Have Been 'Fiddling' Crime Figures for Years," *Telegraph*, 7 January 2014, http://www.telegraph.co.uk/news/uknews /crime/10557155/Lord-Stevens-admits-police-have-been-fiddling-crime-figures -for-years.html, accessed 21 May 2015.

42. David Barrett, "Police Force 'Tricks' to 'Fiddle' Crime Figures," *Telegraph*, 5 December 2009, http://www.telegraph.co.uk/news/uknews/law-and-order/6736505/Police -force-tricks-to-fiddle-crime-figures.html, accessed 21 May 2015.

43. Kate Wilkinson, "Police Wrong to Claim That Crime Index 'Vindicates' Official Crime Statistics," *Africa Check*, 15 November 2013, http://africacheck.org/reports /police-wrong-to-claim-that-crime-index-vindicates-official-crime-statistics/, accessed 21 May 2015.

44. South African singer, songwriter, film actor, and Afrikaner activist Steve Hofmeyer has claimed persistently that whites are "being killed like flies," an extravagantly ill-conceived assertion. For a carefully researched evaluation of his claim, see "Are SA Whites Really Being Killed 'Like Flies'? Why Steve Hofmeyr Is Wrong," researched by Nechama Brodie, edited by Julian Rademeyer, *Africa Check*, 24 June 2013, http://africacheck.org/reports/are-white-afrikaners-really-being-killed-like -flies/, accessed 4 June 2015. See also du Preez (2013, 188).

45. The lack of critical attention to the assumptions built into these techniques is

striking. In his astute study of the social production of statistics by the Canadian Center for Justice Studies, for instance, Haggerty (2001, 31) notes that they "have their limitations." But he says only that they underrepresent corporate, environmental, and "victimless" crimes. GIS has been widely used in fields like geography and urban planning, where there has been some debate about their political implications (see Pickles 1995). To date, however, there seems to be little parallel discussion of their use in crime mapping.

46. That first survey was done with UN aid by the Department for Safety and Security, and involved the participation of Statistics South Africa. Others have also been undertaken since then by independent research organizations, like the ISS (2004).

47. The advent of publications like the *International Review of Victimology* is testimony to the growing concern, as a matter of human rights, with the role of victims in criminal procedure.

48. Victim charters have been promulgated in a number of countries. In Britain, for instance, they were common in the wake of the Thatcherite "social contract." In South Africa, the Law Commission appointed a committee to investigate proposals for victim compensation in the 1990s, very soon after the end of the *ancien régime* (Camerer *et al.* 1998).

49. This recital, which we attended, was held at Pollsmoor on 12 August 2004 under the auspices of YOUTHSA and Youth in Prison.

50. E.g., C. Hooper-Box, "Theft and Corruption Top List of Crimes in SA," *Sunday Independent* (RSA), 7 March 2004, 2; and G. Jepson, "Crime Is in the Eye of the Beholder—Study," *This Day*, 4 March 2004, 3.

51. T. Leggett, "Race Groups' Views on Safety Differ," *Sunday Independent* (RSA), 4 July 2004, 16.

52. Leggett's study, and the debate surrounding it, were most fully covered in Zenzile Khoisan, "Coloureds Twice as Likely to Be Murdered," *Cape Argus*, 26 May 2004, 1.

53. Z. Williams, "So It Wasn't All Sex and Drugs," *Mail & Guardian*, 23–29 July 2004, 16.

54. Tshwete, "Media Statement by the Minister for Safety and Security."

55. Produced by the Human Sciences Research Council GIS Center, the map drew on SAPS data. See E. Sylvester, "Pinpointing Our Crime Hotspots," *Saturday Star*, 13 November 1999, 11.

56. E. Sylvester, "Jo'burg CBD a Paradise for Criminals," *Saturday Star*, 13 November 1999, 11.

57. See John Plummer's letter, "Crime Pays," *Cape Times*, 1 July 2004, 10.

58. See above, n. 3.

59. Van der Spuy, "Came Back to Crime."
60. P. Tyler, "Time to Speak Out, Victims of Crime," *Cape Argus*, 21 July 2003, 11.
61. Our data on the case are based on interviews with Thaisi Medupe (the primary witness), Reggie Mpame (the registrar of the High Court in Mmabatho), Abraham Maeco (the headman of Matlonyane), and several associates of the victim; on visits to the sites at which the events occurred; and on the records of the case. See also Nat Molomo, "Bizarre Zombie Claim in Court," *Mail*, 31 March 1995.
62. "Huge Public Response to Sizzlers Identikits," *Cape Times*, 3 February 2003, 3.
63. P. Dickson and L. Van Zilla, "Memorial Service Held for Gay Club Victims," *Cape Times*, 23 January 2003, 1.
64. K. Maughn, "Sizzlers Pair Fall Out," *Cape Argus*, 4 March 2004, 1.
65. A. Smith, "Gays Outraged by Castration Call on Website," *Cape Argus*, 26 June 2004, 1.
66. "Kidnapping Hell Enters Sixth Day," *Independent Newspapers*, 15 July 2004, 1; and G. Gifford and SAPA, "Call Centre Set Up to Help Find Leigh," *Star*, 15 July 2004, 2.
67. A. Eliseev and R. Philp, "Touched by an Angel," *Sunday Times*, 25 July 2004, 3.
68. R. Philp and A. Eliseev, "Rich Parents Go for Anti-kidnap Training," *Sunday Times* (RSA), 18 July 2004, 3.
69. "Kidnap: South Africa's New Terror," *You* (magazine), 29 July 2004, cover; also "The Matthews Tragedy Has Highlighted an Under-reported Crime in SA—and You Could Be a Victim," 12–13.
70. K. Ajam, "Despair in the Search for Missing Loved Ones," *Independent on Saturday*, 17 July 2004, 1.
71. Rebecca Davis, "Panayiotou, Patel, and Trevor Noah's 'Cousin': The Relative Value of South African Life," *Daily Maverick*, 26 May 2015, http://www.dailymaverick.co.za/article/2015-05-26-panayiotou-patel-and-trevor-noahs-cousin-the-relative-value-of-south-african-life/#.VWRSlU3bInM, accessed 26 May 2015.
72. Fanie van Deventer, cited in Ajam, "Despair in the Search for Missing Loved Ones."
73. See "Kidnapping," Crime Stats SA, http://www.crimestatssa.com/national.php, accessed 6 June 2015.
74. Philp and Eliseev, "Rich Parents Go for Anti-kidnap Training," 3.
75. It was later reported that Rob Matthews dropped an "instalment" (R50,000) of the R300,000 demanded at the designated spot south of Johannesburg. See R. Philp, A. Eliseev, and H. Geldenhuys, "Killers Froze Body of Leigh Matthews," *Sunday Times* (RSA), 22 August 2004, 1.
76. A. Eliseev and R. Philp, "Hope for Leigh Refuses to Die," *Sunday Times* (RSA), 18 July 2004, 3.
77. SAPA, "Country Mourns for Leigh," *Cape Times*, 23 July 2004, 1.

78. E-mail circulated under title "Death Penalty: Do It for Leigh Matthews," 6 August 2004. We thank Shaheen Ariefdien for drawing our attention to this petition.

79. Most recently, at the time of writing, there is the case of Jayde Panayiotou, found murdered on 22 April 2015. See Davis, "Panayiotou, Patel, and Trevor Noah's 'Cousin.'"

80. SAPA, "Find the 'Sick People' Who Killed Leigh—ANC," *IOL News*, 22 July 2004, http://www.iol.co.za/south-africa/find-the-sick-people-who-killed-leigh---anc -217790, accessed 10 August 2004.

81. Rob and Sharon Matthews, "Thank You for Caring about Leigh," *Sunday Times* (RSA), 22 August 2004, 2.

82. Jonathan Ancer, "A Tale of Two Broken Families," *Star*, 8 October 2004, 1.

83. A striking—and strident—instance is the movement that has arisen in response to the murder of farmers (especially white farmers), alleged by those who have taken up the issue to be much more frequent than official statistics, or independent research, would suggest; see n. 44.

Chapter 2.4

1. The term *mabangalala*, literally "those who do not sleep" in isiZulu, did not always carry such violent, counterrevolutionary connotations. In the pre- and early apartheid years, Goodhew (1993) argues, it was associated with left-wing political organizations; see also N. Smith (2013, 14).

2. For an unusually vivid firsthand account of the brute ineptitude and forensic incapacities of the police in dealing with the scene of a violent crime—and with its judicial aftermath—see Gevisser (2014, 245ff).

3. The policy was officially spelled out in *Community Policing: Policy Framework and Guidelines* (South African Police Service 1997); see Minnaar 2013, 63.

4. See Jonny Steinberg, "Policemen Thwarted in Rural Areas," *Business Day*, 20 November 1998, http://www.bday.co.za/98/1120/news/n13.htm, accessed 5 November 2005. This report also gives a useful description of the problems of policing the countryside.

5. As a report on the topic published by the Center for Policy Studies in Johannesburg noted, "'Civil society' is freighted by democracy theorists with the capacity to nurture citizens' democratic capacities. But rather than testing these propositions empirically, there has been a tendency in the democratic transition literature to define civil society in tautological fashion, that is by what it is destined to do (to fill in for the limitations of formal democracy), rather than by what it actually is or how it does it" (Heller and Ntlokonkulu 2001, 4).

6. Quoted in Jonny Steinberg, "Freedom Breeds Crime: Grist for the Authoritarian Mill," *Business Day*, 15 September 1999.

7. Nashira Davids, "Anti-crime Cards Spark Racism Row," *Cape Times*, 10 March 2015, 1–2.

8. *Towards a Safer Khayelitsha—August 2014: Report of the Commission of Inquiry into Allegations of Police Inefficiency and a Breakdown in Relations between SAPS and the Community of Khayelitsha*, http://www.khayelitshacommission.org.za/final-report .html, accessed 27 February 2015. We refer to this document hereafter as *Khayelitsha Commission: Final Report*.

9. Siyavuya Mzantsi, Xolani Koyana, and SAPA, "The Killing Field: Kangaroo Courts' Execution Zone," *Cape Times*, 23 January 2014, 1, 3.

10. Daneel Knoetze, "Commission Finds 'Serious Inefficiencies' in Khayelitsha Policing," *GroundUp*, 26 August 2014, http://www.dailymaverick.co.za/article/2014-08 -26-groundup-commission-finds-serious-inefficiencies-in-khayelitsha-policing /#.VPB_6k0o7IU, accessed 27 February 2015.

11. Mzantsi, Koyana, and SAPA, "The Killing Field: Kangaroo Courts' Execution Zone."

12. Ibid.

13. Knoetze, "Commission Finds 'Serious Inefficiencies' in Khayelitsha Policing."

14. Jenna Etheridge, "Police Wish Khayelitsha Residents 'Good Luck' with Gangs," *Mail & Guardian*, 7 February 2014, http://mg.co.za/article/2014-02-07-police -wish-khayelitsha-residents-good-luck-with-gangs, accessed 27 February 2015.

15. At the time, the Western Cape Province, into which Cape Town (and the Cape Flats) fall, was governed not by the ANC but by its parliamentary opposition, the Democratic Alliance, whose then party leader, Helen Zille, was the provincial premier. It was she who appointed the commission.

16. The groups involved were the Social Justice Coalition, Equal Education, Free Gender, Triangle Project, Ndifuna Ukwazi, and the Treatment Action Campaign, all of which organize significant projects in Khayelitsha. See Knoetze, "Commission Finds 'Serious Inefficiencies' in Khayelitsha Policing."

17. Daneel Knoetze, "Khayelitsha Police, Community and Activists Find Ways to Tackle Crime," *GroundUp*, 28 November 2014, http://groundup.org.za/article/kha yelitsha-police-community-and-activists-find-ways-tackle-crime_2486/, accessed 27 February 2015. See also *Khayelitsha Commission: Final Report*, 152.

18. See Daniel Hartford, "Bringing Lavender to the Hills: Community Policing, Fear and Safety in the Cape," *Daily Maverick*, 19 November 2015, http://www.daily maverick.co.za/article/2015-11-19-op-ed-bringing-lavender-to-the-hills-com munity-policing-fear-and-safety-in-the-cape/, accessed 20 November 2015.

19. Marianne Thamm, "Khayelitsha Commission of Inquiry, Phase One: Putting a

Finger in the Leaking Dike," *Daily Maverick*, 16 September 2014, http://www.daily maverick.co.za/article/2014-09-16-khayelitsha-commission-of-inquiry-phase -one-putting-a-finger-in-a-leaking-dike/#.VPLnFUOo7IU, accessed 28 February 2015.

20. Janis Kinnear, "Plea for Army to Halt Escalating Gang Wars," *Weekend Argus*, 2 May 2015, 6.

21. See Michael Morris, "Gangland (Pty) Ltd," *Cape Argus*, 4 August 2003, 1; and Michael Morris and Ashley Smith, "Gangland's Drug Franchises: Police Tactics on Gangs Blasted by New Report," *Cape Argus*, 18 August 2005, 1. See also A. Standing (2003, 2005).

22. Matthew Savides, "Clueless as List of Cold Cases Grows," *Sunday Times* (RSA), 1 March 2015, 8.

23. *S v. Makwanyane and Another* (cct 3/94 [1995]) was the first major decision handed down by the Constitutional Court of South Africa.

24. Stephen Rule and Bongiwe Mncwango, "Rights or Wrongs? Public Attitudes towards Moral Values," Human Sciences Research Council, n.d., http://www.hsrc.ac .za/uploads/pageContent/1607/Rights%20or%20Wrongs.pdf, accessed 2 March 2015. See also Chantelle Benjamin, "Crime in New SA: Is the Death Penalty Cure or an Illusion?," *Business Day*, 23 October 2003, 1, 3.

25. *Death Penalty Information Center*, International Polls and Studies, http://www .deathpenaltyinfo.org/international-polls-and-studies-0, accessed 3 March 2015. The South African data are for 2006.

26. "South African Can't Go On like This: Kagisho Dikgacoi Calls for Death Penalty following Senzo Meyiwa Murder," *Kickoff.com*, 28 October 2014, http://www.kickoff .com/news/49821/kagisho-dikgacoi-calls-for-death-penalty-following-senzo -meyiwa-murder, accessed 2 February 2015.

27. Aislinn Laing, "Bring Back the Death Penalty, Says South Africa Medical Chief," *Telegraph* (UK), 3 February 2012, http://www.telegraph.co.uk/news/worldnews /africaandindianocean/southafrica/9059555/Bring-back-the-death-penalty-says -South-Africa-medical-chief.html, accessed 22 June 2015. The head of the South African Medical Association at the time was Dr. Norman Mabasa. The second phrase in quotes is a paraphrase. Dr. Mabasa's exact words were "kill and you will be killed."

28. See, e.g., African News Agency, "PE Teacher's Husband Charged with Her Murder," *Cape Times*, 5 May 2015, 1.

29. Pierre de Vos, "Death Penalty: It's Not Even the Beginning of a Solution," *Daily Maverick*, 5 November 2014, http://www.dailymaverick.co.za/opinionista/2014-11

-05-death-penalty-its-not-even-the-beginning-of-a-solution/#.VPSPDkOo7IU, accessed 2 March 2015.

30. See *Mountain Men: Protecting Lives Everyday,* http://www.mountainmen.co.za/, accessed 3 March 2015.

31. See Nomavenda Mathiane, "To Some This Man Is a Saint—to Others Just a Vigilante," *Business Day*, 25 June 1999.

32. See Phomello Molwedi, "Sex Vigilante Guilty of Rape," *Star*, 28 July 2000.

33. Tania Broughton, "Vigilante Farmer Jailed for Killing," *IOL.News*, 14 February 2013, http://www.iol.co.za/news/crime-courts/vigilante-farmer-jailed-for-killing -1.1470066#.VUIxn03D9jo, accessed 1 May 2015.

34. For a carefully researched evaluation of his claim, see "Are SA Whites Really Being Killed 'Like Flies'? Why Steve Hofmeyr Is Wrong," researched by Nechama Brodie, edited by Julian Rademeyer. See also du Preez (2013, 188).

35. All quotations in this paragraph are taken from Genevieve Serra, "Tawwe Tannie: Flats Aunty takes on Dwelm Merts," *Daily Voice*, 10 July 2015, 11. *Tawwe* is Afrikaans for "tough," and *dwelm merts* is Kaaps (Cape Coloured Afrikaans) for "drug merchants/dealers."

36. Because of its accessibility and its empirical richness, we cite many of our evidentiary examples here from the *Khayelitsha Commission: Final Report*; all of them, however, are confirmed by our own research (see, e.g., 2007) and by a growing scholarly literature on informal justice, much of it quoted elsewhere in the present and other chapters. On this particular point, the cry that triggers mass disciplinary action, see Pumla Gobodo-Madikizela and Kelly Gillespie, in *Khayelitsha Commission: Final Report*, 342 and 140, respectively.

37. Pumla Gobodo-Madikizela, in *Khayelitsha Commission: Final Report*, 343.

38. Magnus Persson, in *Khayelitsha Commission: Final Report*, 94–95.

39. Gobodo-Madikizela, in *Khayelitsha Commission: Final Report*, 343.

40. See Geoffrey York, "Vigilante Killings on the 'Field of Death' in a South African Township," *Globe and Mail*, 22 February 2015, http://www.theglobeandmail.com /news/world/vigilante-killings-on-the-field-of-death-in-south-african-township /article17052460/, accessed 4 February 2015.

41. *Khayelitsha Commission: Final Report*, 342.

42. Nathi Olifant and Xoliswa Zulu, "Rape Victim Thankful for 'Vigilante Justice,'" *IOL.News*, 27 October 2006, http://www.iol.co.za/news/south-africa/rape-victim -thankful-for-vigilante-justice-1.300438, accessed 4 March 2015.

43. Francesca Villette, "Rage Directed at Police after Suspect Is Freed," *Cape Times*, 6 March 2015, 3.

44. See Hartford, "Bringing Lavender to the Hills." Both *Southern Eye* and *Supreme*, which include roughly equal numbers of male and female members, patrol neighborhoods, seek to disrupt gang activities, and "provide their own solutions" to crime. *Southern Eye* also holds social events and awareness campaigns to combat gender violence and the local drug trade.

45. According to the legal doctrine of common purpose—also known as, among other things, common design and joint (criminal) enterprise—liability for the consequences of an illegal act may be ascribed to anyone who takes part in it, however indirectly. The effort of the South African justice system to arraign 270 miners at Marikana for the deaths inflicted by the police during the strike was authorized under this doctrine.

46. Naeemah Abrahams, Rachel Jewkes, and Ria Laubscher, "'I Do Not Believe in Democracy in the Home': Men's Relationships with and Abuse of Women," MRC Policy Brief, http://www.mrc.ac.za/gender/nodemocracy.pdf, accessed 3 March 2015.

47. SAPA, "Mom, Daughter in Vigilante Killing," *IOL.News*, 15 January 2015, https://www.google.co.za/?gfe_rd=cr&ei=cbX5VMS7CoOp8weEuIGgDg&gws_rd=ssl#q=Mom%2C+daughter+in+vigilante+killing, accessed 6 March 2015.

48. Ms. Peter and her husband, Isaac Mbadu, both worked for the Social Justice Coalition. They denied the charge, along with three counts of kidnapping, insisting that they had been framed for blowing the whistle on police corruption. The two were found guilty, as were a pair of accomplices, and directed to participate in a process of restorative justice. See *Khayelitsha Commission: Final Report*, 81–82; also GroundUp staff, "Twist in the Angy Peter Trial: None of the Accused Will Go to Jail," *GroundUp*, 27 November 2014, http://groundup.org.za/article/twist-angy-peter-trial-none-accused-will-go-prison_2484, accessed 5 March 2015.

49. Shalo Mbatha, "Frustrated Communities Are Striking Back," *Sunday Independent* (RSA), 4 March 2001, 5. All the quoted speech in this paragraph comes from this report.

50. See "'We'll Show You You're a Woman': Violence and Discrimination against Black Lesbians and Transgender Men in South Africa," *Human Rights Watch*, http://www.hrw.org/sites/default/files/reports/southafrica1211.5_December 2011.pdf, accessed 7 March 2015. The report notes that "between April and July 2007 alone, there were three separate instances of sexual assault and murder of known lesbians; at least eight separate instances of violence against lesbians were recorded in 2008, of which three were cases of sexual assault and murder. These cases, happening in rapid succession, established the targeting of lesbians as a specific problem within the LGBT community" (14).

51. Mandy de Waal, "We'll Make You a 'Real' Woman—Even If It Kills You," *Daily Maverick*, 9 December 2011, http://www.dailymaverick.co.za/article/2011-12-09-well-make-you-a-real-woman-even-if-it-kills-you#.VPtIoE0o7IU, accessed 6 March 2015.

52. "South Africa: Four Men Sentenced to 18 Years for Killing Lesbian Zoliswa Nkonyana," *Global Post*, 1 February 2012, http://www.globalpost.com/dispatch/news/regions/africa/south-africa/120201/south-africa-murder-zoliswa-nkonyana-lesbian-killers-sentenced, accessed 4 March 2015.

53. Witchcraft was no less of an everyday phenomenon in urban areas. But concerted attacks in its name, although not unheard of, were less common there (see Ashforth 2005, 234, 244).

54. *State v. Mutshutshu Samuel Magoro and Others* (CC36/91), Supreme Court of Venda, 1992.

55. While typically older and relatively impoverished, these women, being the most frequent recipients of social grants in cash-strapped communities, were often robbed and attacked.

56. Both forms of this ritual are captured in the film *Heal the Whole Man* (1974, directed by Paul Robinson and Jean Comaroff), a copy of which is held by the Royal Anthropological Institute in London.

57. The National Prayer Day, held in Tshwane on 29 September 2014, for instance, was the central focus of Police Safety Month that year. Hundreds of people gathered at the SAPS memorial at the Union Buildings to pay tribute to the sixty-eight officers who had lost their lives on duty over the previous twelve months. The service focused on "police safety, . . . the reduction of crime in general, and . . . the reduction of gender-based violence." See "SAPS Holding National Prayer Day on Monday," *Gateway News*, 24 September 2014, http://gatewaynews.co.za/saps-holding-national-prayer-day-on-Monday/, accessed 9 April 2015.

58. On the Anti-crime Prayer Day, see Patrick Hlahla, "Churches Urged to Fight Crime," *Pretoria News*, 30 June 2000. Two articles about the Mafikeng Development Forum's *Crime Prevention through Prayer* campaign appeared in the *Mafikeng Mail*, 21 March and 4 April 1997.

59. See the address of the then premier of the North West Province, Popo Molefe, to the *Believers' Summit on Religion and Crime*, reported in "Crime, Violence and Religion," *Mafikeng Mail*, 29 May 1998. The same plea was made, to the same audience, by Mduduzi Mashiyane, of the Institute for Democracy in South Africa; see "Community Policing: Role of the Church," *Mafikeng Mail*, 29 May 1999. Note also the speech delivered by a later premier of the North West Province, Maureen Modiselle, to thousands of Zion Christian Church members who converged on

the stadium in Mafikeng-Mmabatho on 9 May 2010 for a mass prayer service. She urged them to pray for "the reduction and elimination of corruption related crime, [and] the restoration of family values amongst our youth." See "Premier Modiselle Thanks Zion Christian Church (ZCC) for Choosing North West for Prayer," *South African Government*, 11 May 2010, http://www.gov.za/premier-modiselle-thanks -zion-christian-church-zcc-choosing-north-west-prayer-0, accessed 9 April 2010.

60. See Khadija Patel, "Pagad 2.0—Will It Get It Right This Time?," *Daily Maverick*, 22 April 2011, http://www.dailymaverick.co.za/opinionista/2011-04-22-pagad-20 -will-it-get-it-right-this-time/#.VSemoE3D9jo, accessed 7 July 2012.

61. "Pagad, Friend or Foe," *Democracy Watch 5* (1999): 8–9, excerpted from *Mail & Guardian*, 5–11 February 1999.

62. Estelle Ellis, "New Clues Link Pagad to Theron Assassination," *IOL.News*, 2 February 2001, http://www.iol.co.za/news/south-africa/new-clues-link-pagad-to-theron -assassination-1.60024#.VSakBE3D9jo, accessed 2 February 2001.

63. "Vigilante Groups on March with Whips, Guns and Petrol Cans," *ANC Daily News Briefing*, 23 July 1999, http://www.anc.org.za/anc/newsbrief/1999/news0723, accessed 15 February 2000.

64. "Pagad: Vigilantes or Terrorists?," *BBC News*, 13 September 2000, http://news.bbc .co.uk/1/hi/world/africa/923701.stm, accessed 6 June 2006.

65. See, e.g., Rebecca Davis, "Rashied Staggie Release: Leader of the Pack Is Back on the Streets," *Daily Maverick*, 23 September 2013, http://www.dailymaverick.co.za/article/2013 -09-23-rachid-staggie-release-leader-of-the-pack-is-back-on-the-streets/, accessed 6 April 2015.

66. Patel, "Pagad 2.0—Will It Get It Right This Time?" Unless otherwise stated, all quoted passages and phrases in this paragraph are from this source.

67. See "PAGAD: 'People against Gangsterism & Drugs'; Striving towards a Gangster-Free & Drug-Free Society," http://www.pagad.co.za/, accessed 10 April 2015.

68. The release from prison on day-parole of Rashied Staggie, twin brother and comrade-in-arms of the gang leader burnt alive by Pagad agents in 1996 (see above), added further fuel to the mix. See Davis, "Rashied Staggie Release."

69. "Gang Violence: Western Cape Government and City of Cape Town Intervene," *Western Cape Government News*, 19 August 2013, https://www.westerncape.gov.za /news/gang-violence-western-cape-government-and-city-cape-town-intervene, accessed 25 March 2015.

70. See Laila Majiet, "Pagad Support 'Increasing' in Mitchell's Plain," *People's Post*, 11 April 2014, http://www.peoplespost.co.za/MM/edition/138047/edition-article -details/pagad-support, accessed 9 April 2015.

71. "Charges against Pagad Leader Provisionally Withdrawn," *eNews Channel Africa*, 23 April 2013, http://www.enca.com/south-africa/charges-against-pagad-leader -provisionally-withdrawn, accessed 10 April 2015.

72. See, in this respect, but for a predominantly Jewish neighborhood in Johannes-burg, Steinberg (2008, 173); Bloom (2009, 55).

73. *Conquest for Life* home page, http://www.conquest.org.za/Mission.html, accessed 15 April 2015.

74. See Khadija Magardie, "Alternative Justice Settles Disputes," *Mail & Guardian*, 6 April 2000.

75. *Conquest for Life* home page.

76. See Hartford, "Bringing Lavender to the Hills."

77. *Western Cape Network for Community Peace and Development: Empowering Commu-nities and Building Sustainable Peace*, http://peacenetworkwc.org/, accessed 15 April 2015.

78. For two reports, somewhat conflicting, see Gill Gifford, "Emotional Scenes as Soweto Youths Throw Their Weapons Away," *Star*, 13 March 2000; and Selby Bo-kaba, "Ditched Weapons Sink without Trace," *Star*, 14 March 2000. The first re-fers to the Ithutheng Trust as the Student Trust, established by Nelson Mandela, whose director, Jackie Maarohanye, claims that she organized the event after the former president asked her to tackle the crime problem in schools.

79. As Constitutional Court Justice Lourens Ackermann put it: "[In] a constitutional state individuals agree (in principle at least) to abandon their right to self-help in the protection of their rights only because the state, in the constitutional state compact, assumes the obligation to protect those rights. If the state fails to dis-charge this duty adequately, there is a danger that individuals might feel justified in using self-help to protect their rights." See Paul Hoffman, "Vigilantism: The Last Resort of the Unprotected," *Institute for Accountability in South Africa*, 19 November 2012, http://worldjusticeproject.org/blog/vigilantism-last-resort-unprotected, ac-cessed 16 April 2015.

80. Interview with Monhle John Magolego, Acornhoek, 11 March 2000.

81. Peet Bothma, "Mapogo—Refleksie Op Polisie," *Die Beeld*, 26 November 2000, 7.

82. In interviews at the time and subsequently, Magolego has stressed the difficulty of assessing the size of *Mapogo*'s membership.

83. See Phillip Morobi, "Mapogo's Sharp Claws Attract White Members," *City Press*, 5 March 2000, 2; and Jonny Steinberg, "Vigilante Group Splits over Illegal Meth-ods," *Business Day*, 8 October 1998, http://www.bday.co.za/98/1008/news/n29 .htm, accessed 6 May 2000.

84. See Morobi, "Mapogo's Sharp Claws Attract White Members."

85. *Mapogo a Mathamaga: Business and Community Shield*, http://mapogoafrica.co.za/, accessed 1 April 2015.

86. "Security Company to Host Monthly Picnic," *Randfontein Herald*, 2 September 2014, http://randfonteinherald.co.za/162592/security-company-to-host-monthly-picnic/, accessed 4 April 2015.

87. On such occasions, Magolego sometimes dons a ceremonial blazer with gold tassels and leopard-skin epaulets and pockets; see Soggot and Ngobeni (1999, 136); Oomen (2004, 157); and N. Smith (2013, 172).

88. Myths to the contrary, there are no tigers in Africa, outside captivity. But in rural black South African English and Afrikaans, "tiger" (*tier*) is often used to refer to leopards. Tigers entered the popular imagination through the strong impact of Indian symbology during the Age of Empire.

89. When we interviewed him first in 2000, Magolego insisted that the organization was not lucrative. Members were assessed an annual fee, based on what they could afford; the average was between R50 and R100 (at the time, US$1.00 = R6.40). Businesses paid a hefty amount to join and were charged on a monthly basis according to size; the range seems to have been between R100 and R1,000. Much of *Mapogo's* income, he told us, went to legal costs, as its members were often brought before the courts.

90. Jonny Steinberg, "Guilt Is Not the Point for Vigilante Group," *Business Day*, 25 August 1999.

91. *Mapogo a Mathamago: Business and Community Shield.*

92. Oomen (2004, 160) estimated that women made up 68 percent of the membership at the time of her research.

93. Magolego has obviously told this story before; see Soggot and Ngobeni (1999, 134). But there *is* evidence that such things have occurred. Two members of *Mapogo* were charged with murder and accused of having fed a man to crocodiles in the Kruger National Park in January 2001; see "Charged with Murder," *Mail & Guardian*, 25 January 2001.

94. Magolego has drawn vocal support from some highly visible right-wingers, like Gaye Derby-Lewis, wife of Clive Derby-Lewis, who was handed down a life sentence for the murder of ANC leader Chris Hani in 1993. Mrs. Derby-Lewis claims to have helped found the Pretoria branch of *Mapogo* and to have signed up new members in the city; Inigo Gilmore, "Derby-Lewis Joins *Mapogo*," *Sunday World*, 4 July 1999, 1.

95. Steinberg, "Guilt Is Not the Point for Vigilante Group."

96. The United Democratic Movement, founded in 1998, is a prodiversity party led by former homeland and ANC leader General Bantu Holomisa.

97. Evidence wa ka Ngobeni, "Mapogo Goes Mainstream," *Mail & Guardian*, 22 June 2000.

Chapter 2.5

1. *Eina Ivy Security Spikes*, see www.eina-ivy.co.za, accessed 23 March 2012. All the quoted phrases in this paragraph are taken from this website. *Eina* is manufactured in KwaZulu-Natal, South Africa, by Eina Ivy Manufacturing.

2. See, e.g., Julian Rademeyer, "Dodgy Statistics: Just a Means to an End for Steve Hofmeyr and Sunette Bridges," *Daily Maverick*, 31 July 2014, http://www.daily maverick.co.za/opinionista/2014-07-31-dodgy-statistics-just-a-means-to-an-end -for-steve-hofmeyr-and-sunette-bridges/#.U96XCU10w5s, accessed 3 August 2014.

3. Sisonke Msimang, "Caught between the Devil and the Deep Blue Sea: A Nation Beholden to Criminals," *Daily Maverick*, 31 July 2014, http://www.dailymaverick .co.za/opinionista/2014-07-31-caught-between-the-devil-and-the-deep-blue-sea -a-nation-beholden-to-criminals/#.U95cAk10w5s, accessed 4 August 2014. Ms. Msimang currently lives in Mozambique.

4. Ibid.

REFERENCES

Abbott, Edith
    1927   "The Civil War and the Crime Wave of 1865–70." *Social Service Review* 1(2): 212–34.

Adorno, Theodor W., and Max Horkheimer
    1979   *Dialectic of Enlightenment*. Translated by John Cumming. New York: Verso. First published 1944.

Agamben, Giorgio
    1998   *Homo Sacer: Sovereign Power and Bare Life*. Translated by Daniel Heller-Roazen. Stanford, CA: Stanford University Press.

Agozino, Biko
    2003   *Counter-Colonial Criminology: A Critique of Imperialist Reason*. London: Pluto Press.

Ahmed, Sara
    2000   *Strange Encounters: Embodied Others in Postcoloniality*. London: Routledge.

Alexander, Elizabeth, ed.
    2008   *Capitalist Punishment: Prison Privatization and Human Rights*. Atlanta, GA: Clarity Press.

Alexander, Michelle
    2010   *The New Jim Crow: Mass Incarceration in the Age of Colorblindness*. New York: New Press.

Alexander, Peter
    2010   "Rebellion of the Poor: South Africa's Service Delivery Protests—a Preliminary Analysis." *Review of African Political Economy* 37 (123): 25–40.

Altbeker, Antony
    1998   *Solving Crime: The State of the SAPS Detective Service*. Monograph no. 31. Pretoria: Institute for Security Studies.

2005 *The Dirty Work of Democracy: A Year on the Streets with the SAPS*. Johannesburg: Jonathan Ball.

2010 *Fruit of a Poisoned Tree: A True Story of Murder and the Miscarriage of Justice*. Johannesburg: Jonathan Ball.

Althusser, Louis

1971 *Lenin and Philosophy and Other Essays*. Translated by Ben Brewster. New York: Monthly Review Press.

Ambrosio, Célia V.

2005 "Attitudes towards the Death Penalty: A Cross-Cultural Investigation." MA diss., University of the Free State.

Anderson, Benedict

1991 *Imagined Communities: Reflections on the Origin and Spread of Nationalism*. Rev. ed. New York: Verso. First published 1983.

Appadurai, Arjun

1996 *Modernity at Large: The Cultural Dimensions of Globalization*. Minneapolis: University of Minnesota Press.

Arendt, Hannah

1958 *The Human Condition*. Chicago: University of Chicago Press.

Arnold, David

1994 "The Colonial Prison: Power, Knowledge and Penology in Nineteenth-Century India." *Subaltern Studies* 8:148–84.

Arrighi, Giovanni

1994 *The Long Twentieth Century: Money, Power, and the Origins of Our Times*. New York: Verso.

Ashforth, Adam

2005 *Witchcraft, Violence, and Democracy in South Africa*. Chicago: University of Chicago Press.

Aspinall, Edward, and Gerry van Klinken

2010 "The State and Illegality in Indonesia." In *The State and Illegality in Indonesia*, edited by Edward Aspinall and Gerry van Klinken. Leiden: KITLV Press (Brill).

Auletta, Ken

2015 "Fixing Broken Windows." *New Yorker*, 7 September, 38–45.

Austen, Ralph

1986 "Social Bandits and Other Heroic Criminals: Western Models of Resistance and Their Relevance for Africa." In *Banditry, Rebellion and Social Process in Africa*, edited by Donald Crummey. London: Heinemann.

Baghel, Ravi

2010 "Fear of Crime in South Africa: Obsession, Compulsion, Disorder." *Transcience Journal* 1 (2): 71–84.

Ballard, Clare, and Lukas Muntingh

2012 *Commission of Inquiry into Allegations of Police Inefficiency in Khayelitsha and a Breakdown in Relations between the Community and the Police in Khayelitsha.* (Submission for Phase One of Commission of Inquiry.) Community Law Center, University of the Western Cape: Civil Society Police Reform Initiative. http://cspri.org.za/publications/submissions-and-presentations.

Banks, Cyndi

1997 *The Social Construction of Statistics: Criminal Data Collection in Papua New Guinea.* Preliminary Paper no. 2. Boroko, Papua New Guinea: Political and Legal Studies Division of the National Research Institute.

Banton, Michael

1964 *The Policeman in the Community.* London: Tavistock.

Barclay, Gordon, and Cynthia Tavares

2003 *International Comparisons of Criminal Justice Statistics 2001.* London: RDS Communications and Development Unit, Home Office, Government of the United Kingdom. http:www.homeoffice.gov.uk/rds/pdfs2/hosb1203.pdf.

Basson, Adriaan

2010 *Finish & Klaar: Selebi's Fall from Interpol to the Underworld.* Cape Town: Tafelberg.

Baxi, Pratiksha

2014 *Public Secrets of Law: Rape Trials in India.* New Delhi: Oxford University Press.

Bayart, Jean-François, Stephen Ellis, and Béatrice Hibou, eds.

1999 *The Criminalization of the State in Africa.* Bloomington: Indiana University Press; Oxford: James Currey in association with the International African Institute.

Beck, Ulrich

1992 *Risk Society: Towards a New Modernity.* Translated by Mark Ritter. London: Sage Publications.

Becker, Florian Nikolas

2010 "Capitalism and Crime: Brechtian Economies in *The Threepenny Opera* and *Love, Crime and Johannesburg.*" *Modern Drama* 53 (2): 159–86.

Becker, Gary

1968 "Crime and Punishment." *Journal of Political Economy* 76 (2): 196–217.

Beckett, Katherine, and Steve Herbert

2010 *Banished: The New Social Control in Urban America.* New York: Oxford University Press.

Benjamin, Walter

1969 *Illuminations: Essays and Reflections.* Translated by Harry Zohn. New York: Schocken Books.

1978   *Reflections: Essays, Aphorisms, Autobiographical Writings.* Translated by Edmund Jephcott. Edited by Peter Demetz. New York: Schocken Books.

1999a   *The Arcades Project.* Translated by Howard Eiland and Kevin McLaughlin. Edited by Rolf Tiedemann. Cambridge, MA: Harvard University Press.

1999b   "Little History of Photography." In *Walter Benjamin: Selected Writings*, vol. 2, *1927–1934*, translated by Rodney Livingstone et al., edited by Michael W. Jennings, Howard Eiland, and Gary Smith. Cambridge, MA: Belknap Press of Harvard University Press.

Berning, Joey, and Moses Montesh

2012   "Countering Corruption in South Africa: The Rise and Fall of the Scorpions and Hawks." *South African Crime Quarterly* 39:3–10.

Bernstein, Robin

2011   *Racial Innocence: Performing Childhood from Slavery to Civil Rights.* New York: New York University Press.

Bittner, Egon

1990   *Aspects of Police Work.* Boston: Northeastern University Press.

Block de Behar, Lisa

1995   *A Rhetoric of Silence and Other Selected Writings.* Berlin: Mouton de Gruyter.

Bloom, Kevin

2009   *Ways of Staying.* Johannesburg: Picador.

Blundo, Giorgio

2007   "Hidden Acts, Open Talks: How Anthropology Can 'Observe' and Describe Corruption." In *Corruption and the Secret of Law: A Legal Anthropological Perspective*, edited by Monique Nuitjen and Gerhard Anders. Farnham, Surrey: Ashgate.

Bobo, Lawrence, and Ryan A. Smith

1998   "From Jim Crow Racism to Laissez-Faire Racism: The Transformation of Racial Attitudes." In *Beyond Pluralism*, edited by Wendy F. Katkin, Ned Landsman, and Andrea Tyree. Champaign: University of Illinois Press.

Boltanski, Luc

2014   *Mysteries and Conspiracies: Detective Stories, Spy Novels and the Making of Modern Societies.* Translated by Catherine Porter. Cambridge: Polity Press.

Bond, Patrick

2003   *Against Global Apartheid: South Africa Meets the World Bank, IMF and International Finance.* New York: Zed Books.

Booysen, Susan

2007   "With the Ballot and the Brick: The Politics of Attaining Service Delivery." *Progress in Development Studies* 7 (1): 21–32.

Botha, Anneli

  2001 "The Prime Suspects? The Metamorphosis of Pagad." In *Fear in the City: Urban Terrorism in South Africa*, edited by Henri Boshoff, Anneli Botha, and Martin Schönteich. Monograph no. 63. Pretoria: Institute for Security Studies.

Bottoms, Anthony E.

  1995 "The Philosophy and Politics of Punishment and Sentencing." In *The Politics of Sentencing Reform*, edited by Christopher M. V. Clarkson and Rodney Morgan. Oxford: Clarendon Press.

Bratton, William, with Peter Knobler

  1998 *Turnaround: How America's Top Cop Reversed the Crime Epidemic*. New York: Random House.

Breckenridge, Keith

  2005 "The Biometric State: The Promise and Perils of Digital Government in the New South Africa." *Journal of Southern African Studies* 31 (2): 267–82.

  2014a *Biometric State: The Global Politics of Identification and Surveillance in South Africa, 1850 to the Present*. Cambridge: Cambridge University Press.

  2014b "Marikana and the Limits of Biopolitics: Themes in the Recent Scholarship of South African Mining." *Africa* 84 (1): 151–61.

Brewer, Rose M., and Nancy A. Heitzeg

  2008 "The Racialization of Crime and Punishment: Criminal Justice, Color-Blind Racism, and the Political Economy of the Prison Industrial Complex." *American Behavioral Scientist* 51 (5): 625–44.

Brown, Andrew

  2005 *Coldsleep Lullaby*. Cape Town: Zebra Press.

  2008 *Street Blues: The Experience of a Reluctant Policeman*. Cape Town: Zebra Press.

Brown, Wendy

  1995 *States of Injury: Power and Freedom in Late Modernity*. Princeton, NJ: Princeton University Press.

Bruce, David, and Rachel Neild

  2005 *The Police That We Want: A Handbook for Oversight of Police in South Africa*. Johannesburg: Centre for the Study of Violence and Reconciliation, in association with the Open Society Foundation of South Africa and the Open Society Justice Initiative.

Buford, Bill

  1991 *Among the Thugs*. London: Secker & Warburg.

Bulmer, Michael

  2003 *Francis Galton: Pioneer of Heredity and Biometry*. Baltimore: Johns Hopkins University Press.

Bundy, Colin

2014 *Short Changed? South Africa since Apartheid.* Johannesburg: Jacana Media.

Burger, Johan

2006 *Strategic Perspectives on Crime and Policing in South Africa.* Pretoria: Van Schaik.

Butler, Judith

1993a *Bodies That Matter: On the Discursive Limits of Sex.* New York: Routledge.

1993b "Endangered/Endangering: Schematic Racism and White Paranoia." In *Reading Rodney King / Reading Urban Uprising,* edited by Robert Gooding-Williams. New York: Routledge.

Buur, Lars

2010 "Domesticating Sovereigns: The Changing Nature of Vigilante Groups in South Africa." In *Domesticating Vigilantism in Africa: South Africa, Nigeria, Benin, Côte d'Ivoire, Burkina Faso,* edited by Thomas G. Kirsch and Tilo Grätz. Martlesham, UK: James Currey.

Buur, Lars, and Steffen Jensen

2004 "Introduction: Vigilantism and the Policing of Everyday Life in South Africa." *African Studies* 63 (2): 139–52.

Caldeira, Teresa P. R.

2000 *City of Walls: Crime, Segregation, and Citizenship in São Paulo.* Berkeley: University of California Press.

2006 "'I Came to Sabotage Your Reasoning!': Violence and Resignifications of Justice in Brazil." In *Law and Disorder in the Postcolony,* edited by Jean Comaroff and John L. Comaroff. Chicago: University of Chicago Press.

Camerer, Lala

1997 "Victims and Criminal Justice." In *Policing the Transformation: Further Issues in South Africa's Crime Debate,* edited by Mark Shaw, Lala Camerer, Duxita Mistry, Sarah Oppler, and Lukas Muntingh. Monograph no. 12. Pretoria: Institute for Security Studies.

Camerer, Lala, Antoinette Louw, Mark Shaw, Lillian Artz, and Wilfried Scharf

1998 *Crime in Cape Town: Results of a City Victim Survey.* Monograph no. 23. Pretoria: Institute for Security Studies.

Canguilhem, Georges

1989 *The Normal and the Pathological.* Translated by Carolyn R. Fawcett, with Robert S. Cohen. New York: Zone Books.

Castells, Manuel

1996 *The Rise of the Network Society.* Cambridge, MA: Blackwell.

Chanock, Martin

1991 "A Peculiar Sharpness: An Essay on Property in the Customary Law of Colonial Africa." *Journal of African History* 32 (1): 65–88.

2004 "South Africa, 1841–1924: Race, Contract, and Coercion." In *Masters, Servants, and Magistrates in Britain and the Empire, 1562–1955*, edited by Douglas Hay and Paul Craven. Chapel Hill: University of North Carolina Press.

Chapman, Michael

2001 "More than Telling a Story: *Drum* and Its Significance in Black South African Writing." In *The "Drum" Decade: Stories from the 1950s*, edited by Michael Chapman. Pietermaritzburg: University of Natal Press.

Chatterjee, Partha

2002 *A Princely Imposter? The Kumar of Bhawal and the Secret History of Indian Nationalism*. Princeton, NJ: Princeton University Press.

Chesterton, Gilbert Keith

2012 *The Complete Father Brown Stories*. Edited by Michael D. Hurley. London: Penguin Books.

Cho, George

1998 *Geographic Information Systems and the Law*. New York: John Wiley & Sons.

Christie, Thomas

2013 *Notional Identities: Ideology, Genre and National Identity in Popular Scottish Fiction since the Seventies*. Newcastle upon Tyne: Cambridge Scholars Publishing.

Coetzee, John M.

1982 *Waiting for the Barbarians: A Novel*. New York: Penguin Books.

1999 *Disgrace: A Novel*. New York: Penguin Books.

Cohen, David

2004 *People Who Have Stolen from Me: Rough Justice in the New South Africa*. New York: St. Martin's Press.

Cohn, Bernard S.

1987 *An Anthropologist among the Historians and Other Essays*. New York: Oxford University Press.

Cole, Simon A.

2002 *Suspect Identities: A History of Fingerprinting and Criminal Identification*. Cambridge, MA: Harvard University Press.

Comaroff, Jean, and John L. Comaroff

1991 *Of Revelation and Revolution*. Vol. 1, *Christianity, Colonialism, and Consciousness in South Africa*. Chicago: University of Chicago Press.

1999a "Occult Economies and the Violence of Abstraction: Notes from the South African Postcolony." *American Ethnologist* 26 (3): 279–301.

2001 "Millennial Capitalism: First Thoughts on a Second Coming." In *Millennial Capitalism and the Culture of Neoliberalism*, edited by Jean Comaroff and John L. Comaroff. Durham, NC: Duke University Press.

2003 "Reflections on Liberalism, Policulturalism, and ID-ology: Citizenship and Difference in South Africa." *Social Identities* 9 (3): 445–74.

2004a "Criminal Obsessions, after Foucault: Postcoloniality, Policing, and the Metaphysics of Disorder." *Critical Inquiry* 30:800–824.

2006a "Figuring Crime: Quantifacts and the Production of the Un/real." *Public Culture* 18 (1): 209–46.

2012 *Theory from the South; or, How Euro-America Is Evolving toward Africa*. Boulder, CO: Paradigm.

2013 "The Point of Sharp Things." In *Gallery of Disorder*, edited by Helmut Lethen. Vienna: Internationales Forschungszentrum Kulturwissenschaften an der Kunstuniversität Linz.

Comaroff, John L.

2013 Foreword to *Policing and Contemporary Governance: The Anthropology of Police in Practice*, edited by William Garriott. New York: Palgrave Macmillan.

Comaroff, John L., and Comaroff, Jean

1999b Introduction to *Civil Society and the Political Imagination in Africa: Critical Perspectives*, edited by John L. Comaroff and Jean Comaroff. Chicago: University of Chicago Press.

2004b "Criminal Justice, Cultural Justice: The Limits of Liberalism and the Pragmatics of Difference in the New South Africa." *American Ethnologist* 31 (2): 188–204.

2006b "Law and Disorder in the Postcolony: An Introduction." In *Law and Disorder in the Postcolony*, edited by Jean Comaroff and John L. Comaroff. Chicago: University of Chicago Press.

2007 "Popular Justice in the New South Africa: Policing the Boundaries of Freedom." In *Legitimacy and Criminal Justice: International Perspectives*, edited by T. Tyler. New York: Russell Sage Foundation.

2009 *Ethnicity, Inc.* Chicago: University of Chicago Press.

Comaroff, John L., and Simon A. Roberts

1981 *Rules and Processes: The Cultural Logic of Dispute in an African Context*. Chicago: University of Chicago Press.

Comaroff, Joshua, and Ong Ker-Shing

2013 *Horror in Architecture*. San Francisco: ORO Editions.

Conan Doyle, Arthur

2003 *The Complete Sherlock Holmes*. Vol. 2. New York: Barnes and Noble Classics.

Conlan, Edward

2004 *Blue Blood*. New York: Riverhead Books.

Coplan, David

    2001   "Sounds of the 'Third Way': Identity and the African Renaissance in Contemporary South African Popular Traditional Music." *Black Music Research Journal* 21 (1): 107–24.

Couzens, Tim

    1985   *The New African: A Study of the Life and Work of H. I. E. Dhlomo.* Johannesburg: Ravan Press.

Crank, John P.

    1998   *Understanding Police Culture.* Cincinnati, OH: Anderson.

Crawford, Robert

    2004   "Risk Ritual and the Management of Control and Anxiety in Medical Culture." *Health* 8 (4): 505–28.

Cressey, Donald Ray

    2008   *Theft of the Nation: The Structure and Operations of Organized Crime in America.* New Brunswick, NJ: Transaction Publications. First published 1969.

Cullen, Kevin

    2013   *Whitey Bulger: America's Most Wanted Gangster and the Manhunt That Brought Him to Justice.* New York: W. W. Norton.

Daily Maverick

    2014   *Brain Porn: The Best of "Daily Maverick."* Cape Town: Tafelberg.

Dangor, Achmat

    1999   *Kafka's Curse: A Novel.* New York: Pantheon.

    2003   *Bitter Fruit.* London: Atlantic Books.

Dardot, Pierre, and Christian Laval

    2014   *The New Way of the World: On Neoliberal Society.* Translated by Gregory Elliott. New York: Verso.

Davidson, Amy

    2014   "Safer Streets." Talk of the Town. *New Yorker*, 15 December, 21–22.

Davis, Angela Y.

    1999   "From the Prison of Slavery to the Slavery of Prison: Frederick Douglass and the Convict Lease System." In *Frederick Douglass: A Critical Reader*, edited by Bill E. Lawson and Frank M. Kirkland. Malden, MA: Blackwell.

    2007   "Race and Criminalization: Black Americans and the Punishment Industry." In *Race, Ethnicity, and Gender: Selected Readings*, edited by Joseph F. Healey and Eileen O'Brien. Thousand Oaks, CA: Pine Forge Press.

Davis, Natalie Zemon

    1983   *The Return of Martin Guerre.* Cambridge, MA: Harvard University Press.

    1988   "On the Lame." *American Historical Review* 93 (3): 572–603.

de Haas, Mary

2000 "Violence." In *South African Human Rights Yearbook, 1997*, vol. 8. Durban: Centre for Socio-legal Studies, University of Natal.

de Kock, Leon

2015 "From the Subject of Evil to the Evil Subject: 'Cultural Difference' in Post-apartheid South African Crime Fiction." *Safundi: The Journal of South African and American Studies* 16 (1): 28–50.

Deleuze, Gilles, and Félix Guattari

1987 *A Thousand Plateaus: Capitalism and Schizophrenia*. Translated by Brian Massumi. Minneapolis: University of Minnesota Press.

Delius, Peter

1996 *A Lion amongst the Cattle: Reconstruction and Resistance in the Northern Transvaal*. Portsmouth, NH: Heinemann.

Department of Law and Order, Republic of South Africa

1994 *Annual Report of the Commissioner of the South Africa Police, 1 January 1993–31 December 1993*. RP 5-1994 (government document).

Derrida, Jacques

2002 *Acts of Religion*. Edited by Gil Anidjar. New York: Routledge.

2009 *The Beast and the Sovereign*. Vol. 1. Translated by Geoffrey Bennington. Edited by Michel Lisse, Marie-Louise Mallet, and Ginette Michaud. Chicago: University of Chicago Press.

Desmond, Cosmas

1971 *The Discarded People: An Account of African Resettlement in South Africa*. Harmondsworth: Penguin Books.

de Vienne, Philibert

1547 *Le philosophe de court*. Lyon: Jean de Tournes.

Dickens, Charles

2009 *Miscellaneous Papers*. Newcastle upon Tyne: Cambridge Scholars Publishing.

Dixon, Bill

2002 *Cloud over the Rainbow: Crime and Transition in South Africa*. Cape Town: Institute for Justice and Reconciliation.

2004 "Introduction: Justice Gained? Crime, Crime Control and Criminology in Transition." In *Justice Gained: Crime and Crime Control in South Africa's Transition*, edited by Bill Dixon and Elrena van der Spuy. Cape Town: University of Cape Town Press.

Dixon, Bill, and Elrena van der Spuy, eds.

2004 *Justice Gained: Crime and Crime Control in South Africa's Transition*. Cape Town: University of Cape Town Press.

Doane, Mary Ann

2002 *The Emergence of Cinematic Time: Modernity, Contingency, the Archive.* Cambridge, MA: Harvard University Press.

Douglas, Mary

1966 *Purity and Danger: An Analysis of Concepts of Pollution and Taboo.* London: Routledge & Kegan Paul.

Dowd, Douglas

2009 *Inequality and the Global Crisis.* New York: Pluto Press.

Drucker, Ernest

2013 "Drug Law, Mass Incarceration, and Public Health." *Oregon Law Review* 91:1097–1128.

Dubbeld, Bernard

2013 "How Social Security Becomes Social Insecurity: Unsettled Households, Crisis Talk and the Value of Grants in a KwaZulu-Natal Village." *Acta Juridica* 13:197–217.

Du Bois, William Edward Burghardt

1901 "The Spawn of Slavery: The Convict-Lease System in the South." *Missionary Review of the World* 14:737–45.

Duiker, K. Sello

2000 *Thirteen Cents: A Novel.* Cape Town: Ink.

Dumas, Alexandre

1896 *The Two Dianas.* Boston: Estes and Lauriat. First French edition, 1846.

du Preez, Max

2013 *A Rumour of Spring: South Africa after 20 Years of Democracy.* Cape Town: Zebra Press.

During, Simon

2015 "From the Subaltern to the Precariat." *Boundary 2: An International Journal of Literature and Culture* 42 (2): 57–84.

Durkheim, Emile

1938 *The Rules of Sociological Method.* 8th ed. Edited by Sarah A. Solovay and John H. Mueller. Translated by George E. G. Catlin. New York: Free Press.

Durrham, Kevin, Xoliswa Mtose, and Lyndsay Brown

2011 *Race Trouble: Race, Identity and Inequality in South Africa.* Lanham, MD: Lexington Books.

Eagleton, Terry

2015 "Signs for Liars." *Times Literary Supplement*, no. 5879, 4 December, 20.

Eco, Umberto, and Thomas A. Sebeok, eds.

1983 *The Sign of Three: Dupin, Holmes, Peirce.* Bloomington: Indiana University Press.

Ekirch, A. Roger

    1987   *Bound for America: The Transportation of British Convicts to the Colonies, 1718–1775*. Oxford: Clarendon Press.

Eliav-Feldon, Miriam

    2012   *Renaissance Impostors and Proofs of Identity*. New York: Palgrave Macmillan.

Ellison, John

    2006   "Community Policing: Implementation Issues." *FBI Law Enforcement Bulletin* 75 (4): 12–16.

Emmett, Tony

    2000   "Addressing the Underlying Causes of Crime and Violence in South Africa." In *Behind the Mask: Getting to Grips with Crime and Violence in South Africa*, edited by Tony Emmett and Alex Butchart. Pretoria: Human Sciences Research Council.

Emsley, Clive

    2007   "Historical Perspectives on Crime." In *The Oxford Handbook of Criminology*, edited by Mark Maguire, Robert Morgan, and Robert Reiner. Oxford: Oxford University Press.

English, Daylanne K.

    2013   *Each Hour Redeem: Time and Justice in African American Literature*. Minneapolis: University of Minnesota Press.

Eterno, John A., and Eli B. Silverman

    2012   *The Crime Numbers Game: Management by Manipulation*. Boca Raton, FL: CRC Press.

Evans-Pritchard, Edward E.

    1940   "The Nuer of the Southern Sudan." In *African Political Systems*, edited by Meyer Fortes and Edward E. Evans-Pritchard. London: Oxford University Press for the International African Institute.

Farrell, Graham, and Ken Pease, eds.

    2001   *Repeat Victimization*. Crime Prevention Studies, vol. 12. Monsey, NY: Criminal Justice Press.

Farrer, James Anson

    1880   *Crimes and Punishments; Including a New Translation of Beccaria's "Dei delitti e delle pene."* London: Chatto & Windus.

Fassin, Didier

    2013   *Enforcing Order: An Ethnography of Urban Policing*. Cambridge: Polity Press.

Fattah, Ezzat A., ed.

    1986   *From Crime Policy to Victim Policy: Reorienting the Justice System*. New York: St. Martin's Press.

Faulkner, William

    1990   *Light in August.* New York: Vintage. First published, 1932.

Faull, Andrew

    2011   "Corruption in the South African Police Service: Civilian Perceptions and Experiences." Paper no. 226. Pretoria: Institute for Security Studies.

Feinstein, Andrew

    2007   *After the Party: A Personal and Political Journey inside the ANC.* Johannesburg: Jonathan Ball.

Feldman, Allen

    1991   *Formations of Violence: The Narrative of the Body and Political Terror in Northern Ireland.* Chicago: University of Chicago Press.

Ferguson, James

    2006   *Global Shadows: Africa in the Neoliberal World Order.* Durham, NC: Duke University Press.

Fields, Karen E.

    1985   *Revival and Rebellion in Colonial Central Africa.* Princeton, NJ: Princeton University Press.

Fordred-Green, Lesley

    2000   "Tokoloshe Tales: Reflections on the Cultural Politics of Journalism in South Africa." *Current Anthropology* 41 (5): 701–12.

Foucault, Michel

    1980   *Power/Knowledge: Selected Interviews and Other Writings, 1972–1977.* Translated by Colin Gordon, Leo Marshall, John Mepham, and Kate Soper. Edited by Colin Gordon. Brighton, UK: Harvester Press.

    1989   *The Birth of the Clinic: An Archaeology of Medical Perception.* London: Routledge.

    1991   *The Foucault Effect: Studies in Governmentality.* Edited by Graham Burchell, Colin Gordon, and Peter Miller. Chicago: University of Chicago Press.

    1995   *Discipline and Punish: The Birth of the Prison.* Translated by Alan Sheridan. New York: Vintage.

    2008   *The Birth of Biopolitics: Lectures at the College de France, 1978–1979.* Edited by Michel Senellart. Translated by Graham Burchell. New York: Palgrave Macmillan.

Fugard, Athol

    1980   *Tsotsi.* New York: Random House.

Galgut, Damon

    2008   *The Impostor.* Johannesburg: Penguin Books.

Galton, Francis

1890 "Criminal Anthropology; Review of *The Criminal*, Havelock Ellis (London: W. Scott, 1890)." *Nature* 42 (1073): 75–76.

Garland, David

2001 *The Culture of Control: Crime and Social Order in Contemporary Society*. Oxford: Oxford University Press.

Garner, Stanton

1990 "Emerson, Thoreau, and Poe's 'Double Dupin.'" In *Poe and His Times: The Artist and His Milieu*, edited by Benjamin Franklin Fisher IV. Baltimore, MD: Edgar Allan Poe Society.

Garriott, William

2013 "Police in Practice: Policing and the Project of Contemporary Governance." In *Policing and Contemporary Governance: The Anthropology of Police in Practice*, edited by William Garriott. New York: Palgrave Macmillan.

Geertz, Clifford J.

1973 *The Interpretation of Cultures: Selected Essays*. New York: Basic Books.

Gerhart, Gail M., and Clive L. Glaser

2010 *From Protest to Challenge*. Vol. 6, *Challenge and Victory, 1980–1990*. Bloomington: Indiana University Press.

Gevisser, Mark

2014 *Lost and Found in Johannesburg*. Johannesburg: Jonathan Ball.

Gillespie, Kelly

Forthcoming "Anthropology before the Commission: Ethnography as Public Testimony." In *If Truth Be Told*, edited by Didier Fassin. Durham, NC: Duke University Press.

Gillespie, Michael Allen, and John Samuel Harpham

2011 "Sherlock Holmes, Crime, and the Anxieties of Globalization." *Critical Review* 23 (4): 449–74.

Gilmore, Ruth Wilson

2007 *Golden Gulag: Prisons, Surplus, Crisis, and Opposition in Globalizing California*. Berkeley: University of California Press.

Ginzburg, Carlo

1989 *Clues, Myths, and the Historical Method*. Translated by John Tedeschi and Anne C. Tedeschi. Baltimore: Johns Hopkins University Press.

Gladwell, Malcolm

2014 "The Crooked Ladder: The Criminal's Guide to Upward Mobility." *New Yorker*, 11 and 18 August, 36–41.

Glanz, Lorraine

    1989   *Coping with Crime: The South African Public's Perceptions of and Reactions to Crime.* Pretoria: Human Sciences Research Council.

    1994   *Crime in South Africa: Perceptions, Fear and Victimization.* Pretoria: Human Sciences Research Council.

Global Burden of Disease Study

    2015   "Global, Regional, and National Age-Sex Specific All-Cause and Cause-Specific Mortality for 240 Causes of Death, 1990–2013: A Systematic Analysis for the Global Burden of Disease Study 2013." *Lancet* 385:117–71.

Gluckman, Max

    1955   *The Judicial Process among the Barotse of Northern Rhodesia (Zambia).* Manchester: Manchester University Press.

Goffman, Alice

    2014   *On the Run: Fugitive Life in an American City.* Chicago: University of Chicago Press.

Goga, Khalil

    2014   "The Drug Trade and Governance in Cape Town." Paper no. 263. Pretoria: Institute for Security Studies.

Goldberg, David Theo, Michael Musheno, and Lisa C. Brower

    2001   "Shake Yo' Paradigm: Romantic Longing and Terror in Contemporary Sociolegal Studies." In *Between Law and Culture: Relocating Legal Studies,* edited by David Theo Goldberg, Michael Musheno, and Lisa C. Brower. Minneapolis: University of Minnesota Press.

Golden, Renny

    2005   *War on the Family: Mothers in Prison and the Families They Leave Behind.* New York: Routledge.

Goodhew, David

    1993   "The People's Police-Force: Communal Policing Initiatives in the Western Areas of Johannesburg, circa 1930–62." *Journal of Southern African Studies* 19 (3): 447–70.

Gooding-Williams, Robert, ed.

    1993   *Reading Rodney King/Reading Urban Rising.* New York: Routledge.

Gordimer, Nadine

    1984   *Something Out There: Stories.* New York: Viking Press.

Graeber, David

    2012   "The Sword, the Sponge, and the Paradox of Performativity: Some Observations on Fate, Luck, Financial Chicanery, and the Limits of Human Knowledge." *Social Analysis* 56 (1): 25–42.

Graham, Lucie Valerie

2012 *State of Peril: Race and Rape in South African Literature.* Oxford: Oxford University Press.

Gray, John

1998 *False Dawn: The Delusions of Global Capitalism.* London: Granta.

Greenberg, David F.

1993 Untitled introductory note to section entitled "Marx and Engels on Crime and Punishment." In *Crime and Capitalism: Readings in Marxist Criminology,* edited by David F. Greenberg. Philadelphia: Temple University Press.

Greenberg, Udi E.

2009 "Criminalization: Carl Schmitt and Walter Benjamin's Concept of Criminal Politics." *Journal of European Studies* 39 (3): 305–19.

Greenblatt, Stephen

2005 *Renaissance Self-Fashioning: From More to Shakespeare.* Chicago: University of Chicago Press.

Greenhouse, Carol J.

2003 "Solidity and Objectivity: Rereading Durkheim." In *Crime's Power: Anthropologists and the Ethnography of Crime,* edited by Philip C. Parnell and Stephanie C. Kane. New York: Palgrave Macmillan.

Grobler, Liza

2013 *Crossing the Line: When Cops Become Criminals.* Johannesburg: Jacana Media.

Gunning, Tom

2003 "The Exterior as *Intérieur*: Benjamin's Optical Detective." *Boundary 2: An International Journal of Literature and Culture* 30 (1): 105–30.

Gustafson, Kaaryn

2009 "The Criminalization of Poverty." *Journal of Criminal Law and Criminology* 99 (3): 643–716.

Habib, Adam, and Vishnu Padayachee

2000 "Economic Policy and Power Relations in South Africa's Transition to Democracy." *World Development* 28 (2): 245–63.

Hacking, Ian

1990 *The Taming of Chance.* Cambridge: Cambridge University Press.

Hadfield, Gillian K.

2014 "Innovating to Improve Access: Changing the Way Courts Regulate Legal Markets." *Daedalus* 143 (3): 83–95.

Haggerty, Kevin D.

2001 *Making Crime Count.* Toronto: University of Toronto Press.

Hallett, Michael A., and Randall Sheldon

    2006   *Private Prisons in America: A Critical Race Perspective.* Urbana: University of Illinois Press.

Hansen, Miriam Bratu

    1999   "The Mass Production of the Senses: Classical Cinema as Vernacular Modernism." *Modernism/Modernity* 6 (2): 59–77.

Harari, Roberto

    2004   *Lacan's Four Fundamental Concepts of Psychoanalysis: An Introduction.* Translated by Judith Filc. New York: Other Press.

Harris, Bronwyn

    2001   "'As for Violent Crime That's Our Daily Bread': Vigilante Violence during South Africa's Period of Transition." In *Violence and Transition Series*, vol. 1. Johannesburg: Centre for the Study of Violence and Reconciliation.

Haugerud, Angelique

    2013   *No Billionaire Left Behind: Satirical Activism in America.* Stanford, CA: Stanford University Press.

Hay, Douglas, and Paul Craven, eds.

    2004   *Masters, Servants, and Magistrates in Britain and the Empire, 1562–1955.* Chapel Hill, NC: University of North Carolina Press.

Haysom, Nicholas

    1986   *Mabangalala: The Rise of Right-Wing Vigilantes in South Africa.* Occasional Paper. Johannesburg: Centre for Applied Legal Studies, University of the Witwatersrand.

    1989   "Vigilantes: A Contemporary Form of Repression." Seminar no. 4. Johannesburg: Centre for the Study of Violence and Reconciliation. http://www.csvr.org.za/wits/papers/paphaysm.htm.

Heller, Patrick, and Libhongo Ntlokonkulu

    2001   "A Civic Movement, or a Movement of Civics? The South African National Civic Organisation (SANCO) in the Post-apartheid Period." Research Report no. 84. Johannesburg: Centre for Policy Studies.

Herzog, Todd

    2009   *Crime Stories: Criminalistic Fantasy and the Culture of Crisis in Weimar Germany.* New York: Berghahn Books.

Hicks, Robert D.

    1991   *In Pursuit of Satan: The Police and the Occult.* Buffalo, NY: Prometheus Books.

Highmore, Ben

    2002   *Everyday Life and Cultural Theory: An Introduction.* London: Routledge.

Hirschfield, Alex, and Kate Bowers, eds.

    2001 *Mapping and Analysing Crime Data: Lessons from Research and Practice.* New York: Taylor & Francis.

Hirschowitz, Ros, Seble Worku, and Mark Orkin

    2000 *Quantitative Research Findings on Rape in South Africa.* Pretoria: Statistics South Africa.

Hobbes, Thomas

    1994 *Leviathan.* Edited by Edwin Curley, with selected variants from the Latin edition of 1668. Indianapolis, IN: Hackett. First published 1651.

Hobsbawm, Eric

    1959 *Primitive Rebels: Studies in Archaic Forms of Social Movement in the 19th and 20th Centuries.* New York: W. W. Norton.

    1962 *The Age of Revolution, 1789–1848.* New York: New American Library (Mentor Book).

Holden, Paul, and Hennie Van Vuuren

    2011 *The Devil in the Detail: How the Arms Deal Changed Everything.* Pretoria: Institute for Security Studies.

Hornberger, Julia

    2009 "Ma-Slaan-Pa Dockets: Negotiations at the Boundary between the Private and the Public." In *Governance of Daily Life in Africa: Ethnographic Explorations of Public and Collective Services*, edited by Giorgio Blundo and Pierre-Yves Le Meur. Leiden: Brill.

    2013 *Policing and Human Rights: The Meaning of Violence and Justice in the Everyday Policing of Johannesburg.* New York: Routledge.

Hough, Mike

    2008 "Violent Protest at Local Government Level in South Africa: Revolutionary Potential?" *Scientia Militaria: South African Journal of Military Studies* 36 (1): 1–13.

Hron, Madelaine

    2008 "Torture Goes Pop!" *Peace Review: A Journal of Social Justice* 20 (1): 22–30.

Hudson, Barbara

    2006 "Beyond White Man's Justice: Race, Gender and Justice in Late Modernity." *Theoretical Criminology* 10 (1): 29–47.

Huff, Darrell

    1954 *How to Lie with Statistics.* New York: W. W. Norton.

Hurley, Michael D.

    2012 Introduction to *The Complete Father Brown Stories*, by G. K. Chesterton. London: Penguin Books.

Ignatiev, Noel

    1995   *How the Irish Became White*. New York: Routledge.

Indiana University, School of Public and Environmental Affairs

    2014   *Government Outsourcing: A Practical Guide for State and Local Governments*. (Report of an Expert Panel.) http://datasmart.ash.harvard.edu/assets/content/IU_SPEA_Government_Outsourcing_Report.pdf.

Institute for Security Studies (ISS)

    2004   *National Victims of Crime Survey: South Africa, 2003*. Monograph no. 101. Pretoria: Institute for Security Studies.

ISS. *See* Institute for Security Studies.

Jackall, Robert

    2005   *Street Stories: The World of Police Detectives*. Cambridge, MA: Harvard University Press.

Jacobs, Jane

    1961   *The Death and Life of Great American Cities*. New York: Random House.

Jain, Anil K., Patrick Flynn, and Arun A. Ross, eds.

    2008   *Handbook of Biometrics*. New York: Springer.

James, Cyril Lionel Robert

    1993   *American Civilization*. Edited by Anna Grimshaw and Keith Hart. Oxford: Blackwell.

James, Deborah

    2014   *Money from Nothing: Indebtedness and Aspiration in South Africa*. Stanford, CA: Stanford University Press.

Jansen, Jonathan

    2011   *We Need to Talk*. Northcliff and Northlands (Johannesburg): Bookstorm & Pan Macmillan South Africa.

Jauregui, Beatrice

    2013a   "Beatings, Beacons, and Big Men: Police Disempowerment and Delegitimation in India." *Law and Social Inquiry* 38 (3): 643–69.

    2013b   "Dirty Ethnography: Epistemologies of Violence and Ethical Entanglements in Police Ethnography." In *Policing and Contemporary Governance: The Anthropology of Police in Practice*, edited by William Garriott. New York: Palgrave Macmillan.

Johnson, David Cay, ed.

    2014   *Divided: The Perils of Our Growing Inequality*. New York: New Press.

Jules-Macquet, Regan

    2014   *The State of South African Prisons*. NICRO Public Education Series, Edition One. Cape Town: National Institute for Crime Prevention and the Reintegration of Offenders.

Justice Policy Institute

2011 *Gaming the System: How the Political Strategies of Private Prison Companies Promote Ineffective Incarceration Policies.* Washington, DC: Justice Policy Institute. http://www.justicepolicy.org/uploads/justicepolicy/documents/gaming _the_system.pdf.

Karstedt, Susanne

2003 "Legacies of a Culture of Inequality: The Janus Face of Crime in Post-Communist Countries." *Crime, Law and Social Change* 402 (2–3): 295–320.

Katzmann, Robert A.

2014 "When Legal Representation Is Deficient: The Challenge of Immigrant Cases for the Courts." *Daedalus* 143 (3): 37–50.

Keefe, Patrick Radden

2015 "Assets and Liabilities: The Mobster Whitey Bulger Secretly Worked for the F.B.I., or Was It the Other Way Around?" *New Yorker*, 21 September, 94–99.

Keenan, Thomas, and Eyal Weizman

2012 *Mengele's Skull: The Advent of Forensic Aesthetics.* Berlin: Sternberg Press.

Kelly, John K.

1999 "The Other Leviathan: Corporate Investment and the Construction of a Sugar Colony." In *White and Deadly: Sugar and Colonialism*, edited by Pal Ahluwalia, Bill Ashcroft, and Roger Knight. Commack, NY: Nova Science.

Kerman, Piper

2011 *Orange Is the New Black: My Year in a Women's Prison.* New York: Random House.

Kitsuse, John I., and Aaron V. Cicourel

1963 "A Note on the Uses of Official Statistics." *Social Problems* 11 (2): 131–39.

Klatzow, David

2014 *Justice Denied: The Role of Forensic Science in the Miscarriage of Justice.* Cape Town: Zebra Press.

Klein, Kathleen Gregory

1999 Introduction to *Diversity and Detective Fiction*, edited by Kathleen Gregory Klein. Bowling Green, OH: Bowling Green State University Popular Press.

Kohler-Hausmann, Issa

2014 "Managerial Justice and Mass Misdemeanors." *Stanford Law Review* 66 (3): 611–93.

Kondos, Alex

1987 "The Question of 'Corruption' in Nepal." *Mankind* 17 (1): 5–29.

Kracauer, Siegfried

1997 *Theory of Film: The Redemption of Physical Reality.* Princeton, NJ: Princeton University Press. First published 1960.

Kretzmann, Steve

2004 "Bars in Their Eyes: Arrested Development." *The Big Issue* (South Africa), no. 84:16–18.

Kruger, Loren

2001 "Theatre, Crime, and the Edge-City in Post-apartheid Johannesburg." *Theatre Journal* 53 (2): 223–52.

Kuper, Hilda Beemer

1984 "The Diviner and the Detective." In *Rite, Drama, Festival, Spectacle: Toward a Theory of Cultural Performance*, edited by John J. MacAloon. Philadelphia: Institute for the Study of Human Issues.

La Hausse, Paul

1990 "So Who Was Elias Kuzwayo? Nationalism, Identity, and the Picaresque in Natal, c. 1920–1948." Working Paper of the History Workshop, University of the Witwatersrand, Johannesburg.

Lambroso, Cesare

1895 "Criminal Anthropology Applied to Pedagogy." *Monist* 6 (1): 50–59.

1912 *Crime: Its Causes and Remedies*. Translated by Henry P. Horton. Boston: Little, Brown.

Latour, Bruno, and Steve Woolgar

1979 *Laboratory Life: The Social Construction of Scientific Facts*. Beverly Hills, CA: Sage.

Leach, Edmund R.

1961 *Rethinking Anthropology*. London: Athlone Press.

Le Bon, Gustave

1896 *The Crowd: A Study of the Popular Mind*. London: T. Fisher Unwin.

Lebovic, Nitzan

2015 "Biometrics; or, The Power of the Radical Center." *Critical Inquiry* 41 (4): 841–68.

Lefort, Claude

1988 *Democracy and Political Theory*. Translated by David Macey. Minneapolis: University of Minnesota Press.

Leggett, Ted

2002 "Improved Crime Reporting: Is South Africa's Crime Wave a Statistical Illusion?" *SA Crime Quarterly* 1:7–10.

2003 "The Facts behind the Figures: Crime Statistics 2002/3." *SA Crime Quarterly* 6:1–6.

2004a "Race, Risk, and Threat in South Africa." *Reconciliation Barometer* 2 (1): 6–7.

2004b "What's Up in the Cape? Crime Rates in Western and Northern Cape Provinces." *SA Crime Quarterly* 7:15–20.

Lemke, Thomas

2001 "'The Birth of Bio-politics': Michel Foucault's Lecture at the Collège de France on Neo-liberal Governmentality." *Economy and Society* 30 (2): 190–207.

Lepore, Jill

2014 "The Warren Brief: Reading Elizabeth Warren." *New Yorker*, 21 April, 96–101.

Lévi-Strauss, Claude

1969 *The Elementary Structures of Kinship*. Translated by James Harle Bell, Richard von Sturmer, and Rodney Needham. Boston: Beacon Press.

Lichtenstein, Alex

2011 "A 'Labor History' of Mass Incarceration." *Labor: Studies in Working-Class History of the Americas* 8 (3): 5–14.

Linebaugh, Peter

1991 *The London Hanged: Crime and Civil Society in the Eighteenth Century*. London: Penguin Books.

Livingstone, David

1857 *Missionary Travels and Researches in South Africa*. London: Murray.

Locke, John

1988 *Two Treatises of Government*. Cambridge: Cambridge University Press. First published 1690.

1995 *An Essay concerning Human Understanding*. New York: Prometheus Books.

Lockwood, Sarah

n.d. "Taking to the Streets: Explaining Service Delivery Protests in Post-apartheid South Africa." Doctoral research proposal, Department of African and African American Studies, Harvard University.

Lomnitz, Claudio

2014 "Mexico's First Lynching: Sovereignty, Criminality, Moral Panic." *Critical Historical Studies* 1 (1): 85–123.

Louw, Antoinette

1998 "Reporting Crimes to the Police: How South Africa Fares." *Nedcor ISS Crime Index* 2 (4): 13–15.

Louw, Antoinette, and Martin Schönteich

2001 "Playing the Numbers Game: Promises, Policing and Crime Statistics." In *Crime Wave: The South African Underworld and Its Foes*, edited by Jonny Steinberg. Johannesburg: Witwatersrand University Press.

Louw, Antoinette, Mark Shaw, Lala Camerer, and Rory Robertshaw

1998 *Crime in Johannesburg: The Results of a Victim Survey*. Pretoria: Institute for Security Studies.

Macpherson, Crawford Brough

1962   *The Political Theory of Possessive Individualism: Hobbes to Locke*. Oxford: Oxford University Press.

Magnello, M. Eileen

2000   "Biometrics, Biology, Statistical Biology, and Mathematical Statistics." In *Reader's Guide to the History of Science*, edited by Arne Hessenbruch. Chicago: Fitzroy Dearborn.

Maguire, Mike, and John Pointing, eds.

1988   *Victims of Crime: A New Deal?* Milton Keynes, UK: Open University Press.

Makholwa, Angela

2007   *Red Ink*. Johannesburg: Picador Africa.

Malala, Justice

2007   "Losing My Mind." In *At Risk: Writing on and over the Edge of South Africa*, edited by Liz McGregor and Sarah Nuttall. Johannesburg: Jonathan Ball.

Malan, Rian

2002   "Jo'burg Lovesong." In *From Jo'burg to Jozi: Stories about Africa's Infamous City*, edited by Heidi Holland and Adam Roberts. London: Penguin Books.

Mamdani, Mahmood

1996   *Citizen and Subject: Contemporary Africa and the Legacy of Late Colonialism*. Princeton, NJ: Princeton University Press.

Mandel, Ernest

1984   *Delightful Murder: A Social History of the Crime Story*. Minneapolis: University of Minnesota Press.

Manning, Peter K.

1977   *The Social Organization of Policing*. Cambridge, MA: MIT Press.

2003   *Policing Contingencies*. Chicago: University of Chicago Press.

Mariner, Kate

2015   "Intimate Speculation." PhD diss., University of Chicago.

Marling, William

1998   *The American Roman Noir: Hammett, Cain and Chandler*. Athens: University of Georgia Press.

Marsh, Rob

1999   *With Criminal Intent: The Changing Face of Crime in South Africa*. Cape Town: Ampersand Press.

Martin, Jeffrey T.

2000   "Social Orders and Their Guardians: Policing, Ritual, and Tradition in Contemporary Taiwan." PhD diss., University of Chicago.

Marx, Karl
  1993 "The Usefulness of Crime." In *Crime and Capitalism: Readings in Marxist Criminology*, edited by David F. Greenberg. Philadelphia: Temple University Press. Also reprinted in *Karl Marx: Selected Writings in Sociology and Social Philosophy*, edited by Thomas B. Bottomore and Maximilien Rubel (New York: McGraw-Hill, 1964). First published in *Theories of Surplus Value*, vol. 1 (Moscow: Progress Publishers, 1963).

Masco, Joseph
  2010 "'Sensitive but Unclassified': Secrecy and the Counterterrorist State." *Public Culture* 22 (3): 433–63.

Mashele, Prince
  2006 "Will The Scorpions Still Sting? The Future of the Directorate of Special Operations." *South African Crime Quarterly* 17:25–29.

Mason, Cody
  2012 *Too Good to Be True: Private Prisons in America.* Washington, DC: Sentencing Project: Research and Advocacy for Reform. http://sentencingproject.org/doc/publications/inc_Too_Good_to_be_True.pdf.

Masondo, Meshack
  2008 "The Love of Money." In *Bad Company: Stories of Suspense, Intrigue and Thrills*, edited by Joanne Hichens. Johannesburg: Pan Macmillan South Africa.

Masuku, Sibusiso
  2001 "South Africa: World Crime Capital?" *Nedbank ISS Crime Index* 5 (1): 16–21.

Matshikiza, John
  2001 Introduction to *The "Drum" Decade: Stories from the 1950s*, edited by Michael Chapman. Pietermaritzburg: University of Natal Press.

Matthews, Roger
  2005 "The Myth of Punitiveness." *Theoretical Criminology* 9 (2): 175–201.

Matzke, Christine
  2012 "Girls with Guts: Writing a South African Thriller; Angela Makholwa in Conversation." In *Life Is a Thriller: Investigating African Crime Fiction*, edited by Anjan Oed and Christine Matzke. Cologne: Rüdiger Köppe Verlag.

Mauer, Mark (with the Sentencing Project)
  2006 *Race to Incarcerate.* 2nd ed. New York: Free Press.

Mauer, Mark, and Ryan S. King
  2007 *Uneven Justice: State Rates of Incarceration by Race and Ethnicity.* Washington, DC: Sentencing Project: Research and Advocacy for Reform. www.sentencingproject.org/doc/publications/rd_stateratesofincbyraceandethnicity.pdf.

Mauss, Marcel

1985   "A Category of the Human Mind: The Notion of the Person; the Notion of Self." Translated by W. D. Halls. In *The Category of the Person*, edited by Michael Carrithers, Steven Collins, and Steven Lukes. Cambridge: Cambridge University Press. First published 1938.

Mawby, Rob C.

2002   *Policing Images: Policing, Communication and Legitimacy.* Cullompton, UK: Willan.

Mayhew, Patricia, Catriona Mirrlees-Black, and Natalie Aye Maung

1994   *Trends in Crime: Findings from the 1994 British Crime Survey.* Research Findings, no. 14. London: Home Office Research and Statistics Department.

Mazzarella, William

2010   "The Myth of the Multitude; or, Who's Afraid of the Crowd?" *Critical Inquiry* 36 (4): 697–727.

Mbeki, Moeletsi

2009   *Architects of Poverty: Why African Capitalism Needs Changing.* Johannesburg: Picador Africa.

Mbembe, Achille

2001   *On the Postcolony.* Berkeley: University of California Press.

2006   "On Politics as a Form of Expenditure." In *Law and Disorder in the Postcolony*, edited by Jean Comaroff and John L. Comaroff. Chicago: University of Chicago Press.

McCall Smith, Alexander

2002   *The No. 1 Ladies' Detective Agency.* New York: Anchor Books. First published 1998.

McDonald, David A., and John Pape, eds.

2002   *Cost Recovery and the Price of Service Delivery in South Africa.* London: Zed Books.

McLarney, Terry

2009   "Case Closed." In *Homicide*, by David Simon. Edinburgh: Canongate Books. First published 1991.

Meranze, Michael

2003   "Foucault, the Death Penalty and the Crisis of Historical Understanding." *Historical Reflections* 29 (2): 191–209.

Merleau-Ponty, Maurice

1962   *The Phenomenology of Perception.* New York: Routledge.

Merrill, Sarah Bishop

1998   *Defining Personhood: Toward the Ethics of Quality in Clinical Care.* Amsterdam: Editions Rodopi.

Merry, Sally E.

    1998 "The Criminalization of Everyday Life." In *Everyday Practices and Trouble Cases*, edited by Austin Sarat, Marianne Constable, David Engel, Valerie Hans, and Susan Lawrence. Evanston, IL: Northwestern University Press.

Meth, Paula

    2013 "Unsettling Insurgency: Reflections on Women's Insurgent Practices in South Africa." In *Dialogues in Urban and Regional Planning*, vol. 5, edited by Michael Hibbard, Robert Freestone, and Tore Øivin Sager. New York: Routledge.

Meyer, Deon

    2003 *Heart of the Hunter*. Translated by K. L. Seegers. New York: Little, Brown.

    2012 *7 Days*. Translated by K. L. Seegers. London: Hodder & Stoughton.

    2014 *Cobra*. Translated by K. L. Seegers. London: Hodder & Stoughton.

Miller, Arthur

    1949 *Death of a Salesman: Certain Private Conversations in Two Acts and a Requiem*. New York: Viking Press.

Minnaar, Anthony

    2001 "The New Vigilantism in Post–April 1994 South Africa: Crime Prevention or an Expression of Lawlessness?" Institute for Human Rights and Criminal Justice Studies, Technikon SA, Pretoria, http://www.unisa.ac.za/contents/docs/vigilantism.pdf.

    2013 "South Africa." In *Community Policing in Indigenous Communities*, edited by Mahesh K. Nalla and Graeme R. Newman. Boca Raton, FL: CTC Press.

Modisane, Bloke

    1963 *Blame Me on History*. New York: Simon & Schuster.

Mollett, Thomas, and Calvin Mollett

    2014 *Bloody Lies: Citizens Reopen the Inge Lotz Murder Case*. Johannesburg: Penguin Books.

Moodie, T. Dunbar, and Vivienne Ndatshe

    1994 *Going for Gold: Men, Mines, and Migration*. Berkeley: University of California Press.

Moore, Sally Falk

    1986 *Social Facts and Fabrications: "Customary" Law on Kilimanjaro, 1880–1980*. Cambridge: Cambridge University Press.

Moretti, Franco

    2005 *Signs Taken for Wonders: On the Sociology of Literary Forms*. Translated by Susan Fischer, David Forgacs, and David Miller. London: Verso.

Morris, Rosalind C.

2006 "The Mute and the Unspeakable: Political Subjectivity, Violent Crime, and 'the Sexual Thing' in a South African Mining Community." In *Law and Disorder in the Postcolony*, edited by Jean Comaroff and John L. Comaroff. Chicago: University of Chicago Press.

2010 "Accidental Histories, Post-historical Practice? Re-reading *Body of Power, Spirit of Resistance* in the Actuarial Age." *Anthropological Quarterly* 83 (3): 581–624.

Most, Glenn W., and Willian W. Stowe

1983 Introduction to *The Poetics of Murder: Detective Fiction and Literary Theory*, edited by Glenn W. Most and William W. Stowe. New York: Harcourt Brace Jovanovich.

Mpe, Phaswane

2001 *Welcome to Our Hillbrow*. Pietermaritzburg: University of Natal Press.

Msimang, Sisonke

2014 "A Conversation about Violence." In *Brain Porn: The Best of "Daily Maverick."* Cape Town: Tafelberg. First published in *Daily Maverick*, 12 March 2014, http://www.dailymaverick.co.za/opinionista/2014-03-12-crossing-the-street -to-avoid-white-men-a-conversation-about-violence/#.VPQYTU10wnk.

Muehlebach, Andrea

2012 *The Moral Neoliberal: Welfare and Citizenship in Italy*. Chicago: University of Chicago Press.

Muhammad, Khalil Gibran

2010 *The Condemnation of Blackness: Race, Crime, and the Making of Modern Urban America*. Cambridge, MA: Harvard University Press.

Mzobe, Sifiso

2010 *Young Blood*. Cape Town: Kwela Books.

Nalla, Mahesh K., and Graeme R. Newman, eds.

2013 *Community Policing in Indigenous Communities*. Boca Raton, FL: CTC Press.

Ndebele, Njabulo Simakahle

1991 *Rediscovery of the Ordinary: Essays in South African Literature*. Johannesburg: Congress of South African Writers (COSAW).

2003 *The Cry of Winnie Mandela*. Cape Town: David Philip.

Newham, Gareth, and David Bruce

2000 "Racism, Brutality and Corruption Are the Key Human Rights Challenges Facing the Transformation of the SAPS." Centre for the Study of Violence and Reconciliation, Johannesburg. http://www.csvr.org.za/old/wits/articles /artgnd2.htm.

Newham, Gareth, and Andrew Faull

2011 *Protector or Predator? Tackling Police Corruption in South Africa*. Monograph no. 182. Pretoria: Institute for Security Studies.

Nina, Daniel

2000 "*Dirty Harry* Is Back: Vigilantism in South Africa—the (Re) Emergence of the 'Good' and 'Bad' Community." *African Security Review* 9 (1): 18–28.

Nippel, Wilfried

1995 *Public Order in Ancient Rome*. Cambridge: Cambridge University Press.

Nixon, Rob

1994 *Homelands, Harlem, and Hollywood: South African Culture and the World Beyond*. New York: Routledge.

2011 *Slow Violence and the Environmentalism of the Poor*. Cambridge, MA: Harvard University Press.

Nkosi, Lewis

1964 *The Rhythm of Violence*. London: Oxford University Press.

1965 *Home and Exile*. London: Longmans.

1971 "On South Africa (the Fire Sometime)." *Transition* 38:30–34.

Obarrio, Juan

2014 *The Spirit of the Laws in Mozambique*. Chicago: University of Chicago Press.

Obermeyer, Nancy

1995 "The Hidden GIS Technocracy." *Cartography and Geographic Information Systems* 22 (1): 78–83.

Oed, Anja, and Christine Matzke

2012 Introduction to *Life Is a Thriller: Investigating African Crime Fiction*, edited by Anja Oed and Christine Matzke. Cologne: Rüdiger Köppe Verlag.

O'Kane, James M.

1992 *The Crooked Ladder: Gangsters, Ethnicity, and the American Dream*. New Brunswick, NJ: Transaction.

Olsen, Kathryn

2009 "Musical Characterizations of Transformation: An Exploration of Social and Political Trajectories in Contemporary Maskanda." PhD diss., University of KwaZulu-Natal.

Olutola, Adewale A.

2013 "Community Policing: A Panacea or a Pandora's Box to Tackle the Rise in Crimes in Nigeria and South Africa." In *The Evolution of Policing: Worldwide Innovations and Insights*, edited by Melchor C. de Guzman, Aiedeo Mintie Das, and Dilip K. Das. Boca Raton, FL: CRC Press.

Ong, Walter J.

1988 *Orality and Literacy: The Technologizing of the World*. London: Routledge.

Oomen, Barbara

2004 "Vigilantism or Alternative Citizenship? The Rise of *Mapogo a Mathamaga*." *African Studies* 63 (2): 153–71.

2005 *Chiefs in South Africa: Law, Power and Culture in the Post-apartheid Era*. New York: Palgrave.

Orford, Margie

2006 *Like Clockwork: A Clare Hart Novel*. Johannesburg: Jonathan Ball.

2010 *Blood Rose*. London: Atlantic Books.

2011 "The Grammar of Violence." *International Crime Authors: Reality Check*. www .internationalcrimeauthors.com/?p=1300.

2012a *Daddy's Girl*. Johannesburg: Jonathan Ball.

2012b *Gallows Hill*. Cape Town: Corvus Books.

2013 *Water Music*. Johannesburg: Jonathan Ball.

Owen, Oliver

2014 Review of *Enforcing Order: An Ethnography of Urban Policing*, by Didier Fassin (Polity Press, 2013). *Journal of the Royal Anthropological Institute*, n.s., 20 (3): 596–98.

Packer, George

2011 "Coming Apart: After 9/11 Transfixed America, the Country's Problems Were Left to Rot." *New Yorker*, 12 September, 62–71.

Peacock, Steven

2014 *Swedish Crime Fiction: Novel, Film, Television*. Manchester: Manchester University Press.

Pearson, Geoffrey

1983 *Hooligan: A History of Respectable Fears*. New York: Palgrave Macmillan.

Pease, Ken

2000 "What to Do about It? Let's Turn Off Our Minds and GIS." In *Mapping and Analysing Crime Data: Lessons from Research and Practice*, edited by Alex Hirschfield and Kate Bowers. New York: Taylor & Francis.

Peirce, Charles Sanders

1934 *Collected Papers of Charles Sanders Peirce*. Vol. 2, *Elements of Logic*. Edited by Charles Hartshorne and Paul Weiss. Cambridge, MA: Harvard University Press.

Pelser, Eric, Johann Schnetler, and Antoinette Louw

2002 *Not Everybody's Business: Community Policing in the SAPS' Priority Areas*. Monograph no. 71. Pretoria: Institute for Security Studies.

Pensky, Max

1993 *Melancholy Dialectics: Walter Benjamin and the Play of Mourning*. Amherst: University of Massachusetts Press.

Pickles, John, ed.

　1995　*Ground Truth: The Social Implications of Geographical Information Systems*. New York: Guilford Press.

Pierson, David P.

　2014　"Breaking Neoliberal? Contemporary Neoliberal Discourses and Policies in AMC's *Breaking Bad*." In *Breaking Bad: Critical Essays on the Contexts, Politics, Style, and Reception of the Television Series*, edited by David P. Pierson. Plymouth, UK: Lexington Books.

Piketty, Thomas

　2014　*Capital in the Twenty-First Century*. Translated by Arthur Goldhammer. Cambridge, MA: Belknap Press.

Pikoli, Vusi, and Mandy Wiener

　2013　*My Second Initiation: The Memoir of Vusi Pikoli*. Johannesburg: Picador Africa.

Pinault, David

　1992　*Story-Telling Techniques in the Arabian Nights*. Leiden: Brill.

Piot, Charles

　2010　*Nostalgia for the Future: West Africa after the Cold War*. Chicago: University of Chicago Press.

Poe, Edgar Allan

　1975　"The Murders in the Rue Morgue." In *The Complete Tales and Poems of Edgar Allan Poe*. New York: Vintage.

Poll, Ryan

　2014　"The Rising Tide of Neoliberalism: Attica Locke's *Black Water Rising* and 'The New Jim Crow.'" In *Class and Culture in Crime Fiction: Essays on Works in English since the 1970s*, edited by Julie H. Kim. Jefferson, NC: McFarland.

Poovey, Mary

　1998　*A History of the Modern Fact: Problems of Knowledge in the Sciences of Wealth and Society*. Chicago: University of Chicago Press.

Poplak, Richard

　2014　"An Uncontrolled Creep: Zuma, Busted by Madonsela." In *Brain Porn: The Best of "Daily Maverick."* Cape Town: Tafelberg. First published in *Daily Maverick*, 19 March 2013, http://www.dailymaverick.co.za/article/2014-03-19-hannibal -elector-an-uncontrolled-creep-jacob-zuma-busted-by-thuli-madonsela/# .VOYI3010yRQ.

Porter, Theodore M.

　1986　*The Rise of Statistical Thinking, 1820–1900*. Princeton, NJ: Princeton University Press.

　1995　*Trust in Numbers: The Pursuit of Objectivity in Science and Public Life*. Princeton, NJ: Princeton University Press.

Posel, Deborah

   2004 "Afterword: Vigilantism and the Burden of Rights: Reflections on the Paradoxes of Freedom in Post-apartheid South Africa." *African Studies* 63 (2): 231–36.

Posner, Richard

   1980 *The Little Book of Plagiarism*. New York: Pantheon Books.

   1981 *The Economics of Justice*. Cambridge, MA: Harvard University Press.

Proudhon, Pierre-Joseph

   1994 *What Is Property?* Edited and translated by Donald R. Kelley and Bonnie G. Smith. Cambridge: Cambridge University Press. First published 1840.

Provine, Doris Marie, and Roxanne Lynn Doty

   2011 "The Criminalization of Immigrants as a Racial Project." *Journal of Contemporary Criminal Justice* 27 (3): 261–77.

Ralushai, N. V., M. G. Masingi, D. M. M. Madiba, et al.

   1996 *Report of the Commission of Inquiry into Witchcraft Violence and Ritual Murders in the Northern Province of the Republic of South Africa* (To: His Excellency The Honourable Member of the Executive Council for Safety and Security, Northern Province). No publisher given.

Read, Tim

   2001 Foreword to *Mapping and Analysing Crime Data: Lessons from Research and Practice*, edited by Alex Hirschfield and Kate Bowers. New York: Taylor & Francis.

Redpath, Jean

   2004 *The Scorpions: Analysing the Directorate of Special Operations*. Monograph no. 96. Pretoria: Institute for Security Studies.

Reiner, Robert

   2010 *The Politics of the Police*. Oxford: Oxford University Press.

   2012 "Policing and Social Democracy: Resuscitating a Lost Perspective." *Journal of Police Studies* 4/25:91–114.

Reiner, Robert, and Malcolm Cross

   1991 "Introduction: Beyond Law and Order—Crime and Criminology into the 1990s." In *Beyond Law and Order: Criminal Justice Policy and Politics into the 1990s*, edited by Robert Reiner and Malcolm Cross. Basingstoke, UK: Macmillan.

Reiner, Robert, and Tim Newburn

   2007 "Policing and the Police." In *The Oxford Handbook of Criminology*, edited by Mike Maguire, Rod Morgan, and Robert Reiner. Oxford: Oxford University Press.

Robertshaw, Rory, Antoinette Louw, Mark Shaw, Mduduzi Mashiyane, and Sid Brettell

   2001 *Reducing Crime in Durban: A Victim Survey for a Safer City*. Monograph no. 58. Pretoria: Institute for Security Studies.

Robins, Steven

2004 "Grounding 'Globalisation from Below': 'Global Citizens' in Local Spaces." In *What Holds Us Together: Social Cohesion in South Africa*, edited by David Chidester, Phillip Dexter, and Wilmot James. Cape Town: Human Sciences Research Council.

Roeder, Oliver, Lauren-Brooke Eisen, and Julia Bowling

2015 *What Caused the Crime Decline?* New York: Brennan Center for Justice, New York University School of Law.

Roitman, Janet

2005 *Fiscal Disobedience: An Anthropology of Economic Regulation in Central Africa.* Princeton, NJ: Princeton University Press.

2006 "The Ethics of Illegality in the Chad Basin." In *Law and Disorder in the Postcolony*, edited by Jean Comaroff and John L. Comaroff. Chicago: University of Chicago Press.

Rose, Nikolas Simon

1999 *Powers of Freedom: Reframing Political Thought.* Cambridge: Cambridge University Press.

Rose, Nikolas Simon, and Peter Miller

1992 "Political Power beyond the State: Problematics of Government." *British Journal of Sociology* 43 (2): 173–206.

Rubin, Jonah S.

2015 "'They Are Not Just Bodies': Memory, Death, and Democracy in Post-Franco Spain." PhD diss., University of Chicago.

Saito, Satomi

2007 "Culture and Authenticity: The Discursive Space of Japanese Detective Fiction and the Formation of the National Imaginary." PhD diss., University of Iowa.

Salzani, Carol

2007 "The City as Crime Scene: Walter Benjamin and the Traces of the Detective." *New German Critique* 34:165–87.

Samara, Tony Roshan

2011 *Cape Town after Apartheid: Crime and Governance in the Divided City.* Minneapolis: University of Minnesota Press.

Sampson, Robert J., and Stephen W. Raudenbush,

2004 "Seeing Disorder: Neighborhood Stigma and the Social Construction of 'Broken Windows.'" *Social Psychology Quarterly* 67 (4): 319–42.

Scheingold, Stuart

1991 *The Politics of Street Crime: Criminal Process and Cultural Obsession.* Philadelphia: Temple University Press.

Scheper-Hughes, Nancy

2014 "The House Gun: White Writing, White Fears and Black Justice." *Anthropology Today* 30 (6): 8–12.

Schleh, Eugene

1991 *Mysteries of Africa*. Bowling Green, OH: Bowling Green State University Popular Press.

Schmitt, Carl

2007 *The Concept of the Political*. Expanded ed. Translated by George Schwab. Chicago: University of Chicago Press. First German edition, 1927.

Schneider, Jane, and Peter Schneider

2008 "The Anthropology of Crime and Criminalization." *Annual Review of Anthropology* 37:351–73.

Schönteich, Martin

2001 "Crime Trends: A Turning Point?" *SA Crime Quarterly* 1:1–6.

Schreiner, Olive

1959 *Trooper Peter Halket of Mashonaland*. London: Benn. First published 1897.

Schwartz, Hillel

1996 *The Culture of the Copy: Striking Likenesses, Unreasonable Facsimiles*. Cambridge, MA: MIT Press.

Schweitzer, N. J., and Michael J. Saks

2007 "The CSI Effect: Popular Fiction about Forensic Science Affects the Public's Expectations about Real Forensic Science." *Jurimetrics* 47:357–64.

Scott, James C.

1998 *Seeing like a State: How Certain Schemes to Improve the Human Condition Have Failed*. New Haven, CT: Yale University Press.

Sebeok, Thomas Albert, and Jean Umiker-Sebeok

1983 "'You Know My Method': A Juxtaposition of Charles S. Peirce and Sherlock Holmes." In *The Sign of Three: Dupin, Holmes, Peirce*, edited by Umberto Eco and Thomas A. Sebeok. Bloomington: Indiana University Press.

Seltzer, Mark

1997 "Wound Culture: Trauma in the Pathological Public Sphere." *October* 80 (Spring): 3–26.

2004 "The Crime System." *Critical Inquiry* 30: 557–83.

Sen, Atreyee, and David Pratten

2008 "Global Vigilantes: Perspectives on Justice and Violence." In *Global Vigilantes*, edited by David Pratten and Atreyee Sen. New York: Columbia University Press.

Shapiro, David

    2011 *Banking on Bondage: Private Prisons and Mass Incarceration*. New York: American Civil Liberties Union.

Sharp, John S.

    1998 "'Non-racialism and Its Discontents': A Post-apartheid Paradox." *International Social Science Journal* 50 (156): 243–52.

Shaw, Mark

    1997 "Crime in Transition." In *Policing the Transformation: Further Issues in South Africa's Crime Debate*, edited by Mark Shaw, Lala Camerer, Duxita Mistry, Sarah Oppler, and Lukas Muntingh. Monograph no. 12. Pretoria: Institute for Security Studies.

    2002 *Crime and Policing in Post-apartheid South Africa: Transforming under Fire*. Bloomington: Indiana University Press.

Shaw, Mark, and Peter Gastrow

    2001 "Stealing the Show? Crime and Its Impact on Post-apartheid South Africa." *Daedalus* 130 (1): 235–58.

Shaw, Mark, and Antoinette Louw

    1998 "Crime and Policing: Perceptions and Fears." *Nedcor ISS Crime Index* 2 (1): 1–6.

Siegel, James T.

    1998 *A New Criminal Type in Jakarta: Counter-revolution Today*. Durham, NC: Duke University Press.

Simmel, Georg

    1978 *The Philosophy of Money*. Translated by Tom Bottomore and David Frisby. London: Routledge & Kegan Paul.

Simon, Jonathan

    2001 "'Entitlement to Cruelty': Neo-liberalism and the Punitive Mentality in the United States. In *Crime, Risk and Justice: The Politics of Crime Control in Liberal Democracies*, edited by Kevin Stenson and Robert R. Sullivan. Cullompton, UK: Willan.

    2007 *Governing through Crime: How the War on Crime Transformed American Democracy and Created a Culture of Fear*. Oxford: Oxford University Press.

    2014 "Uncommon Law: America's Excessive Criminal Law and Our Common-Law Origins." *Daedalus* 143 (3): 62–72.

Singer, Peter W.

    2003 *Corporate Warriors: The Rise of the Privatized Military Industry*. Ithaca, NY: Cornell University Press.

Smith, Caleb

2009   *The Prison and the American Imagination.* New Haven, CT: Yale University Press.

2013   "Spaces of Punitive Violence." *Criticism* 55 (1): 161–68.

Smith, Nicholas Rush

2013   "The Rights of Others: Vigilantism and the Contradictions of Democratic State Formation in Post-apartheid South Africa." PhD diss., University of Chicago.

Soggot, Mungo, and Evidence wa ka Ngobeni

1999   "'We Must Work on their Buttocks.'" In *The Mail & Guardian Bedside Book, 1999*, edited by D. Macfarlane. Auckland Park: Mail & Guardian.

Soja, Edward J.

1989   *Postmodern Geographies: The Reassertion of Space in Critical Social Theory.* London: Verso.

Sontag, Susan

2009   "The Pornographic Imagination." In *Styles of Radical Will*, by Susan Sontag. London: Penguin Classics. First published 1966.

South African Institute of Race Relations

2015   *Broken Blue Line 2: The Involvement of the South African Police Service in Serious and Violent Crime in South Africa.* Johannesburg: South African Institute of Race Relations.

South African Police Service (SAPS)

1997   *Community Policing: Policy Framework and Guidelines.* Pretoria: Department of Safety and Security, South African Police Service.

2003   *Annual Report of the Commissioner of the South African Police Service, 2002–3.* Pretoria: South African Police Service.

SSA. *See* Statistics South Africa.

Stalcup, Meg

2013   "Interpol and the Emergence of Global Policing." In *Policing and Contemporary Governance: The Anthropology of Police in Practice*, edited by William Garriott. New York: Palgrave Macmillan.

Standing, André

2003   "The Social Contradictions of Organized Crime on the Cape Flats." Occasional Paper no. 74. Pretoria: Institute for Security Studies.

2005   "The Threat of Gangs and Anti-gangs Policy." Policy Discussion Paper no. 116. Pretoria: Institute for Security Studies

Standing, Guy

2011   *The Precariat: The New Dangerous Class.* London: Bloomsbury.

Statistics South Africa (SSA)

2013 *Mortality and Causes of Death in South Africa, 2010: Findings from Death Notification*. Statistical release P0309.3. Pretoria: Statistics South Africa.

2014 *Victims of Crime Survey, 2013/4*. Statistical release P0341. Pretoria: Statistics South Africa.

Steinberg, Jonny

2001 "Introduction: Behind the Crime Wave." In *Crime Wave: The South African Underworld and Its Foes*, edited by Jonny Steinberg. Johannesburg: University of Witwatersrand Press.

2008 *Thin Blue: The Unwritten Rules of Policing South Africa*. Johannesburg: Jonathan Ball.

2011 "Crime Prevention Goes Abroad: Policy Transfer and Policing in Post-apartheid South Africa." *Theoretical Criminology* 15 (3): 349–64.

Stiglitz, Joseph E.

2002 *Globalization and Its Discontents*. New York: Norton.

Stillman, Sarah

2014 "Get out of Jail, Inc.: Does the Alternatives-to-Incarceration Industry Profit from Injustice?" *New Yorker*, 23 June, 48–61.

Stoler, Laura Ann

1985 "Perceptions of Protest: Defining the Dangerous in Colonial Sumatra." *American Ethnologist* 12 (4): 642–58.

1995 *Race and the Education of Desire: Foucault's "History of Sexuality" and the Colonial Order of Things*. Durham, NC: Duke University Press.

Storch, Robert D., and F. Engels

1975 "The Plague of Blue Locusts: Police Reform and Popular Resistance in Northern England, 1840–1857." *International Review of Social History* 20 (1): 61–90.

Sullivan, Robert R

2001 "The Schizophrenic State: Neo-liberal Criminal Justice." In *Crime, Risk, and Justice*, edited by Kevin Stenson and Robert R. Sullivan. Cullompton, UK: Willan.

Summerscale, Kate

2008 *The Suspicions of Mr. Whicher; or, The Murder at Road Hill House*. London: Bloomsbury.

Sunder Rajan, Kaushik

2005 "Subjects of Speculation: Emergent Life Sciences and Market Logics in the United States and India." *American Anthropologist* 107 (1): 19–30.

Super, Gail

2013 *Governing through Crime in South Africa: The Politics of Race and Class in Neoliberalizing Regimes*. Farnham, Surrey: Ashgate.

Switzer, Les, ed.

1997 *South Africa's Alternative Press: Voices of Protest and Resistance, 1880–1960.* Cambridge: Cambridge University Press.

Talbot, Margaret

2014 "Comment: Opened Files." *New Yorker*, 20 January, 19–20.

Teppo, Annika Björnsdotter

2009 "'My House Is Protected by a Dragon': White South Africans, Magic and Sacred Spaces in Post-apartheid Cape Town." *Suomi Anthropologi: Journal of the Finnish Anthropological Society* 34 (1): 19–41.

Thamm, Marianne

2014a "Bad Cops, Assassins, Czech Fugitives: The Meaning of Paul O'Sullivan." In *Brain Porn: The Best of "Daily Maverick."* Cape Town: Tafelberg. First published in *Daily Maverick*, 15 January 2014, http://www.dailymaverick.co.za/article/2014-01-15-bad-cops-assassins-czech-fugitives-the-meaning-of-paul-osullivan/#.VOsywk10yRQ.]

2014b "*Miners Shot Down*: A Film Every South African Should See, and Never Forget." In *Brain Porn: The Best of "Daily Maverick."* Cape Town: Tafelberg. First published in *Daily Maverick*, 4 June 2013, http://www.dailymaverick.co.za/article/2014-06-04-miners-shot-down-the-film-every-south-african-should-see-and-never-forget/#.VOht4E10yRQ.

2014c *To Catch a Cop: The Paul O'Sullivan Story.* Johannesburg: Jacana Media.

Thomas, C. William

2002 "The Rise and Fall of Enron: When a Company Looks Too Good to Be True, It Usually Is." *Journal of Accountancy*, 1 April 2002. http://www.journalofaccountancy.com/Issues/2002/Apr/TheRiseAndFallOfEnron.htm.

Thomas, Keith

1992 "How Britain Made It." *New York Review of Books*, 19 November. http://www.nybooks.com/articles/archives/1992/nov/19/how-britain-made-it/?page=2.

Thomas, Peter

2002 "Poe's Dupin and the Power of Detection." In *The Cambridge Companion to Edgar Allan Poe*, edited by Kevin J. Hayes. Cambridge: Cambridge University Press.

Thompson, Edward P.

1963 *The Making of the English Working Class.* London: Gollancz.

1991 *Customs in Common.* London: Penguin Books.

Thompson, Heather Ann

2011 "Rethinking Working-Class Struggle through the Lens of the Carceral State: Towards a Labor History of Inmates and Guards." *Labor: Studies in Working-Class History of the Americas* 8 (3): 15–45.

Thornton, Robert James

    1999   "What Is 'Civil' about 'Civil Society' in Africa? *PreTexts: Literary and Cultural Studies* 8 (1): 93–112.

Tibbs, Donald T.

    2010   "Who Killed Oscar Grant? A Legal-Eulogy of the Cultural Logic of Black Hyper-policing in the Post–Civil Rights Era. Drexel University Earle Mack School of Law Research Paper no. 1559489, 25 February. http://papers.ssrn.com/sol3/papers.cfm?abstract_id=1559489.

Tilly, Charles

    1985   "War Making and State Making as Organized Crime." In *Bringing the State Back In*, edited by Peter B. Evans, Dietrich Rueschemeyer, and Theda Skocpol. Cambridge: Cambridge University Press.

Tribe, Laurence, and Joshua Matz

    2014   *Uncertain Justice: The Roberts Court and the Constitution*. New York: Henry Holt.

Turner, Ralph H.

    1996   "The Moral Issue in Collective Behavior and Collective Action." *Mobilization: An International Quarterly* 1 (1): 1–15.

Turner, Victor Witter

    1957   *Schism and Continuity in an African Society: A Study of Ndembu Village Life*. Manchester: Manchester University Press for the Institute for African Studies, University of Zambia.

    1967   *The Forest of Symbols: Aspects of Ndembu Ritual*. Ithaca, NY: Cornell University Press.

Twain, Mark

    1902   *A Double-Barreled Detective Story*. New York: Harper & Brothers.

United Kingdom, Office for National Statistics

    2015   *Crime in England and Wales, Year Ending September 2014*. London: National Office for Statistics.

United Nations

    2005   *Report on the World Situation, 2005: The Inequality Predicament*. New York: Department of Economic and Social Affairs, Division for Social Policy and Development, United Nations. http://www.un.org/esa/socdev/rwss/media%2005/cd-docs/media.htm.

Urla, Jacqueline

    1993   "Cultural Politics in an Age of Statistics: Numbers, Nations, and the Making of Basque Identity." *American Ethnologist* 20 (4): 818–43.

Vanderbilt, Tom

 1997 "The Advertised Life." In *Commodify Your Dissent: Salvos from the "Baffler,"* edited by Tom Frank and Matt Weiland. New York: W. W. Norton.

van Dijk, Jan J. M.

 1996 "Crime and Victim Surveys." In *International Victimology: Selected Papers from the 8th International Symposium*, edited by Chris Sumner, Mark Israel, Michael O'Connell, and Rick Sarre. Canberra: Australian Institute of Criminology.

Van Leer, David

 1993 "Detecting Truth: The World of the Dupin Tales." In *The American Novel: New Essays on Poe's Major Tales*, edited by Kenneth Silverman. Cambridge: Cambridge University Press.

van Onselen, Charles

 2014 *Showdown at the Red Lion: The Life and Times of Jack McLoughlin, 1859–1910*. Johannesburg: Jonathan Ball.

van Rooyen, Johann

 2000 *The New Great Trek: The Story of South Africa's White Exodus*. Pretoria: University of South Africa Press.

Vladislavić, Ivan

 2004 *The Exploded View*. Johannesburg: Random House.

 2015 *101 Detectives: Stories*. Century City, RSA: Umuzi.

von Schnitzler, Antina, Goodwill Ditlhage, Lazarus Kgalema, Traggy Maepa, Tlhoki Mofokeng, and Piers Pigou

 2001 "Guardian or Gangster? *Mapogo a Mathamaga*: A Case Study." In *Violence and Transition Series*, vol. 3. Johannesburg: Centre for the Study of Violence and Reconciliation.

Wacquant, Loïc

 2002 "From Slavery to Mass Incarceration: Rethinking the 'Race Question' in the US." *New Left Review* 13 (January–February): 41–60.

 2009a "The Body, the Ghetto and the Penal State." *Qualitative Sociology* 32 (1): 101–29.

 2009b *Punishing the Poor: The Neoliberal Government of Social Instability.* Durham, NC: Duke University Press.

Waddington, P. A. J.

 1999 *Policing Citizens: Authority and Rights*. London: UCL Press.

Warnes, Chris

 2012 "Writing Crime in the New South Africa: Negotiating Threat in the Novels of Deon Mayer and Margie Orford." *Journal of Southern African Studies* 38 (4): 981–91.

Warren, Elizabeth

2014   *A Fighting Chance*. New York: Henry Holt.

Western, Bruce

2006   *Punishment and Inequality in America*. New York: Russell Sage Foundation.

White, Hylton

2004   "Ritual Haunts: The Timing of Estrangement in a Post-apartheid Country-side." In *Producing African Futures: Ritual and Reproduction in a Neoliberal Age*, edited by Brad Weiss. Leiden: Brill.

2013   "Spirit and Society: In Defence of a Critical Anthropology of Religious Life." *Anthropology Southern Africa* 36 (3–4): 139–45.

Wiener, Mandy

2011   *Killing Kebble: An Underworld Exposed*. Johannesburg: Pan Macmillan South Africa.

Wildavsky, Aaron, and Adam Wildavsky

2008   "Risk and Safety." In *The Concise Encyclopedia of Economics*. Library of Economics and Liberty. http://www.econlib.org/library/Enc/RiskandSafety.html.

Williams, Michael

2002   *The Eighth Man*. Cape Town: Oxford University Press.

Wilson, Christopher P.

2000   *Cop Knowledge: Police Power and Cultural Narratives in Twentieth-Century America*. Chicago: University of Chicago Press.

Wilson, Monica Hunter

1951   "Witch Beliefs and Social Structure." *American Journal of Sociology* 56 (4): 307–13.

Wilson, Monica Hunter, and Archie Mafeje

1963   *Langa: A Study of Social Groups in an African Township*. Oxford: Oxford University Press.

Wilson, Richard

2013   "Gangster's Paradise? Framing Crime in Sub-Saharan Africa." *Humanity: An International Journal of Human Rights, Humanitarianism, and Development* 4 (3): 449–71.

Woodson, Dorothy C.

1988   *"Drum": An Index to "Africa's Leading Magazine," 1951–1965*. Bibliographies in African Studies, 2. Madison: University of Wisconsin African Studies Program.

Worger, William H.

2004   "Convict Labour, Industrialists and the State in the US South and South Africa, 1870–1930." *Journal of Southern African Studies* 30 (1): 63–86.

Wright, Alan

2002 *Policing: An Introduction to Concepts and Practice*. Cullompton, UK: Willan.

Wright, Lawrence

1994 *Remembering Satan*. New York: Knopf.

Wright, Richard

1940 *Native Son*. New York: Harper & Brothers.

Young, Malcolm

1991 *An Inside Job: Policing and Police Culture in Britain*. New York: Oxford University Press.

Zapiro [Jonathan Shapiro]

2002 *Bushwhacked: Cartoons from "Sowetan," "Mail & Guardian" and "Sunday Times."* Cape Town: Double Storey Books.

INDEX

Page numbers in italics refer to illustrations